AWS®
Certified Machine Learning Engineer Study Guide

Associate (MLA-C01) Exam

AWS® Certified Machine Learning Engineer Study Guide

Associate (MLA-C01) Exam

Dario Cabianca

Copyright © 2025 by Dario Cabianca. All rights reserved, including rights for text and data mining and training of artificial intelligence technologies or similar technologies.

Published by John Wiley & Sons, Inc., Hoboken, New Jersey.
Published simultaneously in Canada.

No part of this publication may be reproduced, stored in a retrieval system, or transmitted in any form or by any means, electronic, mechanical, photocopying, recording, scanning, or otherwise, except as permitted under Section 107 or 108 of the 1976 United States Copyright Act, without either the prior written permission of the Publisher, or authorization through payment of the appropriate per-copy fee to the Copyright Clearance Center, Inc., 222 Rosewood Drive, Danvers, MA 01923, (978) 750-8400, fax (978) 750-4470, or on the web at www.copyright.com. Requests to the Publisher for permission should be addressed to the Permissions Department, John Wiley & Sons, Inc., 111 River Street, Hoboken, NJ 07030, (201) 748-6011, fax (201) 748-6008, or online at http://www.wiley.com/go/permission.

The manufacturer's authorized representative according to the EU General Product Safety Regulation is Wiley-VCH GmbH, Boschstr. 12, 69469 Weinheim, Germany, e-mail: Product_Safety@wiley.com.

Trademarks: Wiley and the Wiley logo, and the Sybex logo are trademarks or registered trademarks of John Wiley & Sons, Inc. and/or its affiliates in the United States and other countries and may not be used without written permission. AWS is a registered trademark of Amazon Technologies, Inc. All other trademarks are the property of their respective owners. John Wiley & Sons, Inc. is not associated with any product or vendor mentioned in this book.

Limit of Liability/Disclaimer of Warranty: While the publisher and author have used their best efforts in preparing this book, they make no representations or warranties with respect to the accuracy or completeness of the contents of this book and specifically disclaim any implied warranties of merchantability or fitness for a particular purpose. No warranty may be created or extended by sales representatives or written sales materials. The advice and strategies contained herein may not be suitable for your situation. You should consult with a professional where appropriate. Further, readers should be aware that websites listed in this work may have changed or disappeared between when this work was written and when it is read. Neither the publisher nor authors shall be liable for any loss of profit or any other commercial damages, including but not limited to special, incidental, consequential, or other damages.

For general information on our other products and services or for technical support, please contact our Customer Care Department within the United States at (800) 762-2974, outside the United States at (317) 572-3993 or fax (317) 572-4002.

Wiley also publishes its books in a variety of electronic formats. Some content that appears in print may not be available in electronic formats. For more information about Wiley products, visit our web site at www.wiley.com.

Library of Congress Control Number: 2025908052

Paperback ISBN: 9781394319954
ePDF ISBN: 9781394319992
ePub ISBN: 9781394319978

Cover Design: Wiley
Cover Image: © Jeremy Woodhouse/Getty Images

SKY10105695_051625

To my family.

Contents at a Glance

Acknowledgments	*ix*
About the Author	*xi*
About the Technical Editor	*xiii*
Introduction	*xv*
The AWS Certified Machine Learning Engineer – Associate Exam	*xv*
Who Should Buy This Book	*xviii*
Study Guide Features	*xviii*
AWS Certified Machine Learning Engineer Exam Objectives	*xix*
Assessment Test	*xxvii*
Answers to Assessment Test	*xxxii*
Chapter 1	Introduction to Machine Learning	1
Chapter 2	Data Ingestion and Storage	27
Chapter 3	Data Transformation and Feature Engineering	61
Chapter 4	Model Selection	105
Chapter 5	Model Training and Evaluation	185
Chapter 6	Model Deployment and Orchestration	237
Chapter 7	Model Monitoring and Cost Optimization	297
Chapter 8	Model Security	331
Appendix A	Answers to the Review Questions	355
Appendix B	Mathematics Essentials	373
Index		*391*

Acknowledgments

Creating the *AWS Certified Machine Learning Engineer Study Guide Associate (MLA-C01) Exam* has been an extraordinary journey, and I would like to take this opportunity to express my gratitude to those who made this book possible.

In addition to my family, I would like to thank Kenyon Brown, senior acquisition editor at Wiley, who helped get the book started. I am also grateful to Christine O'Connor, managing editor at Wiley, and to Dabian Witherspoon, project manager, for his detailed coordination of all tasks as the book progressed through its stages.

Justin Roberts, the technical editor, did a phenomenal job validating the content I authored and testing the code I created. I am also grateful to Kim Wimpsett, the copyeditor, and Dhilip Kumar Rajendran, the content refinement specialist, for their accurate and comprehensive review of the copyedits and the proofs.

Finally, I would like to thank the late Professor Giovanni Degli Antoni, my doctoral thesis advisor, who always inspired and motivated me to pursue my scientific curiosity during my years at the University of Milan, whose Department of Computer Science has been named in his honor.

About the Author

Dario Cabianca is a computer scientist (PhD, University of Milan), author, and AWS practice director at Trace3, which is a leading IT consultancy offering AI, data, cloud and cybersecurity solutions for clients across industries. At Trace3, Dario oversees the practice nationally, serving customers, building partnerships, and evangelizing Trace3's portfolio of AWS competencies and services. He has worked with a variety of global consulting firms and enterprises for more than two decades and has earned 10 cloud certifications with AWS, Google Cloud, Microsoft Azure, and ISC2.

About the Technical Editor

Justin Roberts is a solutions architect at Amazon Web Services (AWS), where he advises strategic customers on designing and running complex large-scale systems on AWS. Justin has worked for several enterprises over almost two decades across numerous disciplines. He currently holds multiple industry certifications, including 14 AWS certifications, and is a member of the exclusive AWS "Golden Jacket" club for holding all active AWS certifications at once. Justin has a BS from Eastern Kentucky University and an MBA from Bellarmine University.

Introduction

The demand for machine learning (ML) engineers has significantly increased, particularly since 2023, when the introduction of ChatGPT revolutionized the artificial intelligence (AI) landscape. This field has seen a substantial interest and investment, as organizations across various sectors recognize the transformative potential of AI. As ML and AI become progressively more sophisticated, the need for skilled professionals to develop, implement, and maintain these systems has never been greater. To meet this demand, the new AWS Certified Machine Learning Engineer – Associate certification was developed to equip aspiring engineers with the knowledge and skills necessary to excel in this dynamic field.

The AWS Certified Machine Learning Engineer – Associate certification is a testament to the proficiency and expertise required to navigate this ever-evolving field. This certification not only validates an individual's technical skills but also underscores their ability to leverage AWS's extensive suite of ML and AI services to drive innovation. As this technology continues to mature, certified professionals are well-positioned to lead the charge in developing cutting-edge AI solutions.

This study guide adopts a methodical approach by walking you step-by-step through all the phases of the ML lifecycle. The exposition of each topic offers a combination of theoretical knowledge, practical exercises with tested code in Python, and necessary diagrams and plots to visually represent ML models and AI in action.

Throughout this study guide, we will delve into the fascinating world of AWS SageMaker AI (formerly known as Amazon SageMaker) and Amazon Bedrock, exploring their numerous features and functionalities. We will cover the core concepts and practical applications, providing you with the knowledge and tools needed to excel as an AWS Machine Learning Engineer. Whether you are just starting your journey or looking to deepen your expertise, this guide will serve as a comprehensive resource to mastering these platforms and achieving certification.

By obtaining the AWS Certified Machine Learning Engineer – Associate certification, you are not just enhancing your skillset but also contributing to the forefront of technological innovation. Let this study guide be your roadmap to success in this rapidly expanding field.

The AWS Certified Machine Learning Engineer – Associate Exam

The AWS Certified Machine Learning Engineer – Associate Exam is intended to validate the technical skills required to design, build, and operationalize well-architected ML workloads on AWS. The exam covers a wide range of topics, including data preparation, feature engineering, model training, model evaluation, and deployment strategies.

The exam consists of 65 questions and has a duration of 130 minutes. It is available in multiple languages, including English, Japanese, Korean, and Simplified Chinese. The exam costs $150 and can be taken at a Pearson VUE testing center or online as a proctored exam. This certification is valid for 3 years.

Your exam results are presented as a scaled score ranging from 100 to 1,000. To pass, a minimum score of 720 is required. This score reflects your overall performance on the exam and indicates whether you have successfully passed.

The official exam guide is available at https://d1.awsstatic.com/training-and-certification/docs-machine-learning-engineer-associate/AWS-Certified-Machine-Learning-Engineer-Associate_Exam-Guide.pdf.

During the writing of this book, "Amazon SageMaker" was renamed "Amazon SageMaker AI." As a result, the first chapters of this book still use the former name, because at that time this was the correct name in use. In this book, the terms "Amazon SageMaker" and "Amazon SageMaker AI" are used interchangeably to denote the new AWS unified platform for data, analytics, ML, and AI. See https://aws.amazon.com/blogs/aws/introducing-the-next-generation-of-amazon-sagemaker-the-center-for-all-your-data-analytics-and-ai.

Why Become AWS Machine Learning Engineer Certified?

The increasing demand for AWS ML and AI engineers—due to the rapid adoption of ML and AI technologies across industries—has made this a perfect time to pursue the AWS Certified Machine Learning Engineer – Associate certification. Companies are looking for skilled professionals who can harness the power of AWS to build, deploy, and manage ML models efficiently. By earning this certification, you can demonstrate your proficiency in using AWS tools and services to drive impactful ML and AI solutions. This certification not only validates your technical skills but also sets you apart in a competitive job market, making you a valuable asset to potential employers.

One of the key reasons to pursue this certification is the comprehensive knowledge you'll gain about AWS's cutting-edge ML and AI services. While preparing for the exam, you'll master the use of Amazon SageMaker AI, a powerful platform for building, training, deploying and monitoring ML models at scale. You'll also explore the latest additions to Amazon SageMaker AI, which continuously evolves to bring together a broad set of AWS ML, AI, and data analytics services. As a result, you'll become proficient in using Amazon Bedrock, a service that simplifies the deployment of foundation models by offering pre-trained models from leading AI companies. However, due to the relatively new nature of Amazon Bedrock, there is a lack of in-depth material available, making this certification even more valuable as it positions you at the forefront of emerging AI technologies.

Amazon SageMaker AI and Amazon Bedrock are designed for seamless integration with numerous AWS services that are required during the phases of the ML lifecycle. Therefore, the study continues with extensive coverage of such services. These include storage services (e.g., Amazon S3, Amazon Elastic File System [EFS], Amazon FSx for Lustre, and others), ingestion services (e.g., Amazon Data Firehose, Amazon Kinesis Data Streams, Amazon Managed Streaming for Apache Kafka [MSK], and others), deployment services (e.g., Amazon Elastic Compute Cloud [EC2], Amazon Elastic Container Service [ECS], and others), orchestration services (e.g., AWS Step Functions, Amazon Managed Workflows for Apache Airflow [MWAA], and others), monitoring, cost optimization, and security services, just to name a few.

Another significant advantage of becoming AWS Machine Learning Engineer certified is the access to exclusive resources and a supportive community of professionals. By joining the certified AWS community, you'll have the opportunity to network with other professionals, share knowledge, and stay updated on the latest trends and advancements in the field. This certification not only boosts your career prospects, but also keeps you engaged in a dynamic and constantly evolving industry.

How to Become AWS Machine Learning Engineer Certified

Your journey to become AWS Machine Learning Engineer Certified begins with a structured approach that covers foundational knowledge, hands-on practice, and thorough exam preparation. This study guide is crafted to mirror that journey.

Foundational knowledge Start by building a robust understanding of ML concepts, formulate ML problems, and learn algorithms and statistical methods. It's also important to grasp the basics of linear algebra, calculus, probability, and statistics, as they form the mathematical foundation for ML. Additionally, familiarize yourself with AWS services, particularly Amazon SageMaker AI, which provides tools and features for every phase of the ML lifecycle. Learning Python, the primary programming language used in ML, is also essential.

Hands-on practice Engage in practical experience through AWS resources like tutorials, labs, and workshops. Focus on using Amazon SageMaker AI for various phases of the ML lifecycle, including

Data preparation Use Amazon SageMaker Data Wrangler to simplify data preparation and feature engineering.
Model building Leverage Amazon SageMaker Studio for an integrated development environment that supports building, training, and debugging ML models.
Model training Utilize Amazon SageMaker Training to efficiently train models with built-in algorithms or your own custom code.
Model deployment Use Amazon SageMaker Endpoint to deploy trained models for real-time predictions, and Amazon SageMaker Batch Transform for batch predictions.
Model monitoring Employ Amazon SageMaker Model Monitor to continuously monitor the performance of deployed models and ensure that they remain accurate over time.

By working on real-world projects that cover the entire ML lifecycle, you'll gain hands-on experience and deepen your understanding.

Exam preparation   Use AWS's official exam guide to understand key objectives. Utilize practice exams and sample questions to test your readiness. Regular review and practice will ensure that you are well-prepared for the certification exam. On exam day, manage your time effectively and read each question carefully to increase your chances of passing and earning the certification.

Who Should Buy This Book

This book is intended for a broad audience of software, data, and cloud engineers/architects with ideally 1 year of hands-on experience with AWS services. Given the engineering focus of the certification, basic knowledge of the Python programming language—which is the de facto ML programming language—is expected.

Moreover, due to the data-centric nature of ML, having a firm grasp of basic mathematics and statistics is essential, but don't worry—we'll cover the basics in Appendix B (Mathematics Essentials), and provide guidance as needed.

This book comes with tested code in Python, with which you can experiment using Amazon SageMaker Studio. To get the most out this book, an AWS account is highly recommended.

Study Guide Features

This study guide utilizes a number of common elements to help you acquire and reinforce your knowledge. Each chapter includes

Summaries   The summary section briefly explains the key concepts of the chapter, allowing you to easily remember what you learned.

Exam essentials   The exam essentials section highlights the exam topics and the knowledge you need to have for the exam. These exam topics are directly related to the task statements provided by AWS, which are available in the upcoming exam objectives section.

Chapter review questions   A set of questions will help you assess your knowledge and your exam readiness.

Interactive Online Learning Environment and Test Bank

An online learning environment accompanies this study guide, designed to simplify your learning experience. Whether you're preparing at home or on the go, this platform is here to make studying easier and more convenient for you. The following learning resources are included:

Practice tests   This study guide includes a total of 115 questions. All 90 questions in the guide are available in our proprietary digital test engine, along with the 25 questions in the assessment test at the end of this introduction.

Electronic flash cards One hundred questions in a flash card format (a question followed by a single correct answer) are provided.

Glossary The key terms you need to know for the exam are available as a searchable glossary in PDF format along with their definitions.

The online learning environment and the test bank are available at https://www.wiley.com/go/sybextestprep.

Conventions Used in This Book

This study guide uses certain typographic styles in order to help you quickly identify important information and to avoid confusion over the meaning of words such as on-screen prompts.

In particular, look for the following styles:

- *Italicized text* indicates key terms that are described at length for the first time in a chapter. These words are likely to appear in the searchable online glossary. (Italics are also used for emphasis.)
- A monospaced font indicates the contents of a program or configuration files, messages displayed as a text-mode macOS/Linux shell prompt, filenames, text-mode command names, and Internet URLs.

In addition to these text conventions, which can apply to individual words or entire paragraphs, a few conventions highlight segments of text:

A note indicates information that's useful or interesting, but that's somewhat peripheral to the main text. A note might be relevant to a small number of networks, for instance, or it may refer to an outdated feature.

A tip provides information that you should understand for the exam. A tip can save you time or frustration and may not be entirely obvious. A tip might describe how to get around a limitation or how to use a feature to perform an unusual task.

AWS Certified Machine Learning Engineer Exam Objectives

This study guide is designed to comprehensively address each exam objective, reflecting the exam weighting outlined in the official guide, as illustrated in the following table:

Domain	Weight %
Domain 1: Data Preparation for Machine Learning (ML)	28%
Domain 2: ML Model Development	26%
Domain 3: Deployment and Orchestration of ML Workflows	22%
Domain 4: ML Solution Monitoring, Maintenance, and Security	24%

Domain 1: Data Preparation for Machine Learning (ML)

Task Statement 1.1: Ingest and Store Data

Knowledge of	Chapter
Data formats and ingestion mechanisms (for example, validated and non-validated formats, Apache Parquet, JSON, CSV, Apache ORC, Apache Avro, RecordIO)	2, 4, 5, 6
How to use the core AWS data sources (for example, Amazon S3, Amazon Elastic File System [Amazon EFS], Amazon FSx for NetApp ONTAP)	2, 5, 6
How to use AWS streaming data sources to ingest data (for example, Amazon Kinesis, Apache Flink, Apache Kafka)	2
AWS storage options, including use cases and tradeoffs	2

Task Statement 1.2: Transform Data and Perform Feature Engineering

Knowledge of	Chapter
Data cleaning and transformation techniques (for example, detecting and treating outliers, imputing missing data, combining, deduplication)	3, 4
Feature engineering techniques (for example, data scaling and standardization, feature splitting, binning, log transformation, normalization)	3, 4
Encoding techniques (for example, one-hot encoding, binary encoding, label encoding, tokenization)	3

Tools to explore, visualize, or transform data and features (for example, Amazon Amazon SageMaker Data Wrangler, AWS Glue, AWS Glue DataBrew)	3
Services that transform streaming data (for example, AWS Lambda, Spark)	3
Data annotation and labeling services that create high-quality labeled datasets	3

Task Statement 1.3: Ensure Data Integrity and Prepare Data for Modeling

Knowledge of	Chapter
Pretraining bias metrics for numeric, text, and image data (for example, class imbalance [CI], difference in proportions of labels [DPL])	3
Strategies to address CI in numeric, text, and image datasets (for example, synthetic data generation, resampling)	3, 5
Techniques to encrypt data	3, 8
Data classification, anonymization, and masking	3
Implications of compliance requirements (for example, personally identifiable information [PII], protected health information [PHI], data residency)	8
Validating data quality (for example, by using AWS Glue DataBrew and AWS Glue Data Quality)	3
Identifying and mitigating sources of bias in data (for example, selection bias, measurement bias) by using AWS tools (for example, Amazon SageMaker Clarify)	3
Preparing data to reduce prediction bias (for example, by using dataset splitting, shuffling, and augmentation)	3
Configuring data to load into the model training resource (for example, Amazon EFS, Amazon FSx)	2, 3

Domain 2: ML Model Development

Task Statement 2.1: Choose a Modeling Approach

Knowledge of	Chapter
Capabilities and appropriate uses of ML algorithms to solve business problems	1, 4
How to use AWS AI (for example, Amazon Translate, Amazon Transcribe, Amazon Rekognition, Amazon Bedrock) to solve specific business problems	1, 4, 6
How to consider interpretability during model selection or algorithm selection	4, 6
Amazon SageMaker built-in algorithms and when to apply them	4

Task Statement 2.2: Train and Refine Models

Knowledge of	Chapter
Elements in the training process (for example, epoch, steps, batch size)	5
Methods to reduce model training time (for example, early stopping, distributed training)	5
Factors that influence model size	5
Methods to improve model performance	5
Benefits of regularization techniques (for example, dropout, weight decay, L1 and L2)	5
Hyperparameter tuning techniques (for example, random search, Bayesian optimization)	5
Model hyperparameters and their effects on model performance (for example, number of trees in a tree-based model, number of layers in a neural network)	1, 4, 5
Methods to integrate models that were built outside Amazon SageMaker into Amazon SageMaker	5, 6

Task Statement 2.3: Analyze Model Performance

Knowledge of	Chapter
Model evaluation techniques and metrics (for example, confusion matrix, heat maps, F1 score, accuracy, precision, recall, root mean square error [RMSE], receiver operating characteristic [ROC], area under the ROC curve [AUC])	5
Methods to create performance baselines	5
Methods to identify model overfitting and underfitting	5
Metrics available in Amazon SageMaker Clarify to gain insights into ML training data and models	5
Convergence issues	5

Domain 3: Deployment and Orchestration of ML Workflows

Task Statement 3.1: Select Deployment Infrastructure Based on Existing Architecture and Requirements

Knowledge of	Chapter
Deployment best practices (for example, versioning, rollback strategies)	6
AWS deployment services (for example, Amazon SageMaker AI endpoints)	6
Methods to serve ML models in real time and in batches	6
How to provision compute resources in production environments and test environments (for example, CPU, GPU)	6
Model and endpoint requirements for deployment endpoints (for example, serverless endpoints, real-time endpoints, asynchronous endpoints, batch inference)	6

Knowledge of	Chapter
How to choose appropriate containers (for example, provided or customized)	6
Methods to optimize models on edge devices (for example, Amazon SageMaker Neo)	6

Task Statement 3.2: Create and Script Infrastructure Based on Existing Architecture and Requirements

Knowledge of	Chapter
Difference between on-demand and provisioned resources	6
How to compare scaling policies	6
Tradeoffs and use cases of infrastructure as code (IaC) options (for example, AWS CloudFormation, AWS Cloud Development Kit [AWS CDK])	6
Containerization concepts and AWS container services	6
How to use Amazon SageMaker endpoint auto scaling policies to meet scalability requirements (for example, based on demand, time)	6

Task Statement 3.3: Use Automated Orchestration Tools to Set up Continuous Integration and Continuous Delivery (CI/CD) Pipelines

Knowledge of	Chapter
Capabilities and quotas for AWS CodePipeline, AWS CodeBuild, and AWS CodeDeploy	6
Automation and integration of data ingestion with orchestration services	6
Version control systems and basic usage (for example, Git)	6
CI/CD principles and how they fit into ML workflows	6, 7

Deployment strategies and rollback actions (for example, blue/green, canary, linear) — 6

How code repositories and pipelines work together — 6

Domain 4: ML Solution Monitoring, Maintenance, and Security

Task Statement 4.1: Monitor Model Inference

Knowledge of	Chapter
Drift in ML models	7
Techniques to monitor data quality and model performance	7
Design principles for ML lenses relevant to monitoring	7

Task Statement 4.2: Monitor and Optimize Infrastructure and Costs

Knowledge of	Chapter
Key performance metrics for ML infrastructure (for example, utilization, throughput, availability, scalability, fault tolerance)	6, 7
Monitoring and observability tools to troubleshoot latency and performance issues (for example, AWS X-Ray, Amazon CloudWatch Lambda Insights, Amazon CloudWatch Logs Insights)	7, 8
How to use AWS CloudTrail to log, monitor, and invoke retraining activities	7, 8
Differences between instance types and how they affect performance (for example, memory optimized, compute optimized, general purpose, inference optimized)	6, 7
Knowledge of	Chapter
Capabilities of cost analysis tools (for example, AWS Cost Explorer, AWS Billing and Cost Management, AWS Trusted Advisor)	7
Cost tracking and allocation techniques (for example, resource tagging)	7

xxvi Introduction

Task Statement 4.3: Secure AWS Resources

Knowledge of	Chapter
IAM roles, policies, and groups that control access to AWS services (for example, AWS Identity and Access Management [IAM], bucket policies, Amazon SageMaker Role Manager)	8
Amazon SageMaker security and compliance features	8
Controls for network access to ML resources	8
Security best practices for CI/CD pipelines	8

Assessment Test

1. When configuring Amazon S3 for data storage, what best practice should be followed to ensure efficient cost management and data retrieval?

   A. Store all data in the S3 Standard storage class.

   B. Utilize versioning for all objects.

   C. Implement lifecycle policies to transition data to appropriate storage classes.

   D. Enable cross-region replication for all buckets.

2. For high-throughput data ingestion into Amazon S3, which feature can be leveraged to manage large-scale file transfers efficiently?

   A. Amazon S3 Multipart Upload

   B. Amazon S3 Access Points

   C. Amazon S3 Transfer Acceleration

   D. Amazon S3 Batch Operations

3. What is a key advantage of using Amazon FSx for Lustre over Amazon S3 for machine learning workloads requiring high-speed processing?

   A. Better compatibility with Hadoop

   B. Lower cost for large datasets

   C. Support for distributed file systems with high throughput

   D. Seamless integration with Amazon Glacier

4. In the context of feature engineering, what is the primary goal of applying Principal Component Analysis (PCA) to a dataset?

   A. Increase the dimensionality of data

   B. Extract uncorrelated features for better model performance

   C. Normalize the distribution of features

   D. Enhance the interpretability of the dataset

5. When dealing with categorical variables in feature engineering, which method can be used to effectively capture the ordinal relationship between categories?

   A. One-hot encoding

   B. Binary encoding

   C. Ordinal encoding

   D. Frequency encoding

xxviii Introduction

6. For a problem requiring prediction of time-series data, which machine learning algorithm is most suitable?

   A. K-nearest neighbors

   B. DeepAR

   C. Support vector machines

   D. Random forests

7. Which ensemble method combines the predictions of multiple weak learners to improve model performance and robustness?

   A. Decision trees

   B. Neural networks

   C. XGBoost

   D. K-means clustering

8. In the context of model development, what is the purpose of using a regularization technique such as L1 or L2 regularization?

   A. To improve the accuracy of the training dataset

   B. To simplify the model by penalizing large coefficients

   C. To enhance data visualization

   D. To increase the learning rate of the model

9. Which optimization algorithm is commonly used to minimize the loss function during the training of deep learning models?

   A. Gradient descent

   B. Newton's method

   C. Genetic algorithm

   D. Simulated annealing

10. When evaluating a binary classification model, which metric should be used to determine the balance between precision and recall?

    A. Accuracy

    B. F1 score

    C. ROC-AUC

    D. Mean squared error

11. How can cross-validation help in assessing the generalization capability of a machine learning model?

    A. By splitting the dataset into train and test sets multiple times

    B. By using the entire dataset for training

C. By creating synthetic data points for evaluation

D. By reducing the dimensionality of features

12. What is the key benefit of using Amazon SageMaker AI for model deployment and orchestration?

A. Automatic hyperparameter tuning

B. Real-time model monitoring

C. Seamless integration with Amazon SageMaker Pipelines

D. Built-in data visualization tools

13. In the context of deploying machine learning models, what is the purpose of using AWS Step Functions?

A. To perform ETL operations on data

B. To create and manage complex ML workflows with state transitions

C. To monitor model performance in real time

D. To deploy models on edge devices

14. What is the advantage of using Amazon SageMaker Model Monitor for deployed models?

A. Automatic scaling of model endpoints

B. Continuous monitoring of model quality and data drift

C. Real-time training of models

D. Deployment of models across multiple regions

15. How can the detection of data drift help maintain model performance?

A. By retraining the model on the same dataset

B. By identifying changes in data distribution that affect model predictions

C. By increasing the model's learning rate

D. By reducing the number of features used in the model

16. Which AWS services can help secure machine learning models by enforcing access controls and encryption?

A. Amazon VPC and Amazon CloudWatch

B. AWS IAM and AWS Key Management Service (KMS)

C. AWS CloudTrail and Amazon GuardDuty

D. AWS IAM and AWS Config

17. When deploying machine learning models, what is a recommended best practice to prevent unauthorized access to sensitive data?

A. Using private S3 buckets for model storage

B. Storing model credentials in AWS Secrets Manager

xxx Introduction

    C. Enabling encryption at rest and in transit

    D. Allowing restricted network access to model endpoints

18. In feature engineering, which method helps in transforming skewed data distributions into a more Gaussian-like distribution?

    A. Min-max scaling

    B. Log transformation

    C. Label encoding

    D. One-hot encoding

19. What is the purpose of using dropout in training deep learning models?

    A. To improve the accuracy of the model

    B. To prevent overfitting by randomly dropping neurons

    C. To increase the learning rate

    D. To simplify the model architecture

20. Which Amazon SageMaker AI service helps detect bias in machine learning models during post-deployment monitoring?

    A. Amazon SageMaker Model Monitor

    B. Amazon SageMaker Data Wrangler

    C. Amazon SageMaker Clarify

    D. Amazon SageMaker Neo

21. You are tasked with deploying a machine learning model that requires GPU acceleration for inference to achieve optimal performance. Which AWS compute instance type would you select for this purpose?

    A. T2.micro

    B. C5.large

    C. P3.2xlarge

    D. R5.xlarge

22. You need to deploy multiple versions of a machine learning model to evaluate their performance in a live environment. Which AWS service enables you to deploy and manage these multiple model versions effectively?

    A. Amazon SageMaker Model Registry

    B. AWS Glue Data Catalog

    C. Amazon SageMaker Multi-Model Endpoints

    D. Amazon SageMaker Ground Truth

23. A retail company needs to process customer images in real time for personalized shopping experiences using a deep learning model. Which combination of AWS services and configurations would you use to achieve high performance and scalable inference?

A. Amazon SageMaker with Multi-Model Endpoints and Elastic Load Balancing

B. Amazon EC2 with GPU instances and AWS Auto Scaling

C. AWS Lambda with Amazon S3 and API Gateway

D. Amazon SageMaker with Endpoint Variants and Auto Scaling

24. A healthcare company needs to ensure that its deployed machine learning models comply with regulatory standards and maintain high accuracy over time. Which feature of Amazon SageMaker Model Monitor would you leverage to track data quality and model performance, and what key metrics would you monitor to ensure compliance?

A. Baseline constraints and statistics; monitor data distribution and prediction accuracy

B. Model registry; track model versions and updates

C. Hyperparameter tuning; optimize model hyperparameters

D. Feature store; manage and store feature data

25. An organization is looking to simplify the process of managing IAM roles for various Amazon SageMaker users and workloads. It needs to ensure that roles are correctly configured with the necessary permissions while maintaining security best practices. Which feature of Amazon SageMaker Role Manager would you use to achieve this?

A. Automatic role creation

B. Role templates

C. Role auditing

D. Role inheritance

Answers to Assessment Test

1. C. Lifecycle policies in Amazon S3 help manage storage costs by automatically transitioning data to lower-cost storage classes as it becomes less frequently accessed.

2. A. Amazon S3 Multipart Upload allows for efficient, parallel upload of large files by splitting them into smaller parts, which can be uploaded independently and reassembled.

3. C. Amazon FSx for Lustre is designed for high-performance workloads and provides a distributed file system with high throughput and low latency, making it ideal for data-intensive ML tasks.

4. B. PCA reduces the dimensionality of the data by transforming it into a set of uncorrelated principal components, improving model performance by eliminating redundant features.

5. C. Ordinal encoding assigns numerical values to categorical variables while preserving the order of the categories, which is important for algorithms that can leverage this relationship.

6. B. DeepAR is specifically designed to handle sequential data and can capture temporal dependencies, making it suitable for time series prediction.

7. C. XGBoost combines the predictions of multiple weak learners, typically decision trees, to create a strong predictive model by sequentially training each new learner to correct the errors made by the previous ones, effectively "boosting" the overall accuracy through an iterative process of error correction.

8. B. Regularization techniques add a penalty for large coefficients, encouraging simpler models that generalize better to new data and reducing the risk of overfitting.

9. A. Gradient descent is a widely used optimization algorithm in deep learning that iteratively adjusts model parameters to minimize the loss function.

10. B. The F1 score is the harmonic mean of precision and recall, providing a single metric that balances both aspects, particularly useful for imbalanced datasets.

11. A. Cross-validation involves partitioning the data into multiple train and test splits, providing a more reliable estimate of the model's generalization performance.

12. C. Amazon SageMaker Pipelines allows for the creation and management of end-to-end machine learning workflows, facilitating efficient model deployment and orchestration.

13. B. AWS Step Functions enable the orchestration of complex workflows with state transitions, ensuring that each step of the ML process is executed in the correct order.

14. B. Amazon SageMaker Model Monitor continuously tracks model performance and data drift, alerting users to issues that could impact model accuracy and reliability.

15. B. Detecting data drift involves monitoring shifts in data distribution, which can help identify when the model may need retraining to maintain performance.

16. B. AWS IAM enables access control by securely managing identities and access to AWS services and resources. AWS KMS provides encryption keys and manages their lifecycle, ensuring data and model security through encryption at rest and in transit.

17. C. Encrypting data at rest and in transit ensures that sensitive data remains secure, even if accessed without proper authorization.

18. B. Log transformation reduces skewness in data, making distributions more Gaussian-like, which can improve model performance and interpretation.

19. B. Dropout is a technique that prevents overfitting in neural networks. It works by randomly deactivating a percentage of neurons during training. This forces the remaining neurons to compensate, which prevents any one neuron from becoming too dependent on others.

20. C. Amazon SageMaker Clarify detects and measures bias in machine learning models, both before and after deployment, helping to ensure fair and unbiased predictions.

21. C. P3.2xlarge provides GPU acceleration, which is essential for models requiring high computational power for inference, ensuring optimal performance.

22. C. Amazon SageMaker Multi-Model Endpoints allows you to deploy multiple models on a single endpoint, effectively managing different model versions and improving resource utilization, leading to cost savings and simplified deployment management.

23. D. Amazon SageMaker with Endpoint Variants and Auto Scaling allows you to deploy multiple versions of a model with Auto Scaling to handle different traffic loads, providing high performance and scalable inference for real-time image processing.

24. A. Baseline constraints and statistics help ensure that the input data remains consistent with the training data and the model's predictions continue to meet the required accuracy and compliance standards.

25. B. Role templates simplify the assignment of appropriate permissions based on common Amazon SageMaker tasks, ensuring that users have the necessary access while adhering to security best practices and reducing the complexity of role management.

Chapter 1

Introduction to Machine Learning

THE AWS CERTIFIED MACHINE LEARNING (ML) ENGINEER ASSOCIATE EXAM OBJECTIVES COVERED IN THIS CHAPTER MAY INCLUDE, BUT ARE NOT LIMITED TO THE FOLLOWING:

✓ **Domain 2: ML Model Development**
- 2.1 Choose a modeling approach
- 2.2 Train and refine models

Machine learning (ML) has become ubiquitous in our digital world. Whether you need to book a flight, visit your doctor, make an online purchase, pay a bill, or check the weather forecast, behind the scenes any of these actions has started (or is a part of) a process that collects large amounts of data, processes the data, and performs some ML task.

ML is a branch of artificial intelligence (AI) that enables systems to learn and improve from experience without being explicitly programmed.[1] By analyzing large datasets, ML algorithms can identify patterns, make decisions, and predict outcomes.

The integration of ML into various domains has revolutionized industries by enhancing efficiency, accuracy, and decision-making capabilities.

This chapter will provide the ML foundations you need to know for the exam. To better understand ML, we need to set the context where ML originated, which is AI.

Understanding Artificial Intelligence

AI is a branch of computer science whose main focus is to develop systems capable of performing tasks that typically require human intelligence. These tasks include (but are not limited to) recognizing speech, making decisions, solving problems, identifying patterns, and understanding languages. AI systems leverage techniques such as ML, natural language processing (NLP), deep learning, and computer vision to simulate cognitive functions like learning, reasoning, and self-correction. The field of AI is rapidly evolving, with applications spanning various industries, from healthcare and finance to autonomous vehicles and smart cities. Understanding AI involves exploring its fundamental concepts, its historical development, and the ethical implications of its widespread adoption.

AI systems ingest data, such as human-level knowledge, and emulate natural intelligence. ML is a subset of AI, where data and algorithms continuously improve the training model to help achieve higher-quality output predictions. Deep learning is a subset of ML. It is an approach to realizing ML that relies on a layered architecture, simulating the human brain to identify data patterns and train the model.

---

[1] An early ML pioneer and computer scientist, Arthur Samuel, coined the term *machine learning* in 1959 to denote the "field of study that gives computers the ability to learn without being explicitly programmed." Thirty-eight years later, another computer scientist, Tom Mitchell, defined machine learning as "the study of computer algorithms that allow computer programs to automatically improve through experience."

FIGURE 1.1 Deep learning, machine learning, and AI.

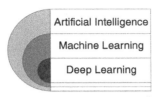

Figure 1.1 illustrates this hierarchy. It all starts with data and how data can be used to extract relevant information, which ultimately produces knowledge

Data, Information, and Knowledge

Data, information, and knowledge form the foundation of understanding and applying AI. *Data* is the raw, unprocessed facts and figures collected from various sources. When data is organized and processed, it transforms into *information*, which provides context and meaning. *Knowledge* is derived from the synthesis of information, enabling comprehension and informed decision-making.

In AI, data serves as the essential input that fuels ML algorithms, enabling the training of models to recognize patterns and make predictions. Information, structured from the data, helps refine these models by offering insights and context. Ultimately, knowledge empowers AI systems to emulate human-like reasoning, enhancing their ability to perform complex tasks, adapt to new situations, and provide valuable solutions across various domains.

Data

Data is defined as a value or set of values representing a specific concept or concepts. Data is the most critical asset of the digital age, fueling advancements in technology and shaping the way we understand and interact with the world. To harness its full potential, it's essential to recognize the different classes of data: structured, semi-structured, and unstructured. Each class has unique characteristics and applications, particularly in the context of AI.

Understanding these classes of data and their peculiarities is crucial for leveraging AI's full potential. Structured data provides the foundation for organized analysis, semi-structured data offers flexibility in handling complex information, and unstructured data unlocks a wealth of untapped insights. Together, they enable AI systems to learn, adapt, and deliver transformative solutions across various domains. Let's review each class in more detail.

Structured Data

Structured data is highly organized and easily searchable in databases. This type of data adheres to a fixed schema, meaning it follows a predefined format with specific fields and records. For example, a spreadsheet containing customer information, such as names, addresses, and purchase histories, is structured data. It allows for efficient querying and analysis, making it invaluable for business intelligence and data-driven decision-making.

4   Chapter 1 ▪ Introduction to Machine Learning

These are examples of structured data:

- Relational databases (e.g., SQL databases)
- Spreadsheets (e.g., Excel files)
- Financial records (e.g., transaction logs)

Semi-Structured Data

Semi-structured data lacks the rigid structure of structured data but still contains some organizational elements, such as tags or markers, that provide context and hierarchy. This class of data is often used for storing and transmitting complex information that doesn't fit neatly into a table format. Semi-structured data is more flexible than structured data, allowing for greater adaptability in handling diverse data types.

These are examples of semi-structured data:

- JavaScript Object Notation (JSON) files
- Extensible Markup Language (XML) documents
- Email messages (headers, body text, attachments)

Unstructured Data

Unstructured data is the most common and diverse type of data, encompassing information that doesn't follow a predefined format or schema. This class of data is often rich in content but challenging to analyze and search. Unstructured data requires advanced AI techniques, such as NLP and computer vision, to extract meaningful insights.

These are examples of unstructured data:

- Text files (e.g., Word documents)
- Multimedia files (e.g., images, videos)
- Social media content (e.g., tweets, posts)

Information

Information bridges the gap between raw data and actionable knowledge. Derived from data, information provides a semantic element in the form of context and meaning, resulting in a transformation of disparate facts and figures into coherent, useful insights.

Information can be understood as data that has been processed, organized, or structured in a way that adds context and relevance. Unlike raw data, which is often unorganized and lacks inherent meaning, information is data presented in a format that is understandable and useful to its recipient(s). For example, a list of temperatures recorded at various times of the day is mere data; when these temperatures are organized into a table showing daily weather patterns, they become information.

The key characteristics of information are accuracy, relevance, completeness, and timeliness:

Accuracy   Information must be precise and free from errors to be valuable. Inaccurate information can lead to misguided decisions and outcomes.

Relevance   Information should be pertinent to the context or problem at hand. Irrelevant information, no matter how accurate, serves little purpose.

Completeness   Information must be comprehensive enough to provide a clear understanding without ambiguity. Incomplete information can result in incorrect conclusions.

Timeliness   Information is most useful when it is available at the right time. Outdated information can be as detrimental as inaccurate information.

In AI, information plays a critical role in training and refining algorithms. AI systems rely on vast amounts of data to learn and make predictions. This data is processed into information that adds context and aids in pattern recognition and decision-making.

For instance, in NLP, raw text data is processed to extract meaningful information, such as sentiment analysis or language translation. Similarly, in computer vision, images are analyzed to identify objects and patterns, turning visual data into actionable information.

Knowledge

Knowledge represents a higher level of understanding that goes beyond mere data and information. It encompasses the insights, experiences, and contextual understanding that enable individuals and systems to make informed decisions, solve problems, and innovate.

Knowledge is derived from the synthesis and application of information. It involves recognizing patterns, understanding relationships, and drawing conclusions based on experience and context. Unlike data, which is raw and unprocessed, or information, which is organized and meaningful, knowledge embodies a deeper comprehension that guides action and thought.

The key characteristics of knowledge are contextuality, applicability, basis in experience, and dynamism.

Contextuality   Knowledge is deeply rooted in context. It involves understanding not just the facts but also the circumstances and nuances that surround them.

Applicability   Knowledge is practical. It involves the ability to apply information to real-world situations, making it actionable and relevant.

Experience-based   Knowledge is often gained through experience. It encompasses lessons learned, insights gained, and the wisdom accumulated over time.

Dynamism   Knowledge is ever-evolving. As new information becomes available and experiences accumulate, knowledge grows and adapts.

In AI, knowledge is crucial for developing systems that can derive inferences, learn, and adapt. AI systems rely on vast amounts of data and information to build knowledge bases that enable them to perform complex tasks and make intelligent decisions.

For example, expert systems in AI were designed to emulate human expertise in specific domains. These systems utilized knowledge bases that contained rules, facts, and relationships, allowing them to provide recommendations and solve problems. Similarly, ML algorithms use data and information to build models that capture knowledge about patterns and trends, enabling predictive analytics and decision-making.

Understanding Machine Learning

ML is a subset of AI that allows computers to learn from existing information, *without being explicitly programmed*, and apply that learning to perform other similar tasks.

Without explicit programming, the machine learns from data and information it feeds. The machine picks up patterns, trends, or essential features from previous data and makes predictions on new data. This aspect of ML, i.e., a machine's ability to learn *without being explicitly programmed*, is important and emphasizes the key difference between ML and classical programming.

Let's say you are tasked by your manager to build a program that translates text from English to Italian. At a very high level, you could pursue a classical programming approach by manually coding rules and exceptions for lexicon, grammar, syntax, and vocabulary. This approach would be extremely complex and not scalable. Instead, with ML, you could leverage models that excel at understanding context, idioms, and nuances in both languages, which are essential for accurate translation. These ML models can continuously improve their translation capabilities with more data, adapting to new expressions, idioms, and evolving language usage.

A real-life ML application is in recommendation systems. For example, Amazon uses ML to recommend books to users based on users' book categories selection and purchase history. Likewise, Spotify uses ML to recommend songs to users based on previously purchased songs and genres to their liking. In both cases, Amazon and Spotify use large amounts of data to train their ML models and derive meaningful inferences in the form or recommendations.

In the upcoming sections, the fundamental concepts of ML will be introduced. These concepts will form the basis you need to master each exam objective. Let's start with the ML lifecycle.

ML Lifecycle

First, you must have a holistic view of the entire ML lifecycle. Because ML is deeply grounded in science, it all starts by questions like "What is the business problem we are trying to solve?" and, most importantly, "How does machine learning address this business need?"

Figure 1.2 illustrates the ML lifecycle. These steps are generally followed in all ML projects, regardless of the cloud provider or the tools in use. Let's review each step.

Define ML Problem

Defining a ML problem is the critical first step in the development of any ML project. It involves understanding and clearly articulating the specific business challenge or question that needs to be addressed using data and ML techniques. This phase includes identifying the problem's scope, the desired outcomes, and the feasibility of applying ML solutions. Crucially, it requires a detailed analysis of the available data, understanding the business

FIGURE 1.2 Machine learning lifecycle.

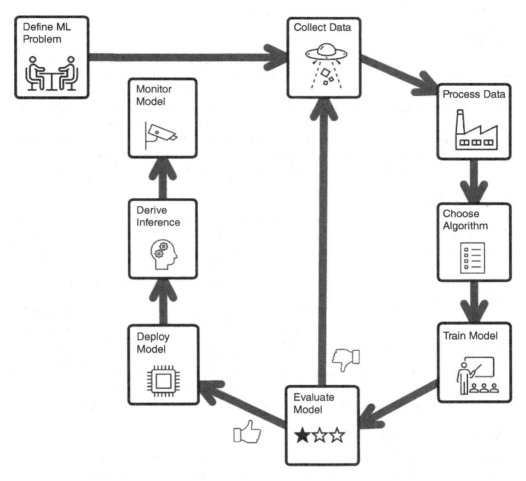

context, and determining the performance metrics that will be used to evaluate success. By establishing a clear and well-defined problem statement, you can ensure that your efforts are focused and aligned with strategic goals, leading to more effective and impactful ML solutions.

What sets an ML problem apart from other problems in computer science/engineering is its reliance on data-driven approaches and statistical models to make predictions or decisions. Traditional programming relies on explicit instructions and algorithms to solve problems, whereas ML leverages patterns and relationships within the data to infer solutions. This shift from *deterministic* algorithms to *probabilistic models* means that ML problems often involve uncertainty and require continuous learning and adaptation from new data, making them

8 Chapter 1 ▪ Introduction to Machine Learning

uniquely dynamic and challenging. This aspect of continuous learning and adaptation from new data is reflected in the cycle represented in Figure 1.2.

Collect Data

The "Collect Data" phase involves gathering the raw data needed for training and testing models. The types of data collected should align with the specific ML problem being addressed. For instance, if the goal is to predict housing prices, numerical data like square footage and year built would be essential. For a customer segmentation task, categorical data like customer demographics and purchase behavior would be relevant. Ensuring that the collected data is relevant and representative of the problem domain sets the foundation for effective model building. Initial efforts should focus on acquiring comprehensive and high-quality data, as this will significantly impact the overall success of the project.

Process Data

The collected data is in a raw state as a result of being ingested from different data sources. In this format, the dataset is not suitable for modeling. First, the dataset may contain missing or noisy data. Second, different data may be in different ranges. Third, not all collected data may be relevant to the model's ability to derive accurate predictions (as you will learn later, also called the target variable, or label). Last, the dataset must be split in three sets: the training, validation, and test datasets.

As a result, the collected data must be adequately transformed to be suitable for model training and evaluation. The "Process Data" step includes normalizing, scaling, and encoding data to ensure consistency and comparability across features. Feature engineering, on the other hand, involves creating new features or modifying existing ones to enhance the model's predictive power. Techniques such as binning numerical data, creating interaction terms, and extracting datetime features are commonly used. The goal of this phase is to clean, refine, and enrich the data, making it ready for effective model training and evaluation.

Choose Algorithm

In the "Choose Algorithm" phase of the ML lifecycle, the focus shifts to selecting the most appropriate algorithm to address the defined problem. This decision is critical because different algorithms are tailored to different types of tasks, such as classification, regression, clustering, or reinforcement learning. Factors like the nature of the data, the complexity of the problem, and the desired outcomes play a significant role in this selection process. For instance, linear regression might be chosen for a straightforward predictive analysis, whereas a deep neural network could be more suitable for complex image recognition tasks.

This phase involves evaluating the strengths and limitations of various algorithms, considering aspects such as accuracy, interpretability, training time, and scalability. It may also include experimenting with multiple algorithms and using cross-validation techniques to compare their performance on the processed data. The goal is to identify the algorithm that offers the best balance of performance and feasibility, ensuring that the model can effectively learn from the data and make accurate predictions. This informed selection sets the stage for the subsequent phases, where the chosen algorithm will be trained, validated, and fine-tuned to achieve optimal results.

Train Model

The "Train Model" phase is a pivotal stage in the ML lifecycle, following the selection of an algorithm. During this phase, the chosen algorithm is applied to the training data to identify patterns and learn the underlying relationships. This process involves feeding the data into the model and iteratively adjusting the model's parameters to minimize errors, assess bias-variance trade-offs, and improve predictive accuracy. Various techniques, such as gradient descent and backpropagation, are employed to optimize the model's performance.

The goal of training the model is to create a robust and accurate predictive model that generalizes well to new, unseen data. This phase is critical because it determines the model's capability to make reliable predictions and drive decision-making in real-world applications. The effectiveness of this phase hinges on the quality and representativeness of the training data, as well as the proper tuning of hyperparameters to avoid overfitting or underfitting.

Evaluate Model

After training, the model is ready for the evaluation phase, whose goal is to assess its performance on a separate *validation dataset* and to ensure that it generalizes well to new, unseen data. Key performance metrics such as accuracy, precision, recall, F1 score, and mean squared error are calculated to gauge the model's effectiveness. This evaluation helps identify any issues like *overfitting* or *underfitting* and provides insights into areas where the model might need improvement.

Evaluation also includes visualizing results through confusion matrices, receiver operating characteristic (ROC) curves, and other diagnostic plots to understand the model's strengths and weaknesses. Based on these evaluations, iterative refinement and tuning of the model may be conducted to enhance its predictive performance. This phase ensures that the model meets the desired criteria and is ready for deployment in real-world applications.

Deploy Model

After you've trained, tuned, and evaluated your model, you can deploy it into production and let your ML application consume it through an endpoint to make predictions. The deployment phase is all about making the trained and validated model available for use in real-world ML applications. It encompasses setting up an infrastructure to host the model, ensuring scalability, reliability, security, sustainability, and cost-effectiveness, which are all pillars of the well-architected ML framework. Figure 1.3 illustrates how each pillar maps to each phase.

10 Chapter 1 ▪ Introduction to Machine Learning

FIGURE 1.3 Well-architected ML lifecycle.

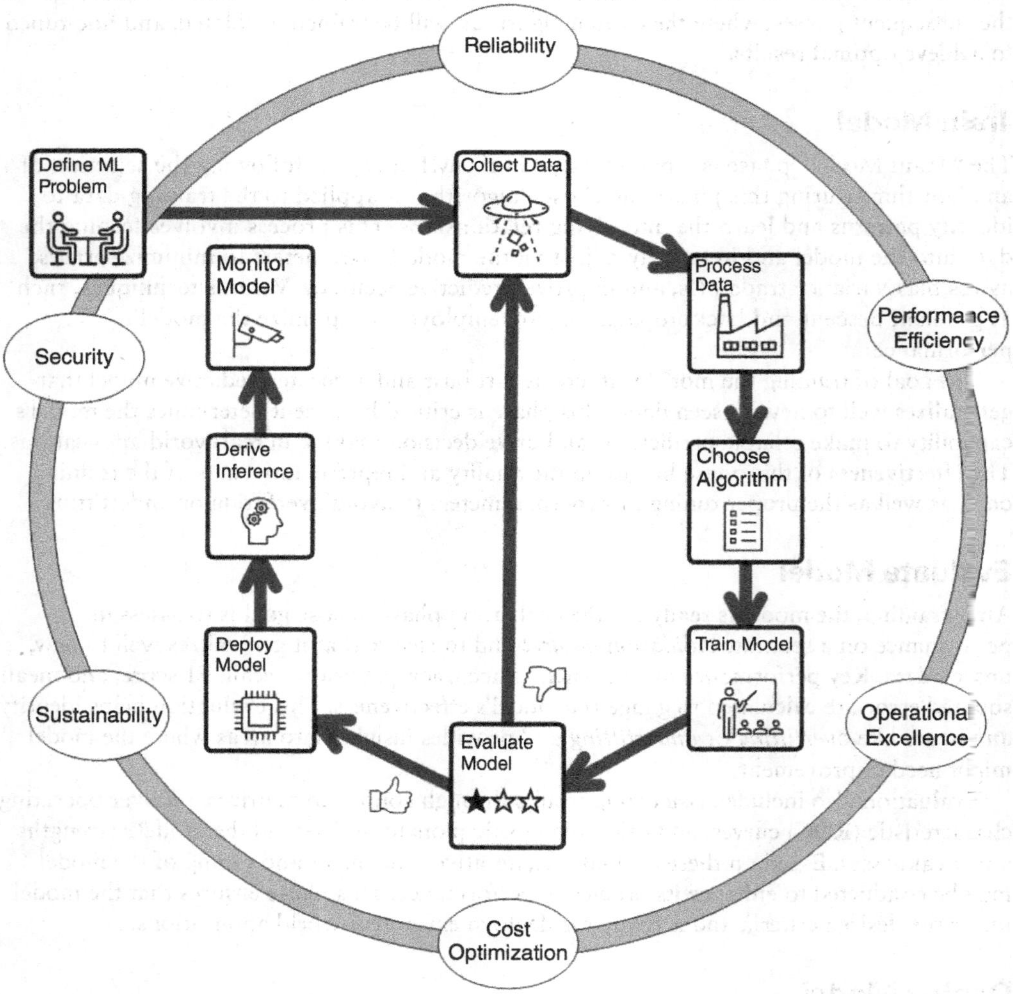

The "Deploy Model" phase in AWS leverages Amazon SageMaker to seamlessly transition from evaluation to deployment. This phase involves using specific SageMaker services tailored to deployment needs.

For real-time predictions, *Amazon SageMaker Real-Time Inference* endpoints are ideal, offering low-latency responses suitable for applications requiring immediate predictions, such as interactive web apps or chatbots. For scenarios where batch processing is sufficient, *Amazon SageMaker Batch Transform* provides an efficient way to handle large datasets, making predictions in a cost-effective manner. Additionally, for workloads with fluctuating traffic, *Amazon SageMaker Serverless Inference* dynamically scales to meet demand without managing servers.

These Amazon SageMaker services ensure that the model remains highly available and performant in production. The deployment phase focuses on making the trained model accessible and usable in real-world applications, ensuring that it delivers value by providing accurate and timely predictions.

Derive Inference

The "Derive Inference" phase, following model deployment, involves using the model to generate predictions or insights from new data in real time or batch mode. This phase is where the model delivers tangible value by applying its learned patterns to make decisions, classify data, or forecast outcomes. In practice, this means feeding the model live data inputs and obtaining actionable outputs that can drive business strategies, optimize operations, or enhance user experiences. The success of this phase hinges on the model's accuracy and relevance, ensuring that it consistently provides reliable and insightful inferences to inform decision-making.

Monitor Model

Deployment is more than just putting the model into operation; it's about maintaining its effectiveness over time. Continuous monitoring is essential to detect any performance degradation or drift in data patterns. This monitoring phase ensures that the model remains accurate and relevant, providing consistent value in its designated tasks.

In AWS, this can be accomplished using *Amazon SageMaker Model Monitor*, which automatically detects data and prediction quality issues. Amazon SageMaker Model Monitor continuously tracks key metrics like accuracy, latency, and data drift, and it generates alerts when deviations occur. Additionally, *Amazon CloudWatch* is used to collect and analyze logs, set alarms, and visualize performance metrics in real time. This proactive monitoring approach helps maintain the model's effectiveness, enabling timely interventions and retraining to address any performance degradation.

By carefully monitoring model deployments, organizations can leverage their ML models to drive impactful business decisions and enhance operational efficiency.

ML Concepts

During this study, we will use many terms related to ML. Therefore, it is essential that you understand this jargon. The key concepts you need to know for the exam are discussed in this section. These concepts will be covered in detail in the upcoming chapters, as your knowledge progresses.

Features

Features—also known as independent variables—are the inputs that the model learns from during training. The model uses the values of these features to make predictions.

Features are derived from observations or measurements recorded in the dataset. Each observation represents a single instance or data point, and the features are the attributes or variables that describe these instances. For example, if you're observing houses, each house (observation) might have features like the number of bedrooms, square footage, and year built.

Target Variable

The *target variable*—also known as the *dependent variable*—is the outcome the model is trying to predict.

In a supervised learning context, the target variable is known beforehand and is used to train the model. Put differently, the entire dataset you feed the model includes features data (independent variables) and target variables data (dependent variables). The model will use this dataset to learn during training.

Target variables are identified during the first step of the ML lifecycle, i.e., "Define ML Problem."

For example, if you're developing a model to predict house prices, the target variable would be the price of the house.

In ML, the terms *target variable, dependent variable,* and *label* are often used interchangeably. They all refer to the output variable that the model aims to predict based on the input features. Whether you're doing regression or classification, this is the variable you're trying to forecast or classify.

Optimization Problem

Optimization problems are central to ML. At its core, ML involves finding the best parameters for a model to minimize error and make accurate predictions. Whether it's through gradient descent, regularization techniques, or hyperparameter tuning, solving optimization problems is essential to training effective models.

Examples of optimization algorithms include gradient descent, stochastic gradient descent (SGD), and mini-batch gradient descent.

For example, consider training a neural network for image classification (neural networks will be introduced in the upcoming sections in this chapter). To achieve the highest accuracy, we use gradient descent to minimize the loss function, which measures the difference between the predicted and actual labels. The optimization algorithm iteratively adjusts the model's weights and biases to reduce this loss, improving the model's performance. Another example of an optimization problem is hyperparameter tuning in ML models. Hyperparameters, like learning rate, batch size, and number of layers in a neural network, significantly impact the model's performance. Finding the optimal combination of these hyperparameters involves searching through a vast space of possible values. Techniques such as grid search, random search, and Bayesian optimization automate this process, systematically exploring different hyperparameter configurations and evaluating their performance on a validation set. These optimization methods help identify the best settings, leading to improved model performance and generalization.

Objective Function

An *objective function*, also known as a *loss function* or *cost function*, is a key concept in ML that defines the goal of the model training process. It's the function that the algorithm aims to minimize (or maximize) during training. By evaluating how well the model's predictions match the actual outcomes, the objective function measures the error or loss. Algorithms use this feedback to adjust the model's parameters iteratively, striving to reduce the error and improve accuracy. Common examples include mean squared error for regression tasks and cross-entropy loss for classification tasks. Understanding and selecting the right objective function is crucial for guiding the learning process effectively.

ML Algorithms vs. ML Models

Throughout this study, we will use the terms *ML models* and *ML algorithms*. These are two distinct concepts, and it is important to understand the differences between the two.

An ML algorithm is the step-by-step list of instructions provided in the form of code, which runs on a particular dataset to analyze data and identify patterns. This algorithm is analogous to general programming code. For example, it could be the geometrical average of a set of numbers. Similarly, in ML, an algorithm can be applied to learn the statistics of a given dataset or to apply current statistics to predict future data.

On the other hand, an ML model is the result of applying an algorithm to a dataset. It represents the learned patterns and relationships within the data in the form of a set of parameters. Once trained, the model can be used to make predictions or decisions based on new, unseen data.

Think of the ML algorithm as the recipe and the ML model as the finished dish created from the recipe.

> Mathematically, the model can be thought of as a function that maps input features to output predictions. The learning process is all about discovering this function by finding the optimal parameters that minimize the difference between the predicted outputs and the actual target values. So, in essence, the ML algorithm helps identify and refine this mathematical function, transforming data into meaningful insights.

ML Algorithm Classification

A general way to classify ML algorithms is by learning type: *supervised learning*, *unsupervised learning*, and *reinforcement learning*. Let's deep dive into each type:

Supervised learning   Supervised learning involves training a ML model using a labeled dataset, which means that each training example is paired with an output label: i.e., the correct prediction. The model learns to map inputs to the correct output by adjusting its parameters to minimize the error between its predictions and the actual labels. Common algorithms include linear regression, logistic regression, and support vector machines. Applications of supervised learning include email spam detection, image classification, and medical diagnosis.

Unsupervised learning   Unsupervised learning deals with unlabeled data. The goal here is to uncover hidden patterns or intrinsic structures within the data. Without predefined labels, the model tries to learn the underlying distribution or clustering of the data. Common algorithms include k-means clustering, hierarchical clustering, and principal component analysis (PCA). Applications of unsupervised learning include market basket analysis, customer segmentation, and anomaly detection.

Reinforcement learning   Reinforcement learning is inspired by behavioral psychology and involves training an agent to make decisions by rewarding desired behaviors and punishing undesired ones. The agent learns to maximize cumulative rewards over time by interacting with its environment and receiving feedback. Key components include the policy, reward signal, and value function. Applications of reinforcement learning include game playing (like AlphaGo), robotics, and autonomous driving.

Another way to classify ML algorithms is by predictive task. You need to understand the following two categories for the exam. More details will be provided in Chapter 4, where Amazon SageMaker's built-in algorithms will be covered in detail, with examples, code, and plots to show you how they work.

Classification   Algorithms that predict a discrete category, like "apple" or "orange" (e.g., logistic regression, decision trees)

Regression   Algorithms that predict a continuous value, like price or temperature (e.g., linear regression, support vector regression)

Differences Between ML and AI

AI and ML are often used interchangeably, but they represent distinct concepts within the field of computer science. AI is the broader concept, encompassing any technique that enables machines to simulate human intelligence, including reasoning, learning, problem-solving, and decision-making. AI can be rule-based systems, expert systems, or even simple automation tasks, aiming to replicate various aspects of human cognition.

ML, a subset of AI, specifically focuses on the ability of machines to learn from data and improve its performance over time without being explicitly programmed. ML involves training algorithms on datasets to identify patterns and make predictions. It includes techniques like supervised learning, unsupervised learning, and reinforcement learning, each serving different purposes in teaching machines to become smarter.

FIGURE 1.4 AWS ML stack.

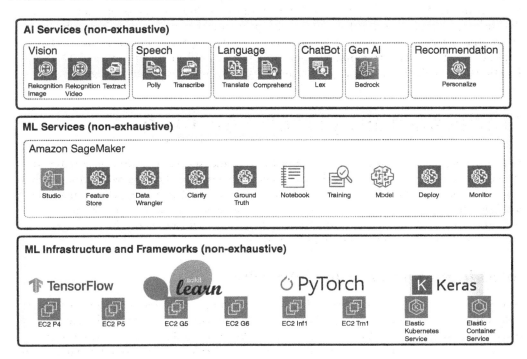

For your workloads in AWS, you can choose from three different levels of ML and AI capabilities: ML Infrastructure and Frameworks, ML Services, and AI Services. This is called the *AWS ML stack*, as illustrated in Figure 1.4.

The AWS ML stack is a comprehensive suite of tools and services designed to support every stage of the ML lifecycle. At the base is the ML Infrastructure and Frameworks layer, which provides powerful computing resources like EC2 instances (P4, P5, G5, G6, Inf1, and Trn1) optimized for ML, as well as preconfigured environments like AWS Deep Learning AMIs that support popular ML frameworks such as TensorFlow, PyTorch, and Keras.

Moving up, the ML Services layer centers around Amazon SageMaker, a fully managed service that streamlines the processes of building, training, and deploying ML models. Amazon SageMaker is a family of services that offer features such as data labeling, model tuning, model evaluation, and deployment, significantly reducing the complexity and effort required for ML projects. You will learn the specific Amazon SageMaker services for each task in the upcoming chapters.

At the top, the AI Services layer provides *ready-to-use* AI capabilities that developers can easily integrate into their applications without ML or deep learning expertise. These AI services use prebuilt algorithms, use prebuilt models (already trained by AWS), and support a wide range of use cases: Amazon Rekognition for image and video analysis, Amazon Poll for text-to-speech conversion, Amazon Textract for extracting text and data from documents, Amazon Translate for real-time language translation, Amazon Transcribe for converting speech to text, and Amazon Bedrock for building and scaling generative AI applications. These services enable businesses to quickly implement sophisticated AI functionalities, enhancing their applications with powerful and scalable intelligence.

Understanding Deep Learning

Deep learning (DL) is a specialized subset of ML that focuses on algorithms inspired by the structure and function of the brain, known as *neural networks*. Whereas ML encompasses a wide array of algorithms such as regression, classification, and clustering, DL distinguishes itself through its use of deep neural networks with many layers. These networks have revolutionized fields by automatically learning to represent data in ways that are often more accurate and effective than traditional ML methods.

Introduction to Neural Networks

Neural networks are the backbone of DL. They are composed of interconnected compute units called *neurons* that work together to process and learn from data. Each neuron receives input, processes it through an *activation function*, and passes the output to the next layer of neurons. This structure allows neural networks to learn complex patterns and representations in data, making them powerful tools for tasks like image and speech recognition.

Structure of a Neural Network

Neural networks are composed of interconnected neurons, which are grouped in layers. Let's dive deeper into each of these components.

Neuron

A neuron, also known as a *node* or a *perceptron* in the context of artificial neural networks, is the fundamental building block of neural networks. It simulates the function of a biological neuron found in the human brain, albeit in a simplified and mathematical form.

The neuron's mathematical operations enable it to transform input features into meaningful predictions. By adjusting weights and biases through training, the neuron learns to make accurate predictions based on patterns and relationships in the data.

The components of a neuron are represented in Figure 1.5. Let's go over each.

FIGURE 1.5 Mathematical representation of a neuron.

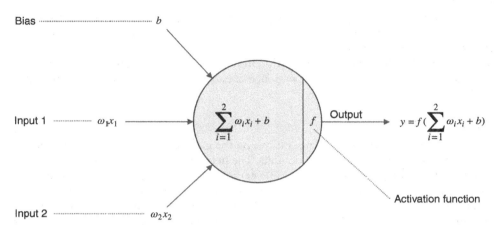

Inputs These are the data features or signals that the neuron receives. Each input represents a specific observation for that feature. In Figure 1.5, the neuron receives two inputs, x_1 and x_2.

Weights Weights are values that determine the importance or contribution of each input to the neuron's output. During training, the network adjusts these weights to improve accuracy. In Figure 1.5, the input x_1 uses the weight ω_1, and the input x_2 uses the weight ω_2.

Bias The bias is an additional parameter that allows the activation function to shift. It helps the neuron make adjustments to the weighted sum before applying the activation function. In Figure 1.5, the bias is denoted with the symbol b.

Weighted sum With reference to Figure 1.5, the neuron calculates a weighted sum of the inputs and the bias: $\sum_{i=1}^{2} \omega_i x_i + b$.

Activation function The activation function f introduces nonlinearity into the model. It takes the weighted sum and produces the neuron's output. Common activation functions include sigmoid, Rectified Linear Unit (ReLU), and Hyperbolic Tangent (Tanh). In a neural network, the choice of activation function for each neuron is made by the data scientists or ML engineers designing the model and is informed by experimentation to determine the most effective configuration for the specific task at hand.

Output The output y is the final result produced by the neuron after applying the activation function to the weighted sum. The neuron sends its output to the next layer of neurons or to the final output layer.

Input Layer

The input layer is the first layer of the neural network. Its primary function is to receive the initial data that will be processed by the network. Each neuron in the input layer corresponds to a feature in the dataset.

For example, in a housing price prediction model, the features might be the size of the house, the number of bedrooms, the location, etc. Each of these features is an input to the input layer.

Hidden Layers

Hidden layers perform complex computations on the input data to detect patterns and relationships that aren't immediately obvious. The network can have one or more hidden layers. Each hidden layer consists of multiple neurons, and the outputs of the neurons in one layer become the inputs for the neurons in the subsequent layer. This process continues through all the hidden layers until it reaches the output layer. Neurons in hidden layers use activation functions (like ReLU, Sigmoid, and Tanh) to introduce nonlinearity. This allows the network to capture complex relationships in the data.

Continuing with our housing price prediction model, hidden layers might learn to identify patterns like the relationship between the size of the house and the number of bedrooms or the influence of the location on the price.

Output Layer

The output layer is the final layer of the neural network. Its primary function is to produce the final prediction or classification based on the processed data from the hidden layers. The output layer consists of neurons, each representing a possible outcome or class. The choice of activation function for each neuron in the output layer depends on the type of problem Regression problems are characterized by continuous value predictions. For regression a linear activation function or no activation function might be used. Classification problems are characterized by discrete value predictions. For classification problems, a softmax or sigmoid activation function is commonly used to produce probabilities for each class.

In our housing price prediction model, the output layer might have a single neuron that produces the predicted price.

How Neural Networks Work

In a complex neural network, the generated model is a combination of weights and biases for each neuron. Here's a bit more detail on how this process works.

A neural network generates a model through the sophisticated interplay of weights and biases within its neurons, enhanced by the *backpropagation* algorithm. Backpropagation is the key algorithm in training a neuron. During the training phase, input data is fed into the network, where each neuron calculates a weighted sum of its inputs. This sum, combined with a bias, is passed through an activation function to produce the neuron's output. The weights determine the influence each input (feature) has on the output (prediction), and the bias shifts the activation function to better fit the data. By adjusting these weights and biases through backpropagation, the network learns to map inputs to outputs accurately. Backpropagation calculates the error at the output layer using a *loss function* and then propagates this error backward through the network. By computing the gradient of the loss function with respect to the weights and biases, it uses optimization algorithms like gradient descent to update these parameters, thereby minimizing the error and improving predictive accuracy.

As the network trains, it progressively fine-tunes the weights and biases across all its neurons, effectively capturing complex patterns in the data. Each layer of neurons transforms the input data through a series of weighted sums, biases, and activation functions, with backpropagation ensuring these transformations lead to minimized error. The final layer's output is the model's prediction, whether it's a classification label or a continuous value. This combination of numerous neurons, each with its own set of weights and biases, facilitated by backpropagation, creates a powerful model capable of handling a wide range of tasks, from image recognition to NLP. The resulting model is a finely tuned machine, shaped by the continuous adjustment of weights and biases, enabling it to make accurate and reliable predictions.

Weights and biases are parameters that the model learns during training. They are adjusted through optimization processes like gradient descent and backpropagation to minimize the loss function and improve the model's predictions. Hyperparameters, on the other hand, are set *before* the training process begins and are not learned from the data. They control the training process and the structure of the model. Examples of hyperparameters include learning rate, number of epochs, number of hidden layers and units, batch size, and regularization parameters (to prevent overfitting by adding constraints to the model). More details will be provided in the "Hyperparameter Tuning" section in Chapter 5.

Neural Networks Types

Neural networks come in various types, each designed to tackle specific tasks and data structures. Artificial neural networks (ANNs), deep neural networks (DNNs), convolutional neural networks (CNNs), and recurrent neural networks (RNNs) are some of the most prominent types you need to know for the exam. These different neural network architectures enable diverse applications across various domains, from image and video recognition to NLP and sequential data analysis.

Artificial Neural Networks

Artificial neural networks (ANNs) are the simplest form of neural networks, consisting of an input layer, one hidden layer, and an output layer. These layers are fully connected, meaning each neuron in one layer is connected to every neuron in the next layer. ANNs are capable of learning from data by adjusting the weights of these connections to minimize error. Despite their simplicity, ANNs can perform a wide range of tasks, from classification to regression.

Deep Neural Networks

Deep neural networks (DNNs) build upon the concept of ANNs by adding more hidden layers; hence the term *deep*. This depth allows them to model more complex patterns in the data, which is essential for solving sophisticated tasks. Each layer in a DNN learns to extract increasingly abstract features from the data, culminating in a powerful representation that can be used for tasks like object detection and natural language understanding. Figure 1.6 illustrates a DNN with three inputs, two hidden layers, and one output.

Convolutional Neural Networks

Convolutional neural networks (CNNs) are a type of DNN specifically designed for processing grid-like data, such as images. Because images are composed of pixels arranged in a grid format—where each pixel represents a specific color or intensity—CNNs utilize convolutional layers that apply filters to the input data, effectively capturing spatial hierarchies and patterns. This architecture makes CNNs exceptionally good at tasks like image classification, object detection, and even playing complex games.

Recurrent Neural Networks

Recurrent neural networks (RNNs) are another type of DNN tailored for sequential data, such as time series or natural language. Unlike traditional neural networks, RNNs have connections that form directed cycles, allowing them to maintain a memory of previous inputs. This makes them highly effective for tasks that involve sequences, such as language modeling, speech recognition, and machine translation. Variants like long short-term

FIGURE 1.6 Deep neural network with two hidden layers.

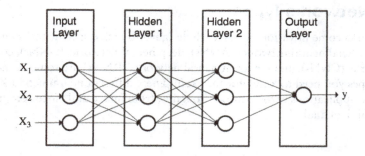

memory (LSTM) networks and gated recurrent units (GRUs) address some of the limitations of standard RNNs by better capturing long-term dependencies in the data.

Differences Between DL and ML

ML is a broad field encompassing various techniques that enable machines to learn from data and make predictions without being explicitly programmed. It includes algorithms like linear regression, decision trees, and clustering, often requiring manual feature engineering and preprocessing.

On the other hand, DL is a specialized subset of ML and uses neural networks with multiple layers (deep neural networks) to automatically learn representations from raw data and generate predictions from the data.

Whereas traditional ML models might rely on handcrafted features, DL models excel at processing large volumes of unstructured data, such as images and text, by extracting features autonomously. This depth and complexity allow DL models to achieve higher accuracy in tasks like image recognition and NLP, at the expense of significant amount of computational resources and longer training times.

As an AWS ML engineer, your job is to determine the trade-offs between the quality of your models and the costs related to training, deployment, and maintenance.

Case Studies

The following two case studies highlight how AWS's powerful compute solutions can enhance DL applications across different industries.

Case Study 1: Mobileye's Autonomous Driving Technology

Mobileye, a driving automation technology provider, develops self-driving technology and advanced driver-assistance systems using cameras, computer chips, and software.

Application   Mobileye uses Amazon EC2 DL1 instances to train DL models for computer vision tasks like object detection, tracking, and segmentation. These models are critical for building autonomous driving solutions that adapt to changing road conditions.

Impact   By leveraging AWS, Mobileye improved price performance by 40%, accelerated its development cycle, and managed more than 250 production workloads daily. This allowed Mobileye to deploy more efficient and cost-effective autonomous driving solutions.

For more information, visit:

```
https://aws.amazon.com/solutions/case-studies/mobileye-ec2-dl1-
case-study
```

Case Study 2: Leidos' Healthcare ML Applications

Leidos, a science and technology solutions leader, builds ML applications to help public and private health organizations accelerate diagnosis and treatment.

Application   Leidos migrated its ML workloads to Amazon EC2 DL1 instances, which are powered by Gaudi accelerators from Habana Labs. This migration improved performance and reduced compute costs for NLP and computer vision use cases.

Impact   Leidos achieved 66% cost savings on model training, increased precision scores to 95–97%, and cut model training time from 8 hours to less than 1 hour for about 2,200 cases a day. This significantly improved patient outcomes and streamlined claim processing.

For more information, visit:

`https://aws.amazon.com/solutions/case-studies/leidos-case-study`

Summary

In this chapter, you learned how ML is a subset of AI that focuses on developing algorithms and statistical models that enable computers to learn and make predictions without explicit programming.

The distinctive element of ML when compared with traditional programming is the ability of ML models to learn from data and improve their performance over time without being explicitly programmed for specific tasks, allowing them to adapt and generalize to new use cases and unseen data more effectively.

The ML lifecycle was introduced with a description of each phase, from the definition of an ML problem to the deployment and monitoring of an ML model. You learned how features are the input of an ML algorithm, whereas the target variable is the output the algorithm is trying to predict. The concept of objective (loss) function was also introduced as a means to measure how well the model's predictions match the actual outcomes. Emphasis was provided on how ML algorithms differ from ML models, the former defining the specific procedures or rules used to train models by adjusting parameters based on input data, and the latter representing the outcome of this training process, encapsulating learned patterns and making predictions on new data.

You learned how AWS offers a wide spectrum of AI and ML services logically organized in the AWS ML stack. This representation includes at the lowest level compute infrastructure specifically designed and built for optimized ML applications, in the middle level the Amazon SageMaker ecosystem of services, and at the highest level a broad selection of fully managed AI services for a variety of different use cases.

At the end of the chapter, an introduction to deep learning—as a specialized branch of ML—was provided. DL uses neural networks to automatically extract high-level features from raw data, making them particularly effective for tasks such as image and speech recognition, and NLP. DL models, with their ability to learn intricate patterns and representations, have significantly advanced the capabilities of AI systems. Thus, whereas AI encompasses the broader goal of creating intelligent agents, ML and DL provide the tools and methods to achieve these objectives, with DL pushing the boundaries of what's possible in terms of complexity and accuracy.

Exam Essentials

Know the difference between data, information, and knowledge. Data is a collection of raw, unprocessed facts and figures without context or meaning. Information is data that has been processed, interpreted, and given context, making it useful for decision-making. Information is characterized by accuracy, relevance, completeness, and timeliness. Knowledge is information that has been assimilated, understood, and interpreted through experience, leading to insights, wisdom, or expertise.

Know the difference between structured, semi-structured, and unstructured data. Structured data is organized in accordance to a predefined schema and is easily searchable. Examples include Excel files and relational databases. Semi-structured data does not conform to a strict schema but still contains tags or markers to separate semantic elements, providing a degree of organization (e.g., JSON, XML documents). Unstructured data is often rich in information but requires advanced tools, such as natural language processing and ML, to extract meaningful insights because it lacks a predefined structure or schema.

Understand the machine learning lifecycle. ML is an iterative process, where models are continuously refined and improved based on new data and feedback, enabling the system to adapt and enhance its performance over time. The phases of the ML lifecycle are define ML problem, collect data, process data, choose algorithm, train model, evaluate model, deploy model, derive inference, and monitor model.

Know the difference between supervised, unsupervised, and reinforcement ML algorithms. With supervised ML algorithms, models are trained to predict outcomes using labeled data, where each data point is tagged with a corresponding label or outcome (i.e., the correct prediction). In contrast, unsupervised ML algorithms work with unlabeled data. The objective is to identify hidden patterns, structures, or relationships within the data. Reinforcement ML algorithms force agents to learn how to predict outcomes through trial and error.

Know the difference between an ML algorithm and an ML model. An ML algorithm is a set of rules or procedures used to create and train a model. It defines how the model will learn from the input data by adjusting its parameters. Examples include linear regression, logistic regression, decision trees, and k-Nearest Neighbors (k-NN). An ML model is the output generated *after* the training process using an ML algorithm. It represents the learned patterns and relationships derived from the training data. These patterns and relationships are codified in the form of a mathematical function, which essentially expresses in an unambiguous way the learned model. Once trained, the model can make predictions or classifications on new, unseen data.

Understand what a neural network is. A neural network is a computational model used in DL that simulates the human brain, consisting of interconnected neurons in layers. It processes input data, adjusts weights and biases through learning algorithms, and produces output to recognize patterns and make predictions.

Review Questions

1. Which of the following is *not* an example of semi-structured data?
   A. NoSQL database
   B. JSON document
   C. XML document
   D. PDF document

2. Which phase immediately precedes the model evaluation in the ML lifecycle?
   A. Derive inference
   B. Gradient descent
   C. Deploy model
   D. Train model

3. What are the inputs to a machine learning algorithm?
   A. Target variables
   B. Weights
   C. Bias
   D. Features

4. Which of the following is *not* a type of machine learning algorithm?
   A. Supervised learning
   B. Gradient descent
   C. Unsupervised learning
   D. Reinforcement learning

5. What distinguishes a machine learning model from a machine learning algorithm?
   A. The model is a set of rules, and the algorithm is the learned patterns.
   B. The model performs predictions, and the algorithm defines how it learns.
   C. The model is the learning process, and the algorithm is the final output.
   D. The model is a hyperparameter, and the algorithm is an optimization technique.

6. In the context of machine learning, what is a hyperparameter?
   A. A parameter that the model learns from the data
   B. A parameter that is set before the training process begins
   C. A variable that holds the final output of the model
   D. A metric used to evaluate the model's performance

7. What is the primary purpose of using activation functions in neural networks?

    A. To initialize the weights

    B. To introduce nonlinearity into the model

    C. To reduce the dimensionality of the data

    D. To perform gradient descent optimization

8. What is the primary function of backpropagation in a neural network?

    A. To forward propagate the input data through the network

    B. To update the weights and biases of each neuron to minimize error

    C. To visualize the data

    D. To remove outliers from the dataset

9. Which type of neural network is best suited for processing sequential data, such as time series or text?

    A. Convolutional neural network (CNN)

    B. Recurrent neural network (RNN)

    C. Artificial neural network (ANN)

    D. Deep neural network (DNN)

10. What is a key difference between deep learning and machine learning?

    A. DL algorithms require less data than ML algorithms to perform well.

    B. DL relies on neural networks with multiple layers to automatically extract features, whereas ML often requires manual feature engineering.

    C. ML algorithms are always more accurate than DL algorithms.

    D. DL algorithms cannot be used for image and speech recognition tasks.

Chapter 2

Data Ingestion and Storage

THE AWS CERTIFIED MACHINE LEARNING (ML) ENGINEER ASSOCIATE EXAM OBJECTIVES COVERED IN THIS CHAPTER MAY INCLUDE, BUT ARE NOT LIMITED TO, THE FOLLOWING:

✔ **Domain 1: Data Preparation for Machine Learning**
  - 1.1 Ingest and store data

Introducing Ingestion and Storage

Data ingestion and storage are the two core elements of the Collect Data phase of the machine learning (ML) lifecycle, as shown in Figure 2.1.

As you learned in Chapter 1, your ML solution requires data to train the selected model and generate inference. Data may come in different forms (structured, semi-structured or unstructured), from different sources, and at different times.

Ingestion is the process responsible for collecting the data for your ML solution and pushing it into AWS. You—as an AWS machine learning engineer—will need to select the best AWS data ingestion service to gather the data from different sources based on volume, velocity, and variety.

Upon collection, you will need to store the ingested data in a suitable and secure location to ensure the durability and availability requirements are met. With this approach, your ML solution will have access to the data to train your ML model when it's needed (availability) and as long as it's needed (durability).

Ingesting and Storing Data

Before delving into ingestion and storage, let's take a step back to better understand all the elements of an ML problem.

Machine learning is part of a broader discipline known as data engineering. In this context, ML is one of the three ways data is served.

Figure 2.2 illustrates the data engineering lifecycle. The first step is generation, which is focused on where the data originates from. Data can be generated by a variety of different source system such as a database, an Internet of Things (IoT) device, a streaming system, and more. A data engineer designs processes to consume data from source systems but might not be able to control them.

Upon generation, data is ingested in its raw format(s) into a storage system located in AWS, where it is stored and subsequently processed. For the exam, it is necessary to ensure an appropriate data store is chosen. The choice is based on the specific use case

Ingesting and Storing Data 29

FIGURE 2.1 The ML lifecycle.

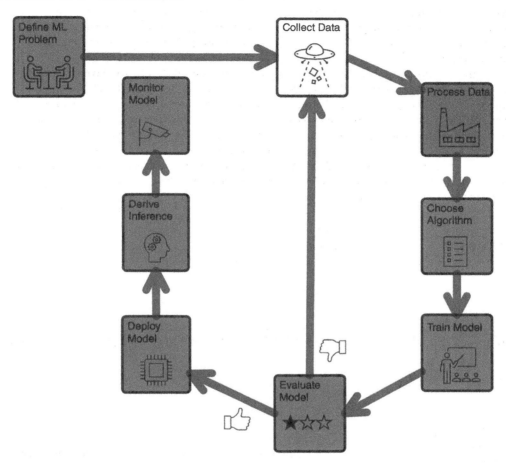

FIGURE 2.2 The data engineering lifecycle.

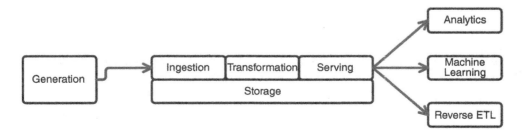

Chapter 2 ▪ Data Ingestion and Storage

For example, you may want to store your raw data as object storage in an S3 bucket because your data is produced in batches, and this type of storage is relatively cheap compared to other means. Conversely, if your data was produced and consumed in near real time, you may want to store it in a streaming storage medium, such as Amazon Kinesis Data Streams.

Figure 2.3 shows a hierarchical view of storage layers in AWS. The top layer illustrates storage at a conceptual level by listing different types of storage abstractions. The middle layer describes storage at a logical level, with some of the most commonly used storage systems and types. The bottom layer lists the underlying infrastructure components that make the storage systems, and the corresponding storage abstractions, work. For each storage system, several AWS services are generally available.

For the exam it is also required that you understand how to extract the stored data and how to prepare it for your selected ML algorithm, which will be used to train your model and derive inferences. These tasks will be covered in the next chapters.

FIGURE 2.3 AWS storage systems.

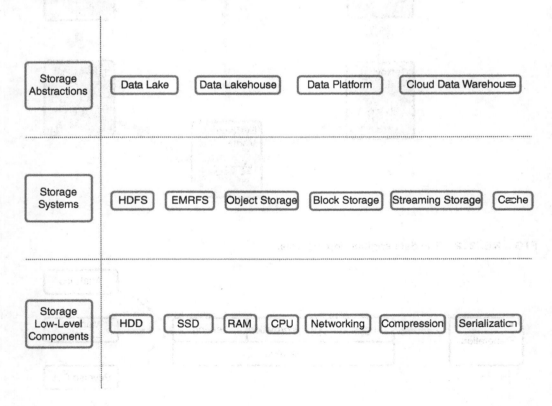

Ingesting and Storing Data   **31**

In the upcoming sections, you will learn how to choose the most appropriate data store to collect and host the data for your ML solution. The core AWS services to ingest data from different sources into AWS will be covered, as well as the main use cases that apply to them.

Data Formats and Ingestion Techniques

There are many different data formats to efficiently ingest and store data for your ML model. By using the right data format and algorithm, you—as a machine learning engineer—can optimize performance, improve scalability, and reduce processing time.

AWS supports a variety of data formats to cater to different use cases and services. These are some of the commonly used data formats to ingest and store data in AWS:

- Comma-separated values (CSV)
- JavaScript Object Notation (JSON)
- Apache Parquet
- Apache Optimized Row Columnar (ORC)
- Apache Avro
- RecordIO

CSV is widely used to store structured data in tabular format, whereas JSON is ideal for document-based, semi-structured data.

Apache Parquet and Apache ORC are columnar data formats and are designed to optimize storage operations (read, writes) for large datasets. The values in each column are stored in contiguous memory locations, providing the following benefits:

- Column-specific compression is efficient in storage space.
- Column-specific encoding and compression techniques can be used.
- Queries that fetch specific column values do not need to read the entire row, thus improving performance.

Unlike Apache Parquet and Apache ORC, Apache Avro is designed to store data in a row-based format. Avro data relies on schemas. When Avro data is read, the schema used when writing it is always present. This permits each data component to be written with no per-value overheads, making serialization both fast and small. This also facilitates use with dynamic scripting languages, because data, together with its schema, is fully self-describing. When Avro data is stored in a file, its schema is stored with it as well so that files may be processed later by any program. If the program reading the data expects a different schema, this can be easily resolved, because both schemas are present.

Last, RecordIO is a data format used primarily by Apache MXNet, a deep learning framework. The basic idea is to divide the data into individual chunks, called *records*, and then prepend to every record its length in bytes, followed by the data. As a result, RecordIO implements a file format for a sequence of records.

32 Chapter 2 ▪ Data Ingestion and Storage

A key driver in the decision of what data format to choose is the format supported by the ML algorithm you intend to use for your ML problem. This ML algorithm will be trained on your data, so ensuring compatibility between the data format and the algorithm's requirements is crucial for optimal performance and efficiency. By aligning your data format with the algorithm's capabilities, you can streamline the data ingestion process, reduce preprocessing overhead, and achieve more accurate and faster results in your ML workflow.

Table 2.1 lists built-in Amazon SageMaker algorithms along with their accepted data formats. Chapter 4 will cover in detail each one of these algorithms.

Another important driver to consider is your *data access pattern*. A data access pattern defines how producers and consumers interact with data to meet business needs. It involves understanding and documenting the ways data is queried, stored, and retrieved. The following are the main factors that define your data access pattern:

Data size.   Knowing the volume of data helps in determining effective data partitioning.

Data shape.   Organizing data to match query requirements can enhance speed and scalability.

Data velocity.   Understanding peak query loads helps in optimizing data partitioning for better I/O capacity.

TABLE 2.1   Data format support for built-in ML algorithms in Amazon SageMaker.

Algorithm	Accepted data formats
BlazingText	Text file (one sentence per line)
DeepAR forecasting	JSON Lines, Parquet
Factorization Machines	RecordIO-protobuf, CSV
Image classification	RecordIO, image files (.jpg, .png)
IP Insights	CSV
K-means	RecordIO-protobuf, CSV
K-nearest neighbors (k-NN)	RecordIO-protobuf, CSV
Linear learner	RecordIO-protobuf, CSV
LDA	RecordIO-protobuf, CSV
Neural topic model	RecordIO-protobuf, CSV
Object detection	RecordIO, image files (.jpg, .png)

Ingesting and Storing Data **33**

Algorithm	Accepted data formats
PCA	RecordIO-protobuf, CSV
Random cut forest	RecordIO-protobuf, CSV
Semantic segmentation	RecordIO, image files (. pg, .png)
Seq2Seq	RecordIO-protobuf, text file
XGBoost	CSV, LibSVM, Parquet

TABLE 2.2 Example of a data access pattern.

Field	Example
Data Access Pattern Name	Find orders
Data Access Pattern Description	Find orders by Customer ID and Time Interval
Priority	Medium
Operation (Read/Write)	Read
Type (Single Item/Multiple Items/All)	Multiple
Filter	Customer ID = 123, Time Interval = 24 hours ago
Sort	Time descending

Table 2.2 illustrates an example of what you should look for in a data access pattern.

In essence, data access patterns help in designing efficient and scalable data ingestion solutions by aligning your organization data with access requirements.

Put differently, the way your raw data is consumed from different sources and is ingested and stored into AWS will help you determine the data format and the AWS service to use.

Table 2.3 shows how AWS services are grouped based on whether your data is structured, semi-structured, or unstructured.

As you may have noticed, Amazon S3 is the most flexible service because it can be used for all three different data categories. Additionally, you can supplement Amazon S3 with Amazon Athena and query your data directly from S3 without formatting the data or managing the infrastructure.

34 Chapter 2 ▪ Data Ingestion and Storage

TABLE 2.3 AWS services for structured, semi-structured, and unstructured data.

Structured	Semi-structured	Unstructured
Amazon RDS	Amazon DynamoDB	Amazon S3
Amazon Aurora	Amazon DocumentDB	Amazon Rekognition
Amazon Redshift	Amazon Athena	Amazon Transcribe
Amazon S3	Amazon S3	Amazon Comprehend
Amazon Athena		

In the next sections, we will deep dive into these services as they relate to ingestion and storage.

Choosing AWS Ingestion Services

When it comes to ingestion services, AWS offers a broad spectrum of options. What service best fits your use case is driven by a number of factors:

Scalability. Your ingestion solution must be able to support the velocity and volume of your data as it becomes available from all its data sources.

Resilience. Your ingestion solution must be able to recover from failures and be able to resume seamlessly from when the failure occurred.

Security and compliance. The data must be properly secured during the ingestion process so that no unauthorized actor is allowed to ever consume it while in transit or while it is stored. Moreover, the ingestion process must comply with industry-specific regulations, e.g., Payment Card Industry Data Security Standard (PCI DSS), Health Insurance Portability and Accountability Act (HIPAA), and so on. Additional considerations must be examined to ensure data is ingested and stored in accordance with data residency requirements.

Cost. With the cloud pay-as-you-go delivery model, you always want to make sure cost is under control. This is even more true when dealing with streaming data, which virtually never stops. As a result, costs incurred to ingest and store data to train your ML models can quickly grow. You, as an ML engineer, need to choose an AWS ingestion service that supports the most cost-effective pricing model for your use case.

Flexibility. Your ingestion solution must be able to adapt to changes. AWS services are highly customizable. Make sure you tailor your data ingestion pipelines to meet your business and technical requirements, but also consider change as an additional element to be addressed in the architecture of your solution.

Let's start our study with AWS data ingestion services for streaming data.

Amazon Data Firehose

Amazon Data Firehose (formerly known as Amazon Kinesis Data Firehose) is a fully managed service that allows you to collect, transform, and deliver data streams to data lakes, data warehouses, and analytics services in near real time (within seconds).

As a fully managed service, Amazon Data Firehose continuously processes the stream, automatically scales based on the volume of data available, and delivers it to its destination within seconds.

To use Amazon Data Firehose, you configure a data stream with a source, a destination, and the transformations your data needs prior to reaching its destination.

You must select the *source* for your data stream, such as a topic in Amazon Managed Streaming for Kafka (MSK) or a stream in Kinesis Data Streams, or you can directly write data using the Firehose Direct PUT application programming interface (API). Amazon Data Firehose is integrated into more than 20 AWS services so you can set up a data stream from sources such as Amazon CloudWatch Logs, AWS Web Application Firewall (WAF) web ACL logs, AWS Network Firewall Logs, Amazon Simple Notification Services (SNS), or AWS IoT.

You must select a *destination* for your stream, such as Amazon S3, Amazon OpenSearch Service, Amazon Redshift, Splunk, Snowflake, or a custom HTTP endpoint.

You can optionally specify whether you want to convert your data stream into a format such as Parquet or ORC, decompress the data, perform custom data transformations using your own AWS Lambda function, or dynamically partition input records based on attributes to deliver into different locations.

Use Cases

Typical use cases include the following:

Streaming into data lakes and warehouses. You can stream data into Amazon S3, Amazon Redshift, and other destinations, converting it into formats like Parquet for analysis without building complex processing pipelines.

Security observability. You can monitor network security in real time and create alerts when potential threats arise using supported security information and event management (SIEM) tools.

Machine learning applications. You can enrich data streams with ML models to analyze data and predict outcomes as the data moves to its destination.

Amazon Kinesis Data Streams

Amazon Kinesis Data Streams is another managed service to ingest and store data streams for processing, with the value-add of performing *real-time* data streaming as well as providing extensive integration with the AWS ecosystem of data engineering services.

Amazon Kinesis Data Streams lets you build custom, real-time applications using the Amazon Managed Service for Apache Flink or other popular frameworks like Apache Spark. You can also stream your data directly to consumer applications running on Amazon EC2 instances. Additionally, AWS Lambda can be used as a consumer to process data in near real time without the need to manage servers.

With Amazon Kinesis Data Streams, your data is put into Kinesis data streams, which ensures *durability* and *elasticity*. The delay between the time a record is put into the stream and the time it can be consumed (put-to-get delay) is typically less than one second. Put differently, a Kinesis Data Streams application can start consuming the data from the stream almost immediately after the data is added. Because Amazon Kinesis Data Streams is a managed service, you don't need to worry about creating and running a data intake pipeline.

The elasticity of Kinesis Data Streams enables you to automatically scale the stream up or down so that you never lose data records before they expire.

Use Cases

Typical use cases for Amazon Kinesis Data Streams include the following:

Accelerated log and data feed intake and processing.   You can have producers push data directly into a stream without having to worry about your data being lost if the application server fails. Amazon Kinesis Data Streams provides accelerated data feed intake because you don't batch the data on the servers before you submit it for intake.

Real-time metrics and reporting.   You can use data collected into Amazon Kinesis Data Streams for simple data analysis and reporting in real time. For example, your data-processing application can work on metrics and reporting for system and application logs as the data is streaming in, rather than wait to receive batches of data.

Real-time data analytics.   This combines the power of parallel processing with the value of real-time data. For example, process website clickstreams in real time, and then analyze site usability engagement using multiple different Kinesis Data Streams applications running in parallel.

Complex stream processing.   You can create sophisticated data streams applications that combine multiple data streams into new data streams for downstream processing.

Amazon Managed Streaming for Apache Kafka (MSK)

If you are familiar with the Apache Kafka event streaming platform, the good news is that you can build and run applications that use Apache Kafka on AWS with limited effort and minimal administration. AWS offers Amazon MSK, which enables you to securely ingest and process streaming data in real time with a fully managed, highly available Apache Kafka service.

Amazon MSK provides the control plane to let you create, update, and delete Apache Kafka clusters. For on-demand streaming and zero-operations use cases, you can choose Amazon MSK *Serverless*, which automatically provisions and scales capacity while managing the partitions in your topic, so you can stream data without worrying about right-sizing or scaling clusters. With Amazon MSK serverless, you pay only for what you use.

Amazon MSK also lets you use Apache Kafka's data plane operations, such as those for producing and consuming data.

Additionally, Amazon MSK runs open-source versions of Apache Kafka. As a result, existing applications, tooling, and plugins from partners and the Apache Kafka community are supported without requiring changes to application code.

The exam does not expect you to master every aspect of Amazon MSK. Nonetheless, you will be required to know the main components of Amazon MSK's architecture and their intended purpose:

Broker nodes. These are the worker nodes that perform the "heavy-duty" tasks, including ingesting, storing (in topic partitions), and processing your streaming data. When creating an Amazon MSK cluster, you specify how many broker nodes you want Amazon MSK to create in each Availability Zone. Some of these broker nodes are elected for you as the controller nodes and are responsible for managing the states of partitions and replicas, performing administrative tasks like reassigning partitions, and maintaining the leader-follower relationship between brokers for partitions. The minimum is one broker node per Availability Zone. Each Availability Zone has its own virtual private cloud (VPC) subnet.

ZooKeeper nodes. Amazon MSK also creates the Apache ZooKeeper nodes for you. Apache ZooKeeper is an open-source server that enables highly reliable distributed coordination between the broker nodes.

KRaft controllers. The Apache Kafka community developed KRaft to replace Apache ZooKeeper for metadata management in Apache Kafka clusters. In KRaft mode, cluster metadata is propagated within a group of Kafka controllers, which are part of the Kafka cluster, instead of across ZooKeeper nodes. KRaft controllers are included at no additional cost and require no additional setup or management from you.

Producers, consumers, and topic creators. Amazon MSK enables you to use Apache Kafka's data-plane operations to create topics and to produce and consume data.

Cluster operations. You can use the AWS Management Console, the AWS Command Line Interface (AWS CLI), or the APIs in the SDK to perform control plane operations. For example, you can create or delete an Amazon MSK cluster, list all the clusters in an account, view the properties of a cluster, and update the number and type of brokers in a cluster.

Use Cases

Typical use cases for Amazon MSK include the following:

Ingesting, storing, processing, and delivering real-time event streams. Amazon MSK enables you to capture and process in real time high-volume application and database events and continuously ingest them into a data lake or to a variety of supported destinations for further processing.

System of record for streaming data. Amazon MSK can act as a single source of truth for the state of your data. This means that all changes to the data are captured and stored in Amazon MSK durable topics, allowing different applications to access and update the state consistently.

38 Chapter 2 ▪ Data Ingestion and Storage

Powering your event-driven architectures on AWS. You can leverage the versatility of Apache Kafka to develop and build modern, secure event-driven applications on AWS.

Amazon Managed Service for Apache Flink

With Amazon Managed Service for Apache Flink (formerly known as Amazon Kinesis Data Analytics), you can leverage the Apache Flink framework to process and analyze streaming data in real time. Apache Flink is an open-source stream processing framework for stateful computations and complex analytics.

Unlike Apache Kafka, Apache Flink does not provide its own data storage system. However, it is fully integrated with various external storage systems to manage state and process data, such as Amazon S3, Amazon MSK, Amazon Kinesis Data Streams, and other data sources.

Some of the unique capabilities offered by Apache Flink are its robust support for data streaming workloads at scale, fault tolerance, and strong guarantees of exactly-once correctness. This is particularly appealing to global enterprises, which require reliable and performant infrastructure to transfer large volumes of data in the form of real-time events.

Moreover, the service offers access to Apache Flink's expressive APIs, and through Amazon Managed Service for Apache Flink Studio, you can interactively query data streams or launch stateful applications in only a few steps. With this managed service, you can get started with Apache Flink and quickly deploy and operate your data stream processing applications.

Just like Apache MSK and most of the AWS fully managed services, there are no servers and clusters to manage, and there is no compute infrastructure to set up. You pay only for the resources you use.

Use Cases

Typical use cases for Amazon Managed Service for Apache Flink include the following:

Streaming data pipelines. Continuously ingest, enrich, and transform data streams, loading them into destination systems for timely action (versus batch processing). Examples include data lake ingestion, ML pipelines, and streaming extract, transform, load (ETL).

Stream and batch analytics. Amazon Managed Service for Apache Flink supports traditional batch queries on bounded datasets and real-time, continuous queries from unbounded, live data streams. Examples include usage metering and billing, network monitoring, feature engineering, and campaign performance.

Event-driven applications. You can leverage the capabilities of Apache Flink to easily develop and maintain event-driven applications on AWS. An event-driven application is a stateful application that ingests events from one or more event streams and reacts to incoming events by triggering computations, state updates, or external actions. Examples include fraud detection, business processes monitoring, and geo-fencing.

AWS DataSync

AWS DataSync is a data transfer and discovery service that simplifies data migration and helps you quickly, easily, and securely transfer your file or object data to, from, and between AWS storage services.

AWS DataSync achieves data discovery by using a DataSync agent to connect to your source storage system's management interface. The agent collects information about your storage resources, including performance metrics and capacity utilization. This data is then sent to AWS DataSync Discovery, which analyzes the information and provides recommendations for migrating your data to AWS storage services. This automated process helps you understand your storage utilization and plan your migration more effectively.

With AWS DataSync, you can also transfer data between other cloud storage systems or on-premises storage systems and AWS services. In this context, cloud storage systems can include the following:

- Self-managed storage systems, such as an NFS file server in your VPC within AWS
- Storage systems or services hosted by another cloud provider
- Storage systems or services hosted on-premises in your company data center(s)

AWS DataSync supports the following storage systems:

- Network File System (NFS)
- Server Message Block (SMB)
- Hadoop Distributed File Systems (HDFS)
- Object storage (Google Cloud Storage, Azure Blob Storage, Wasabi Cloud Storage, and self-managed object storage compatible with the Amazon S3 API)

AWS DataSync supports the following AWS storage services:

- Amazon S3
- Amazon EFS
- Amazon FSx for Windows File Server
- Amazon FSx for Lustre
- Amazon FSx for OpenZFS
- Amazon FSx for NetApp ONTAP
- AWS Snowcone
- AWS Snowball Edge

By using DataSync, you can achieve the following benefits:

Simplify migration planning. With automated data collection and recommendations, DataSync Discovery can minimize the time, effort, and costs associated with planning your data migrations to AWS. You can use recommendations to inform your budget planning and rerun discovery jobs to validate your assumptions as you approach your migration.

40 Chapter 2 ▪ Data Ingestion and Storage

Automate data movement. DataSync makes it easier to transfer data over the network between storage systems and services. DataSync automates both the management of data-transfer processes and the infrastructure required for high performance and secure data transfer.

Transfer data securely. DataSync provides end-to-end security, including encryption and integrity validation, to help ensure that your data arrives securely, intact, and ready to use. DataSync accesses your AWS storage through built-in AWS security mechanisms, such as AWS Identity and Access Management (IAM) roles. It also supports VPC endpoints, giving you the option to transfer data without traversing the public Internet and further increasing the security of data copied online.

Move data faster. DataSync uses a purpose-built network protocol and a parallel, multi-threaded architecture to accelerate your transfers. This approach speeds up migrations, recurring data-processing workflows for analytics and ML, and data protection processes.

Reduce operational costs. Move data cost-effectively with the flat, per-gigabyte pricing of DataSync. Avoid having to write and maintain custom scripts or use costly commercial transfer tools.

Use Cases

Typical use cases for AWS DataSync include the following:

Discover data. Get visibility into your on-premises storage performance and utilization AWS DataSync Discovery can also provide recommendations for migrating your data to AWS storage services.

Migrate data. Transfer active datasets rapidly over the network into AWS storage services. DataSync includes automatic encryption and data integrity validation to help make sure your data arrives securely, intact, and ready to use.

Archive cold data. Move cold data stored in on-premises storage directly to durable, highly available, and secure long-term storage classes such as S3 Glacier Flexible Retrieval and S3 Glacier Deep Archive. Doing so can free up on-premises storage capacity and shut down legacy systems.

Replicate data. Copy data into any Amazon S3 storage class, choosing the most cost-effective storage class for your needs. You can also send data to Amazon EFS, FSx for Windows File Server, FSx for Lustre, or FSx for OpenZFS for a standby file system.

Transfer data for timely in-cloud processing. Transfer data in or out of AWS for processing. This approach can speed up critical hybrid cloud workflows across many industries. These include ML in the life-sciences industry, video production in media and entertainment, big-data analytics in financial services, and seismic research in the oil and gas industry.

AWS Glue

The process to prepare your data to be ready for a selection of an ML algorithm is a key step in the ML lifecycle. AWS Glue is a cloud-optimized ETL serverless service, which allows you to discover, prepare, move, and integrate data from multiple sources across your business so your data is ready for use.

AWS Glue is different from other ETL services in four important ways:

Serverless. You don't need to provision, configure, or spin up servers or manage their lifecycle.

Automatic schema inference. AWS Glue comes with crawlers, which parse your datasets, discover your file types, extract the schema, and store all this metadata in a centralized catalog for later querying and analysis.

Automatic ETL scripts generation. AWS Glue automatically generates the scripts you need to extract, transform, and load your data from source to target.

Extensive connectivity. AWS Glue offers a wide range of connectors to integrate with various data sources. It provides built-in support for commonly used data stores such as Amazon Redshift, Amazon Aurora, Microsoft SQL Server, MySQL, MongoDB, MariaDB, and PostgreSQL. Additionally, AWS Glue allows the use of custom JDBC drivers to integrate with other data sources.

With the aforementioned benefits, AWS Glue makes data preparation simple, fast, secure, and cost-effective. Your team of ML and data engineers can leverage AWS Glue to visually create, run, and monitor ETL pipelines to load data into your data lakes and prepare your data to select an ML algorithm. Additionally, AWS Glue is expressive and flexible, enabling the development of custom ETL scripts using popular frameworks like Spark, PySpark, Scala, and Ray (AWS Glue for Ray). This allows for tailored data processing solutions that can meet the unique needs of your ML projects, ensuring both efficiency and precision in data preparation.

Use Cases

Typical use cases for AWS Glue include the following:

Complex ETL pipeline development. Because of its Auto Scaling capability, AWS Glue is the ideal service to run data processing for ETL jobs with uneven compute demands, an unpredictable amount of data, and a large number of data sources.

Data discovery. AWS Glue's native capabilities make it easy to identify data across AWS, on premises, and on other clouds and then make it instantly available for querying and transforming.

Support for data processing frameworks. With AWS Glue, you can connect to more than 70 diverse data sources, implement a variety of workload types (batch, micro-batch, and streaming), and manage your data in a centralized data catalog.

Simplified data engineering experience. Using AWS Glue interactive sessions, data and ML engineers can interactively explore and prepare data using the integrated development environment (IDE) or notebook of their choice.

Choosing AWS Storage Services

The data you will use to train your ML model will need to be persisted in its raw format using a suitable storage service. This is crucial as it ensures that your data is readily accessible and in an optimal state for preprocessing and model training. Additionally, storage is essential not only for training data but also for storing the artifacts resulting from the training process, such as model parameters, weights, and other derived data. These artifacts are vital for making accurate predictions, enabling you to deploy and operationalize your ML models effectively. Proper storage management facilitates seamless transitions between data ingestion, model training, model evaluation, and model deployment, thereby supporting the end-to-end ML lifecycle.

The following are the main factors you need to consider in selecting the appropriate storage service:

Durability.   Addresses the question "For how long do you need to keep your data?" Durability measures the ability of a storage service to persist data when faced with the challenges of normal operation over its lifetime.

Availability.   Addresses the question "How soon do you need to use your data?" Availability measures the percentage of time that the storage service is available for use, where "available for use" means that it performs its agreed function when required. Availability (also known as service availability) is a commonly used metric to quantitatively measure reliability.

Storage type.   Addresses the question "In which format do you need your data to be effectively used for the preparation process?" Storage types include Object, Block, File, and other specific types based on use cases.

Cost.   Addresses the question "How much money are you willing to spend to store your data?" Cost is one of the pillars of the Well-Architected Framework and applies to any solution you design, architect, and build in the cloud. In the next sections, we will cover the cost factor for each AWS storage service relevant to the ML lifecycle.

Security.   Addresses the question "What type of protection is required for your data at rest?" Security is another pillar of the Well-Architected Framework and applies to any solution you design, architect, and build in the cloud. The sensitivity of your data determines what data protection security controls are required while your data is stored, i.e., at rest.

In the upcoming sections, the main storage services offered by AWS for ML workloads will be covered. We will start with the three storage services that are natively integrated with Amazon SageMaker: Amazon S3, Amazon Elastic File System (EFS), and Amazon FSx for Lustre.

Amazon Simple Storage Service (S3)

Amazon S3 is an object storage service that provides industry-leading durability, availability, scalability, security, and performance.

Object storage is a storage type that persists and manages data in an unstructured format called *objects*. As organizations embark in their digital transformation journey, their ability to store large amounts of unstructured data such as photos, videos, email, web pages, sensor data, and audio files has become a key aspect of their digital transformation.

Amazon S3 distributes this data across multiple physical devices but allows users to access the content efficiently from a unique identifier, i.e., the object's *Uniform Resource Identifier* (URI).

The major benefits of object storage are the virtually unlimited scalability and the lower cost of storing large amounts of data for use cases such as data lakes, cloud native applications, analytics, log files, and ML.

Object storage also delivers greater data durability and resilience because it stores objects on multiple devices, across multiple systems, and even across multiple Availability Zones and regions. This allows for virtually unlimited scale and also improves resilience and availability of the data.

With its native integration with Amazon SageMaker, Amazon S3 is one of the most cost-effective and user-friendly storage options for ML operations in AWS. It offers a range of storage classes to suit different access patterns and budgets, making it a versatile choice for storing both training data and model artifacts. Moreover, Amazon S3's integration with various AWS services—such as AWS Lambda, Amazon Elastic Container Services (ECS), and Amazon Elastic Kubernetes Services (EKS)—simplifies the process of building, training, and deploying ML models.

Figure 2.4 illustrates a simple workflow that highlights how Amazon S3 and Amazon SageMaker can interact with each other during the ML lifecycle.

For the exam, make sure you have a good understanding of the Amazon S3 storage classes, as described in Table 2.4.

Amazon Athena

Amazon Athena is a serverless, interactive query service that allows you to analyze data directly in Amazon S3 using standard SQL.

With Amazon Athena, you can perform SQL queries against data stored in S3. Examples include CSV, JSON, or columnar data formats such as Apache Parquet and Apache ORC.

FIGURE 2.4 Amazon S3 use in the ML lifecycle.

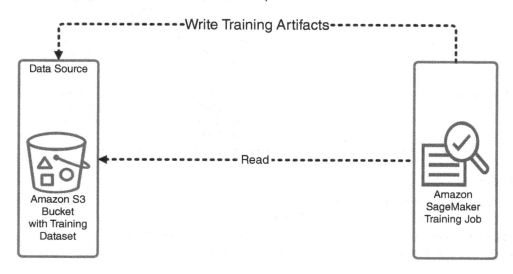

Chapter 2 ▪ Data Ingestion and Storage

TABLE 2.4 Amazon S3 storage classes.

S3 storage class	Description
S3 Standard	Designed for frequently accessed data
S3 Intelligent-Tiering	Optimizes costs by automatically moving data between two access tiers based on changing data access patterns
S3 Express One Zone	High-performance, single Availability Zone storage class delivering consistent single-digit millisecond data access for latency-sensitive applications
S3 Standard-IA (infrequent access)	Suitable for data that is less frequently accessed but requires rapid access when needed at lower cost compared to S3 Standard
S3 One Zone-IA	Ideal for infrequently accessed data that doesn't require multiple Availability Zone resilience, offering lower storage costs
S3 Glacier Instant Retrieval	Designed for long-lived, rarely accessed data that requires immediate access, providing low retrieval times and costs
S3 Glacier Flexible Retrieval	Used for archival data with flexible access times ranging from minutes to hours, offering low-cost storage
S3 Glacier Deep Archive	Provides the lowest cost storage for long-term data archiving, with retrieval times of up to 12 hours
S3 Outposts	Brings S3 storage to your on-premises environments, ensuring consistent performance and meeting data residency requirements

Use Cases

Built on a resilient architecture specifically designed to persist large amounts of unstructured data, Amazon S3 is best suited for the following use cases:

Data lakes and ML. A data lake is a centralized repository that allows you to store all your data in its raw format at any scale. You can use a data lake to run data processing, data analytics, ML, and high-performance computing (HPC) applications to unlock the value of your data.

Data backup and restore. With Amazon S3's robust replication and data protection capabilities, you can build applications that meet your recovery time objective (RTO), recovery point objective (RPO), and compliance requirements.

Data archival. You can retain your "cold" data (infrequently accessed data that must be retained for compliance) to the Amazon S3 Glacier storage classes to lower costs, eliminate operational complexities, and meet your organization's data archival requirements.

Generative artificial intelligence (AI). At the time of writing this book, Amazon S3 stores exabytes of data for more than 350 trillion objects and averages more than 100 million requests per second. With this massive level of scalability, Amazon S3 is the ideal storage service to prepare and train your large language models (LLMs). LLMs are trained to learn statistical relationships from vast amounts of data during a self-supervised and semi-supervised training process. We will cover these concepts in the upcoming chapters.

Amazon Elastic File System (EFS)

Amazon EFS is a serverless, fully elastic AWS *file-based* storage service. Its serverless feature means there is no administration required to manage, configure, and create its underlying infrastructure; AWS will perform these tasks for you.

Amazon EFS enables you to create and configure distributed file systems on AWS and mount them to a variety of AWS compute resources, including Amazon EC2 instances, Amazon EKS clusters, Amazon ECS, AWS Lambda functions, and others. No provisioning, deploying, patching, or maintenance is required.

It also supports the popular NFS versions 4.0 and 4.1 (NFSv4) protocols, resulting in seamless integration with workloads requiring NFS.

You can then share these files, optimize costs with Amazon EFS lifecycle management, and further protect your data with AWS Backup and Amazon EFS replication.

Its elastic ability means the service will scale workloads *on demand* to petabytes of storage and gigabytes per second of throughput out of the box.

With a *pay-as-you-go* pricing model, you can reduce total cost of ownership (TCO) by leveraging its built-in lifecycle management feature, which is designed to intelligently move "cold" data to cost-optimized Infrequent Access and Archive EFS storage classes.

As an alternative to Amazon S3, if your training data already resides in Amazon EFS, you can easily access and use this data within Amazon SageMaker for model training. This integration streamlines the workflow, allowing you to leverage the scalable and high-performance storage capabilities of Amazon EFS while developing and deploying your ML models in Amazon SageMaker efficiently.

Figure 2.5 illustrates an example workflow that shows how Amazon EFS can be used to store training data and learning artifacts during the ML lifecycle.

When deciding between Amazon EFS and Amazon S3 for ML storage in AWS, it's essential to consider their distinct benefits tailored to specific use cases. Amazon EFS offers

FIGURE 2.5 Amazon EFS use in the ML lifecycle.

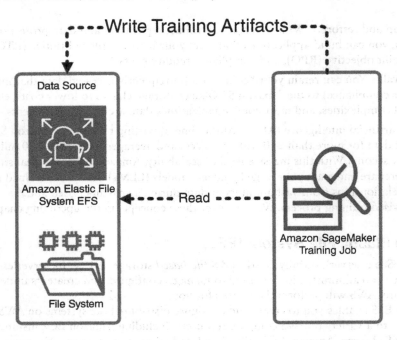

a file system interface with strong consistency, file locking, and support for NFS protocols, making it ideal for applications requiring traditional file system semantics and fast access to training datasets. However, it is important to note that setting up Amazon EFS with Amazon SageMaker requires some DevOps work, as you need to configure an interface VPC endpoint to ensure secure connectivity. This involves creating the endpoint in your VPC, configuring security groups, and ensuring proper IAM policies are in place.

In contrast, Amazon S3 is a versatile object storage service that excels in handling large, unstructured datasets and supporting various data storage needs for your ML workloads.

Although S3 is often more cost-effective for general storage, the choice between Amazon EFS and Amazon S3 should be based on your application's specific requirements. Amazon EFS is preferable for workloads that need quick access to training data stored in a shared file system, with strong consistency, whereas S3 is better suited for cost-effective object storage and large-scale data storage solutions.

Use Cases

Given its serverless, scalability, and reliability features, Amazon EFS is best suited for use cases where unpredictable amounts of file data need to be shared across multiple consumers. These include the following:

Data science and ML.   Amazon EFS offers the performance and consistency needed for ML and big data analytics workloads.

Modern application development. Amazon EFS allows developers to share code and other files in a secure, organized way to increase DevOps agility and respond faster to customer feedback. Its highly available distributed file server capabilities allow developers to share data from their AWS containers and serverless applications with zero management required.

Content management systems (CMSs). As a highly available, serverless, elastic, and distributed file server, Amazon EFS simplifies storage for modern CMS workloads, resulting in accelerated go-to-market, increased reliability, increased security, and cost reduction.

Amazon FSx for Lustre

Amazon FSx for Lustre is a fully managed storage service providing a high-performance, scale-out file system. Built on the open-source Lustre parallel, distributed file system, this storage service is designed for compute-intensive workloads, providing submillisecond latencies, up to hundreds of gigabytes of throughput, and millions of input/output per second (IOPS), making it ideal for ML, HPC, video processing, and financial modeling. By offering scalable, secure, and durable storage, Amazon FSx for Lustre enables you to process large datasets quickly and cost-effectively.

Just like Amazon S3 and Amazon EFS, Amazon FSx for Lustre can also natively integrate with Amazon SageMaker. This integration allows you to use this storage service as a data source for your ML training jobs, significantly speeding up the training process. By eliminating the need to download data from Amazon S3 to the training instances, Amazon FSx for Lustre ensures faster startup and training times, enhancing overall efficiency. As illustrated in Figure 2.6, the training instances are unaware that the training data is being pulled from S3 because Amazon FSx for Lustre acts as an abstraction layer between the S3 bucket

FIGURE 2.6 Amazon FSx for Lustre use in the ML lifecycle.

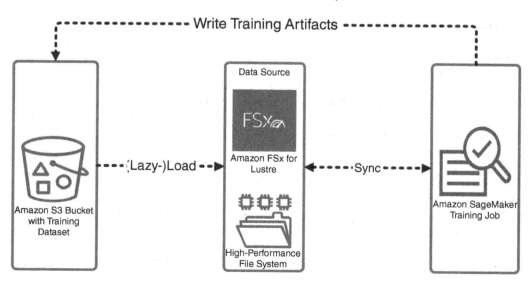

48   Chapter 2 ▪ Data Ingestion and Storage

and the training instances, resulting in a high-performance file system interface that can be configured as a buffer cache. This highlights FSx for Lustre's role in abstracting the data transfer process, ensuring that the training instances interact with a high-performance file system without needing to manage the data fetching from S3 directly.

Amazon FSx for Lustre supports two data loading design patterns: a *one-time load* from S3 to Lustre, and *lazy loading*, which gradually loads data from S3 as it is accessed. The former is a great option when you need to quickly make a large dataset available for processing, offering superior performance at a higher initial cost due to the rapid data transfer. The latter is ideal for scenarios where you want to minimize initial data transfer and costs, as data is loaded only as it is needed, although it may result in slightly longer access times for the first use of each piece of data. This flexibility makes Amazon FSx for Lustre an excellent choice for workloads that require high throughput and low-latency access to data.

In addition to its performance benefits, Amazon FSx for Lustre supports multiple deployment options, including *scratch* and *persistent* file systems, to accommodate your ML applications' different data processing needs. Scratch file systems are ideal for ephemeral storage and shorter-term processing, whereas persistent file systems are better suited for longer-term storage and throughput-focused workloads.

With its robust integration capabilities (Amazon SageMaker native connectivity), expressive configurability (one-time load and lazy loading), and flexible deployment options (scratch and persistent file systems), Amazon FSx for Lustre is a powerful storage service for ML applications requiring high-performance, scalable, and low-latency data access.

So far, you have learned the three AWS storage services that offer native integration with Amazon SageMaker's training ingestion mechanism. These are Amazon S3, Amazon EFS, and Amazon FSx for Lustre. For the exam, make sure you understand the different trade-offs between training times, performance, and costs. Each of these storage services has unique features that can impact your ML workflows. Amazon S3 is highly scalable and cost-effective, making it suitable for large datasets and long-term storage. Amazon EFS provides a simple, scalable, and fully managed file storage for use with AWS Cloud services and on-premises resources, offering shared access and flexibility. Amazon FSx for Lustre is optimized for high-performance, low-latency computing, and ML workloads, offering different data loading access patterns and deployment options.

As shown in Figure 2.7, when comparing the three storage services against training times as the only dimension, Amazon FSx for Lustre is your best option. However, if cost is a critical factor, Amazon S3 is the most economical choice, followed by Amazon EFS, which balances cost and performance effectively.

Use Cases

As a fully managed service built on the Lustre high-performance file system, Amazon FSx for Lustre is best suited for the following use cases:

Machine learning.   With its native integration with Amazon SageMaker, FSx for Lustre is perfect for ML training jobs that require submillisecond latencies to access large datasets. By using FSx for Lustre as a data source, ML engineers and data scientists can significantly reduce the time required for model training due to the high-speed access and processing

FIGURE 2.7 Training data load times comparison.

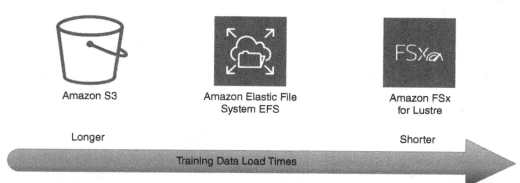

capabilities. The flexibility of loading data from Amazon S3—through either one-time loads or lazy loading—enhances the efficiency of ML workflows, making it an excellent choice for tasks that require rapid data access and high throughput.

High-performance computing.   Amazon FSx for Lustre is also ideal for HPC workloads that demand massive amounts of data processing power with low latency. This includes applications such as scientific research, simulations, and computational tasks like weather modeling and genomic sequencing, enabling researchers and engineers to perform complex calculations and analyses quickly and efficiently.

Media processing.   Amazon FSx for Lustre excels in media processing applications such as video rendering, transcoding, and editing, where substantial data throughput and low latency are critical. The high-performance characteristics of Amazon FSx for Lustre enable media professionals to process large media files efficiently, meeting the demanding requirements of production environments. This ensures faster completion of tasks and a smoother workflow, making it an excellent storage service for the media and entertainment industry.

Amazon FSx for NetApp ONTAP

Amazon FSx for NetApp ONTAP is another fully managed AWS storage service that utilizes *file* as its storage type and is built on NetApp's popular ONTAP operating system.

Amazon FSx for NetApp ONTAP delivers high-performance file storage that enables the use of ONTAP's unified data management capabilities, including the following:

- Unified storage management that can span flash, disk, and cloud running storage area network (SAN), network attached storage (NAS), and object workloads
- Low-latency access
- Data compression
- Data deduplication
- Storage scalability

Chapter 2 ▪ Data Ingestion and Storage

Data compression and deduplication result in cost savings by reducing the size of data that needs to be stored.

Use Cases

Typical use cases for Amazon FSx for NetApp ONTAP include the following:

Workload migration.   Seamlessly migrate workloads running on NetApp or other NFSs, SMB, iSCSI, and NVMe-over-TCP servers to AWS without modifying application code or how you manage data.

Business continuity and disaster recovery (BDCR).   Achieve secure backup, archive, and data replication from on-premises file servers or across AWS Regions.

High-performance database workloads.   With submillisecond latencies and scalability to up to millions of IOPS per file system, Amazon FSx for NetApp ONTAP delivers highly available shared file storage for your high-performance database workloads. Additionally, Amazon FSx for NetApp ONTAP allows you to scale out file systems by spreading customers' workloads across multiple file servers.

Amazon FSx for Windows File Server

Amazon FSx for Windows File Server is a fully managed service that provides highly reliable, scalable, and performant Windows-based file storage. It seamlessly integrates with your existing Windows applications and environments, offering native support for the Windows Server Message Block (SMB) protocol. This makes it an ideal solution for shared file storage in use cases such as home directories, user profiles, and enterprise applications requiring file storage. With Active Directory integration, it ensures secure access control and user management, and data deduplication features help reduce storage costs by eliminating duplicate files.

This storage service offers robust performance with SSD storage options, ensuring low-latency access to your files and high IOPS for demanding applications. Its flexible scalability allows you to easily adjust the file system size to meet your growing storage needs, making it a powerful and efficient storage solution for Windows-based environments.

Use Cases

Typical use cases for Amazon FSx for Windows File Server include the following:

Windows file server migration.   By providing a fully managed, native Windows file system that supports the SMB protocol and Active Directory integration, Amazon FSx for Windows File Server allows organizations to seamlessly move their existing file systems to AWS without modifying their applications, ensuring a smooth transition with minimal disruption.

SQL Server cost savings.   Amazon FSx for Windows File Server enables high-availability deployments without requiring SQL Enterprise licensing, leading to significant cost savings. This is especially beneficial for organizations centered around SQL Server that are considering migrating to AWS.

Virtual desktops and application streaming. With Amazon FSx for Windows File Server, you can store user profile data on shared, persistent storage accessible from Amazon WorkSpaces and Amazon AppStream 2.0. This storage service can simplify virtual desktop user experiences by reducing login times and improving overall productivity.

Amazon FSx for OpenZFS

Amazon FSx for OpenZFS is a fully managed storage service that allows you to operate and scale OpenZFS file systems on AWS, combining the familiar features and performance of OpenZFS with the scalability and simplicity of AWS. It supports access from Linux, Windows, and macOS compute instances and containers via the NFS protocol (v3, v4, v4.1, and v4.2), delivering IOPS in excess of a million and submillisecond latencies, leveraging the latest AWS compute, disk, and networking technologies for high-performance workloads.

Use Cases

Typical use cases for Amazon FSx for OpenZFS include the following:

Workload migration. The main use case for this storage service, as the name suggests, is migrating workloads running on ZFS (or other Linux-based file servers) to AWS without needing to modify application code or data management practices.

Data-intensive applications. With the advanced features of the OpenZFS file system and the extensive NFS support, Amazon FSx for OpenZFS is best suited for developing data-intensive applications on AWS.

Amazon Elastic Block Storage (EBS)

Amazon EBS is a high-performance AWS *block* storage service, which can be used as a cloud SAN.

Amazon EBS storage comes in the form of EBS volumes, which are similar to virtual disks in the cloud and can be attached to Amazon EC2 instances. EBS volumes can be solid-state drives (SSDs) or hard disk drives (HDDs). SSD-based volumes are optimized for transactional workloads involving frequent read/write operations with small I/O size, where the key performance metric is IOPS, whereas HDD-based volumes are optimized for large streaming workloads where the key performance metric is throughput.

With Amazon EBS you can also take snapshots, which are point-in-time backups of EBS volumes that can be used to restore new volumes.

Use Cases

Typical use cases for Amazon EBS include the following:

Block-level storage migration. Migrate mid-range, on-premises SAN workloads to AWS. Attach high-performance and high-availability block storage for mission-critical applications.

52 Chapter 2 ▪ Data Ingestion and Storage

RDBMs and NoSQL workloads. Deploy and scale your choice of databases, including SAP HANA, Oracle, Microsoft SQL Server, PostgreSQL, MySQL, Cassandra, and MongoDB.

Big data analytics workloads. Easily resize clusters for big data analytics engines, such as Hadoop and Spark, and freely detach and reattach volumes.

Amazon Relational Database Service (RDS)

Amazon RDS is a managed relational database service available in eight different engines: Amazon Aurora PostgreSQL-Compatible Edition, Amazon Aurora MySQL-Compatible Edition, RDS for PostgreSQL, RDS for MySQL, RDS for MariaDB, RDS for SQL Server, RDS for Oracle, and RDS for Db2.

Because you get to choose the database engine, the code, applications, and tools you already use today with your existing databases can be also used with Amazon RDS. For example, there is no need to refactor your SQL Server stored procedure, to recode your application (other than the means your application uses to connect to your database), or even to use another SQL editing tool.

As a managed service, Amazon RDS handles database management tasks for you, such as provisioning, patching, backup, recovery, failure detection, and repair.

Amazon RDS offers three different deployment environments, including deploying in the cloud with Amazon Aurora or Amazon RDS, deploying hybrid workloads with Amazon RDS on AWS Outposts, and deploying with privileged access with Amazon RDS Custom.

As with all AWS services, there are no up-front investments required, and you pay only for the resources you use.

Use Cases

Typical use cases for Amazon RDS include the following:

Modern web and mobile applications. Amazon RDS is an excellent choice to build well-architected applications, because it offers a secure storage solution with high availability, performance, and scalability with limited administration. Additionally, its pay-per-use pricing model allows you to effectively manage the cost of persisting your data in a relational database running in AWS.

Legacy database migration. Migrating on-premises legacy databases to Amazon RDS is the natural choice for organizations that look to modernize their workloads during their digital transformation journey. In addition to improved scalability and reliability, cost reduction is a critical factor to consider due to a significant saving in license fees as well as the benefit of the pay-per-use pricing model.

Amazon DynamoDB

Amazon DynamoDB is a serverless NoSQL database service with consistent single-digit-millisecond performance at any scale.

Its serverless feature means you don't need to provision any infrastructure, or patch, manage, install, maintain, or operate any software. DynamoDB also comes with zero-downtime maintenance.

As a NoSQL database, DynamoDB is designed and built to deliver high performance, scalability, manageability, and flexibility compared to relational databases. To support a broad spectrum of use cases, with DynamoDB you can use both key-value and document data models. To help you build enterprise-grade applications, Amazon DynamoDB provides strong read consistency and ACID (atomicity, consistency, isolation, and durability) transactions support.

To achieve consistent single-digit-millisecond performance, DynamoDB is optimized for high-performance workloads and provides APIs that encourage efficient database usage. It omits features that are inefficient and nonperforming at scale: for example, JOIN operations. DynamoDB delivers consistent single-digit-millisecond performance for your applications, whether there are 100 or 100 million users.

Use Cases

DynamoDB is ideal for use cases that require consistent performance at any scale with minimal operational overhead, including but not limited to the following:

Financial service applications. Amazon DynamoDB transactions can be used to achieve ACID across one or more tables with a single request. ACID transactions are ideal for workloads that process financial transactions or fulfill orders. Amazon DynamoDB instantly adjusts to workloads as they spike up and down, enabling you to efficiently scale your database for market conditions, such as trading hours.

Gaming applications. Because of its ability to scale in and scale out, its consistent performance, and the ease of operations provided by its serverless architecture, Amazon DynamoDB can be used to efficiently persist all data element of any game platforms, such as game state, player data, session history, and leaderboards. This scalability optimizes your architecture's efficiency whether you're scaling out for peak traffic or scaling in when gameplay usage is low.

Data streaming applications. Amazon DynamoDB is widely used by media and entertainment companies as a metadata index for content management services or to serve near-real-time sports statistics. Amazon DynamoDB is also used to perform user watchlist and bookmarking services and to process billions of daily customer events for recommendations generation. These customers benefit from DynamoDB's scalability, performance, and resilience. DynamoDB's built-in elasticity enables streaming media use cases that can support any levels of demand.

Troubleshooting

Troubleshooting and debugging data ingestion and storage issues related to capacity and scalability in AWS involves several steps and best practices. Here are some key strategies you need to know for the exam:

Monitoring and logging. Use CloudWatch to monitor your AWS resources and applications. Set up alarms to notify your data operations team of any anomalies in metrics such as

54 Chapter 2 ▪ Data Ingestion and Storage

CPU usage, memory usage, and I/O operations. Enable CloudTrail to log API calls and track changes to your AWS resources. This helps in identifying the root cause of issues.

Scaling and performance optimization. Implement auto scaling for your EC2 instances and other scalable resources to automatically adjust capacity based on demand. Use read replicas and Aurora's auto-scaling capabilities to handle increased read traffic and improve performance.

Data ingestion optimization. To optimize the performance of your data pipelines, use techniques such as data partitioning, caching, and parallel processing. For real-time data ingestion, leverage Amazon MSK, Amazon Manage Service for Apache Flink, Amazon Kinesis Data Streams, or Amazon Data Firehose to handle large volumes of streaming data. Additionally, consider supplementing these services with AWS Lambda functions to process data in real time and scale automatically based on the volume of ingested data.

Storage management. Use Amazon S3 for enterprise-scale object storage. Implement lifecycle policies to move data to different storage classes based on data access patterns. Monitor Amazon EBS volumes for performance and adjust volume types or sizes as needed to meet capacity and performance requirements.

Database optimization. Ensure your database queries are optimized and indexes are properly configured to improve performance. Consider sharding your database to distribute the load across multiple instances. With Amazon DynamoDB, refrain from using scan operations whenever possible, due to their inefficient performance compared to other query operations.

Cost management. Use AWS Cost Explorer to monitor and analyze your AWS spending. Identify areas where you can optimize costs by adjusting resource usage. Consider purchasing reserved instances or savings plans for predictable workloads to reduce costs. Leverage spot instances for elastic ephemeral workloads to minimize costs.

By implementing these strategies, you can effectively troubleshoot and debug data ingestion and storage issues related to capacity and scalability in AWS.

Summary

In this chapter, we covered data ingestion and data storage, which are the two key components of the collection phase of the machine learning lifecycle.

With ingestion, you aggregate the data for your ML solution from different sources and push it into AWS in its raw format. Data ingestion can occur in batches or in real time. Amazon Data Firehose, Amazon Kinesis Data Streams, Amazon MSK, and Amazon Managed Service for Apache Flink are used to ingest real-time data. AWS DataSync and AWS Glue are used to ingest batch data.

With storage, you persist the ingested data in a suitable AWS data store, where it will remain until it's ready for processing. Storage comes in three different types: object, file, and block. Amazon S3 is used to store object data, Amazon EBS is used to store block data, and Amazon EFS and the Amazon FSx family of services are used to store file data.

The drivers to select the appropriate ingestion and storage service depend on the specifics of your use case and include scalability, resilience, security, and cost.

The chapter also covered the different data formats you need to know for the exam, which can be used to further optimize performance, improve scalability, and reduce processing time. An important factor to consider when selecting a data format to train your model is whether this format is supported by the ML algorithm you intend to use for your ML problem.

Exam Essentials

Know the difference between data ingestion and data storage. Data ingestion is about aggregating data from different sources, whereas storage is about persisting data in a data store hosted in AWS.

Understand the different data formats. CSV is used to store structured data in tabular format, whereas JSON is used for document-based, semi-structured data. Apache Parquet and Apache ORC are columnar data formats, whereas Apache Avro is a row-based format. RecordIO is a data format used primarily by Apache MXNet, a deep learning framework.

Understand ingestion services for streaming data. These include Amazon Data Firehose, Amazon Kinesis Data Streams, Amazon MSK, and Amazon Streaming Service for Apache Flink. Amazon Kinesis Data Streams is more suited for real-time, custom data processing, whereas Amazon Data Firehose is ideal for efficiently loading streaming data into selected AWS data stores with minimal setup and management. Amazon MSK is best suited for managing and distributing streaming data (e.g., log aggregation, real-time analytics, and event sourcing), whereas Amazon Managed Service for Apache Flink is designed for processing and analyzing data in real time.

Understand ingestion services for data migration/batch/ETL data. These include AWS DataSync and AWS Glue. The former is ideal for data transfer/migration of data into AWS and the latter for ETL and development of data pipelines.

Understand storage services for object data. Amazon S3 is the most versatile and widely used object storage service on AWS. It provides industry-leading scalability, data availability, security, and performance. Object data contains the data itself, metadata, and a unique identifier. Object storage is accessed via APIs, making it suitable for cloud-native applications. Amazon S3 is natively supported by Amazon SageMaker as a data source for training ML models.

Understand storage services for file data. Amazon EFS and the Amazon FSx family of services (Amazon FSx for Lustre, for NetApp ONTAP, for Windows File Server, and for OpenZFS) are used to store data as file storage type. File storage organizes data in a

56 Chapter 2 ▪ Data Ingestion and Storage

hierarchical manner and is ideal to persist shared data such as data in a company directory, media storage, and content management systems. Amazon EFS and Amazon FSx for Lustre are file-based storage services natively supported by Amazon SageMaker as data sources for training ML models.

Understand storage services for block data. Amazon EBS is the block storage service on AWS. Block storage divides data into fixed-size blocks, each with a unique address but without metadata. Block storage delivers high performance and low latency, making it ideal for transactional workloads.

Understand storage services natively integrated with Amazon SageMaker. Amazon SageMaker natively integrates with Amazon S3 for object storage, and Amazon EFS and Amazon FSx for Lustre for file system storage, facilitating seamless access to data for training, learning, and efficient management of ML workflows.

Review Questions

1. You need to store unprocessed data from IoT devices for a new machine learning pipeline. The storage solution should be a centralized and highly available repository. What AWS storage service do you choose to store the unprocessed data?

   A. Amazon Elastic File System (EFS)

   B. Amazon S3

   C. Amazon DynamoDB

   D. Amazon Relational Database Service (RDS)

2. You are designing a highly scalable data repository for your machine learning pipeline. You need immediate access to the processed data from your pipeline for 6 months. Your unprocessed data must be accessible within 12 hours and stored for 6 years. The storage solution must support SQL querying capabilities. What is the most cost-effective storage solution?

   A. Amazon S3 and Amazon Athena

   B. Amazon S3

   C. Amazon DynamoDB

   D. Amazon Redshift

3. You are using an Amazon Data Firehose delivery stream to ingest GZIP compressed data records from an on-premises application. You need to configure a solution for your data scientist to perform SQL queries against the data stream for real-time insights. What solution meets these requirements?

   A. Amazon S3 and Amazon Athena

   B. Amazon Managed Service for Apache Flink and a Lambda function

   C. Amazon Managed Streaming for Apache Kafka and a Lambda function

   D. Amazon Redshift and Amazon Athena

4. You are a machine learning engineer, and you need to process a large amount of customer data, analyze the data, and get insights so that analysts can make further decisions. To accomplish this task, you need to store the data in a data structure that can handle large volumes of data and efficiently retrieve it as fast as possible. What solution meets these requirements?

   A. Amazon EMR with HDFS

   B. Amazon S3 and a Lambda function

   C. Amazon DynamoDB and a Lambda function

   D. Amazon Redshift and Amazon Athena

58 Chapter 2 ▪ Data Ingestion and Storage

5. You have been asked to redesign and reduce operational overhead and use AWS services to detect anomalies in transaction data and assign anomaly scores to malicious records. The records are streamed in real time and stored in an Amazon S3 data lake for processing and analysis. What is the most efficient solution?

    A. Amazon Data Firehose to stream transaction data and the Amazon Managed Service for Apache Flink RANDOM_CUT_FOREST function to detect anomalies

    B. Amazon Data Firehose to stream transaction data into Amazon S3 with the SageMaker RANDOM_CUT_FOREST function to detect anomalies

    C. Amazon Kinesis Data Stream to stream transaction data and the Amazon Managed Service for Apache Flink RANDOM_CUT_FOREST function to detect anomalies

    D. Amazon Kinesis Data Stream to stream transaction data into Amazon S3 with the SageMaker RANDOM_CUT_FOREST function to detect anomalies

6. You've been asked to improve the time to ingest and store geolocation data in Amazon Redshift to conduct near-real-time analytics. What's the most cost-effective solution?

    A. Amazon Kinesis Data Stream to ingest the geolocation data. Load the streaming data into the Amazon Redshift cluster using Amazon Redshift Streaming Ingestion.

    B. Amazon Managed Streaming for Apache Kafka to ingest the geolocation data. Load the streaming data into the Amazon Redshift cluster using Amazon Redshift Spectrum.

    C. Amazon Data Firehose to ingest the geolocation data. Load the streaming data into the Amazon Redshift cluster using Amazon Redshift Streaming Ingestion.

    D. Amazon Managed Service for Apache Flink to ingest the geolocation data. Load the streaming data into the Amazon Redshift cluster using Amazon Redshift Streaming Ingestion.

7. You are migrating a data analysis solution to AWS. The application produces the data as CSV files in near real time. You need a solution to convert the data format to Apache Parquet before saving it to an S3 bucket. What is the most efficient solution?

    A. Amazon Kinesis Data Streams and create a streaming AWS Glue ETL job to convert the data into Apache Parquet

    B. Amazon Managed Streaming for Apache Kafka and a Lambda function

    C. Amazon Data Firehose and a Lambda function

    D. Amazon Managed Service for Apache Flink and a Lambda function

8. You are using Amazon Data Firehose to ingest data records from on premises. The records are compressed using GZIP compression. How can you efficiently perform SQL queries against the data stream to gain real-time insights and reduce the latency for queries?

    A. Amazon Managed Service for Apache Flink and a Lambda function

    B. Amazon Kinesis Data Streams, a Lambda function, and Amazon OpenSearch

    C. Amazon Managed Streaming for Apache Kafka and a Lambda function

    D. Amazon Kinesis Data Streams, a Lambda function, and Amazon Redshift

9. Your team is working on training a large-scale image recognition model that requires high throughput and low-latency access to a dataset stored in Amazon S3. Which storage service would best optimize training performance in Amazon SageMaker?

A. Amazon S3

B. Amazon EFS

C. Amazon FSx for Lustre

D. Amazon FSx for Windows File Server

10. You need a cost-effective solution for storing and frequently accessing a large amount of sensor data for an IoT analytics project in Amazon SageMaker. Which storage service should you choose?

A. Amazon FSx for Lustre

B. Amazon EFS

C. Amazon S3

D. Amazon FSx for OpenZFS

Chapter 3

Data Transformation and Feature Engineering

THE AWS CERTIFIED MACHINE LEARNING (ML) ENGINEER ASSOCIATE EXAM OBJECTIVES COVERED IN THIS CHAPTER MAY INCLUDE, BUT ARE NOT LIMITED TO THE FOLLOWING:

✓ **Domain 1: Data Preparation for Machine Learning**
- 1.2 Transform data and perform feature engineering
- 1.3 Ensure data integrity and prepare data for modeling

Chapter 3 ■ Data Transformation and Feature Engineering

Introduction

In Chapter 2, you learned how to ingest data from different sources and how to store this data in AWS. Now that you have collected the data and secured it in AWS, your job as a machine learning (ML) engineer is to make it ready to train your ML model. This step is illustrated in the Process Data phase of the ML lifecycle, as shown in Figure 3.1.

Your data is usually stored in its raw state in a *data lake*. A data lake architecture can provide a solid foundation on which to build a ML solution because it's designed to store massive amounts of data in a central repository, so it's readily available to be categorized, processed, enriched, and consumed by diverse groups within your organization.

The following are the key characteristics of a data lake:

Storage at scale. A data lake must be able to accommodate data coming in any time, whether it be at predefined time intervals or in real time, in small payloads, or in large batches.

Data movement. Just like a real lake has a river inlet that brings water into the lake, and a river outlet that moves water out of the lake, a data lake must allow for data movement in and out of the data lake.

Raw data. Data moved into the data lake may come from different sources and may be structured, semi-structured, or unstructured. The format of the data is irrelevant during the ingestion and the storage phases of the data collection.

Security. Because sensitive data may be imported into the data lake, it is critical that no unauthorized user has access to this data. As a result, the data lake must be protected by robust identity and access management (IAM) security controls. Encryption in use and in transit is no less important than encryption at rest. Therefore, security guardrails should be established and enforced to protect the data while it is produced and consumed.

Catalog. Data lakes must allow you to store relational data (e.g., operational databases, line-of-business application data), and nonrelational data (e.g., data from mobile apps, IoT devices, and social media). They also give you the ability to understand what data is in the lake through crawling, cataloging, and indexing of data.

Introduction 63

FIGURE 3.1 The ML lifecycle.

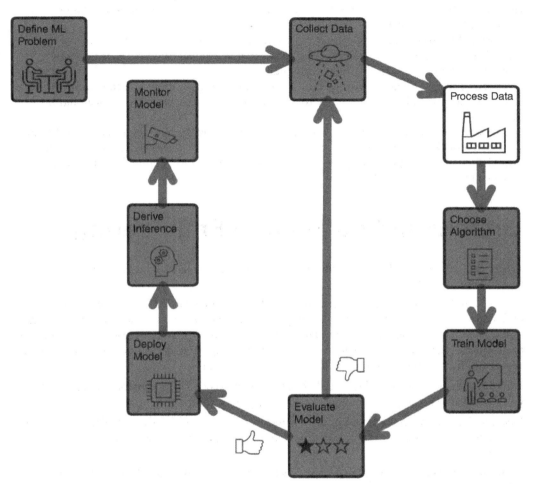

To create a data lake in AWS, you would typically use a combination of the following services: Amazon S3 (for storage), AWS Glue (for cataloging), Amazon Athena (for querying), and AWS Lake Formation (for central management of IAM, data security, and governance).

Except for AWS Lake Formation, we already covered these services in the previous chapter. For the exam, you need to know that Amazon S3 is the preferred storage option with a data lake on AWS because it provides highly durable (99.999999999%), highly available, secure storage and seamless integration with a number of data processing services and ML platforms on AWS. Amazon S3 can be used as a single source of truth storage for most AWS ML services. Additionally, with Amazon S3's Intelligent-Tiering storage class, you can reduce storage cost by letting AWS automatically determine when to move data to the most suitable storage class.

AWS Lake Formation nicely supplements the aforementioned AWS services by centralizing data permissions, simplifying security management and governance at scale, monitoring data access, and ensuring compliance.

In the upcoming sections, you will learn the techniques that allow you to process the data in your data lake and make it suitable to train your ML model, resulting in meaningful inferences.

The ultimate goal of the Process Data phase is to produce quality data to effectively train your ML model so it will learn faster from your data and it will produce accurate predictions. The higher the quality of your training dataset, the more accurate the inferences produced by your ML model.

Understanding Feature Engineering

Before deep diving into feature engineering, let's focus on understanding the different types of data:

Categorical data. Categorical data contains a finite number of distinct categories, where each category is represented with a string. Categorical data might have a logical order, such as the size of a shirt: Small, Medium, Large, X-Large. This type of categorical data is referred to as *ordinal*. Alternatively, categorical data without a logical order is referred to as *nominal*. For example, the 50 US states are categorical nominal data.

Numerical data. Numerical data in ML refers to any type of data that can be represented with numbers. This includes discrete data and continuous data.

Discrete data has a countable number of values between any two values. A discrete variable is always numeric, such as the number of customer complaints or the number of flaws or defects.

Continuous data has an infinite number of values between any two values. A continuous variable can be numeric or date/time, such as the length of a part or the date and time a payment is received.

Textual data. Textual data refers to written content that can be processed and analyzed. This can include everything from sentences and paragraphs in articles or books to social media posts, reviews, and more. It's used in various natural language processing (NLP) tasks like sentiment analysis, language translation, and text classification.

Image data. Image data consists of pixel values that can be analyzed to extract features like edges, shapes, colors, and patterns. Image data is often used in computer vision tasks, such as object detection, facial recognition, and image classification.

Time-series data. Time-series data refers to a collection of observations or measurements recorded over regular intervals of time. In this type of data, each observation is associated with a specific timestamp or time period, creating a sequence of data points ordered chronologically. The order of the data points is crucial for understanding trends, patterns, and variations occurring over that time period.

The ability to understand the different types of data is a first step toward our goal of training an ML model. This is a necessary step considering the fact that the data in your data lake is the combination of multiple datasets ingested from different data sources. Each dataset may be composed of structured, semi-structured, or unstructured data. And even if all your datasets are made up of structured data, it is not guaranteed that the schema is the same for all the datasets. As a result, this data needs to be properly transformed to be ready to be fed to an ML algorithm.

This is where feature engineering comes into play. Feature engineering is the science (and art) of extracting more information from existing data to improve your ML model's prediction power and help your ML model learn faster. You are not adding any new data during featuring engineering, but rather, you are making the data you already have more useful. By rearranging your data into a set of *features* that can be fed directly into an ML algorithm, your ML model will derive better inferences. Feature engineering often relies on domain knowledge of the data for your ML model to produce more effective outcomes.

The types of data you just learned (categorical, numerical, textual, image, time-series) will determine the most appropriate feature engineering approach.

Defining Features

In ML, *features* are individual measurable properties or characteristics of the data you're analyzing. Every unique attribute of the data is considered a *feature* (also known as an *attribute*). Think of them as inputs that your model uses to make predictions. For example, in a dataset of sales data, features might include the date, the number of visitors, and the number of orders (sales).

Figure 3.2 illustrates a simplified dataset of sales data.

FIGURE 3.2 Example of a dataset.

Date	Visitors	Sales	
Oct-05-24	8567	3134	**37% of customers made a purchase**
Oct-06-24	8219	2917	
Oct-07-24	3567	177	
Oct-08-24	3908	204	**5% of customers made a purchase**
Oct-09-24	4135	219	

FIGURE 3.3 Adding a feature to a dataset.

Day of Week	Date	Visitors	Sales
Saturday	Oct-05-24	8567	3134
Sunday	Oct-06-24	8219	2917
Monday	Oct-07-24	3567	177
Tuesday	Oct-08-24	3908	204
Wednesday	Oct-09-24	4135	219

Assume your ML model will use this data to predict sales in a given day. At first sight, you may have noticed that the first two rows have a number of sales significantly higher than the remaining three rows. Further analysis indicated that customers are more prone to purchasing during weekends. As a result, it's the day of the week that is influencing purchasing habits. So we can engineer a feature that calls out the day of the week and then write a simple script that imputes that data automatically, as shown in Figure 3.3.

This simple example showed how "hidden" information from your dataset can help your ML model learn faster. Feature engineering is all about discovering where this information is and how to transform your dataset to make the best use of it.

Selecting Features for Model Training

The following are the main feature engineering areas of focus:

- Feature extraction
- Feature selection
- Feature creation and transformation

The goal of feature extraction and feature selection is to reduce the dimensionality of your dataset. The term *dimensionality* indicates the number of features (or inputs) you have in your dataset. The higher the dimensionality of a dataset, the harder the task to effectively train your ML model. Models will be challenged to find the patterns you want them to recognize when there are many different dimensions of data (many features) to sort through.

This is why performing feature extraction and selection is important.

Feature Extraction

Feature extraction is the process of automatically reducing the dimensionality of your dataset by creating new features from existing features. Feature extraction is a common process with datasets that have a large number of features, most often seen when working with image, audio, or text data.

Figure 3.4 shows an example of image recognition.

Before the introduction of neural networks, one of the ways to analyze image datasets was to extract features from the individual images. If the image is a car, you extract some of the useful aspects of the image like the windshield, headlight, turn signals, and tires as independent features. So instead of having raw pixels making up your dataset, you have features or columns such as `windshield_present` and `headlight_present` in your dataset, as displayed in Figure 3.5. These features will make it easier for the ML algorithm to learn from the image data and eventually start to recognize faces.

In most cases, the data itself will help you determine what specific feature extraction technique to use.

For image data, it might be extracting key features like we saw earlier. In NLP, it could be extracting useful features like the most popular words from text other than articles or prepositions.

FIGURE 3.4 Example of image recognition.

FIGURE 3.5 Extracting features from an image.

Feature	Value
headlight_present	true
turn_signal_present	true
windshield_present	true
tire_present	true

68   Chapter 3 ▪ Data Transformation and Feature Engineering

Feature Selection

Feature selection is another technique to reduce the dimensionality of your dataset and is commonly used in conjunction with feature extraction.

Feature selection ranks the dataset existing features according to their predictive significance and selects only the ones that are most relevant based on the ranking.

Because your dataset contains raw data stored in a data lake, some features will likely be more important than others with respect to the model accuracy. Some features will also be redundant due to data correlation to other features.

In the example in Figure 3.6, revenue shifts in parallel to sales, so it is not likely to provide much more insight to the model than it's already getting from the sales data.

The features that are irrelevant to the problem need to be removed. Feature selection addresses these problems by *filtering out* irrelevant or redundant features from your dataset. As a result, only a subset of features that are most useful to the problem is made available to your ML algorithm.

Filtering algorithms may use a statistical measure to help identify features that have a strong relationship with the target variable. In the example, the target variable we want our ML model to predict is sales for a given day, so net profits from sales are probably not relevant to that prediction. As a result, we can remove that feature.

Remember, ML algorithms are not only used for typical structured datasets. Often, we're dealing with unstructured datasets in the form of images, audio, or video, for instance. These types of data formats require filtering techniques to reduce the dimensionality of the dataset.

Feature Creation and Transformation

Unlike feature extraction and selection, feature creation and transformation is not a dimensionality reduction technique. Instead, feature creation and transformation is the process of generating new features from existing features. For example, say we have "date" as a feature, and it's formatted as a two-digit day, two-digit month, and two-digit year (dd-mm-yy).

You might find that combining the day, month, and year into one feature is not very helpful for your predictions. Instead, you could generate three different features, one for day, one for

FIGURE 3.6   Performing feature selection.

Day of Week	Date	Visitors	Sales	Revenue	Net
Saturday	Oct-05-24	8567	3134	47814	4512
Sunday	Oct-06-24	8219	2917	44561	4191
Monday	Oct-07-24	3567	177	3473	305
Tuesday	Oct-08-24	3908	204	3851	376
Wednesday	Oct-09-24	4135	219	4015	391

Redundant   Irrelevant

Data Cleaning and Transformation **69**

month, and one for year, and this way potentially discover a meaningful relationship between one of these features and the target variable you want your ML model to predict.

Using Amazon SageMaker Feature Store

Because features are inputs (or variables) to ML models during training, wouldn't it be nice to have a central location where you could select, refine, store, and manage all the features of your dataset?

This is where Amazon SageMaker Feature Store comes into play. Amazon SageMaker Feature Store is a fully managed repository to store, share, and manage features for ML models. For example, in an application that recommends books for a given topic, features could include book affinity to the topic, book ratings, and book publishing date.

Features are constantly used by multiple teams (data scientists as well as data and ML engineers), and feature quality is critical to the accuracy of your ML model. Also, when features used to train models offline in batch are made available for real-time inference, it's hard to keep the two feature stores synchronized. Amazon SageMaker Feature Store provides a secured and unified store to process, standardize, and use features at scale across the ML lifecycle.

In the next section, we will cover the preprocessing work that is necessary prior to feature engineering. This work starts by transforming your dataset to address inconsistency data issues, such as managing outliers, inputting missing data, and removing duplication.

Data Cleaning and Transformation

Data cleaning is a fundamental preprocessing step that ensures your dataset is in the best possible shape for feature engineering.

With an effective data cleaning approach, you set the stage for feature engineering by transforming "dirty" data into a structured, accurate, and reliable foundation. This allows you to focus on creating and selecting the most relevant and powerful features for your ML model.

Here's how it provides the necessary groundwork:

Managing missing values. This step addresses any gaps in your dataset, whether by imputing missing values, deleting incomplete records, or otherwise managing them. Clean data ensures that the features you engineer do not suffer from bias or inaccuracies caused by gaps in the data.

Detecting and treating outliers. By identifying and managing outliers, you can prevent them from skewing the feature distribution and impacting model performance. Clean data provides a more realistic representation of the data distribution, which is crucial for effective feature engineering.

Performing deduplication. Removing duplicate records and redundant data points helps streamline the dataset, making feature engineering more efficient and less prone to overfitting.

Chapter 3 · Data Transformation and Feature Engineering

Reformatting and standardization. Ensuring uniform data types, units, and formats allows for more straightforward feature creation. For example, standardizing date formats and measurement units ensures consistency and comparability across features.

Removing noise and errors. Data cleaning involves identifying and correcting errors or inconsistencies within the data. This ensures that the features you create are based on accurate and reliable data, leading to more robust models.

Managing Missing Values

It is not uncommon that your dataset has missing data. For example, some columns in your dataset may be missing values due to a data collection error, or maybe the data was simply unavailable from your data source.

Missing data can make it difficult for the selected ML algorithm to accurately interpret the relationship between the related feature and the target variable. Therefore, it is important to deal with the issue.

Unfortunately, most ML algorithms cannot deal with missing values automatically. Human knowledge is required to replace missing values with something meaningful and relevant to the problem.

The approaches to address missing data vary based on the amount of missing data. The main techniques are as follows:

Collect. If the amount of missing data is substantial and multiple features are impacted, you should try to recollect the data. However, the data ingestion process can be expensive and time-consuming. In this case, you need to determine what the trade-offs are among the cost of recollecting data, the cost of having a low-performance ML model, and alternatives such as imputation or dropping.

Impute. If you are dealing with a small number of missing values, which are randomly distributed throughout the features of your dataset, this could be due to a failure in the data ingestion process. In this case, *imputation* is likely a good option. With imputation, you populate the missing data with the mean, the median, or the most frequent value observed for your feature. If the data distribution for your feature is normal, then use the mean; otherwise, use the median or the most frequent value.

Drop. If the amount of missing data is substantial but is limited to the same feature, you may consider dropping the entire feature. You have to be careful, though, because when you drop too many features, you may not have enough data to feed the ML model.

With Amazon SageMaker, you can use Python libraries like `SimpleImputer` from `sklearn` to fill in missing values. The following snippet shows how this function works:

```
from sklearn.impute import SimpleImputer
import numpy as np

# Create a sample dataset
A = np.array([[1, 2], [None, 4], [5, None]])
```

```
# Create a SimpleImputer object
imputer = SimpleImputer(strategy='mean')

# Fit and transform the data
B = imputer.fit_transform(A)

print(B)
```

The following input array

```
[[1, 2], [None, 4], [5, None]]
```

has been transformed into this:

```
[[1, 2], [3, 4], [5, 3]]
```

AWS Glue DataBrew can also be used to fill missing values using a number of built-in transformations.

Detecting and Treating Outliers

An *outlier* is a data point in your dataset distinct from all other data points for having a significant deviation from the mean.

What does "significantly" mean, exactly? Although the answer depends on the type of data and its probability distribution, the general consensus is that a data point is considered an outlier if it lies more than three standard deviations away from the mean. This is based on the properties of the normal distribution, where approximately 99.7% of data lies within three standard deviations from the mean.

ML algorithms are very sensitive to the distribution and the range of the values of your features. Because outliers drift from the pattern of all other data points, they have a tendency to mislead the ML algorithm during training.

For example, consider the following dataset:

```
[x,y] = [[4, 11], [3.8, 12], [4.5, 12.5], [8, 8], [9, 8.5], [9.5, 7.5],
[13, 5], [14, 4.7], [13.7, 6], [25, 23]]
```

In this example, assume x indicates your water consumption rate per day, whereas y indicates the energy consumption rate per day. These numbers are just for illustration purposes.

As you can see in Figure 3.7, this dataset is distributed in three groups.

One data point clearly stands out and is acting as an outlier.

Although some outliers are caused by artificial errors, others just appear in your dataset as a result of natural phenomena. A natural outlier is not the result of some artificial error but instead is reflective of some truth in the data.

FIGURE 3.7 Example of an outlier.

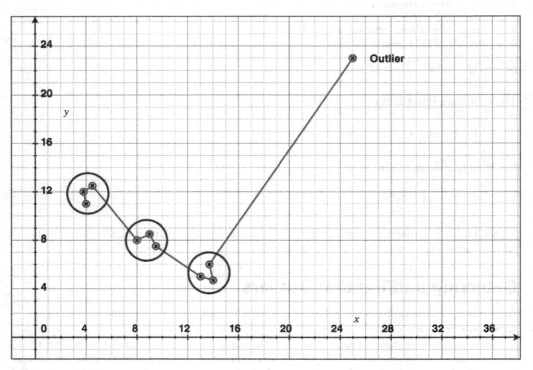

Your job as an ML engineer is to determine whether an outlier should stay in your dataset or needs to be changed or removed. You make this decision by leveraging statistical techniques that help you understand how relevant the outlier is with respect to the other data points in your dataset.

It is important to distinguish between noise and outliers. The former denotes a group of erroneous data points, whereas the latter refers to data points that significantly deviate from the mean of your dataset. In the rest of the chapters, you will learn how to leverage the extensive ecosystem of AWS ML services to determine what "significantly" means.

The treatment of outliers relies on three main approaches:

Delete. If outliers are due to noise or artificial errors, you can simply delete them from your dataset without impacting the quality and the accuracy of your ML model.

Logarithmic transform. By replacing the outlier with its logarithm in a given base (e.g., base e, base 2, base 10, and so on), you are compressing the range of values for a feature, resulting in a reduction of the extreme variation between the values. As a result, the outlier won't be too far off from the other values for that feature. For example, the logarithm base 10 (log_{10}) of 1000 is 3. That's because $10^3 = 1000$, which brings it closer to other smaller values without losing its significance.

Impute. Just as for missing values, you could use the mean of the feature, for instance, and impute that value to replace the outlier value. This would be an excellent approach if the outlier was caused by artificial errors.

Outliers often create a skewed distribution, as shown in Figure 3.7. Log transformation can help normalize this distribution, making it more symmetrical and improving the performance of your ML model.

Figure 3.8 illustrates the same dataset after representing the ordinate axis y using a logarithmic scale. The outlier data point [25, 23] has x = 25 and y = 23. Because log_{10} (23) = 1.37172724, you can see how this data point no longer deviates significantly from the mean.

For the exam, you need to know the AWS services that help you detect and treat outliers, which are Amazon SageMaker Data Wrangler and AWS Glue DataBrew.

You can use Amazon SageMaker Jupyter notebooks to load your dataset using Python libraries like pandas.

FIGURE 3.8   Outlier treatment with logarithmic transformation.

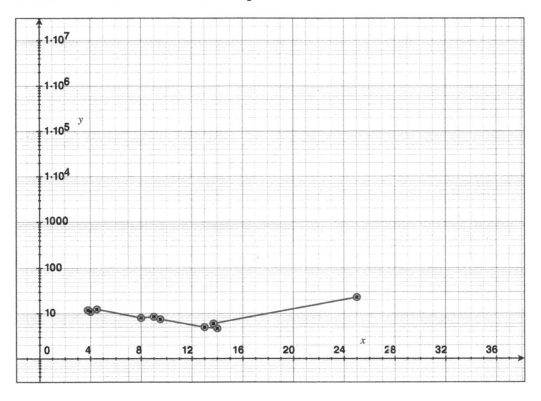

74 Chapter 3 ▪ Data Transformation and Feature Engineering

To determine which outlier detection algorithm to use, you need to analyze the histogram for each feature. Figure 3.9 illustrates the histograms for our dataset generated using the following Python snippet:

```python
import numpy as np
import pandas as pd
import matplotlib.pyplot as plt
import seaborn as sns

# Load dataset
data = np.array([[4, 11], [3.8, 12], [4.5, 12.5], [8, 8], [9, 8.5],
[9.5, 7.5], [13, 5], [14, 4.7], [13.7, 6], [25, 23]])
df = pd.DataFrame(data, columns=['Feature1', 'Feature2'])

# Plot histograms
plt.figure(figsize=(12, 5))

plt.subplot(1, 2, 1)
sns.histplot(df['Feature1'], kde=True)
plt.title('Water Usage Distribution (m³/day)')

plt.subplot(1, 2, 2)
sns.histplot(df['Feature2'], kde=True)
plt.title('Energy Usage Distribution (kWh/day)')

plt.show()
```

FIGURE 3.9 Histograms for water and energy usage.

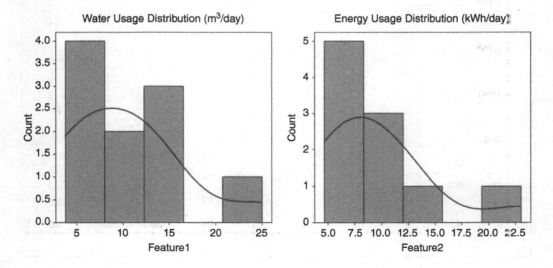

Data Cleaning and Transformation   **75**

In Figure 3.9, the histograms show a right-skewed data distribution for both features. A right-skewed data distribution means that the majority of our data points are clustered toward the lower end of the range, with a long tail extending to the right. This tail represents a small number of data points that have much higher values than the rest of the dataset. Essentially, most values are low, and only a few are exceptionally high, which is exactly our scenario with the data point [25, 23] representing the highest value pair.

For skewed data, the interquartile range (IQR) method is often considered one of the best approaches for detecting outliers. The IQR is less affected by skewness and provides a robust measure to identify extreme values.

Assuming $Q1$ and $Q3$ denote the first and the third quartiles of our dataset, here's a quick overview of how it works:

- Compute $Q1$ and $Q3$.
- Compute $IQR = Q3 - Q1$.

Any data point whose value is smaller than $Q1 - 1.5 * IQR$ or greater than $Q3 + 1.5 * IQR$ is considered an outlier.

In our example, we can leverage the built-in `quantile` method, available from the `DataFrame` class in both the `numpy` and `pandas` libraries, to detect outliers from the dataset, as illustrated in the following snippet:

```
import numpy as np
import pandas as pd

# Load dataset
data = np.array([[4, 11], [3.8, 12], [4.5, 12.5], [8, 8], [9, 8.5],
[9.5, 7.5], [13, 5], [14, 4.7], [13.7, 6], [25, 23]])
df = pd.DataFrame(data, columns=['Feature1', 'Feature2'])

# Calculate IQR
Q1 = df.quantile(0.25)
Q3 = df.quantile(0.75)
IQR = Q3 - Q1

# Define outlier conditions
outliers = ((df < (Q1 - 1.5 * IQR)) | (df > (Q3 + 1.5 * IQR))).any(axis=1)
df['Outlier'] = outliers

print("Original Data with Outlier Flags:")
print(df)

# Treat outliers by removing them
df_cleaned = df[~df['Outlier']].drop(columns='Outlier')

print("\nCleaned Data without Outliers:")
print(df_cleaned)
```

76 Chapter 3 ▪ Data Transformation and Feature Engineering

FIGURE 3.10 Detecting and treating outliers.

```
● (booksession) Darios-Mac-Studio:matplotlib_project dariocabianca$ /Users/dariocabianca/ml/matplotlib_project/bo
  oksession/bin/python /Users/dariocabianca/ml/matplotlib_project/detect_outliers.py
  Original Data with Outlier Flags:
     Feature1  Feature2  Outlier
  0     4.0      11.0     False
  1     3.8      12.0     False
  2     4.5      12.5     False
  3     8.0       8.0     False
  4     9.0       8.5     False
  5     9.5       7.5     False
  6    13.0       5.0     False
  7    14.0       4.7     False
  8    13.7       6.0     False
  9    25.0      23.0      True

  Cleaned Data without Outliers:
     Feature1  Feature2
  0     4.0      11.0
  1     3.8      12.0
  2     4.5      12.5
  3     8.0       8.0
  4     9.0       8.5
  5     9.5       7.5
  6    13.0       5.0
  7    14.0       4.7
  8    13.7       6.0
○ (booksession) Darios-Mac-Studio:matplotlib_project dariocabianca$
```

This program produces the output shown in Figure 3.10, where you can see how the script detected the data point [25, 23] as an outlier and subsequently removed it.

For normally distributed data, the Z-score method is highly effective for detecting outliers. Here's a quick rundown:

- Compute the mean μ of your dataset.
- Compute the standard deviation σ of your dataset.
- For each data point x, the Z-score $z = (x-\mu)/\sigma$.

Because a normal distribution is characterized by the following,

- One standard deviation covers around 68% of the data.
- Two standard deviations covers around 95% of the data.
- Three standard deviations covers around 99.7% of the data.

data points with Z-scores greater than 3 or less than −3 are considered outliers. In other words, it is statistically safe to assume the 0.3% data points whose Z-score is greater than 3 or less than −3 are far enough from the mean to be considered outliers.

The Z-score outlier detection method can also be calculated programmatically. The following snippet shows you how:

```
import numpy as np
import pandas as pd
from scipy import stats

# Load dataset
data = np.array([[4, 11], [3.8, 12], [4.5, 12.5], [8, 8], [9, 8.5],
    [9.5, 7.5], [13, 5], [14, 4.7], [13.7, 6], [25, 23]])
```

```
df = pd.DataFrame(data, columns=['Feature1', 'Feature2'])

# Detect outliers using Z-score
z_scores = np.abs(stats.zscore(df))
outliers = (z_scores > 3).any(axis=1)
df['Outlier'] = outliers

print("Original Data with Outlier Flags:")
print(df)

# Treat outliers by removing them
df_cleaned = df[~df['Outlier']].drop(columns='Outlier')

print("\nCleaned Data without Outliers:")
print(df_cleaned)
```

The preceding code produces the output represented in Figure 3.11.

As you can see, the Z-score method failed to detect the outlier [25, 23]. This is because the distribution of data points in our dataset is not normal, but it's right-skewed.

With AWS Glue DataBrew, you can also detect outliers in your data and handle them using various transformations. This approach includes replacing, removing, rescaling, or flagging outliers using the methods you just learned, i.e., Z-score and IQRs.

Performing Deduplication

Deduplication is the process to remove duplicate data points from your dataset. Deduplication is not just about tidying up your data—it's about making your models more accurate, more performant, and more reliable.

FIGURE 3.11 Failing outlier detection.

```
● (booksession) Darios-Mac-Studio:matplotlib_project dariocabianca$ /Users/dariocabianca/ml/matplotlib_project/bo
  oksession/bin/python /Users/dariocabianca/ml/matplotlib_project/fail_outliers.py
  Original Data with Outlier Flags:
     Feature1  Feature2  Outlier
  0      4.0      11.0    False
  1      3.8      12.0    False
  2      4.5      12.5    False
  3      8.0       8.0    False
  4      9.0       8.5    False
  5      9.5       7.5    False
  6     13.0       5.0    False
  7     14.0       4.7    False
  8     13.7       6.0    False
  9     25.0      23.0    False

  Cleaned Data without Outliers:
     Feature1  Feature2
  0      4.0      11.0
  1      3.8      12.0
  2      4.5      12.5
  3      8.0       8.0
  4      9.0       8.5
  5      9.5       7.5
  6     13.0       5.0
  7     14.0       4.7
  8     13.7       6.0
  9     25.0      23.0
○ (booksession) Darios-Mac-Studio:matplotlib_project dariocabianca$ █
```

From a data quality standpoint, duplicate data can skew the results and lead to inaccurate predictions. Removing duplicates ensures that the data used to train models is clean and accurate.

Model performance and reliability are key factors to be accounted for in the model evaluation and deployment phases of the ML lifecycle. Duplicates can cause overfitting, where the model learns noise rather than the signal. Clean, deduplicated data helps create more generalizable models.

From a reliability standpoint, duplicates can introduce bias, particularly if certain entries are repeated more often than others, leading to imbalanced training data.

As a result, an effective deduplication strategy is critical to ensuring the quality of your ML model training data.

For simplicity and ease of use, AWS Glue DataBrew is probably your best bet for removing duplicates from your dataset. AWS Glue DataBrew offers a straightforward, visual interface to clean and prepare your data without the need for complex code. AWS Glue DataBrew is user-friendly and efficient, making data cleaning tasks like removing duplicates quick and hassle-free.

Standardizing and Reformatting

By implementing standardization, you are preventing features with large values from disproportionately impacting the model compared to features with smaller values. This technique is particularly important for ML algorithms that are sensitive to feature scales, like linear regression and support vector machines, which will be covered in the next chapter.

Reformatting in ML means restructuring your data into a consistent and suitable format for analysis. It includes converting data types, harmonizing formats, and ensuring all data entries follow the same structure.

To perform standardization and reformatting with AWS, you can use Amazon SageMaker and AWS Glue. The main steps are outlined here:

Load data. You can use SageMaker notebooks to load your dataset from an S3 bucket, as shown in the following snippet:

```
import pandas as pd
data = pd.read_csv('your_dataset.csv')
```

Standardize data. You can use the StandardScaler class from the sklearn. preprocessing module to standardize your features, as shown in the following snippet:

```
from sklearn.preprocessing import StandardScaler
scaler = StandardScaler()
data_scaled = scaler.fit_transform(data)
```

More normalization and standardization techniques will be covered in the upcoming sections.

Export data. You can save the standardized dataset to S3.

Create AWS Glue job. Create an AWS Glue job to reformat the data as needed.

Load clean data. Use the cleaned and standardized data to train your ML model.

Removing Noise and Errors

Natural noise and artificial errors were briefly introduced earlier. Because the primary goal of feature engineering is to produce the best possible amount of training data for your ML model, one of the key aspects of this process is the ability to handle noise and errors.

By creating new features or transforming existing ones, you make the training data more informative and relevant for your ML model. This process helps improve model accuracy, efficiency, and generalization, which will result in an increased predictive power of your model.

A model trained on noisy data often learns specific quirks or errors present in the training dataset rather than the underlying patterns. This leads to *overfitting*, where the model performs very well on training data but poorly on new, unseen data. By properly handling noise and errors, you help ensure the model generalizes better to real-world scenarios. We will cover in detail methods to address overfitting in Chapter 5.

Feature Engineering Techniques

In the previous section, the methods to clean your dataset were introduced. Data cleaning is a preliminary step toward preparing your training data for your model.

The objective of the next step is effectively transforming the raw data into meaningful features that improve the performance of your ML model. This is feature engineering's main focus. Ultimately, after feature engineering, your ML model will be ready for training.

Mastering feature engineering is crucial to demonstrate your expertise in building and deploying scalable and efficient ML solutions on AWS. The upcoming sections will cover the feature engineering techniques you need to know for the exam.

We will start with techniques for structured data, and then we will proceed with techniques for unstructured data in the form of images, text, and time-series.

Techniques for Structured Data

With structured data, you can use a number of feature extraction techniques to reduce the dimensionality of your dataset. One of the things you should be careful of when you use feature extraction is that when you put this model into production or automate the pipeline, these features can be replicated easily but still reduce the high dimensions in the data.

Feature Engineering for Numerical Data

Numerical data is ultimately the type of data you want to feed your ML model. Whether your data is categorical, textual, or image, your feature engineering outcomes will need to be in the form of a distinct and well-organized set of numbers that can be used to train your ML algorithm.

The way you engineer these set of numbers into meaningful features may have a significant impact on your model performance and accuracy.

Chapter 3 ▪ Data Transformation and Feature Engineering

In the upcoming sections, we will dive into the feature engineering concepts previously introduced.

Normalization

Normalization is an approach to feature engineering that brings numerical data for all your features into a consistent scale, usually between 0 and 1. This has several key benefits:

Equal weighting. Normalization ensures that no single feature dominates the model due to its scale. This is particularly important for ML algorithms that are sensitive to the scale of your data, such as k-nearest neighbors (k-NN) and neural networks, which compute distances between data points.

Faster convergence. In gradient descent optimization, normalized data helps the ML algorithm converge faster by ensuring that all features contribute equally to the gradient. This leads to more efficient training and better performance for your ML model.

Enhanced interpretability. Normalized data makes it easier to interpret feature importance and model coefficients, as all features are on a comparable scale.

This technique is useful when you want your data to be on a common scale but it doesn't necessarily need to be centered around zero.

As a result of normalization, ML models perform better when all features of your dataset are on the same scale. Normalization can lead to higher accuracy and stability, especially n distance-based algorithms.

Normalization is typically implemented with the MinMax scaler function, which will be covered in detail in the upcoming "Scaling" section.

Standardization

Standardization transforms features to have a mean of 0 and a standard deviation of 1. It's used when you want to ensure that your feature data is centered around the mean (μ) and scaled according to the standard deviation (σ).

This technique is ideal for ML algorithms that assume normally distributed data, such as linear regression, logistic regression, or algorithms that use gradient descent.

You implement standardization by using the Z-score function.

Z-score. This solution transforms the feature dataset to have a mean of 0 and a standard deviation of 1 with the following formula:

$$z = \frac{(x - \mu)}{\sigma}$$

where

- x is your feature data point.
- μ is the mean of your feature dataset.
- σ is the standard deviation of your feature dataset.

The resulting standard deviation is 1 because of the nature of the transformation.

When you subtract the mean (μ) from each data point (x), you center the data around 0. Each data point is adjusted relative to the average value of the dataset.

Dividing by the standard deviation (σ) scales the data points relative to the spread of the data. This step ensures that the variance (which is the square of the standard deviation) of the standardized data becomes 1.

Scaling

Scaling is the general term for adjusting the range or distribution of features. Because normalization's main concern is the range of the transformed dataset (scale 0 to 1 for all features), whereas standardization is focused on distribution (0 as mean μ, and 1 as standard deviation σ of the transformed dataset), these two techniques you just learned are part of scaling.

If your feature data is not normally distributed, you need techniques that handle skewness or outliers differently from Z-score standardization. The ones you need to know for the exam are as follows:

Robust scaling. Robust scaling centers the feature dataset by subtracting the median and scales it according to the IQR. This makes it particularly useful for datasets with outliers, as it ensures the central tendency and spread are robust to them. As a result, this standardization technique is less sensitive to outliers and works well with skewed data.

You can use the `RobustScaler` class from the `sklearn.preprocessing` module to scale your features with this technique, as shown in the following example:

```
import numpy as np
import pandas as pd
from sklearn.preprocessing import RobustScaler

# Load dataset
data = np.array([[4, 11], [3.8, 12], [4.5, 12.5], [8, 8], [9, 8.5],
[9.5, 7.5], [13, 5], [14, 4.7], [13.7, 6], [25, 23]])
df = pd.DataFrame(data, columns=['Feature1', 'Feature2'])

# Apply RobustScaler
scaler = RobustScaler()
data_scaled = scaler.fit_transform(df)

# Convert the scaled data back to a DataFrame for easier viewing
df_scaled = pd.DataFrame(data_scaled, columns=['Feature1', 'Feature2'])

print("Original Data:")
print(df)
print("\nScaled Data:")
print(df_scaled)
```

The preceding code produces the output represented in Figure 3.12.

82 Chapter 3 ▪ Data Transformation and Feature Engineering

FIGURE 3.12 Robust scaling.

```
● (booksession) Darios-Mac-Studio:matplotlib_project dariocabianca$ /Users/dariocabianca/ml/matplotlib_project/bo
  oksession/bin/python /Users/dariocabianca/ml/matplotlib_project/standardize_robust_scaler.py
  Original Data:
     Feature1  Feature2
  0    4.0      11.0
  1    3.8      12.0
  2    4.5      12.5
  3    8.0       8.0
  4    9.0       8.5
  5    9.5       7.5
  6   13.0       5.0
  7   14.0       4.7
  8   13.7       6.0
  9   25.0      23.0

  Scaled Data:
     Feature1  Feature2
  0 -0.644172  0.511628
  1 -0.668712  0.697674
  2 -0.582822  0.790698
  3 -0.153374 -0.046512
  4 -0.030675  0.046512
  5  0.030675 -0.139535
  6  0.460123 -0.604651
  7  0.582822 -0.660465
  8  0.546012 -0.418605
  9  1.932515  2.744186
○ (booksession) Darios-Mac-Studio:matplotlib_project dariocabianca$ []
```

As you can see in Figure 3.12, with robust scaling the scaled data frame is less sensitive to outliers than the original data frame. As a result of the transformation, outliers like [25, 23] don't skew the new dataset for your feature.

MinMax scaling.   This standardization technique transforms features to a fixed range, usually between 0 and 1. This technique preserves the relationships between the features but does not address skewness.

You can use the `MinMaxScaler` class from the `sklearn.preprocessing` module to scale your features with this approach, as shown in the following snippet:

```
import numpy as np
import pandas as pd
from sklearn.preprocessing import MinMaxScaler

# Sample data
data = np.array([[1, 2], [3, 4], [5, 6], [7, 8], [-1, -2], [-3, -4]])
df = pd.DataFrame(data, columns=['Feature1', 'Feature2'])

# Initialize MinMaxScaler
scaler = MinMaxScaler()

# Fit and Transform
data_scaled = scaler.fit_transform(df)
df_scaled = pd.DataFrame(data_scaled, columns=['Feature1', 'Feature2'])

# Print results
print("Original Data:\n", df)
print("\nScaled Data:\n", df_scaled)
```

Feature Engineering Techniques **83**

MaxAbs scaling. MaxAbs scaling is a technique used to standardize data by scaling each feature data point to its maximum absolute value. As a result, each data point falls within the range [–1, 1].

This technique is best suited to standardize sparse datasets or datasets with many 0 data points, because it preserves 0 entries while maintaining the original data distribution.

You can use the `MaxAbsScaler` class from the `sklearn.preprocessing` module to scale your features with this approach, as shown in the following snippet:

```
import numpy as np
import pandas as pd
from sklearn.preprocessing import MaxAbsScaler

# Sample data
data = np.array([[1, 2], [3, 4], [5, 6], [7, 8], [-1, -2]  [-3, -4]])
df = pd.DataFrame(data, columns=['Feature1', 'Feature2'])

# Initialize MaxAbsScaler
scaler = MaxAbsScaler()

# Fit and Transform
data_scaled = scaler.fit_transform(df)
df_scaled = pd.DataFrame(data_scaled, columns=['Feature1', 'Feature2'])

# Print results
print("Original Data:\n", df)
print("\nScaled Data:\n", df_scaled)
```

Power transformations (Box-Cox, Yeo-Johnson). The variance of a dataset is the square of the standard deviation (σ^2). By definition, the variance is always a positive number and measures the spread of data points in a dataset, telling you how far each point is from the mean (μ). Mathematically, it's the average of the squared differences from the mean. A high variance means data points are spread out from the mean; a low variance means they are close to the mean.

Power transformations help stabilize variance and make data more normally distributed. Two common types are the Box-Cox transformation and the Yeo-Johnson transformation. The former works only on positive data, whereas the latter handles both positive and negative data.

You can use the `PowerTransformer` class from the `sklearn.preprocessing` module to scale your features with this approach, as shown in the following snippet:

```
import numpy as np
import pandas as pd
from sklearn.preprocessing import PowerTransformer

# Sample data
data = np.array([[1, 2], [3, 4], [5, 6], [7, 8], [-1, -2], [-3, -4]])
df = pd.DataFrame(data, columns=['Feature1', 'Feature2'])
```

84 Chapter 3 ▪ Data Transformation and Feature Engineering

```
# Initialize Yeo-Johnson Transformation
pt = PowerTransformer(method='yeo-johnson')

# Fit and Transform
data_scaled = pt.fit_transform(df)
df_scaled = pd.DataFrame(data_scaled, columns=['Feature1', 'Feature2'])

# Print results
print("Original Data:\n", df)
print("\nScaled Data:\n", df_scaled)
```

Power transformations make your data more suitable for modeling by reducing skewness and stabilizing variance, leading to more robust and accurate models.

Logarithmic Transformation

As you learned previously, logarithmic transformation is a method to detect and manage outliers. It helps as a feature engineering technique for numerical data by reducing skewness, limiting the impact of outliers, and enhancing linear relationships. Here's how:

Reducing skewness. Many real-world datasets are right-skewed, meaning most data points cluster around lower values with a few outliers extending the "tail" toward higher values. Common examples include income distribution, where a small number of high earners create a long right tail, or test scores on a difficult exam where most students score lower with a few high achievers at the top. Applying a logarithmic transformation compresses this tail, making the distribution more symmetrical and closer to a normal distribution, which many ML algorithms handle better.

Limiting the impact of outliers. High-value outliers can dominate and distort the scale of numerical data. Logarithmic transformation reduces the magnitude of these outliers, bringing them closer to the bulk of the data without outright removal.

Enhancing linear relationships. For some data, the relationship between features and the target variable may be multiplicative or exponential rather than linear. Logarithmic transformation can linearize these relationships, making it easier for linear models to capture the underlying patterns.

For example, consider the following dataset:

```
[x,y] = [[3, 1], [4, 10], [5, 100], [6, 1000]]
```

By transforming y to the $log_{10}(y)$, the new dataset becomes as follows:

```
[x,y] = [[3, 0], [4, 1], [5, 2], [6, 3]]
```

By converting the data to a logarithmic scale, variations become more manageable, and the overall structure of the data is clearer. This transformation can significantly boost the performance and accuracy of many models.

Logarithmic transformation can't be directly applied to features with values of 0 or negative numbers because the logarithm of 0 and negative numbers is undefined, regardless of its base. In such scenarios, consider shifting your data to ensure all values are positive numbers, or use alternative transformations (e.g., cube root), which might be more suitable for your data.

Square or Cube Root

To handle high variance in numeric datasets (in addition to the power transformation covered earlier), consider using square-root or cube-root transformations. The square and cube root of a feature have an effect on the feature distribution. However, that impact is not as significant as logarithmic transformation. The cube root has its own advantage. It can be applied to negative values including 0. The square root can be applied only to positive values and 0.

Binning

Binning (also referred to as *bucketing*) is the process of dividing numerical, continuous data into discrete intervals or "bins." This technique can simplify ML model development and make models more robust to outliers and noise. With binning, you transform numerical data into categorical data.

For example, if you're looking at automobiles data, you can convert the vehicle weight into five columns: is_minicompact, is_subcompact, is_compact, is_midsize, and is_large.

Feature Engineering for Categorical Data

Categorical data can capture important information about the relationships and characteristics of your data that numerical data might miss. Properly engineered categorical features can significantly enhance the performance of your ML models.

Feature engineering for categorical data starts with *encoding*, which is the process of transforming your feature data from string format to a numerical format. The numerical format may be an integer, an array of integers, a matrix, or even a tensor of integers. Encoding is performed to allow ML algorithms to interpret and use this data as input, as most algorithms only understand numerical values.

For example, if your categories are White, Black, and Red, you may encode this data into three vectors: [1, 0, 0] to represent White, [0, 1, 0] to represent Black, and [0, 0, 1] to represent Red.

Label Encoding

Label encoding—as the name suggests—labels each category of your categorical feature to a unique integer. For example, the categorical feature "Color" with values like this

```
["White", "Black", "Red"]
```

86   Chapter 3 ▪ Data Transformation and Feature Engineering

becomes this

```
[0, 1, 2]
```

Although simple, this technique can be problematic for algorithms that assume ordered relationships in data, as it imposes an ordinal structure on categorical values.

This encoding technique is best suited for tree-based ML algorithms because these algorithms can handle the ordinal relationship implied by label encoding.

One-Hot Encoding

One-hot encoding converts a categorical feature into a set of binary features, where each binary feature represents one possible category, with a value of 1 if the category is present and 0 if it's not.

You can use the `OneHotEncoder` class from the `sklearn.preprocessing` module to encode your features with this approach, as shown in the following snippet:

```
import pandas as pd
from sklearn.preprocessing import OneHotEncoder

# Sample data
data = {'Color': ['White', 'Black', 'Red', 'Blue', 'Green', 'Yellow', 'Pink',
'Brown', 'White', 'Black']}
df = pd.DataFrame(data)

# Initialize OneHotEncoder
encoder = OneHotEncoder(sparse_output=False)

# Fit and transform the data
one_hot = encoder.fit_transform(df[['Color']])

# Convert to DataFrame for easier viewing
one_hot_df = pd.DataFrame(one_hot,
columns=encoder.get_feature_names_out(['Color']))

# Print results
print("Original Data:\n", df)
print("\nOne-Hot Encoded Data:\n", one_hot_df)
```

Figure 3.13 shows the result produced by this program.

As you can see, the original dataset had one categorical feature, "Color," with 10 data points (categories): White, Black, Red, Blue, Green, Yellow, Pink, Brown, White, and Black.

The one-hot encoded dataset has been transformed into eight numerical features, equal to the number of distinct colors: Color_Black, Color_Blue, Color_Brown, Color_Green, Color_Pink, Color_Red, Color_White, and Color_Yellow. Each of them has 10 data points.

FIGURE 3.13 One-hot encoding.

```
● (booksession) Darios-Mac-Studio:matplotlib_project dariocabianca$ /Users/dariocabianca/ml/matplotlib_project/bo
  oksession/bin/python /Users/dariocabianca/ml/matplotlib_project/one_hot_encoder.py
Original Data:
    Color
0   White
1   Black
2   Red
3   Blue
4   Green
5   Yellow
6   Pink
7   Brown
8   White
9   Black

One-Hot Encoded Data
   Color_Black  Color_Blue  Color_Brown  Color_Green  Color_Pink  Color_Red  Color_White  Color_Yellow
0      0.0         0.0          0.0          0.0          0.0        0.0         1.0          0.0
1      1.0         0.0          0.0          0.0          0.0        0.0         0.0          0.0
2      0.0         0.0          0.0          0.0          0.0        1.0         0.0          0.0
3      0.0         1.0          0.0          0.0          0.0        0.0         0.0          0.0
4      0.0         0.0          0.0          1.0          0.0        0.0         0.0          0.0
5      0.0         0.0          0.0          0.0          0.0        0.0         0.0          1.0
6      0.0         0.0          0.0          0.0          1.0        0.0         0.0          0.0
7      0.0         0.0          1.0          0.0          0.0        0.0         0.0          0.0
8      0.0         0.0          0.0          0.0          0.0        0.0         1.0          0.0
9      1.0         0.0          0.0          0.0          0.0        0.0         0.0          0.0
○ (booksession) Darios-Mac-Studio:matplotlib_project dariocabianca$ []
```

One-hot encoding is a good choice for features with a small set of categorical data and for non-tree-based ML algorithms, such as linear regression, k-NN, and neural networks. These algorithms will be covered in the next chapter.

One-hot encoding increases the dimensionality of your feature dataset. This can become a problem, especially when dealing with high-cardinality features (those with many unique categories). However, the impact largely depends on the ML algorithm you're using and the nature of your data. You can mitigate the risk of high dimensionality by performing techniques like binary encoding instead, as explained in the next section. Another approach is to use the principal component analysis (PCA) algorithm after one-hot encoding. See Chapter 4 for more information.

Binary Encoding

Binary encoding is an effective technique to handle categorical data without "exploding" the dimensionality of your feature dataset as one-hot encoding might. It works by converting each category value to its corresponding binary number and then splitting the binary number into individual bits as separate features (columns).

Think of binary encoding as a way to compact the number of features resulting from the one-hot-encoding technique.

88   Chapter 3 ▪ Data Transformation and Feature Engineering

In the following example, we used the `BinaryEncoder` class from the `category_encoders` module to binary-encode the same dataset in the previous example:

```python
import category_encoders as ce
import pandas as pd

# Sample data
data = {'Color': ['White', 'Black', 'Red', 'Blue', 'Green', 'Yellow', 'Pink',
'Brown', 'White', 'Black']}
df = pd.DataFrame(data)

# Initialize Binary Encoder
encoder = ce.BinaryEncoder(cols=['Color'])

# Fit and Transform the data
df_binary_encoded = encoder.fit_transform(df)

# Print results
print("Original Data:\n", df)
print("\nBinary Encoded Data:\n", df_binary_encoded)
```

Figure 3.14 displays the output of this transformation.

As a result of binary-encoding our 10 non-distinct categories, the new dataset has only four numerical features (instead of eight).

Why four? Because the original dataset had eight distinct categories, which can be represented in binary format using four bits. Notice how the number of data points (10) doesn't change upon transforming the data.

FIGURE 3.14   Binary encoding.

```
● (booksession) Darios-Mac-Studio:matplotlib_project dariocabianca$ /Users/dariocabianca/ml/matplotlib_project/bo
oksession/bin/python /Users/dariocabianca/ml/matplotlib_project/binary_encoder.py
Original Data:
       Color
0   White
1   Black
2     Red
3    Blue
4   Green
5  Yellow
6    Pink
7   Brown
8   White
9   Black

Binary Encoded Data:
   Color_0  Color_1  Color_2  Color_3
0        0        0        0        1
1        0        0        1        0
2        0        0        1        1
3        0        1        0        0
4        0        1        0        1
5        0        1        1        0
6        0        1        1        1
7        1        0        0        0
8        0        0        0        1
9        0        0        1        0
○ (booksession) Darios-Mac-Studio:matplotlib_project dariocabianca$ []
```

Feature Engineering Techniques **89**

Binary encoding is best suited to address the shortcomings of one-hot encoding, because it mitigates the dimensionality "explosion" resulting from creating one new feature for each unique category.

However, when compared to one-hot encoding, binary encoding can lead to a loss of information within categorical data, which could have a negative impact on your model performance. This is because binary encoding compresses categorical data into fewer bits, causing distinctions between categories to be blurred.

Feature Hashing

This technique uses a hash function to convert high-cardinality categorical data into a fixed number of numerical features that you, as an ML engineer, get to choose.

Feature hashing is efficient and highly scalable because the result of the transformation is a fixed-size vector, keeping memory usage in check. Here's how it works at a high level:

Input feature. The feature hash function receives a feature value, which could be a word, a category, or any other identifiable attribute from your data.

Hash function application. The feature is processed by the hash function, which returns a unique integer value (hash value) based on the value of the feature.

Modulo operation (optional). To ensure the hash value falls within the desired range (usually the size of the feature vector), the hash value is often taken modulo a predefined number.

Vector update. The calculated hash value is used as an index to update the corresponding element in the feature vector.

By leveraging a hash function, this approach transforms data rapidly, thus making it suitable for large datasets. Although collisions can occur, the aggregation of values usually mitigates the impact, especially with large enough hash buckets.

As a result, feature hashing strikes a balance between preserving information and maintaining computational efficiency. It is an excellent solution to feature engineer high-cardinality categorical data in an efficient yet cost-effective manner.

You can use the FeatureHasher class from the sklearn.feature_extraction module to hash your features with this approach, as shown in the following snippet:

```
import pandas as pd
from sklearn.feature_extraction import FeatureHasher

# Sample data
data = [{'Color': 'White'}, {'Color': 'Black'}, {'Color': 'Red'}, {'Color':
'Blue'}, {'Color': 'Green'}, {'Color': 'Yellow'}, {'Color': 'Pink'}, {'Color':
'Brown'}, {'Color': 'White'}, {'Color': 'Black'}]

# Convert to DataFrame for viewing before transformation
df = pd.DataFrame(data)

print("Original Data:")
print(df)
```

Chapter 3 • Data Transformation and Feature Engineering

```python
# Initialize FeatureHasher
hasher = FeatureHasher(n_features=3, input_type='dict')

# Fit and transform the data
hashed_features = hasher.transform(data)

# Convert the hashed features to a DataFrame for easier viewing
hashed_df = pd.DataFrame(hashed_features.toarray(), columns=[f'feature_{i}'
for i in range(hashed_features.shape[1])])

print("\nHashed Data:")
print(hashed_df)
```

Figure 3.15 displays the hashed features generated by this program.

Notice how the `FeatureHasher` class applies feature hashing to convert the categorical data (10 categories) into a fixed-size vector for each category. In this example, we set the number of features in the constructor of the `FeatureHasher` class. This number has been set to 3.

As a result, the 10 categories have been hashed into 10 vectors. Each vector comprises of three integers, one for each of the three features.

Feature Engineering for Time-Series Data

Time-series data was introduced at the beginning of this chapter and is different from standard tabular data because it is captured repeatedly over time, with each successive data point dependent on its past values. Think of a time series like watching a movie—each scene depends on the previous ones. The time dimension plays a key role in time-series data.

FIGURE 3.15 Feature hashing.

```
● (booksession) Darios-Mac-Studio:matplotlib_project dariocabianca$ /Users/dariocabianca/ml/matplotlib_project/bo
  oksession/bin/python /Users/dariocabianca/ml/matplotlib_project/feature_hasher.py
  Original Data:
        Color
  0     White
  1     Black
  2       Red
  3      Blue
  4     Green
  5    Yellow
  6      Pink
  7     Brown
  8     White
  9     Black

  Hashed Data:
     feature_0  feature_1  feature_2
  0        0.0       -1.0        0.0
  1        0.0        1.0        0.0
  2       -1.0        0.0        0.0
  3        0.0       -1.0        0.0
  4        0.0        0.0       -1.0
  5        0.0        0.0        1.0
  6        0.0        0.0       -1.0
  7        0.0        0.0       -1.0
  8        0.0       -1.0        0.0
  9        0.0        1.0        0.0
  ○ (booksession) Darios-Mac-Studio:matplotlib_project dariocabianca$ []
```

Amazon SageMaker Data Wrangler provides a low-code solution to time-series data processing with the ability to clean, transform, and prepare data faster. It also enables data scientists to engineer time-series data in adherence to their forecasting model's input format requirements.

To perform feature engineering on a time-series dataset, we need first to understand the patterns present in our dataset. Amazon SageMaker Data Wrangler offers a number of visualizations, which provide valuable leads to data scientists and analysts into existing patterns and can help you choose a modeling strategy. After we understand the patterns present in our dataset, we can start to engineer new features aimed at increasing the accuracy of the forecasting models.

Featurize Datetime

It's best practice to start the feature engineering process for time-series data by disambiguating date/time features. Date/time features are created from the `timestamp` column and provide an optimal way for ML engineers to start the feature engineering process. The *Featurize datetime* time-series transformation lets us break down a date/time feature by adding the `date_month`, `date_day`, `date_week_of_year`, `date_day_of_year`, and `date_quarter` new features to our dataset. Because we're providing the date/time components as separate features, we enable ML algorithms to detect patterns for improving prediction accuracy.

Encode Categorical

Date/time features aren't limited to integer values. You may also choose to consider certain extracted date/time features as categorical variables and represent them as one-hot-encoded features, with each column containing binary values. To do so, leverage the *One-hot encode* transformation. The newly created `date_quarter` feature contains values from 0 to 3 and can be one-hot encoded using four binary columns, one column for each of the four quarters.

Lag Feature

To increase model accuracy, it is best practice to create *lag features* for the target variable (or label). Lag features are values at prior timestamps that are helpful in predicting future values. They also help identify autocorrelation (also known as *serial correlation*) patterns in the residual series by quantifying the relationship of the observation with observations at previous time steps. Autocorrelation is similar to regular correlation but between the values in a series and its past values. Amazon SageMaker Data Wrangler provides the *Lag features* transformation, which helps create multiple lag features over a specified window size.

Rolling Window Features

Amazon SageMaker Data Wrangler implements automatic time-series feature extraction capabilities using the open-source `tsfresh` package. With the time-series feature extraction transformation, you can automate the feature extraction process. This eliminates the time and effort otherwise spent manually implementing signal processing libraries. For the exam, you need to know that features can be extracted using the *Rolling window features* transformation, which computes statistical properties across a set of observations defined by the window size.

Chapter 3 · Data Transformation and Feature Engineering

After feature engineering the time-series dataset, we are ready to use the transformed dataset as input for a forecasting ML algorithm.

Techniques for Unstructured Data

Unstructured data, such as images, text, audio, and videos, doesn't fit neatly into tables and often lacks a predefined format. AWS offers a comprehensive ecosystem of products and services that make feature engineering for unstructured data more manageable and efficient.

In the upcoming sections, we will cover the techniques you need to know for the exam that apply to image and textual data.

Feature Engineering for Image Data

Just like structured data, feature engineering for image data is a critical step in developing effective ML models. This process involves extracting meaningful features from images, such as edges, textures, and colors, to improve the performance of image recognition and classification tasks by providing the model with more relevant information about the data.

For example, at the beginning of the chapter, we used an image of a car (Figure 3.4) to show you what features could be extracted from this unstructured data.

To perform feature extraction on images, you primarily leverage pre-trained vision models within Amazon SageMaker JumpStart, often by processing them through a convolutional neural network (CNN) and retrieving the resulting feature vectors. These pre-trained vision models include models for object detection, image classification, and many others.

You can also use services like Amazon Rekognition for basic image analysis and feature extraction, depending on your use case. Amazon Rekognition can detect objects, scenes, text, and faces in images, providing high-level features without the need for extensive manual effort. For instance, Amazon Rekognition can identify and extract features such as labels and bounding boxes around objects, which are essential for tasks like object detection and image classification.

Once features are extracted, transforming them into a suitable format is essential. Amazon SageMaker Data Wrangler allows you to perform exploratory data analysis (EDA) and apply transformations like normalization and dimensionality reduction. This step ensures your features are optimized for model training. For example, you can normalize pixel values to a common scale or apply PCA to reduce the dimensionality of your feature set.

Efficiently storing and managing your engineered features is crucial for streamlined workflows. As you learned at the beginning of the chapter, Amazon SageMaker Feature Store provides a centralized repository for feature storage, making it easy to share and reuse features across different models and projects. This ensures consistency and saves time, as you don't have to re-extract features for every new model.

Feature Engineering for Textual Data

In today's data-driven world, textual data is everywhere, from social media posts to customer reviews and beyond. Extracting meaningful insights from this unstructured data requires effective feature engineering. AWS provides a powerful ecosystem of products and services to streamline this process and turn raw text into valuable features for ML models.

Amazon Comprehend is a powerful tool for extracting high-level features from text. It can detect entities, key phrases, sentiment, and language, providing rich insights without extensive manual effort. Additionally, Amazon Textract can extract text from documents, turning unstructured data into structured information.

For more customized feature extraction, Amazon SageMaker offers built-in algorithms and frameworks. These algorithms can be used to train models and extract specific features like word embeddings (e.g., Word2Vec) or perform topic modeling (e.g., Latent Dirichlet Allocation). These algorithms will be discussed in detail in Chapter 4.

The following are some essential techniques you need to know for the exam.

Tokenization

Tokenization is the process of splitting text into smaller units, such as words or phrases, called *tokens*. This is the first step in preparing text data for modeling.

For example, the sentence "Machine learning is fascinating" is tokenized into ["Machine", "learning", "is", "fascinating"].

Tokenization is a key component used by Amazon Bedrock foundation models (FMs) to understand and process user prompts. By breaking down the input text into smaller tokens, these models can effectively interpret the meaning and context of the user's request. For example, a prompt like "Generate an image of a sunset" would be divided into individual words and symbols, allowing the model to analyze each element and understand the overall directive. This token-based approach ensures that the model can handle complex and nuanced instructions with high accuracy and relevance.

Moreover, tokenization plays a key role in the pricing model for using Amazon Bedrock FMs. The cost of utilizing these models is determined by the number of input tokens processed and the output tokens generated. This token-based billing system ensures that users are charged fairly based on the actual computational resources consumed. For example, a longer and more detailed prompt would require more tokens and thus incur a higher cost compared to a shorter, simpler prompt. In Chapter 4, we will introduce a practical example demonstrating how to generate an image from a simple prompt using an FM available in Amazon Bedrock, showcasing the efficiency and effectiveness of token-based processing.

Stop-Words Removal

Stop words are common words (e.g., "the", "is", "and") that often do not contribute meaningful information. Removing them can reduce noise and improve model performance.

For example, removing "is" and "the" from "The cat is on the mat" would result in ["cat", "on", "mat"].

Stemming and Lemmatization

These techniques reduce words to their base or root form. Stemming cuts off prefixes/suffixes, whereas lemmatization uses linguistic rules.

For example, "running" becomes "run".

N-grams

N-grams are contiguous sequences of n items from a given text. They capture context and relationships between words.

For example, for a bi-gram (i.e., a contiguous sequence of two words), the sentence `"Machine learning is fun"` is transformed to `[("Machine", "learning"),` `("learning", "is"), ("is", "fun")]`.

Word Embeddings

Word embeddings like Word2Vec and GloVe convert words into continuous vectors that capture semantic meaning, preserving relationships between words. This makes the data more suitable for ML models.

For example, `"King"` and `"Queen"` might be close in vector space, reflecting their semantic similarity.

Data Labeling

In the realm of ML, data labeling and feature engineering are two intertwined processes that are fundamental to building effective models. They both transform raw data into a structured form that ML algorithms can understand and learn from.

Feature engineering is focused on selecting, modifying, and creating new features from raw data to improve model performance, whereas data labeling involves enriching raw data with metadata in the form of meaningful labels that denote the actual predictions or specific attributes. For supervised learning, this step is fundamental as it provides the ground truth that models learn from. By labeling data, you provide the model with the "correct answers" to learn from and predict against.

Labels act as a reference point, guiding the learning process of algorithms. They define what the model is supposed to predict or classify. For example, in a dataset of animal images, labeling each image as "cat" or "dog" allows the model to learn to distinguish between these animals.

Amazon SageMaker Ground Truth

With AWS, you perform data labeling using Amazon SageMaker Ground Truth, a service specifically designed to streamline and enhance the data labeling process. This service combines advanced automation with human-in-the-loop capabilities to deliver high-quality labeled datasets efficiently. Here is the high-level process:

Store data.   Upload your raw data (images, text, etc.) to Amazon S3. Create separate folders or buckets to organize your data based on the type or project.

Create a labeling job.   In Amazon SageMaker Ground Truth, define the task and instructions.

Automated labeling. Choose the type of data you are labeling (e.g., image classification, text classification, object detection), and specify the input dataset stored in S3. Select Automated Data Labeling to use pre-trained ML models to label a subset of your data, and configure the labeling algorithm settings and parameters.

Human review. Annotators review and correct the labels, ensuring accuracy. This step can be performed by Amazon Mechanical Turk, a private workforce, or third-party vendors. Amazon Mechanical Turk (MTurk) is a crowdsourcing marketplace that connects businesses with a global workforce of workers to complete tasks that are difficult for computers to do, data labeling being one of them.

Data labeling and validation. Amazon SageMaker Ground Truth provides a user-friendly interface for labelers to annotate data. Annotators review and correct the automated labels, adding tags, bounding boxes, or other relevant annotations as needed. You can even implement quality control measures, such as consensus labeling (multiple annotators label the same data) and audit sampling (a subset of labels is reviewed by experts).

Store labeled data. You can keep the labeled data in your S3 bucket, or you can automatically save it in Amazon SageMaker Feature Store for easy access during model training and inference. Either way, make sure you keep the labeled data versioned to track changes.

Model training. Use the labeled data to train your models in Amazon SageMaker.

With the right mix of automation and human labeling intervention, Amazon SageMaker Ground Truth provides a robust solution for creating accurate and reliable labeled datasets, which are crucial for building high-performing ML models.

Managing Class Imbalance

So far, you have learned how to transform your dataset by first cleaning the raw data, then performing feature engineering on your data, and finally labeling the data. This last step is a fundamental aspect of ML because it focuses on providing the correct predictions to each data point so that your ML model can quickly learn during training.

With your ML problem framed and your data carefully processed, you would think you are now ready to select an ML algorithm and start the training process, right? Not quite yet!

Your dataset may look good syntactically as a result of selecting, extracting, and creating features, but not semantically due to an uneven distribution of labels. For examples, in a healthcare use case, consider a dataset where the majority class represents healthy individuals and the minority class represents patients with a rare disease. The goal of your ML problem is to predict a disease accurately. When your dataset presents a disproportionate class of labels—just like in this scenario with a majority class with healthy individuals—you are dealing with a *class imbalance*.

Class imbalance leads to a model that is biased toward the majority class. This can significantly impact the performance and fairness of the model, particularly in cases where the minority class is of critical importance, like in our healthcare use case.

The good news is that AWS offers a comprehensive suite of products and services to address class imbalance, ensuring that your models are not only accurate but also ethical and unbiased.

Before delving into how AWS addresses this challenge, let's review what approach you can pursue to tackle class imbalance and the resulting biases.

Class-Imbalance Mitigation Techniques

Data augmentation is generally considered a best practice to generate more minority labeled data, thereby bridging the gap between majority and minority classes. Techniques like image augmentation (rotations, flips, and color adjustments) for image data, or text augmentation (synonym replacement, random insertion) for text data, can create diverse and representative samples. However, data augmentation may not always be feasible due to cost, compute resources availability, and time constraints. In such scenarios, consider using the following options:

Oversampling. This technique involves increasing the number of data points of the minority class by duplicating existing examples or generating synthetic ones. The synthetic minority over-sampling technique (SMOTE) is a popular method that creates synthetic samples by interpolating between existing minority class examples. This helps balance the dataset without simply duplicating records.

Undersampling. This technique works by randomly removing data points from the majority class, thereby making the class distribution more even with the minority class. Although it can be effective, undersampling may lead to a loss of valuable information, potentially impacting the model's performance.

Class weighting. While computing loss during training, this technique assigns higher weights to the ML algorithm for misclassifying the minority class, thereby forcing the model to pay more attention to it.

> Data augmentation is different from synthetic data. Data augmentation artificially creates new data from the existing training data, whereas synthetic data is generated data that does not use the original dataset.

Amazon SageMaker Clarify

Amazon SageMaker Clarify helps address class imbalance by providing pre-training bias metrics to detect and mitigate bias in your datasets. Each metric corresponds to a different notion of fairness.

These metrics are critical to ensure your models are fair and unbiased from the start. Table 3.1 shows two of the most commonly used metrics: Class Imbalance (CI) and Difference in Proportions of Labels (DPL).

In the context of class imbalance biases with Amazon SageMaker Clarify, a *facet* denotes a specific feature in your dataset that you want to analyze for potential bias.

Facets are used to identify and measure how different subgroups within your data might be affected by class imbalance. With Amazon SageMaker Clarify, *facet a* denotes the feature value that defines a demographic that bias favors, and *facet d* denotes the feature value that defines a demographic that bias disfavors.

For example, if you're analyzing a dataset of credit card transactions, facets may include features like is_fraudulent whose value can be 1 (true) or 0 (false). Let's say this feature has 99.9% values of 0 to indicate that 99.9% of the transactions in the dataset are not fraudulent. By examining these facet values (1 or 0), Amazon SageMaker Clarify can help you understand if certain subgroups of any of these feature values are underrepresented or overrepresented in your training data, which could lead to biased model predictions.

Other pre-training bias metrics can be found at https://docs.aws.amazon.com/sagemaker/latest/dg/clarify-measure-data-bias.html.

Even though the range of each metric varies, all of them have the common characteristic that a value 0 (or near 0) denotes no class imbalance.

By computing these pre-training bias metrics, you can determine the next course of actions for your dataset in preparation for training. In our example, assuming *facet a* is 0, we would likely obtain a CI close to 1. As a result, we would need to undersample.

TABLE 3.1 Examples of pre-training bias metrics.

Bias metric	Interpretation
Class Imbalance (CI)	■ Normalized range: [−1, +1] ■ 0: no class imbalance ■ +1: complete imbalance toward majority class ■ −1: complete imbalance toward minority class
Difference in Proportions of Labels (DPL)	■ Range for normalized binary and multicategory facet labels: [−1, +1] ■ Range for continuous facet labels: [−∞, +∞] ■ 0: equal proportion of positive outcomes between facets ■ +1: facet a has a highest proportion of positive outcomes ■ −1: facet d has a highest proportion of positive outcomes
Equal opportunity difference (EOD)	Object detection bias
Predictive parity difference (PPD)	Image classification bias

The `BiasConfig` class is part of the `sagemaker.clarify` library. This library helps you detect and mitigate bias in ML models. The `BiasConfig` class is used to configure the bias analysis settings for your dataset.

Data Splitting

After managing class imbalance, your data is finally ready to be split into training, validation, and test datasets.

Data splitting refers to dividing your dataset into separate subsets for training, validation, and testing purposes. This is a critical step in ML to ensure that your model is trained effectively and evaluated accurately. Let's see what should be part of each dataset and, most important, what their intended purpose is:

Training dataset. The training dataset is used to teach the model. It's where the model learns patterns and relationships within the data. During training, the model uses this data to adjust its parameters and iteratively learns to minimize errors and improve predictions. For example, you may feed a model numerous labeled examples of emails (spam versus not spam) to teach it how to classify incoming emails.

Validation dataset. The validation dataset is used to evaluate the model's performance by fine-tuning the model's hyperparameters. One of the benefits of using a validation dataset is to prevent a model from overfitting by ensuring the model generalizes well to unseen data.

Test dataset. The test dataset is (and should be) made up of data the model has never seen before. After training and validation, the model's performance is measured on the test dataset to attain an unbiased evaluation of how well the model generalizes to new data. For example, you may create a test dataset by using a separate set of emails that the model hasn't seen before to test its accuracy in classifying spam versus not spam.

In summary, the training dataset is used to build the model, the validation dataset helps tune the model and prevents overfitting, whereas the test dataset provides an unbiased evaluation of the model's performance.

Think of training, validation, and test datasets as stages in preparing for an important exam. The training dataset is like the study materials you use to learn the subject thoroughly, allowing you to understand and internalize the information. The validation dataset resembles the practice exams you take to assess your readiness, identify areas for improvement, and make necessary adjustments without it influencing your core learning process. Finally, the test dataset is similar to the actual exam you take at a test center with a proctor, objectively evaluating your knowledge and performance based on unseen questions, ensuring you are well prepared for real-world scenarios. This metaphor highlights the distinct yet interconnected roles each dataset plays in developing a successful and reliable ML model.

To effectively split data for ML—according to best practices—consider allocating approximately 60–80% for training to ensure the model learns and acquires a comprehensive understanding of the data. Use 10–20% for validation to fine-tune model parameters without influencing the training process, ensuring unbiased performance evaluation. The final 10–20% is reserved for testing, serving as the ultimate gauge of the model's ability to generalize to new, unseen data. Proper partitioning is a key aspect of feature engineering, as it prevents data leakage, avoids overfitting, and provides an accurate measure of how well your ML model will perform in real-world scenarios, impacting its overall reliability and effectiveness.

Data leakage occurs when some test data "leaks" into the training dataset. This is a common pitfall that can severely compromise the integrity of ML models. When data leakage happens, the model learns information that it would not have access to in a real-world scenario, leading to artificially inflated performance metrics and poor generalization to new, unseen data. Avoiding data leakage is crucial to ensure that the model's performance is accurately evaluated and that it can generalize well to real-world situations. Effective techniques to prevent data leakage include maintaining a clear separation between training and test datasets, using cross-validation, and carefully monitoring data preprocessing steps. As a best practice, always normalize/standardize your data *after* you have already split your data into training and test datasets. If data leakage is detected, it is essential to re-evaluate the model using a properly separated dataset to obtain a fair assessment of its performance.

AWS offers Amazon SageMaker Data Wrangler to help you with dataset splitting. Let's see how in more detail.

Amazon SageMaker Data Wrangler

In addition to being your one-stop shop for feature engineering, Amazon SageMaker Data Wrangler can assist you by splitting your dataset into training, validation, and test datasets with minimal to no code. Moreover, specifically you can use the split data transformation based on these four commonly used techniques:

Random split. This technique ensures that each subset (training, validation, test) has a similar distribution of categories, preventing bias toward any particular class. This method is particularly useful when you don't need to preserve the order of your input data.

Order split. This technique ensures that data is split in a way that order is preserved, preventing data leakage by ensuring that past or future information doesn't overlap across the train, validation, and test datasets. This is particularly useful for time-series data or any scenario where the order of data points is critical.

100 Chapter 3 ▪ Data Transformation and Feature Engineering

Stratified split.   This technique ensures that each subset maintains the same proportion of categories as the original dataset. This is particularly useful for classification problems with imbalanced data, as it helps maintain the distribution of classes across all subsets, leading to more reliable model evaluation and training.

Split by key.   This technique ensures that no combination of values across the input columns occurs in more than one of the splits. This is particularly useful for avoiding data leakage in unordered data. It also enables consistent grouping by keeping related data together, thereby preserving the integrity of the splits.

After choosing the split data transformation technique, you can specify the percentages for the training, validation, and test datasets. For example, you might allocate 70% for training, 20% for validation, and 10% for testing. You can finally apply the split data transformation, and Amazon SageMaker Data Wrangler will automatically split your dataset into the specified subsets.

Summary

In this chapter, you learned what you need to do to prepare your raw dataset as a meaningful set of features, which stores the relevant content of your data, in a suitable format that can be fed to and ultimately understood by an ML algorithm to produce accurate and reliable predictions.

The different types of data (categorical, numerical, textual, image, time-series) were introduced to logically group the different data transformation techniques.

By engineering your data with feature selection and extraction, you learned how to pursue a minimalistic approach (dimensionality reduction) to selectively choose the relevant features that matter to your ML model. All aspects of data cleaning were covered, with emphasis on outliers detection and removal, as well as missing-data-imputation methods. Feature engineering techniques for numerical, categorical, time-series, and unstructured data were provided, with examples in the Python programming language.

You learned how Amazon SageMaker Data Wrangler and Amazon SageMaker Feature Store are best suited to perform feature engineering and to store, share, and manage the resulting features, respectively.

Finally, you learned how to develop an effective labeling strategy with Amazon SageMaker Ground Truth, how to mitigate class imbalance with Amazon SageMaker Clarify, and how to split your processed dataset into training, validation, and test datasets by using Amazon SageMaker Data Wrangler.

In the next chapters, you will learn how to choose a modeling approach, how to train and refine your model, and how to evaluate its performance.

Exam Essentials

Know the feature engineering techniques that handle outliers. To handle outliers in feature engineering, it's essential to apply techniques that mitigate their impact on your ML model. These methods include removing outliers altogether (whenever possible) or transforming them using approaches such as logarithmic transformation, which can reduce the skewness of your data. Additionally, imputation methods such as replacing outliers with the median or mean value can be effective in maintaining the integrity of the dataset while reducing their impact on the resulting ML model.

Know the feature engineering techniques that handle skewness. To handle skewness, techniques like logarithmic transformation, square root transformation, and Box-Cox or Yeo-Johnson transformations are excellent choices. These techniques can help normalize distributions and make them more suitable for statistical analysis, especially when dealing with skewed data where the majority of values are clustered toward one side of the distribution with a long tail on the other.

Know the feature engineering techniques that do not handle skewness. Z-score standardization doesn't directly address skewness. It scales the data to have a mean of 0 and a standard deviation of 1, but if the original data is skewed, it remains skewed after transformation.

MinMax scaling doesn't directly address skewness either. It resizes data to fit within a specific range, typically from 0 to 1, but doesn't transform the data distribution. If your data is skewed, skewness remains even after scaling.

Know when to perform feature engineering with normalization versus standardization. Normalization is useful when scale matters, whereas standardization is preferred when the distribution is key.

Know the feature engineering techniques that are used for standardization. For standardization—whose purpose is to ensure that each feature in your dataset contributes equally to the ML model's performance—consider using Z-score for normally distributed data.

Know the feature engineering techniques that are used for normalization. For normalization—whose purpose is to scale each feature in your dataset to the same range (usually 0 to 1)—consider using the MinMax scaling technique.

Know the feature engineering techniques that are used for categorical data. Use label encoding for categorical ordinal data and tree-based ML models. Use one-hot encoding for small sets of categorical, nominal data and non-tree-based ML models. Use binary encoding to reduce the dimensionality caused by one-hot-encoding techniques. Use feature hashing for high-cardinality categorical data, especially in use cases where compute resources need to be optimized and the solution must be cost-effective.

Know the feature engineering techniques that are used for image data. For image data you can extract features from your raw dataset with Amazon SageMaker JumpStart. Amazon Rekognition is also a valid option for basic image analysis and feature extraction, depending on your use case. After extracting your relevant features from the dataset, you can leverage Amazon SageMaker Data Wrangler to transform your dataset for normalization and dimensionality reduction. Finally, you can store your features in Amazon SageMaker Feature Store.

Know the feature engineering techniques that are used for textual data. For textual data, you can extract features from your raw dataset with Amazon Comprehend or Amazon Textract. For more customized feature extraction, Amazon SageMaker allows you to use tokenization, stemming, and lemmatization to perform basic selection of words or to reduce words to their root form for subsequent semantic analysis.

Know the AWS services that are used for data labeling. For data labeling—whose purpose is to enrich your dataset with the actual predictions or meaningful metadata that helps your model to learn faster—consider using Amazon SageMaker Ground Truth.

Know how to manage class imbalance. To mitigate the risks introduced by class imbalance, select a feature that is sensitive to bias (facet), and consider computing the pre-training bias metrics (provided by Amazon SageMaker Clarify) for that feature, such as Class Imbalance (CI) or Difference in Proportions of Labels (DPL). Determine the appropriate strategy accordingly. This can be data oversampling, undersampling, or class weighting.

Know the differences between training, validation, and test datasets. The training dataset is where the model learns patterns, relationships, and features from the data. Essentially, it's where the model gets its "education." After the model has been trained, the validation dataset helps in adjusting hyperparameters and tuning the model to improve its performance and generalization to unseen data. It's like a practice test before the final exam. The test dataset is used to evaluate the model's overall performance. It provides an unbiased assessment of how well the model generalizes to new, unseen data. Think of it as the final exam that determines the model's grade.

Review Questions

1. You are preparing a dataset that contains numerical, categorical, and ordinal features. To train a predictive model and to increase its prediction accuracy, you need to transform the categorical features into numerical values. Which feature engineering solution is best suited for this use case?
   A. One-hot encoding
   B. Feature scaling
   C. Feature extraction
   D. Date formatting

2. You want to convert a column in your training data into binary values. Which technique is best suited for this transformation?
   A. One-hot encoding
   B. Tokenization
   C. Label encoding
   D. Feature hashing

3. During data preparation, you discover missing values on some columns of a dataset containing categorical features. You need to ensure that this will not misrepresent the data and reduce the model reliability. What solution is best suited for this use case?
   A. Amazon SageMaker Clarify
   B. Multiple imputations
   C. Drop the feature
   D. Recollect the data

4. You are training a model, and during data analysis you observe different input variables that vary significantly. You want to ensure that your dataset does not have features with a larger value that greatly influence the model's predictive capability. Which transformation is best suited in this scenario?
   A. Normalization
   B. Standardization
   C. Binning
   D. One-hot encoding

5. You are preparing a dataset that has several categorical features, each with high cardinality. You want to efficiently feature-engineer the dataset in a cost-effective way. What solution fits best this use case?
   A. Label encoding
   B. Lag features
   C. Binary encoding
   D. Feature hashing

104 Chapter 3 ▪ Data Transformation and Feature Engineering

6. A model trained to recognize cars is not performing well. You need to re-engineer the features in the image dataset to ensure better performance. What solution best fits this scenario?

    A. Tokenization using Amazon SageMaker Data Wrangler

    B. Lag feature using Amazon SageMaker Data Wrangler

    C. Binning using Amazon SageMaker Data Wrangler

    D. Amazon SageMaker JumpStart

7. Which advanced technique is commonly used in feature engineering for textual data to convert words into numerical vectors that capture semantic meaning?

    A. One-hot encoding

    B. Tokenization

    C. Word embeddings

    D. Normalization

8. What is the most common technique used to handle class imbalance in machine learning datasets?

    A. Data encoding

    B. Data augmentation

    C. Feature scaling

    D. Data splitting

9. Which AWS services can be used for data labeling in AWS?

    A. Amazon Comprehend

    B. Amazon SageMaker Ground Truth

    C. Amazon Rekognition

    D. Amazon SageMaker Clarify

10. What is the purpose of splitting a dataset into training, validation, and test datasets in machine learning?

    A. To improve the model's accuracy

    B. To ensure the model has diverse data

    C. To prevent overfitting and evaluate model performance

    D. To simplify data processing

Chapter 4

Model Selection

THE AWS CERTIFIED MACHINE LEARNING (ML) ENGINEER ASSOCIATE EXAM OBJECTIVES COVERED IN THIS CHAPTER MAY INCLUDE, BUT ARE NOT LIMITED TO THE FOLLOWING:

✓ **Domain 2: ML Model Development**
- 2.1 Choose a modeling approach
- 2.2 Train and refine models

Chapter 4 • Model Selection

In the previous chapter, we explored the important steps of data transformation and feature engineering, laying the groundwork for effective machine learning (ML) applications. In this chapter, we move into the exciting phase of selecting a model based on your ML problem.

With reference to the ML lifecycle (Figure 4.1), in this chapter our focus is on choosing a suitable ML algorithm (or AI service) tailored to your specific ML requirements.

You will learn how to select an ML algorithm that is best suited for your specific use case and how to implement it effectively to initiate the model development process. Remember, the model development process is iterative in nature, involving continuous refinement and evaluation to ensure the best possible performance and accuracy of your model. By mastering this iterative approach, you'll be well-equipped to tackle complex data challenges and drive impactful results.

This chapter will guide you through the intricate yet fascinating process of transforming raw data into powerful predictive models that can drive actionable insights and decisions.

The selection of an appropriate ML algorithm is a pivotal step in the model development process. This decision hinges on a clear understanding of your use case, the nature of your data, and the specific problem you aim to solve. Whether you're dealing with a classification task, a regression problem, or clustering needs, choosing the right algorithm involves balancing factors like interpretability, accuracy, computational efficiency, scalability, and cost. We'll delve into various algorithm types, providing guidelines on when to use each and how to match them to your unique requirements.

Following the ML lifecycle, once the algorithm is selected, the journey of training begins. Here, we'll cover the basic steps of feeding data into the algorithm. In the next chapter, you will learn how to fine-tune hyperparameters and iteratively refine the model to enhance its performance. We'll also discuss techniques to avoid common pitfalls such as overfitting and underfitting, ensuring that your model generalizes well to new, unseen data.

By the end of this chapter, you'll have a comprehensive understanding of the model selection phase, equipped with the knowledge to choose the most appropriate algorithm or AI service for your ML problem and the confidence to implement your selections effectively.

FIGURE 4.1 The machine learning lifecycle.

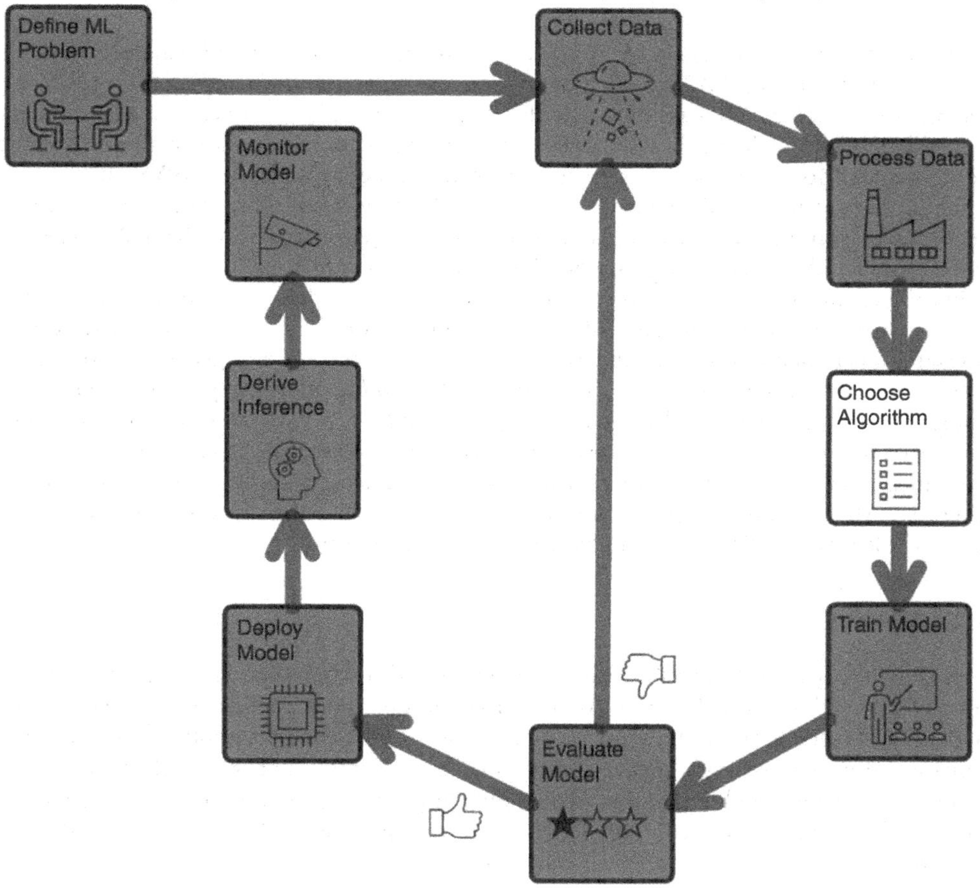

Understanding AWS AI Services

AWS AI services are powerful, prebuilt, and pretrained ML models that help developers and ML engineers seamlessly integrate AI into their applications without requiring in-depth knowledge of ML. These services cover a wide range of AI capabilities, including computer vision, natural language processing (NLP), speech recognition, generative AI, and predictive analytics. For instance, Amazon Rekognition allows users to analyze images and videos to

108 Chapter 4 ▪ Model Selection

identify objects, people, text, scenes, and activities. Meanwhile, Amazon Comprehend performs NLP tasks such as sentiment analysis and entity recognition, enabling businesses to gain insights from unstructured text data.

One of the key advantages of AWS AI services is their ease of use and scalability. They come with fully managed APIs, which developers can call from their applications to leverage sophisticated ML capabilities with minimal effort. These services are also designed to handle large-scale data processing, ensuring that applications can meet high-performance requirements. Moreover, AWS AI services integrate seamlessly with other AWS offerings, enabling users to build end-to-end ML workflows from data collection and processing to model training and deployment. This holistic approach helps streamline the development process and accelerates the adoption of AI across various industries.

For the exam, you need to know which AWS AI services address various AI and ML use cases, such as text analysis, image and video recognition, speech synthesis and recognition, translation, personalized recommendations, document processing, and generative AI. This includes understanding services like *Amazon Comprehend* for text analysis, *Amazon Rekognition* for image and video recognition, *Amazon Polly* for speech synthesis, *Amazon Transcribe* for speech recognition, *Amazon Translate* for translation, *Amazon Personalize* for recommendations, *Amazon Textract* for document processing, and *Amazon Bedrock* for generative AI. Knowing the specific use cases and applications of each service is key to effectively leveraging AWS AI capabilities in different scenarios.

Vision

AWS provides powerful tools for visual content analysis through services like Amazon Rekognition and Amazon Textract. Amazon Rekognition helps analyze images and videos to identify objects, faces, and text, offering capabilities that enhance applications such as security and media analysis. Amazon Textract excels at extracting text and data from scanned documents, enabling automated document processing. Together, these services empower businesses to unlock valuable insights from their visual data efficiently and effectively.

Amazon Rekognition

Amazon Rekognition is a versatile image and video analysis service powered by deep learning algorithms, designed to identify a wide range of objects, people, text, scenes, and activities within visual media. One of its standout features is facial analysis, which includes face detection, comparison, and recognition. This enables developers to create applications capable of recognizing individual faces in real time or from stored media. Additionally, Amazon Rekognition can detect text within images and videos, allowing for comprehensive analysis and extraction of textual information.

The service is user-friendly, providing an easy-to-use API that allows developers to add image and video analysis functionalities to their applications without requiring extensive knowledge of ML. Its scalability ensures that it can handle large volumes of data efficiently, making it suitable for both small-scale projects and enterprise-level solutions. By leveraging

Amazon Rekognition, developers can build sophisticated applications that can analyze visual content to extract valuable insights, automate processes, and improve user experiences.

Use Cases

Amazon Rekognition is leveraged for various critical applications across different industries. It helps detect inappropriate content in images and videos, ensuring safe and compliant media for platforms. This service is also used for verifying identities online, enhancing security and user validation processes for digital services. Media companies can use this service to streamline their analysis by automatically tagging and categorizing content, making it easier to manage and retrieve specific assets. Moreover, Amazon Rekognition can send smart alerts to connected homes, recognizing specific faces or objects and notifying homeowners of unusual activities, thereby enhancing home security and automation systems. These use cases showcase Amazon Rekognition's versatility and its significant role in transforming how visual data is utilized across various sectors.

Amazon Textract

Amazon Textract is a sophisticated AI service designed to extract text, forms, tables, and other data from scanned documents. Unlike traditional optical character recognition (OCR) technologies, Amazon Textract uses ML to understand the layout and structure of documents, capturing semantic relationships between different elements. This advanced capability allows this AI service to accurately interpret complex information, making it particularly useful for processing large volumes of documents quickly and effectively, transforming unstructured data into structured formats that can be analyzed and utilized efficiently.

One of the key features of Amazon Textract is its ability to recognize and extract data from tables and forms within documents, understanding the context and relationships between different pieces of data. This goes beyond merely reading text; Amazon Textract can differentiate between headers, rows, and columns in a table, ensuring that the extracted data maintains its original structure and meaning. This semantic understanding is crucial for applications that require precise data extraction and interpretation, such as financial reporting, legal documentation, and healthcare records, where the context of data is as important as the data itself.

Amazon Textract also integrates seamlessly with other AWS services, enabling users to build comprehensive data processing pipelines. For example, extracted data can be stored in Amazon S3, analyzed with Amazon Athena, or fed into Amazon SageMaker for ML applications. This flexibility allows organizations to leverage Amazon Textract as part of a broader data strategy, enhancing their ability to gain insights and drive decision-making from their document data. By automating the extraction and processing of information and preserving the semantic relationships, Amazon Textract helps reduce manual effort, minimize errors, and increase operational efficiency.

Use Cases

Amazon Textract is widely used across various industries to streamline document processing and data extraction. In the financial sector, it helps automate the extraction of data from invoices, receipts, and tax documents, enabling faster and more accurate financial reporting. In healthcare, Amazon Textract is used to digitize patient records, making it easier to retrieve and analyze medical information. Legal firms can leverage Amazon Textract to process large volumes of contracts and legal documents, ensuring that critical information is accurately captured and accessible. Moreover, in the public sector, Amazon Textract can assist in managing and analyzing government forms and applications, improving the efficiency of administrative processes. These use cases highlight Amazon Textract's adaptability and its significant impact on automating data extraction and processing across diverse industries.

Speech

AWS AI services offer comprehensive speech capabilities designed to transform how applications interact with users through voice. These services provide tools for both generating speech from text and converting spoken language into text, enabling more natural and accessible user experiences. For speech use cases, the main two services are Amazon Polly for converting text to natural-sounding speech and Amazon Transcribe for turning spoken language into accurate text.

Amazon Polly

Amazon Polly is a text-to-speech service that uses advanced deep learning technologies to convert written text into natural-sounding speech. It offers a wide variety of lifelike voices in multiple languages and supports different accents, providing developers with the flexibility to create engaging, localized experiences for their users. Whether it's for interactive voice response (IVR) systems, news reading applications, or audiobooks, Amazon Polly enhances user engagement by making applications more accessible and interactive.

Amazon Polly excels at delivering fast, real-time speech synthesis, ensuring minimal latency for applications that require immediate responses. Amazon Polly also supports Speech Synthesis Markup Language (SSML), allowing developers to control aspects like speech pitch, rate, and pronunciation for a more tailored auditory experience. With Amazon Polly, you can easily and efficiently create dynamic and natural-sounding voice interactions.

Use Cases

Amazon Polly is a versatile text-to-speech service with a wide array of use cases. It's ideal for creating engaging voice interactions in IVR systems, ensuring customers receive clear and natural-sounding responses. Polly is also perfect for generating audiobooks, offering readers an immersive experience with lifelike narration. Additionally, it enhances accessibility by converting text-based content into speech for visually impaired users, making information more accessible. In e-learning platforms, Polly can bring educational content to life with dynamic narration, improving comprehension and retention. Overall, Amazon Polly is a powerful tool for any application that benefits from high-quality, natural-sounding speech.

Amazon Transcribe

Amazon Transcribe is a powerful automatic speech recognition (ASR) service that converts spoken language into written text. It's designed to provide high-accuracy transcriptions for a variety of audio and video formats, making it an essential tool for generating searchable text from recorded speech. Whether used for creating subtitles for video content, generating transcripts for podcasts and interviews, or enabling real-time captioning for live events, Amazon Transcribe enhances accessibility and searchability. It also supports multiple languages and dialects, ensuring broad applicability across different regions and contexts. With features like speaker identification, punctuation restoration, and custom vocabularies, Amazon Transcribe helps users obtain accurate and comprehensive transcripts for diverse applications.

Use Cases

Amazon Transcribe caters to a wide range of applications. It's perfect for creating accurate subtitles and captions for video content, making media more accessible and engaging. Podcasters and interviewers can use it to generate transcripts, enabling easy content archiving and searchability. In live settings, Transcribe can provide real-time captioning, enhancing accessibility for audiences with hearing impairments. It's also valuable for customer service call centers, where it can transcribe conversations to improve analysis and compliance. By converting audio to text efficiently, Amazon Transcribe enhances the usability and accessibility of spoken content across diverse industries.

Language

AWS language AI services are designed to enhance and simplify a wide range of NLP tasks, providing tools for understanding, generating, and translating human language. These services enable developers to build applications that can interact with users in a more intuitive and natural way, automate text analysis, and support multilingual communication. Notably, Amazon Translate offers real-time language translation, and Amazon Comprehend provides insights through text analysis, including sentiment detection and entity recognition.

Amazon Translate

Amazon Translate is a neural machine translation service that provides fast, high-quality, and affordable language translation. It supports dozens of languages, enabling businesses and developers to translate large volumes of text efficiently and integrate translation capabilities directly into their applications. Amazon Translate can handle real-time translation for applications such as websites and mobile apps, making it easier for global users to interact with content in their native languages. The service also supports batch translation, which is useful for translating large documents or datasets quickly.

Amazon Translate is designed to preserve the context and meaning of the original text, ensuring that translations are not only semantically accurate but also natural-sounding. It uses advanced deep learning models trained on a vast array of multilingual data, allowing it

Chapter 4 ▪ Model Selection

to continuously improve over time. Amazon Translate is highly scalable and cost-effective, making it accessible for businesses of all sizes. It also integrates seamlessly with other AWS services, allowing users to build comprehensive solutions that leverage translation capabilities alongside other AI and cloud tools.

Use Cases

Amazon Translate serves a broad range of use cases, making it an invaluable tool for businesses and developers needing multilingual communication. It's widely used for translating website content, enabling global users to access and interact with the information in their native languages. E-commerce platforms leverage Amazon Translate to provide product descriptions in multiple languages, enhancing user experiences and expanding market reach. In customer support, it helps translate chat and email communications, ensuring seamless service across different regions. Amazon Translate also plays a crucial role in translating documents, reports, and user manuals, facilitating global collaboration and information sharing. Additionally, it supports real-time translation for applications like social media and instant messaging, fostering instant and effective communication worldwide.

Amazon Comprehend

Amazon Comprehend is an NLP service that uses ML to uncover insights and relationships within text. It allows businesses to understand the sentiment behind customer reviews, extract key phrases, identify named entities, and even detect the language of the input text. Amazon Comprehend can analyze large volumes of text quickly and accurately, making it an excellent choice for processing customer feedback, social media posts, and other unstructured data. The service can also organize documents by identifying key topics and categorizing content, helping organizations better manage and understand their data.

Amazon Comprehend is a highly configurable service that allows for the creation of custom models tailored to specific business needs. These custom models enable more precise entity recognition and classification based on the unique terminology and context of different industries. Just like other AWS AI services, Amazon Comprehend integrates seamlessly with the AWS ecosystem, enabling users to build comprehensive text analysis pipelines and automate workflows. Whether it's enhancing customer service by analyzing support tickets or improving content recommendation systems, Amazon Comprehend provides powerful tools for turning text into actionable insights.

For organizations requiring more advanced capabilities, Amazon SageMaker offers sophisticated topic modeling algorithms out of the box. These algorithms will be discussed in detail later in the chapter.

Use Cases

Amazon Comprehend can be applied to a wide range of use cases across different industries. Businesses often use it for sentiment analysis, helping them understand customer feedback and social media sentiment to improve products and services. In the healthcare industry,

Amazon Comprehend can analyze medical records to extract valuable insights and identify key entities such as medications, conditions, and treatments. It's also used in content management systems to automatically tag and organize large volumes of documents, making them easier to search and manage. In customer service, Amazon Comprehend can analyze support tickets to identify common issues and improve response times. Moreover, it aids in fraud detection by analyzing communication patterns and identifying suspicious activities. Overall, Amazon Comprehend enables organizations to unlock valuable insights from text data, enhancing decision-making and operational efficiency.

Chatbot

AWS offers powerful chatbot capabilities through services that enable businesses to create engaging, interactive, and intelligent conversational interfaces. These chatbots can be used in various applications, from customer support to interactive applications and internal help desks. AWS provides tools like Amazon Lex, which uses advanced NLP to understand user input and manage complex conversations.

Amazon Lex

Amazon Lex is a powerful service designed to build conversational interfaces into any application using voice and text. Leveraging the same deep learning technologies that power Amazon Alexa, Amazon Lex provides advanced natural language understanding capabilities. This allows developers to create sophisticated, interactive chatbots that can understand and respond to user inputs with a high degree of accuracy. By integrating with other AWS services such as AWS Lambda, Amazon Lex enables seamless execution of backend logic, making it possible to build complex, end-to-end conversational applications.

Amazon Lex has the ability to handle multiturn conversations, enabling chatbots to maintain context and manage complex dialogues. This is particularly useful for customer service applications, where a bot may need to gather information across several interactions to resolve an issue. Amazon Lex also supports built-in integrations with Amazon Connect— AWS's AI-powered contact center service—allowing businesses to create automated call center agents that can assist customers 24/7, reducing the load on human agents and improving response times. Additionally, Amazon Lex can be used to build chatbots for a variety of platforms, including web applications, mobile apps, and social media channels, providing consistent and scalable user experiences across different touchpoints.

From an engineering standpoint, Amazon Lex offers a user-friendly console and development environment, where developers can define the bot's interaction model, including intents, slots, and responses, without needing extensive experience in ML or NLP. Moreover, Amazon Lex provides built-in tools for testing and monitoring chatbot performance, helping developers iterate and improve their bots over time. With its robust capabilities and seamless integration with other AWS services, Amazon Lex is a comprehensive solution for building intelligent, conversational interfaces that enhance user engagement and streamline business processes.

114   Chapter 4 ▪ Model Selection

Use Cases

Amazon Lex is mainly used to improve customer service experiences. Customers leverage Amazon Lex by creating sophisticated chatbots that handle inquiries, provide information, and resolve issues, minimizing the need for human agents and reducing response times. In e-commerce, Lex-powered bots can assist customers with product searches, order tracking, and personalized recommendations, enhancing the shopping experience. Healthcare organizations use Amazon Lex to automate appointment scheduling, provide medical information, and conduct patient prescreening. Finally, Amazon Lex is employed in internal business operations for creating virtual assistants that help employees with tasks such as IT support, HR queries, and workflow automation. Overall, Amazon Lex empowers businesses to build intelligent, conversational interfaces that enhance user engagement and streamline administrative processes.

Recommendation

Recommendation capabilities are provided by AWS through its suite of AI services. These capabilities are aimed at enhancing user experiences by delivering personalized content.

At the core of these capabilities is Amazon Personalize, which allows developers to integrate real-time, tailored recommendations into their applications easily. Amazon Personalize utilizes sophisticated ML algorithms to analyze user data, such as browsing history, purchase behavior, and preferences, to generate highly relevant recommendations.

Amazon Personalize

Amazon Personalize operates by leveraging advanced ML algorithms to analyze user data and generate highly personalized recommendations. The process begins with gathering item interaction data from users, such as clicks, views, and purchases, as well as additional contextual information like item metadata (e.g., genre, price) and user demographics (e.g., age, gender). This data is then fed into the ML models, which are trained to identify patterns and relationships between users and items. The models can be continually updated with real-time interaction data, ensuring that recommendations remain accurate and relevant as user preferences evolve.

A key, unique feature of Amazon Personalize is its use of generative AI techniques to enhance the recommendation process. Generative AI models can simulate new data points based on existing ones, effectively filling gaps in the dataset and improving the accuracy of predictions. This is particularly useful when dealing with sparse data or new users and items that have limited interaction history. By generating synthetic data points, the system can better understand user preferences and provide more precise recommendations, even in scenarios where traditional models might struggle. Moreover, Amazon Personalize allows for customization based on your unique data. You can choose the best ML algorithms suited to your specific use case and data characteristics and provide contextual metadata about users and items for more informed recommendations.

Furthermore, Amazon Personalize employs sophisticated algorithms to handle various recommendation tasks, such as *collaborative filtering*, content-based filtering, and hybrid approaches. Collaborative filtering relies on the collective behavior of users to identify similar users and recommend items they liked. Content-based filtering focuses on the attributes of items to suggest similar products to those a user has shown interest in. Hybrid models combine these approaches to leverage the strengths of both, providing robust and well-rounded recommendations. By using these advanced AI and generative techniques, Amazon Personalize delivers highly personalized and effective recommendations that enhance user engagement and satisfaction. Its flexibility and ease of integration ensure that businesses can tailor the service to their specific needs, delivering optimal results.

Use Cases

Amazon Personalize is widely used across various industries to enhance user experiences through personalized recommendations. In e-commerce, it suggests products based on users' browsing history and purchase behavior, increasing conversion rates and customer satisfaction. Streaming services and news platforms leverage it to recommend movies, TV shows, and articles tailored to individual interests, keeping users engaged. Businesses also use it for targeted marketing campaigns, personalizing email content to promote relevant products and offers, thereby improving engagement. Additionally, customer support teams utilize Amazon Personalize to recommend relevant support articles, helping users resolve issues more efficiently.

By delivering highly relevant and timely recommendations, Amazon Personalize empowers businesses to enhance user engagement and drive better outcomes across various sectors.

Generative AI

Generative AI represents a cutting-edge advancement in artificial intelligence, enabling systems to *generate* (here is where "generative" AI comes from) new content, such as text, images, or even entire multimedia experiences, from learned data patterns. With Amazon Bedrock, AWS brings generative AI capabilities to developers, offering a seamless and scalable platform for building, fine-tuning, and deploying generative AI models. Amazon Bedrock provides access to a variety of powerful foundation models (FMs) from leading AI innovators, along with the tools needed to customize and integrate these models into applications effortlessly. By using Amazon Bedrock, businesses can leverage the potential of generative AI to innovate and enhance their digital solutions, driving creativity and efficiency across various domains.

Amazon Bedrock

Amazon Bedrock is a fully managed service that simplifies the process of building and scaling generative AI applications using FMs. It provides access to a wide range of high-performing FMs from leading AI companies like AI21 Labs, Anthropic, Cohere, Meta, Mistral AI, and Stability AI, as well as Amazon's own models, including the newly released Nova FMs.

General-purpose FMs are versatile models that can handle a variety of tasks such as text generation, translation, summarization, and more. These models are suitable for a broad range of applications across different industries. With a single API, developers can experiment with different models, customize them with their own data using techniques like fine-tuning and retrieval augmented generation (RAG), and deploy them securely within their applications. Amazon Bedrock's serverless architecture eliminates the need to manage infrastructure, allowing developers to focus on innovation and delivering value to their users. The Converse API, part of Amazon Bedrock, provides a consistent and simplified interface for developers to interact with these FMs, making it easy to integrate conversational AI capabilities into applications for enhanced user experiences and natural interactions.

> Not all FMs are supported by the Converse API. For a detailed list of supported models and features, visit https://docs.aws.amazon.com/bedrock/latest/userguide/conversation-inference-supported-models-features.html.

One of the standout features of Amazon Bedrock is its marketplace, which offers a broad selection of specialized FMs for various use cases. Specialized FMs are tailored to specific tasks or domains, providing more accurate and efficient performance for particular applications. These models can be highly beneficial for industries such as healthcare, finance, and entertainment, where specialized knowledge and precision are critical. The marketplace enables developers to discover, test, and integrate these specialized models seamlessly into their ML workflows. Whether it's text generation, image creation, or complex multimodal tasks, Amazon Bedrock provides the tools and flexibility needed to build powerful generative AI applications. By leveraging Amazon Bedrock, businesses can stay at the forefront of AI innovation, ensuring that their applications are both cutting-edge and secure. The Converse API further enhances this capability by offering a straightforward way to interact with these models, making the integration process seamless and efficient.

When selecting a foundational model, it's essential to consider the specific capabilities you need for your application. If your task primarily involves text generation, analysis, or translation, models like Amazon Titan Text G1 – Premier, Amazon Titan Text G1 – Express, and Amazon Titan Text G1 – Lite are ideal. These models are integrated with Amazon Bedrock and support a wide range of text-related tasks, including open-ended question answering, code generation, summarization, and conversational chat. For creative applications, models like Amazon Nova Canvas excel in generating detailed images from text descriptions, making them perfect for art and design tasks. For multimodal capabilities, models like Amazon Nova Lite and Amazon Nova Pro can handle both text and image inputs, providing versatile solutions. For simple use cases and low budgets, Amazon Nova Micro is a text-only model suitable for scenarios that require low-latency text processing without the need for multimodal input. Evaluating the capabilities of these models in the context of your application's specific needs will help you choose the most effective foundational model.

Another criterion to consider when selecting a model is its availability in the region where your generative AI application will operate. This ensures optimal performance, compliance with local regulations, and reduces latency, providing a seamless user experience.

> FMs are available on a per-region basis. To find out which models are supported in your region, visit https://docs.aws.amazon.com/bedrock/latest/userguide/models-regions.html.

For the exam, be aware that some models may not be available in your region, but they can still be used with *cross-region inference* if this feature is supported on your region. Cross-region inference enables you to seamlessly manage unplanned traffic bursts by utilizing compute across different AWS regions. With cross-region inference, you can distribute traffic across multiple AWS regions, enabling higher throughput and enhanced resilience during periods of peak demands. To use cross-region inference, you need to create a cross-region inference profile. To learn more, visit https://docs.aws.amazon.com/bedrock/latest/userguide/inference-profiles-support.html.

Last, just like for any well-architected application (generative AI applications are no different in this regard), you need to consider pricing. Amazon Bedrock pricing is based on two main models:

- On-Demand and Batch
- Provisioned Throughput

With the On-Demand and Batch mode, you pay for the number of input and output tokens processed, where a *token* is a sequence of characters that the model interprets as a single unit of meaning. For Provisioned Throughput, you commit to a specific level of throughput for a period of time, which can be more cost-effective for applications with consistent usage. For more information, visit https://aws.amazon.com/bedrock/pricing.

The following section will provide a simple example of how to programmatically use generative AI.

Using Nova Canvas to Generate an Image

The Nova FMs were recently announced at AWS re:Invent 2024. In this use case, we are going to use Nova Canvas—a state-of-the-art image generation model—to generate an image from a textual prompt. This example will show you how to implement this use case programmatically.

As a design consideration, my AWS account's default region is us-east-2 (Ohio). Because Nova Canvas is not natively supported in my default region (and I don't want to implement cross-region inference), I am going to create my Python client in us-east-1 (N. Virginia)—where the model is currently natively supported. From the AWS Console, we open Amazon

118 Chapter 4 ▪ Model Selection

FIGURE 4.2   Requesting access to Nova Canvas.

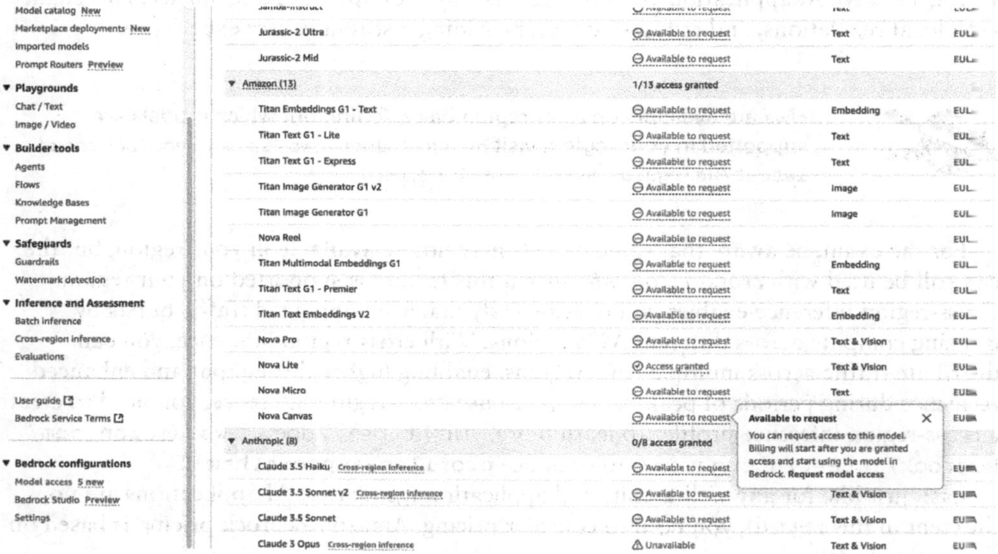

Bedrock and select us-east-1 (N. Virginia) as our working region. We then request access to the model, as shown in Figure 4.2.

The following Python program uses the `boto3` module to create an Amazon Bedrock client in us-east-1 and subsequently interact with the Nova Canvas FM to request the generation of an image. We run this program using the Code Editor application in Amazon SageMaker Studio in us-east-1.

> **NOTE** Amazon SageMaker Studio is a web-based integrated development environment (IDE) for your end-to-end ML pipelines. It comes out of the box with most of the ML libraries you need, and it provides a seamless Visual Studio (VS) Code developer experience.

To get started with Amazon SageMaker Studio, you need to create a domain in the region where your program will run (in our case, in us-east-1). Once your domain is available, you can open Amazon SageMaker Studio, as shown in Figure 4.3. Figure 4.4 illustrates the Studio home page, where you can create a space. A space is a managed instance that Amazon SageMaker Studio uses to launch the Code Editor application. In Figure 4.4, I started a space `dario-ai-space` that uses an instance type `ml.t3.medium` with 5 GB of storage. To develop your ML applications, you need to create and start your space, as displayed in Figure 4.5. Your space has an Elastic File System (EFS) attached to it, where your

Understanding AWS AI Services 119

FIGURE 4.3 Amazon SageMaker Studio.

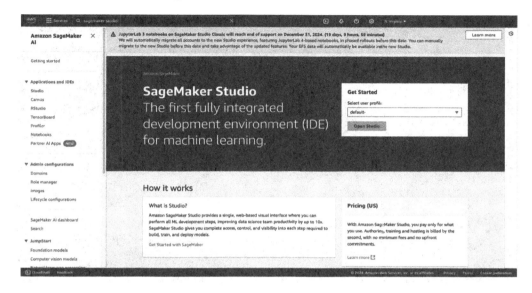

FIGURE 4.4 Amazon SageMaker Studio Space.

Chapter 4 ▪ Model Selection

FIGURE 4.5 Amazon SageMaker Studio Code Editor.

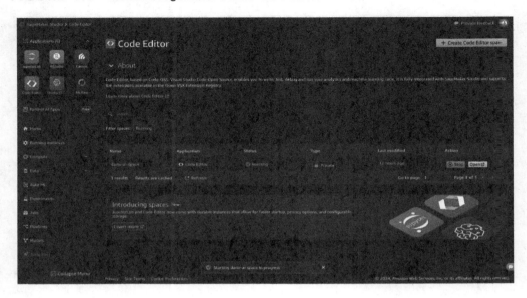

applications' code and other artifacts are saved. To avoid incurring in unwanted cost, make sure you stop your space when you are done coding.

```
import base64
import io
import json
import logging
import os
import boto3
from PIL import Image
from botocore.config import Config
from botocore.exceptions import ClientError

class ImageError(Exception):
    "Custom exception for errors returned by Amazon Nova Canvas"
    def __init__(self, message):
        self.message = message

logger = logging.getLogger(__name__)
logging.basicConfig(level=logging.INFO)

def generate_image(model_id, body):
    """
    Generate an image using Amazon Nova Canvas model on demand.
```

Understanding AWS AI Services   121

```python
    Args:
        model_id (str): The model ID to use.
        body (str) : The request body to use.
    Returns:
        image_bytes (bytes): The image generated by the model.
    """
    logger.info(f"Generating image with Amazon Nova Canvas model {model_id}")

    bedrock = boto3.client(
        service_name='bedrock-runtime',
        config=Config(read_timeout=300)
    )

    accept = "application/json"
    content_type = "application/json"

    response = bedrock.invoke_model(
        body=body, modelId=model_id, accept=accept, contentType=content_type
    )
    response_body = json.loads(response.get("body").read())

    base64_image = response_body.get("images")[0]
    base64_bytes = base64_image.encode('ascii')
    image_bytes = base64.b64decode(base64_bytes)

    finish_reason = response_body.get("error")

    if finish_reason is not None:
        raise ImageError(f"Image generation error. Error is {finish_reason}")

    logger.info(f"Successfully generated image with Amazon Nova Canvas model
{model_id}")

    return image_bytes

def main():
    """
    Entrypoint for Amazon Nova Canvas example.
    """
    logging.basicConfig(level=logging.INFO,
                        format="%(levelname)s: %(message)s")

    model_id = 'amazon.nova-canvas-v1:0'
    prompt = "Generate an image of a white sand beach at sunset."

    body = json.dumps({
        "taskType": "TEXT_IMAGE",
        "textToImageParams": {
            "text": prompt
        },
```

Chapter 4 ▪ Model Selection

```python
        "imageGenerationConfig": {
            "numberOfImages": 1,
            "height": 1024,
            "width": 1024,
            "cfgScale": 8.0,
            "seed": 0
        }
    })

    try:
        image_bytes = generate_image(model_id=model_id, body=body)
        image = Image.open(io.BytesIO(image_bytes))

        # Create directory if it doesn't exist
        efs_directory = '/home/sagemaker-user/ch04/images'
        if not os.path.exists(efs_directory):
            os.makedirs(efs_directory)

        # Save the image to the EFS attached file system
        output_image_path = os.path.join(efs_directory, "white_sand_beach_
sunset.png")
        image.save(output_image_path)
        print(f"Image saved to {output_image_path}")

    except ClientError as err:
        message = err.response["Error"]["Message"]
        logger.error(f"A client error occurred: {message}")
        print(f"A client error occurred: {message}")
    except ImageError as err:
        logger.error(err.message)
        print(err.message)
    else:
        print(f"Finished generating image with Amazon Nova Canvas model
{model_id}.")

if __name__ == "__main__":
    main()
```

I saved this program in the Code Editor as test_nova_canvas.py.

This program utilizes the boto3 module to build a client object named bedrock that interacts with Amazon Bedrock in us-east-1, where Nova Canvas is natively supported. As shown in the generate_image method, this client uses the invoke_model method to send a prompt (encapsulated as a text property of the body parameter) to create an image of a white sand beach at sunset.

When run in Amazon SageMaker Studio, this code generates the requested image, as shown in Figures 4.6 and 4.7.

Once the image is generated, the program decodes the base64 image data and saves it as white_sand_beach_sunset.png in the /home/sagemaker-user/ch04/images folder of the EFS mounted on your Amazon SageMaker Studio instance.

FIGURE 4.6 Program output.

 Amazon SageMaker Studio instances come with EFS mounted by default, so any files saved in local directories within the instance will be stored on the attached EFS. This ensures that our generated image will be readily available and persistent across different sessions within Amazon SageMaker Studio.

The program also includes comprehensive error handling to ensure a smooth process, logging meaningful messages along the way. This setup ensures that the image is both generated and stored efficiently, ready for further use or display.

 During the writing of this book, Amazon SageMaker was renamed Amazon SageMaker AI. For the exam, be aware of this name change. Whenever the book mentions Amazon SageMaker (the service), it means Amazon SageMaker AI (https://aws.amazon.com/blogs/aws/introducing-the-next-generation-of-amazon-sagemaker-the-center-for-all-your-data-analytics-and-ai).

FIGURE 4.7 An image generated by Nova Canvas.

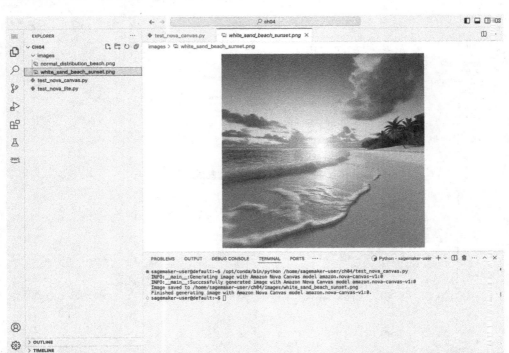

Use Cases

Amazon Bedrock is an excellent choice for developers looking to build generative AI applications with robust foundational models. It's ideal for tasks such as text generation, image creation, and multimodal processing, thanks to its integration with high-performing models like Amazon Titan and Amazon Nova. If you need scalable, reliable, and easy-to-use AI capabilities with managed infrastructure, Amazon Bedrock provides a seamless environment for both experimentation and deployment. Additionally, Amazon Bedrock's pay-as-you-go pricing makes it accessible for projects of varying sizes, from small startups to large enterprises.

Conversely, Amazon Bedrock might not be the best fit if your application requires highly specialized or domain-specific models that are not available within the platform or marketplace. If you need models trained on proprietary data, have strict data residency, or have latency requirements that demand highly specialized solutions, other platforms or custom-built models might be more appropriate. Additionally, if cost is a primary concern and your project has minimal AI needs, simpler, more cost-effective solutions might suffice without the advanced capabilities of Amazon Bedrock.

Developing Models with Amazon SageMaker Built-in Algorithms

Although AWS AI services like Amazon Rekognition, Comprehend, and Personalize offer powerful, prebuilt solutions for common tasks such as image analysis, text processing, and recommendation systems, they may not provide the flexibility needed for specialized use cases. These managed services are designed to be easy to use and require minimal ML expertise, making them suitable for quick deployments and standard applications. However, when your project demands custom feature engineering, advanced model architectures, or optimization for specific performance metrics, Amazon SageMaker's built-in algorithms offer the tools and flexibility needed to achieve these goals.

Choosing to build models with Amazon SageMaker's built-in algorithms offers several advantages, particularly when you require greater control and customization over your ML projects. Amazon SageMaker's built-in algorithms are highly optimized for speed, scale, and accuracy, allowing you to efficiently train, refine, and deploy models tailored to your specific business needs. This approach is ideal when you need to fine-tune hyperparameters, incorporate domain-specific knowledge, or handle unique data preprocessing requirements. By leveraging Amazon SageMaker's built-in algorithms, you can achieve a higher degree of precision and performance, especially in complex or bespoke applications where off-the-shelf solutions may fall short.

Additionally, Amazon SageMaker provides seamless integration with the broader AWS ecosystem, ensuring a cohesive workflow from data preparation to model deployment. You can easily import data from Amazon S3, Amazon EFS, or Amazon FSx for Lustre; utilize AWS Lambda functions for preprocessing; and deploy models using Amazon SageMaker endpoints or AWS Lambda for real-time inference. This tight integration simplifies the ML lifecycle, enhances operational efficiency, and reduces the time and effort required to manage different components of the ML pipeline. It also allows you to take advantage of Amazon SageMaker's distributed training capabilities, which can significantly accelerate model training on large datasets.

In this section, we will explore the built-in algorithms offered by Amazon SageMaker, their appropriate use cases, and how to effectively utilize them to build robust ML models. Figure 4.8 can help you map built-in algorithms to specific ML problem types, input formats, and use cases.

Supervised ML Algorithms

As you learned in Chapter 1, supervised ML is a type of algorithm that learns from labeled training data to make predictions or decisions. In supervised learning, each training example includes input data in the form of a set of features, along with the corresponding output or label. The algorithm uses these labeled examples to learn the mapping between inputs and outputs, and it can then apply this learned mapping to new, unseen data to predict outcomes.

126 Chapter 4 ▪ Model Selection

FIGURE 4.8 Amazon SageMaker built-in algorithms.

Use case	Learning type	Problem type (non exhaustive)	Input format	Built-in algorithms
Pre-trained models and pre-built solution templates provided by Amazon SageMaker JumpStart. Example: Question answering: chatbot that outputs an answer for a given question.	Pre-built	• Image, Tabular, Text Classification • Tabular Regression • Object Detection • Image, Text Embedding	Image, Text, Tabular	Popular algorithms, including Mobilenet, YOLO, Faster-R-CNN, BERT, lightGBM, and CatBoost
Predict if an item belongs to a category. Example: an email spam filter.	Supervised learning	Binary/multi-class classification	Tabular	AutoGluon-Tabular, CatBoost, Factorization Machines, Nearest Neighbors (k-NN), LightGBM, Linear Learner, TabTransformer, XGBoost with Amazon SageMaker
Predict a numeric/continuous value. Example: estimate the value of a house		Regression	Tabular	
Based on historical data for a behavior, predict future behavior. Example: predict sales on a new product based on previous sales data.		Time-series forecasting	Tabular	Amazon SageMaker DeepAR forecasting algorithm
Convert high-dimensional objects into low-dimensional space. Example: identify duplicate support tickets.		Embeddings	Tabular	Object2Vec
Drop columns from a dataset that have a weak relation with target variable. Example: the color of a car when predicting its mileage.	Unsupervised learning	Feature engineering: dimensionality reduction	Tabular	Principal Component Analysis (PCA)
Detect abnormal behavior in application. Example: detect when an IoT sensor is sending abnormal readings.		Anomaly detection	Tabular	Random Cut Forest (RCF)
Protect your application from suspicious users. Example: detect if an IP address consuming a service is from a bad actor.		IP anomaly detection	Tabular	IP Insights
Group similar data points together. Example: find low-spending customers from their transaction histories.		Clustering	Tabular	K-Means
Organize a set of documents into topics (not known in advance). Example: tag a document as a medical category based on matched terms.		Topic modeling	Text	Latent Dirichlet Allocation (LDA), Neural Topic Model (NTM)
Assign pre-defined categories to documents in a corpus. Example: categorize books in a library into academic disciplines.	Textual analysis	Text classification	Text	BlazingText algorithm, Text Classification - TensorFlow
Convert text from one language to other. Example: Italian to English.		Machine translation algorithm	Text	Sequence-to-Sequence Algorithm
Summarize a long text corpus. Example: an abstract for a research paper.		Text summarization	Text	Sequence-to-Sequence Algorithm
Convert audio files to text. Example: transcribe call center conversations for further analysis.		Speech-to-text	Text	Sequence-to-Sequence Algorithm
Label an image based on content. Example: alerts about adult content in an image.	Image processing	Image and multi-label classification	Image	Image Classification - MXNet
Classify something in an image using transfer learning.		Image classification	Image	Image Classification - TensorFlow
Detect people and objects in an image. Example: police review a large photo gallery for a missing person.		Object detection and classification	Image	Object Detection - MXNet, Object Detection - TensorFlow
Tag every pixel of an image individually with a category. Example: self-driving cars prepare to identify objects in their way.		Computer vision	Image	Semantic Segmentation Algorithm

This approach is particularly useful when there is a clear and predefined relationship between the input features and the corresponding label, also known as the *target variable*. Common applications of supervised learning include tasks such as regression, where the goal is to predict a continuous value (e.g., predicting house prices based on features like size and location), and classification, where the goal is to categorize data into discrete classes (e.g., identifying whether an email is spam or not).

Supervised learning should be used when labeled data is available and the objective is to make accurate predictions based on this data. Within supervised learning, there are several pathways depending on the nature of your ML problem.

For regression problems, algorithms like linear regression, decision trees, and XGBoost can be employed to predict continuous values.

In binary classification, algorithms such as logistic regression, support vector machines, and k-nearest neighbors (k-NN) help in distinguishing between two classes.

For multiclass classification, where data needs to be categorized into more than two classes, approaches like decision trees, random forests, and neural networks are commonly used.

Additionally, supervised learning encompasses time-series forecasting algorithms like DeepAR, which predicts future values based on past observations. Moreover, algorithms like Object2Vec are used for creating embeddings that capture semantic information from objects or entities, enhancing the performance of downstream tasks such as recommendation systems or semantic search.

General Regression and Classification Algorithms

This section introduces the most common regression and classification supervised ML algorithms provided by Amazon SageMaker.

Linear Learner

We will start with the Amazon SageMaker Linear Learner algorithm, which provides a solution for both classification and regression problems.

In linear regression use cases, you feed the algorithm labeled samples (x, y). x is a high-dimensional vector of feature values $x_1, x_2, \ldots, x_n$, and y is a real number denoting the label associated to the sample data point.

For binary classification problems, the label must be either 0 or 1.

For multiclass classification problems, the labels must be from 0 to num_classes − 1.

The algorithm learns a linear function or, for classification problems, a linear threshold function and maps a vector x to an approximation of the label y.

The Linear Learner algorithm requires a data matrix, with rows representing the observations (or your data points) and columns representing the dimensions of the features. It also requires an additional column that contains the labels that match the data points. At a minimum, Amazon SageMaker's Linear Learner requires you to specify input and output data locations and objective type (classification or regression) as arguments. The feature dimension is also required. For more information, see https://docs.aws.amazon.com/sagemaker/latest/APIReference/API_CreateTrainingJob.html.

Amazon SageMaker's linear learner algorithm requires input data to be in CSV file or RecordIO-protobuf format.

You can specify additional parameters in the *HyperParameters* string map of the request body. These parameters control the optimization procedure or specifics of the objective function that you train on such as the number of epochs, regularization, and loss type.

Let's deep dive into Linear Regression and Logistic Regression, which are the most common linear modeling use cases, respectively, for regression and classification ML problems. Support vector machines (SVMs) are also included as another selection of a Linear Learner algorithm.

Linear Regression

Linear regression is one of the simplest and most widely used algorithms in supervised ML. The primary goal of linear regression is to model the relationship between a dependent variable (also known as the *target* or *output variable*) and one or more independent variables (known as *features* or *predictors*). It does this by fitting a linear equation to the observed data. The linear equation can be written in the following form:

$$y = \beta_0 + \beta_1 x_1 + \cdots + \beta_n x_n + \epsilon$$

128   Chapter 4 ▪ Model Selection

where y is the actual observed output, β_0 is the intercept, $\beta_1, \beta_2, \ldots, \beta_n$ are the coefficients (or weights) of the features $x_1, x_2, \ldots, x_n$, and ϵ represents the error, also referred to as the *residual* (the difference between the actual and predicted values).

Your goal is to predict the coefficients β_1 the model will learn to minimize the error ϵ across the entire dataset.

When evaluating the model, we look at the residuals to understand how well the model is performing. In linear regression the model aims to find the linear function that minimizes the mean squared error (MSE). The formula for MSE is as follows:

$$\text{MSE} = \frac{1}{n} \sum_{i=1}^{n} \left(y_i - \widehat{y}_i \right)^2$$

where n denotes the number of observations in your dataset, y_i denotes the actual value for the observation i, and $\widehat{y}_i$ denotes the predicted value for the observation i.

Minimizing the MSE helps ensure that the predictions are as close as possible to the actual values, effectively reducing the overall error.

You can use the `LinearRegression` class from the `sklearn.linear_model` module to build a linear regression model from a dataset, as shown in the following snippet:

```python
import numpy as np
import matplotlib.pyplot as plt
from sklearn.linear_model import LinearRegression

# Generate some sample data
np.random.seed(0)
X = 2 * np.random.rand(100, 1)
y = 4 + 3 * X + np.random.randn(100, 1)

# Fit a linear regression model
model = LinearRegression()
model.fit(X, y)
y_pred = model.predict(X)

# Plot the data points
plt.scatter(X, y, color='blue', label='Data Points')

# Plot the regression line
plt.plot(X, y_pred, color='red', label='Regression Line')

# Plot the residuals
for i in range(len(X)):
    plt.plot([X[i], X[i]], [y[i], y_pred[i]], color='green', linestyle='--')

plt.xlabel('X')
plt.ylabel('y')
plt.title('Linear Regression with Residuals')
```

```
plt.legend()
plt.show()

# Print Mean Squared Error
mse = np.mean((y - y_pred) ** 2)
print(f"Mean Squared Error: {mse}")
```

Let's see how this program works:

Data generation We generate a matrix X with 100 rows (samples) and 1 column (feature). Each row denotes the value (observation or sample) of a single feature, which is a random number uniformly distributed between 0 and 2. Then we define a linear relationship $y = 4 + 3X + \epsilon$ with some added residual. In the program, y represents the vector of target variables corresponding to each sample.

Model fitting We create and fit a linear regression model using `LinearRegression` from `scikit-learn`.

Visualization As illustrated in Figure 4.9, we scatter the data points, and we plot the regression line. We finally draw dashed lines to show the residuals (the differences between actual and predicted values) for each data point (100 in total).

MSE We calculate and print the MSE to quantify the model's performance.

FIGURE 4.9 Linear regression.

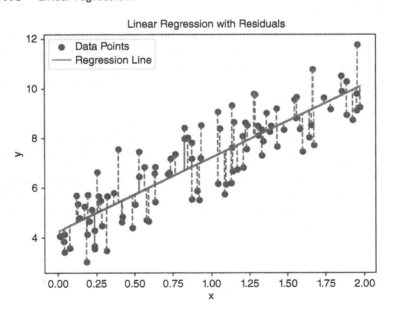

Logistic Regression

Despite the name, logistic regression is a classification algorithm, which allows you to model the probability of a correct category prediction using a linear combination of input features. This algorithm is particularly useful when the dependent variable is binary, meaning it can take on only two possible outcomes: correct category prediction or incorrect category prediction.

Logistic regression works by applying a *logistic function* to the linear combination of the input features, which transforms the output to fall within the range of 0 and 1. This output can then be interpreted as the probability of the event occurring, with a threshold (commonly 0.5) used to classify the event into one of the two possible categories.

The logistic function, also known as the *sigmoid function*, is key to logistic regression and is defined as follows:

$$\sigma(z) = \frac{1}{1 + e^{-z}}$$

In the formula, z is the linear combination of the input features and their corresponding coefficients:

$$z = \beta_0 + \beta_1 x_1 + \cdots + \beta_n x_n + \epsilon$$

As illustrated in Figure 4.10, the logistic function maps any real-valued number into a probability measure—i.e., the unit interval (0, 1)—making it suitable for probability estimation. The S-shaped curve of the sigmoid function ensures that as the input z becomes very large or very small, the output approaches 1 or 0, respectively, but never actually reaches these extreme values. This characteristic is crucial for modeling probabilities, as it ensures that the predicted probabilities are always within a valid range.

The best way to understand how an algorithm works is with a simple example. The following program in Python uses the Iris dataset to predict whether a flower is of the species *Iris-virginica* based on the sepal length and width. The program uses a logistic regression algorithm and plots the decision boundary, as well as the probability estimates provided by the sigmoid function.

> **NOTE** The Iris dataset is a popular dataset containing measurements of different features of Iris flowers (sepal length, sepal width, petal length, petal width) from three species (*Iris-setosa, Iris-versicolor, Iris-virginica*). This dataset is available in the `load_iris` class from the `sklearn.datasets` module. For more information, visit https://scikit-learn.org/1.5/auto_examples/datasets/plot_iris_dataset.html.

```
import numpy as np
import matplotlib.pyplot as plt
from sklearn import datasets
from sklearn.linear_model import LogisticRegression
from sklearn.model_selection import train_test_split
```

FIGURE 4.10 Logistic function.

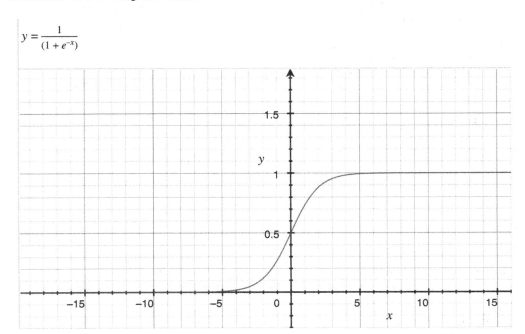

$y = \dfrac{1}{(1+e^{-x})}$

```
# Load the Iris dataset
iris = datasets.load_iris()
X = iris.data[:, :2]  # Using only sepal length and sepal width
y = (iris.target == 2).astype(int)   # Only interested in whether it is
Iris-Virginica or not

# Split the data into training and test sets
X_train, X_test, y_train, y_test = train_test_split(X, y, test_size=0.2,
random_state=42)

# Train the Logistic Regression model
model = LogisticRegression()
model.fit(X_train, y_train)

# Generate grid of points to plot the sigmoid function
x_min, x_max = X[:, 0].min() - 1, X[:, 0].max() + 1
y_min, y_max = X[:, 1].min() - 1, X[:, 1].max() + 1
xx, yy = np.meshgrid(np.arange(x_min, x_max, 0.01), np.arange(y_min,
y_max, 0.01))

# Calculate the probabilities
Z = model.predict_proba(np.c_[xx.ravel(), yy.ravel()])[:, 1]
Z = Z.reshape(xx.shape)
```

132 Chapter 4 ▪ Model Selection

```
# Plot the decision boundary and sigmoid probabilities
contour = plt.contourf(xx, yy, Z, alpha=0.8, cmap=plt.cm.Greys, levels=np.
linspace(0, 1, 11))

# Update scatter plot with different markers for each class
plt.scatter(X[y == 0, 0], X[y == 0, 1], c='white', edgecolors='k', marker='o',
s=40, label='Not Iris-Virginica')
plt.scatter(X[y == 1, 0], X[y == 1, 1], c='white', edgecolors='k', marker='s',
s=40, label='Iris-Virginica')

plt.colorbar(contour, label='Probability of Iris-Virginica')
plt.xlabel('Sepal length')
plt.ylabel('Sepal width')
plt.title('Logistic Regression Sigmoid Function Visualization')

# Add legend
plt.legend()

plt.show()
```

Let's see first how this program works:

Load and preprocess the data   The Iris dataset is loaded, and only the sepal length and sepal width features are selected. The target variable is converted to a binary format, indicating whether the flower is *Iris-virginica*.

Split the data   The data is split into training and test sets using `train_test_split`. This helps in evaluating the model's performance on unseen data.

Train the logistic regression model   A logistic regression model is instantiated. The model is trained on the training data using the `fit` method.

Generate a grid of points   A grid of points covering the feature space (sepal length and sepal width) is created using `np.meshgrid`. This grid will be used to visualize the decision boundary and probabilities.

Calculate probabilities   The trained model is used to predict the probability of each data point in the grid belonging to the *Iris-virginica* class using the `predict_proba` method. These probabilities are then reshaped to match the grid.

Plot the results   The decision boundary and the probabilities are plotted using `contourf`. The data points are plotted on top of this using `scatter`. A color bar is added to indicate the probability scale, and a legend is included to denote what the circle and square data points represent (Not Iris-Virginica and Iris-Virginica).

This program demonstrates logistic regression's ability to create a linear decision boundary and visualize how the model's probabilities vary across the feature space. Figure 4.11 displays the plot generated by this program.

In Figure 4.11, square data points indicate true *Iris-virginica* data samples, whereas circle data points indicate other Iris species (*Iris-setosa* or *Iris-versicolor*). Notice how probability ranges are separated with each other by lines. This is because the logistic regression

FIGURE 4.11 Probability ranges calculated with logistic regression.

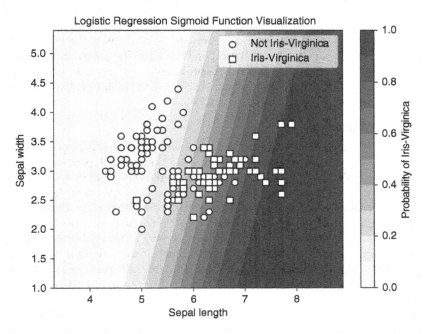

algorithm tries to correlate features (in this case, sepal length and sepal width) using a linear equation. During training, a logistic regression algorithm tries to find a linear decision boundary that separates the two classes. Let's elaborate a little more.

Mathematically, the logistic regression algorithm fits a linear combination of the input features to the log-odds of the binary outcome.

In our example, the binary outcome is the event that a data sample is actually an *Iris-virginica*, and p denotes the probability that such event occurs:

$$z = \beta_0 + \beta_1 x_1 + \cdots + \beta_n x_n + \epsilon = \log\left(\frac{p}{1-p}\right)$$

The last part of the equation is referred to as the *logit function* and returns the log-odds of p, which is then passed through the logistic (sigmoid) function to produce a probability between 0 and 1:

$$\sigma(z) = \frac{1}{1 + e^{-z}}$$

Because the logit z is a linear combination of the features, the decision boundary created by logistic regression will also be linear. This boundary represents the points where the model predicts a 50% probability (i.e., $z = 0$). Data points on one side of the line will have probabilities greater than 50%, and data points on the other side will have probabilities less than 50%.

In Figure 4.11, the contour lines you see represent the probability thresholds generated by the logistic regression model. Each line corresponds to a specific probability value. Because the underlying equation used to calculate these probabilities is linear, the contour lines are parallel and evenly spaced. These lines indicate regions with similar probabilities and help visualize how the model separates different classes.

Support Vector Machines

SVMs are versatile supervised learning algorithms that can be used for both classification and regression tasks, offering powerful solutions for a range of ML problems.

In classification, SVMs work by finding the optimal *hyperplane* that separates the classes in the feature space with the maximum margin. This margin is the distance between the hyperplane and the nearest data points from either class, known as *support vectors*. By maximizing this margin, SVMs aim to achieve better generalization on unseen data. SVMs can handle both linear and nonlinear classification problems by using *kernel tricks* to transform the feature space into higher dimensions, making it possible to draw a linear boundary in this transformed space. Commonly used kernels include linear, polynomial, and radial basis function (RBF) kernels, each suited to different types of data distributions.

For regression tasks, SVMs are adapted into support vector regression (SVR). The primary goal of SVR is to find a function that deviates from the actual target values by a value no greater than a specified margin and at the same time, is as flat as possible. In other words, SVR tries to fit the best possible line within a margin of tolerance (e) for the target values. This method uses a similar concept to support vectors in SVM classification, identifying key data points that define the optimal regression line or curve while ignoring any points that fall within the margin. The result is a robust and flexible model that can handle outliers and noise effectively. Like SVM for classification, SVR also benefits from kernel functions to capture complex relationships between features and the target variable, making it a powerful tool for regression analysis.

Use Cases

Linear regression is best used when there is a clear, linear relationship between the dependent variable and one or more independent variables. It's ideal for simple to moderately complex problems where the goal is to predict a continuous outcome, such as predicting house prices based on square footage and number of bedrooms. Linear regression is easy to implement and interpret, making it suitable for scenarios where model transparency is important. However, it may not be the best choice for more complex relationships that involve nonlinearity or interactions between variables. In such cases, using linear regression can lead to poor model performance and inaccurate predictions. Additionally, linear regression is sensitive to outliers and multicollinearity, which can distort the results. Therefore, it's less appropriate for datasets with significant outliers, high-dimensional data, or where the assumption of a linear relationship does not hold. For these more complex scenarios, other algorithms like polynomial regression, decision trees, or gradient boosting might be more effective.

Logistic regression is a go-to method for binary classification problems, where the outcome variable is categorical with two possible outcomes, such as spam detection, disease diagnosis (positive/negative), or predicting customer churn (yes/no). It's suitable when the relationship between the independent variables and the log-odds of the dependent variable is linear. Logistic regression is easy to implement and interpret, providing not only classification but also the probability of class membership. However, it is less effective for complex datasets with nonlinear relationships or interactions between variables. In such cases, its performance might lag behind more advanced techniques like decision trees, SVMs, or neural networks, which can model more intricate patterns. Additionally, logistic regression assumes the absence of multicollinearity among independent variables and requires a sufficiently large dataset to produce reliable results, making it less appropriate for small, highly correlated, or very high-dimensional data.

Multicollinearity refers to a situation in statistical modeling, specifically in multiple regression analysis, where two or more predictor variables are highly correlated. This high correlation means that one predictor variable can be nearly linearly predicted from the others. This creates redundancy and can cause issues in estimating the coefficients of the regression model reliably. One way to address multicollinearity is with regularization techniques, which add a penalty to the linear regression model for having learned large coefficients that do not generalize well to unseen data. Regularization will be covered in Chapter 5.

SVMs are powerful supervised learning models used primarily for classification tasks, although they can also be applied to regression problems. They are particularly effective when dealing with high-dimensional datasets and cases where the classes are well-separated by a clear margin. SVMs are advantageous when the number of features exceeds the number of samples, as they are less prone to overfitting in such scenarios.

In ML, overfitting occurs when a model learns the training data too well, capturing noise and outliers in addition to the underlying patterns. This results in a model that performs exceptionally well on the training data but poorly on unseen data, as it fails to generalize to new examples. Overfitting can be mitigated through techniques such as cross-validation, pruning in decision trees, using regularization methods, or simplifying the model to ensure it captures only the relevant patterns without the noise. We will cover overfitting and the techniques to address it in Chapter 5.

136   Chapter 4 ▪ Model Selection

However, SVMs are not ideal for large datasets due to their computational intensity, which can lead to longer training times and higher memory usage. Additionally, SVMs may struggle with noisy datasets and overlapping classes, where they might not perform as well compared to more flexible algorithms like random forests or gradient boosting. They also require careful tuning of hyperparameters such as the kernel type and regularization parameters to achieve optimal performance. In summary, SVMs are best used for small to medium-sized (up to approximately 10,000 samples), high-dimensional datasets with clear class separations, and less suited for large, noisy datasets or problems requiring quick training and predictions.

K-Nearest Neighbors

The k-NN algorithm is a simple yet effective supervised ML method used for classification and regression problems. The core idea behind k-NN is that similar data points are likely to be close to each other in the feature space. When making a prediction, k-NN identifies the k-nearest neighbors of a given data point and uses their labels to determine the label of the new point. For classification, the algorithm assigns the most common label among the k-nearest neighbors, whereas for regression, it averages the labels of the neighbors.

The value of k is set before the learning process begins and represents the number of nearest data points—neighbors—to consider when making a prediction for a new data point. This is a crucial *hyperparameter* in the k-NN algorithm. A small value of k (e.g., $k = 1$) makes the model highly sensitive to noise in the data, as it considers only the closest neighbor. Conversely, a large value of k (e.g., $k = 10$) smooths out predictions by averaging over more neighbors, which can be beneficial for noisy data but may overlook local patterns. Choosing the right value of k involves balancing these factors and is typically done using techniques like cross-validation, which will be discussed in Chapter 5. Essentially, k determines the "neighborhood" around a data point that influences its prediction.

Despite its simplicity, k-NN can be computationally expensive, especially with large datasets, because it requires calculating the distance between the query data point and all other points in the dataset. Various distance metrics, such as Euclidean, Manhattan, and Minkowski distances, can be used to measure distances. The choice of distance metric can significantly affect the performance of the algorithm and should align with the nature of the data and the problem at hand.

The following example visually demonstrates how k-NN works for a classification problem by using a simplified, two-dimensional version of the Iris dataset:

```
import numpy as np
import matplotlib.pyplot as plt
from sklearn.datasets import load_iris
from sklearn.model_selection import train_test_split
from sklearn.neighbors import KNeighborsClassifier
from matplotlib.colors import ListedColormap
```

```python
# Load the Iris dataset
iris = load_iris()
X = iris.data[:, :2]  # Use only the first two features for visualization
y = iris.target

# Split the data into training and testing sets
X_train, X_test, y_train, y_test = train_test_split(X, y, test_size=0.2,
random_state=42)

# Create and train the k-NN classifier
k = 3
knn = KNeighborsClassifier(n_neighbors=k)
knn.fit(X_train, y_train)

# Plot the decision boundary
x_min, x_max = X[:, 0].min() - 1, X[:, 0].max() + 1
y_min, y_max = X[:, 1].min() - 1, X[:, 1].max() + 1
xx, yy = np.meshgrid(np.arange(x_min, x_max, 0.1), np.arange(y_min,
y_max, 0.1))
Z = knn.predict(np.c_[xx.ravel(), yy.ravel()])
Z = Z.reshape(xx.shape)

plt.figure(figsize=(8, 6))
plt.contourf(xx, yy, Z, alpha=0.3, cmap=ListedColormap(('gray', 'lightgray',
'darkgray')))

# Colors and markers for the classes
training_markers = ['o', 's', '^']
test_markers = ['o', 's', '^']
colors = ['black', 'black', 'black']
labels = ['Iris-setosa', 'Iris-versicolor', 'Iris-virginica']

# Plot training data points
for i, (color, marker) in enumerate(zip(colors, training_markers)):
    mask = y_train == i
    plt.scatter(X_train[mask, 0], X_train[mask, 1], c=color, label=f'Training
{labels[i]}', marker=marker, edgecolor='k')

# Plot testing data points
for i, marker in enumerate(test_markers):
    mask = y_test == i
    plt.scatter(X_test[mask, 0], X_test[mask, 1], facecolors='none',
edgecolors='k', label=f'Test {labels[i]}', marker=marker)

# Add legend for the classes
plt.xlabel(iris.feature_names[0])
plt.ylabel(iris.feature_names[1])
plt.title(f'k-NN Classification (k={k})')
plt.legend()
plt.show()
```

138   Chapter 4 ▪ Model Selection

Here is an explanation on how this program works:

Data loading In this step, we load the Iris dataset and select the first two features for easy visualization: i.e., sepal length and sepal width.

Data splitting We split the dataset into training and testing sets.

Model training We create a k-NN classifier with $k = 3$ and fit it to the training data.

Plot the decision boundary The decision boundary in the plot is the result of the k-NN prediction with $k = 3$ and is visually displayed in Figure 4.12 by the three regions in the two-dimensional feature space of our Iris dataset. The region on the left side of Figure 4.12 indicates *Iris-setosa* predictions, the region at the bottom indicates *Iris-versicolor* predictions, and the region on the right side indicates *Iris-virginica* predictions.

Plot training and test data points Similarly, the shape of each data point directly corresponds to its actual class label (i.e., the true value of the class: *Iris-setosa*, *Iris-versicolor*, or

FIGURE 4.12   Fitting k-NN to 2D Iris dataset.

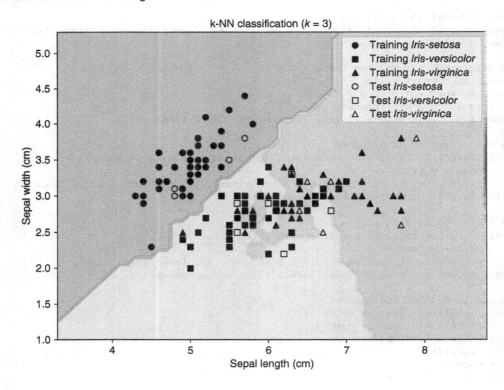

Iris-virginica), allowing you to visually distinguish between predictions and labels for different data points in the plot. Test data points are plotted with white fill and black contours using `facecolors='none'` and `edgecolors='k'`.

> Notice in Figure 4.12 how a few *Iris-virginica* training data points are located in the bottom area of the feature space (i.e., the *Iris-versicolor* area) to denote how our k-NN algorithm (with $k = 3$) mistakenly classified these *Iris-virginica* data points as *Iris-versicolor*. As a result, this model didn't perform well. More information will be provided in Chapter 5 when you will learn how to evaluate a model's performance by tuning the value of the model's hyperparameter, like k.

To use the k-NN algorithm in Amazon SageMaker, you first need to prepare your dataset and upload it to a suitable storage location (e.g., Amazon S3, Amazon EFS, or Amazon FSx for Lustre). You can then configure an *estimator* with the k-NN algorithm by specifying parameters like the number of neighbors k and the distance metric. After configuring the estimator with the necessary hyperparameters and input data paths, you initiate the training job, which Amazon SageMaker will handle, including provisioning and scaling the required infrastructure. Once the training is complete, the model can be deployed as an endpoint on Amazon SageMaker to make real-time predictions. This integrated approach leverages Amazon SageMaker's robust infrastructure to efficiently train and deploy k-NN models.

Use Cases

k-NN is best suited for classification and regression ML problems when the dataset is relatively small (fewer than 1,000 samples) to moderately sized (ranging from 1,000 to approximately 10,000 samples) and the decision boundaries are not overly complex.

It's particularly effective when the data has a clear, intuitive proximity in the feature space that makes the concept of "nearness" meaningful. k-NN should also be considered when the cost of model *interpretability* is high. This is because k-NN is inherently considered a very interpretable algorithm, meaning you can easily understand how it makes predictions based on the proximity of data points in the feature space, making it a good choice when explainability is a primary concern.

However, k-NN is less suitable for large datasets due to its high computational cost and memory usage. It performs poorly with high-dimensional data (the "curse" of dimensionality) as the distance metric becomes less meaningful, and it can struggle with noisy data unless carefully tuned. Additionally, k-NN requires significant preprocessing, such as feature scaling, to work effectively. If the dataset contains many irrelevant or highly correlated features, k-NN's performance may degrade, making it necessary to consider alternative algorithms like SVMs or random forests in these cases.

Decision Trees (Random Forest and XGBoost)

Decision tree algorithms are among the most popular and widely used methods in ML for both classification and regression tasks. Their intuitive nature and ability to handle various types of data make them a go-to choice for many data scientists and ML engineers.

A decision tree is a tree-like model of decisions and consists of nodes, branches, and leaves. The *root node* is the starting point that represents the entire dataset, *internal nodes* are points where the data is split based on certain conditions, and *leaves* are terminal points that represent the final outcomes or predictions. Branches are paths representing the outcomes of the decisions.

Decision trees operate by recursively partitioning the dataset into subsets based on feature values, which result in a tree structure. The goal is to create branches such that the data within each subset (node) is as homogeneous as possible. Homogeneity means that each subset of data (or node) resulting from a split should contain data points that are as similar to each other as possible. Ultimately, you want to achieve high *purity* within each node, to indicate that the data points in each node belong to the same class (in classification tasks) or have similar values (in regression tasks).

This process involves several key steps:

Feature selection   The algorithm selects the best feature to split the data at each node. The selection is based on metrics like Gini impurity, information gain (entropy), and variance reduction, depending on the type of task (classification or regression). The formula to calculate the variance is as follows:

$$\text{Variance} = \frac{1}{n} \sum_{i=1}^{n} \left(y_i - \widehat{y}_i \right)^2$$

Data splitting   The dataset is split into subsets based on the selected feature. Each subset then becomes a new node in the tree, and the process repeats recursively.

Stopping criteria   The recursive splitting stops when a predefined condition is met. This could be a maximum tree depth, a minimum number of samples per node, or when no further improvement in purity is possible.

Pruning   To prevent overfitting, decision trees can be pruned. Pruning involves removing branches that have little significance and do not contribute to the model's performance. This can be done through techniques like cost-complexity pruning.

Although decision trees are interpretable and versatile in their ability to capture complex, nonlinear relationships in the data, they also have the disadvantage of being highly sensitive to the training dataset. As a result, the algorithm could generate completely different predictions given a change of any single data point. To address this limitation, ensemble methods like random forest and gradient boosting are used. Random forests combine multiple decision trees, each trained in parallel on different subsets of the data, to improve accuracy and robustness, whereas Gradient boosting builds trees sequentially, with each tree correcting the errors of the previous ones.

Random Forest

With random forests, several data points are chosen randomly from the training dataset to create a new dataset. For each data point, a few features are selected for building the decision tree for the new dataset. This process is referred to as *bootstrapping*. The random forest algorithm involves using a number of decision trees—hence the name, as a forest is composed of multiple trees, and each tree is trained on a random subset of the data, contributing to an aggregated, more accurate, and robust prediction by voting for the most popular class in classification tasks, or averaging predictions in regression tasks.

Random forest algorithms have the advantage of training multiple decision trees in parallel, resulting in significantly faster training times. However, because each decision tree is generated independently, the model may not fully optimize for errors made by individual trees, potentially missing out on the benefits of sequential learning and gradient-based adjustments that more advanced algorithms like XGBoost provide.

XGBoost

The XGBoost algorithm (extreme gradient boosting), known for its efficiency and performance, is a powerful, tree-based ML algorithm. The primary objective of training an XGBoost model is to build an ensemble of decision trees that *sequentially* improve the accuracy of predictions by correcting the errors of previous trees. One key outcome of this training process is the determination of the most important features in the dataset. Feature importance is crucial as it helps in understanding which attributes of the data contribute the most to the predictive power of the model. This understanding can inform feature selection and model tuning, as well as provide insights into the underlying patterns in the data.

When comparing XGBoost with random forest, both algorithms are ensemble methods that utilize decision trees, but they differ significantly in their approach and performance. As illustrated in Figure 4.13, random forest builds multiple independent decision trees in parallel and aggregates their predictions, which helps reduce variance and improve robustness. It is particularly effective for handling large datasets with high variance but does not always capture complex patterns in the data as effectively as gradient boosting methods.

On the other hand, XGBoost constructs decision trees sequentially, each tree aiming to correct the errors of the previous ones. This sequential boosting process helps XGBoost reduce both bias and variance, leading to more accurate models, especially on complex datasets. Moreover, XGBoost's advanced optimization techniques and regularization make it more efficient and less prone to overfitting compared to random forest.

The provided Python code demonstrates how to train an XGBoost model on the Iris dataset. It showcases the steps involved in preparing the data, training the model, and evaluating feature importance. By plotting feature importance, the code reveals which features are most influential in making predictions.

FIGURE 4.13 Random forest versus XGBoost comparison.

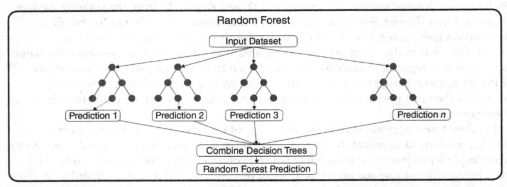

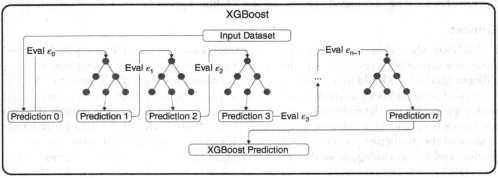

```
import numpy as np
import matplotlib.pyplot as plt
import xgboost as xgb
from sklearn.datasets import load_iris
from sklearn.model_selection import train_test_split
from sklearn.metrics import accuracy_score

# Load the Iris dataset
iris = load_iris()
X = iris.data
y = iris.target

# Split the data into training and testing sets
X_train, X_test, y_train, y_test = train_test_split(X, y, test_size=0.2,
random_state=42)

# Create a DMatrix, the internal data structure for XGBoost
dtrain = xgb.DMatrix(X_train, label=y_train)
dtest = xgb.DMatrix(X_test, label=y_test)
```

Developing Models with Amazon SageMaker Built-in Algorithms

```python
# Define the parameters for the XGBoost model
params = {
    'max_depth': 3,
    'eta': 0.1,
    'objective': 'multi:softprob',  # Multiclass classification
    'num_class': 3
}

# Train the model
num_round = 50
bst = xgb.train(params, dtrain, num_round)

# Prepare new data points for prediction
new_data = np.array([
    [5.1, 3.5, 1.4, 0.2],  # Example data point 1
    [6.2, 3.4, 5.4, 2.3]   # Example data point 2
])

# Create a DMatrix for the new data
dnew = xgb.DMatrix(new_data)

# Make predictions
preds = bst.predict(dnew)
predictions = [np.argmax(pred) for pred in preds]

# Define the class names
class_names = {0: 'Iris-setosa', 1: 'Iris-versicolor', 2: 'Iris-virginica'}

# Print the predictions with class names and detailed output, including the
actual data points
for i, (data_point, pred) in enumerate(zip(new_data, predictions)):
    class_label = class_names[pred]
    print(f'Prediction for datapoint {i+1} ({data_point}): {class_label}')

# Feature importance plot
fig, ax = plt.subplots(figsize=(10, 6))
xgb.plot_importance(bst, ax=ax)

# Add custom legend for features
features = ['sepal length (cm)', 'sepal width (cm)', 'petal length (cm)',
'petal width (cm)']
feature_labels = {f'f{i}': feature for i, feature in enumerate(features)}

# Create custom legend entries
handles = [plt.Line2D([0], [0], marker='o', color='w', label=f'{key}: {value}',
                      markersize=10, markerfacecolor='gray') for key, value in
feature_labels.items()]
ax.legend(handles=handles, title='Feature Legend', loc='upper right')

plt.show()
```

FIGURE 4.14 Feature importance using XGBoost.

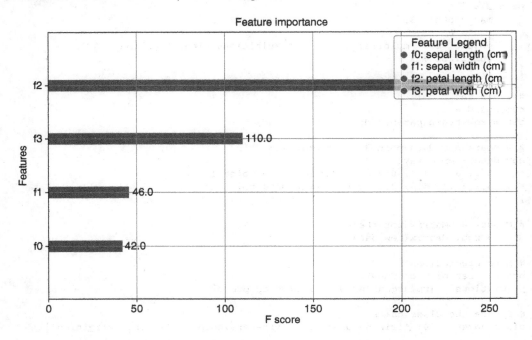

FIGURE 4.15 XGBoost predictions for two data points.

```
(booksession) Darios-Mac-Studio:matplotlib_project dariocabianca$ /Users/dariocabianca/ml/matplotlib_project/bo
oksession/bin/python /Users/dariocabianca/ml/matplotlib_project/predict_using_xgboost.py
Prediction for datapoint 1 ([5.1 3.5 1.4 0.2]): Iris-setosa
Prediction for datapoint 2 ([6.2 3.4 5.4 2.3]): Iris-virginica
2024-11-20 10:04:40.714 Python[10019:67228] +[IMKClient subclass]: chose IMKClient_Modern
2024-11-20 10:04:40.714 Python[10019:67228] +[IMKInputSession subclass]: chose IMKInputSession_Modern
2024-11-20 22:57:01.589 Python[10019:67228] The class 'NSSavePanel' overrides the method identifier.  This meth
od is implemented by class 'NSWindow'
(booksession) Darios-Mac-Studio:matplotlib_project dariocabianca$ []
```

In Figure 4.14, the petal length (f2) emerges as a significant feature, indicating its strong correlation with the target classes in the dataset.

After identifying the most important features, the XGBoost model can be used to make predictions on new, unseen data. Figure 4.15 displays the predictions for two data points, each made up of four numeric values expressed in "cm" (centimeters) corresponding to the features f0, f1, f2, and f3.

The code also illustrates how to prepare new data points, run predictions using the trained model, and interpret the results. This process ensures that the model is not only robust in terms of its training performance but also effective in real-world applications where new data is continuously encountered. By leveraging the insights gained from feature

Developing Models with Amazon SageMaker Built-in Algorithms **145**

importance and the predictive capabilities of XGBoost, ML engineers can develop highly accurate and reliable ML models for various structured data problems.

To use the XGBoost algorithm in Amazon SageMaker, you first need to prepare your dataset and upload it to a suitable storage location (e.g., Amazon S3, Amazon EFS, or Amazon FSx for Lustre). You then configure an XGBoost *estimator* by specifying essential hyperparameters such as the objective function (e.g., `binary:logistic` for binary classification or `reg:squarederror` for regression), the number of boosting rounds, and the learning rate. Other important hyperparameters include `max_depth` to control the depth of each tree, `subsample` to specify the fraction of samples to be used for training each tree, and `colsample_bytree` to determine the fraction of features to be used in constructing each tree. A detailed list of hyperparameters is available at `https://docs.aws.amazon.com/sagemaker/latest/dg/xgboost_hyperparameters.html`.

After setting up the estimator with these hyperparameters, you initiate the training job, and Amazon SageMaker manages the infrastructure needed for the training process. Once the training is complete, the trained XGBoost model can be deployed as an endpoint in Amazon SageMaker, allowing you to make real-time predictions on new, unseen data.

Use Cases

Decision trees are a suitable choice when interpretability is a critical aspect of your ML problem. They are easy to understand and visualize, making them ideal for scenarios where explaining the model's decisions to stakeholders is essential. Decision trees work well with both numerical and categorical data and do not require extensive data preprocessing. However, they are prone to overfitting, especially with complex datasets, leading to poor generalization on new data. Therefore, they are less suitable for tasks involving large, noisy datasets or those requiring high predictive accuracy.

Random forests should be considered when the goal is to improve predictive performance while mitigating the overfitting issue associated with individual decision trees. By averaging the results of multiple trees, random forests provide more robust and accurate predictions. They are particularly effective for large datasets with high variance and when feature importance insights are needed. However, random forests can become computationally intensive with large numbers of trees and deep models, making them less ideal for applications requiring real-time predictions or environments with limited computational resources.

XGBoost is the algorithm of choice when high predictive accuracy and efficiency are paramount. It excels in handling large datasets and complex feature interactions due to its sequential tree-building process and advanced regularization techniques (regularization is a technique to address overfitting and will be covered in detail in Chapter 5). XGBoost is particularly useful in competitive ML tasks and scenarios requiring the best possible model performance. However, it requires careful tuning of hyperparameters and can be more complex to implement compared to decision trees and random forests. Additionally, XGBoost's complexity and computational demands might be overkill for simpler tasks where interpretability and quick deployment are more critical than achieving the highest accuracy.

146 Chapter 4 ▪ Model Selection

Recommendation

Recommendation systems are pivotal in delivering personalized experiences across various industries. One effective approach within Amazon SageMaker is using the factorization machines algorithm, which excels at handling high-dimensional sparse data common in recommendation tasks. By learning latent factors representing user-item interactions, factorization machines can predict user preferences accurately. A key aspect of these models is *embeddings*, which are continuous-valued feature representations that capture the semantic relationships within the data, enabling efficient processing and improved performance. Amazon SageMaker's Object2Vec algorithm further enhances this capability by learning embeddings that can represent diverse types of objects, facilitating sophisticated recommendation systems that can understand and predict complex user behaviors and preferences effectively.

Factorization Machines

The Amazon SageMaker Factorization Machines algorithm is a powerful tool designed to handle high-dimensional sparse datasets, which are common in recommendation systems and click prediction tasks. This algorithm is particularly effective at capturing interactions between features that may otherwise be missed by traditional linear models. Factorization machines extend the capabilities of matrix factorization, allowing for a broader range of interactions between variables. By breaking down the complex relationships within the data into simpler, more manageable components, the algorithm can efficiently learn from vast amounts of data and provide accurate predictions. The implementation in Amazon SageMaker supports both classification and regression tasks, making it versatile for various applications.

One of the key advantages of the Amazon SageMaker Factorization Machines algorithm is its ability to handle sparsity efficiently. Sparse datasets, where many features are zero or missing, can pose significant challenges for many ML algorithms. However, factorization machines leverage latent factors to model these interactions compactly, reducing the dimensionality of the problem and improving performance. This makes the algorithm particularly suited for tasks like user-item recommendations, where the data matrix can be very large but also very sparse.

To use the Factorization Machines algorithm in Amazon SageMaker, you first need to prepare your dataset and upload it to a suitable storage location (e.g., Amazon S3, Amazon EFS, or Amazon FSx for Lustre). You then configure an estimator for the factorization machines algorithm by specifying essential hyperparameters. These include the `predictor_type` (`binary_classifier` or regressor), the number of factors to capture feature interactions, `feature_dim` (total number of features), `mini_batch_size`, and epochs for training duration. Additionally, you may set regularization parameters such as `bias_lr` (learning rate for bias term), `linear_lr` (learning rate for linear term), and `factor_lr` (learning rate for factor term) to control overfitting. To learn more about factorization machines' hyperparameters, visit `https://docs.aws.amazon.com/sagemaker/latest/dg/fact-machines-hyperparameters.html`.

Once the estimator is configured with these hyperparameters, initiate the training job, and Amazon SageMaker will manage the necessary infrastructure. After training, deploy the trained model as an endpoint in Amazon SageMaker to make real-time predictions on new data.

Use Cases

The primary use cases for Amazon SageMaker factorization machines include recommendation systems and predictive modeling in e-commerce. For instance, they can be used to predict user preferences in online retail by analyzing past purchase behavior and product interactions. Additionally, factorization machines are highly effective in click-through rate (CTR) prediction for online advertising, where understanding user interactions with ads can significantly impact ad targeting and personalization. Overall, the versatility and efficiency of the factorization machines algorithm make it a valuable tool for any scenario involving large-scale, sparse datasets.

Object2Vec

Amazon SageMaker's Object2Vec is a versatile neural embedding algorithm designed to generate low-dimensional dense embeddings from high-dimensional data. These embeddings capture the semantic relationships between objects, making them useful for tasks like nearest-neighbor search, clustering, and feature representation in downstream supervised learning tasks. Object2Vec generalizes the well-known Word2Vec technique, optimized for various types of structured and unstructured data.

To configure Object2Vec's hyperparameters in Amazon SageMaker, you need to specify several key parameters. These include `enc0_max_seq_len` (maximum sequence length for the enc0 encoder), `enc0_vocab_size` (vocabulary size of enc0 tokens), `dropout` (dropout probability for network layers), `early_stopping_patience` (number of consecutive epochs without improvement before early stopping), and `enc_dim` (dimension of the output embedding layer). Additionally, you can customize the comparator list (`comparator_list`) to define how embeddings are compared, and set the learning rate (`learning_rate`), mini-batch size (`mini_batch_size`) and optimizer type (`optimizer`). These hyperparameters allow you to fine-tune the algorithm to your specific use case, ensuring optimal performance and accuracy. To learn more about Object2Vec's hyperparameters, visit `https://docs.aws.amazon.com/sagemaker/latest/dg/object2vec-hyperparameters.html`.

Use Cases

Object2Vec in Amazon SageMaker is ideal for scenarios where you need to generate high-quality embeddings from complex, high-dimensional data to capture semantic relationships. It's particularly useful in recommendation systems, similarity searches, and clustering, and as input features for downstream supervised learning tasks. However, Object2Vec may not be the best choice if your primary goal is to perform simple linear transformations or if your dataset is not sparse and doesn't benefit from capturing intricate interactions. Additionally, for applications requiring real-time training or extremely large-scale datasets with strict latency constraints, other algorithms optimized for such tasks might be more suitable. Overall, Object2Vec excels in situations requiring robust, interpretable embeddings for complex, structured, or unstructured data.

Forecasting

Forecasting with Amazon SageMaker offers robust solutions for predicting future values based on historical data, enabling businesses to make data-driven decisions. Amazon SageMaker provides DeepAR as a built-in algorithm for time-series forecasting. Let's see how it works.

DeepAR

The DeepAR algorithm in Amazon SageMaker is a powerful tool designed for time-series forecasting. It leverages recurrent neural networks (RNNs) to capture complex temporal patterns and dependencies within data. Unlike traditional statistical methods, DeepAR can handle large-scale datasets with multiple time series, making it particularly effective for forecasting tasks involving diverse products or locations. By training on related time series, the algorithm can learn shared patterns and improve the accuracy of individual forecasts. which is especially beneficial for applications like demand forecasting, inventory management, and financial predictions.

DeepAR is designed to provide *probabilistic forecasts*. This means it not only predicts a single point estimate but also quantifies uncertainty by generating a range of possible future values. Mathematically speaking, DeepAR outputs a probability distribution around a predicted future value rather than just a single point estimate, allowing users to understand the uncertainty associated with their predictions. DeepAR's ability to produce probabilistic forecasts is critical for decision-making processes that need to account for various outcomes and their associated probabilities. This allows businesses to better manage risks and optimize resources by understanding the full spectrum of potential future scenarios.

When configuring DeepAR from Amazon SageMaker, several key hyperparameters need to be considered. The `epochs` hyperparameter determines the number of times the model will iterate over the training data, influencing the training duration and performance. The `context_length` hyperparameter specifies the number of time steps the model uses from the past to make forecasts. The `prediction_length` hyperparameter defines the number of future time steps the model will predict. Additionally, `num_layers` and `num_cells` control the depth and size of the RNN, respectively, impacting the model's ability to learn complex patterns. Other important hyperparameters include `mini_batch_size` for training efficiency and `learning_rate` for adjusting the model weights during training. Proper tuning of these hyperparameters is essential to optimize the model's performance and accuracy for specific forecasting tasks. For a complete list of DeepAR hyperparameters, visit https://docs.aws.amazon.com/sagemaker/latest/dg/deepar_hyperparameters.html.

Use Cases

Use DeepAR for time-series forecasting when dealing with large-scale datasets comprising multiple related time series, especially when you need probabilistic forecasts that quantify uncertainty in predictions. It's particularly effective for applications like demand forecasting, inventory management, and financial predictions, where capturing complex patterns

Developing Models with Amazon SageMaker Built-in Algorithms **149**

and dependencies is critical. However, avoid using DeepAR if your dataset is small or consists of simple, single-variable time series where traditional statistical methods (like ARIMA or exponential smoothing) may suffice. Also, if real-time training or very low-latency predictions are required, other algorithms optimized for such tasks might be more appropriate.

Unsupervised ML Algorithms

If you ever played crosswords, you know the satisfaction of filling in the blanks and seeing words come together. Now, imagine a more challenging version called "Diagramless Crosswords," where you not only have to solve the clues but also figure out the grid's structure. This intriguing puzzle is a perfect metaphor for understanding unsupervised ML. Just like in diagramless crosswords, where the solver must uncover the hidden grid and the words, unsupervised ML algorithms work without predefined labels, searching for patterns and structures directly from the data.

In the domain of unsupervised ML, there are several key algorithms, each serving different purposes. One popular technique is *clustering*, with K-means being a classic example. K-means groups data points into clusters based on their similarities, much like sorting puzzle pieces into coherent sections. Another essential method is *dimensionality reduction*, exemplified by principal component analysis (PCA). PCA simplifies complex datasets by reducing the number of dimensions, akin to folding a large map to focus on a specific area. *Topic modeling* is another excellent application of unsupervised ML, with algorithms like latent Dirichlet allocation (LDA) and neural topic model (NTM). These algorithms uncover hidden themes within large text datasets, similar to revealing the underlying story in a jumble of words.

Additionally, *anomaly detection* is a critical application of unsupervised ML used to identify outliers or unusual patterns in data. Algorithms like random cut forest (RCF) and IP insights excel in this domain, spotting anomalies that might indicate fraud or other irregular activities. Together, these algorithms showcase the versatility of unsupervised ML, providing powerful tools to explore and understand your data's hidden structures without needing predefined labels or guidance.

Clustering

In unsupervised ML, a dataset is explored to uncover hidden patterns, group similar data points into *clusters*, and identify intrinsic structures without predefined labels, providing valuable insights into the data's underlying characteristics and relationships. Clustering, in particular, facilitates the transition from raw data to valuable information by organizing data into meaningful groups. This organization transforms isolated data points into insightful information, which can then be interpreted and analyzed to generate knowledge. By understanding these clusters, one can derive actionable knowledge and insights that drive informed decision-making and strategic planning.

150 Chapter 4 ▪ Model Selection

K-Means Clustering

The K-means algorithm is a popular unsupervised ML approach used for clustering data into a predefined number of clusters, k.

The algorithm works iteratively by assigning each data point to one of the k clusters based on the similarity of data points.

Similarity in this context is typically defined using a measure of distance. The most common distance metric used is Euclidean distance, which calculates the straight-line distance between two points in a multidimensional space (our feature space). The algorithm minimizes the sum of squared distances from each point to the centroid of the cluster it is assigned to. A *centroid* is the central point of a cluster, calculated as the mean of all points within that cluster. It represents the center of mass for the cluster and is used to assign data points to clusters.

One common challenge is determining the appropriate number of clusters for a given dataset. The *elbow method* is a heuristic used to estimate the number of clusters by plotting the within-cluster sum of squares (WCSS) against the number of clusters. As the number of clusters increases, the WCSS decreases, but there is a point where the rate of decrease sharply slows down, forming an "elbow" in the plot. This elbow point suggests an optimal number of clusters, balancing between underfitting and overfitting. Mathematically, the WCSS for a set of clusters is calculated as the sum of the squared distances between each data point and its corresponding cluster centroid.

Given a set of clusters $C_1, C_2, ..., C_k$, with centroids $\mu_1, \mu_2, ..., \mu_k$, the WCSS is calculated as follows:

$$\text{WCSS} = \sum_{j=1}^{k} \sum_{i \in C_j} ||x_i - \mu_j||^2$$

where k is the number of clusters, C_j is the set of data points in the j-th cluster, x_i is a data point in the j-th cluster, μ_j is the centroid of the j-th cluster, and $||x_i - \mu_j||^2$ is the Euclidean distance squared between the data point x_i and the centroid μ_j.

Elbow Method Visualization

To help you understand the elbow method, the following Python program plots the elbow function for the Iris dataset using the KMeans class from the `sklearn.cluster` module

```python
import os
import matplotlib.pyplot as plt
from sklearn.cluster import KMeans
from sklearn.datasets import load_iris
from sklearn.preprocessing import StandardScaler

# Create images directory if it doesn't exist
images_dir = './images'
```

```
os.makedirs(images_dir, exist_ok=True)

# Load the Iris dataset
iris = load_iris()
data = iris.data

# Standardize the data
scaler = StandardScaler()
scaled_data = scaler.fit_transform(data)

# List to hold the within-cluster sum of squares (WCSS)
wcss = []

# Run K-Means for 1 to 10 clusters
for k in range(1, 11):
    kmeans = KMeans(n_clusters=k, random_state=0)
    kmeans.fit(scaled_data)
    wcss.append(kmeans.inertia_)

# Plot the WCSS values to visualize the elbow method
plt.figure(figsize=(8, 5))
plt.plot(range(1, 11), wcss, marker='o')
plt.title('Elbow Method for Determining Optimal Number of Clusters')
plt.xlabel('Number of Clusters')
plt.ylabel('Within-Cluster Sum of Squares (WCSS)')
plt.grid(True)

# Save the plot to the images directory
plot_file = os.path.join(images_dir, 'elbow_method_plot.png')
plt.savefig(plot_file)
print(f"Elbow method plot has been saved to '{plot_file}'")
```

Most of the statements in this program are straightforward and self-explanatory, but what happens inside the loop?

Model initialization `KMeans(n_clusters=k, random_state=0)` initializes the K-means model with k clusters and a specified random state for reproducibility.

Model training `kmeans.fit(scaled_data)` trains the K-means model on the `scaled_data`. During this process, the following steps are performed:

- **Cluster centroids initialization:** The algorithm initially assigns random positions to the cluster centroids.

- **Data point assignment:** Each data point is assigned to the nearest cluster centroid based on the Euclidean distance.

- **Centroid update:** The centroids are recalculated as the mean of all data points assigned to that cluster.

- **Reiteration:** The process of data point assignment and centroid update is repeated until convergence (i.e., the centroids no longer change significantly).

152 Chapter 4 ■ Model Selection

Compute WCSS   After the model is trained, `kmeans.inertia_` is appended to the `wcss` list. `kmeans.inertia_` is an attribute of the `KMeans` class (in the `sklearn.cluster` module) that represents the WCSS. This attribute measures the *compactness* of the clusters: the lower the WCSS, the closer the data points within a cluster are to their cluster centroid.

When run in Amazon SageMaker Studio, this code generates the elbow plot and saves it as `elbow_method_plot.png` in the `./images` folder of the EFS mounted on your Amazon SageMaker Studio instance.

> Amazon SageMaker Studio instances come with EFS mounted by default, so any files saved in local directories within the instance will be stored on the attached EFS. This ensures that your generated plot will be readily available and persistent across different sessions within Amazon SageMaker Studio.

The elbow plot is displayed in Figure 4.16, and it effectively illustrates the optimal number of clusters by highlighting the point where the WCSS begins to decrease more slowly, forming an "elbow" shape. This visual cue helps in determining the appropriate number of clusters for the dataset.

FIGURE 4.16   Elbow function.

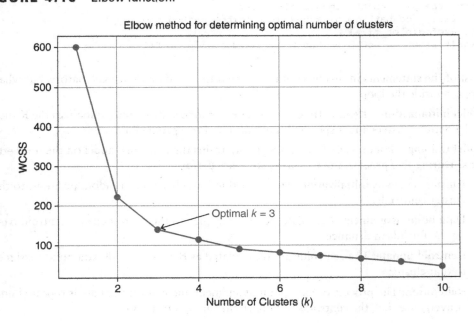

Based on the data in Figure 4.16, $k = 3$ is the optimal number of clusters. This means adding more clusters beyond $k = 3$ does not provide substantial improvement in the compactness of the clusters. In the case of the Iris dataset, this optimal clustering effectively captures the natural grouping of the different species, thus balancing simplicity and accuracy without overfitting.

Let's now put the K-means algorithm to work and see how effectively our data points are grouped in three clusters. Keep in mind the Iris dataset is a four-dimensional feature space with 150 data points. As a result, a plot illustrating the clustering cannot be visually represented unless the dimensionality is reduced from four to three (or two). We will learn another unsupervised ML technique intended to reduce the dimensionality of a dataset in the next section. To provide a comprehensive view while keeping the visualization intuitive and accessible, we are going to perform the K-means algorithm with a simplified, three-dimensional version of the Iris dataset.

A more accurate way to cluster the Iris dataset will be covered in the upcoming section, when we cover the PCA algorithm, which is designed to reduce the dimensionality of your feature dataset while maintaining the maximum possible variance in the data.

The following Python program performs the K-means clustering on three features of the Iris dataset (sepal length, petal length, petal width) and saves the plot with the clusters and centroids as kmeans_iris_3d_plot.png in the ./ch04/images folder of the EFS mounted on your Amazon SageMaker Studio instance:

```
import os
import numpy as np
import matplotlib.pyplot as plt
from mpl_toolkits.mplot3d import Axes3D
from sklearn.datasets import load_iris
from sklearn.preprocessing import StandardScaler
from sklearn.cluster import KMeans

# Define the output directory and file path
output_dir = './ch04/images'
output_file = os.path.join(output_dir, 'kmeans_iris_3d_plot.png')

# Create the output directory if it doesn't exist
os.makedirs(output_dir, exist_ok=True)

# Load Iris dataset
iris = load_iris()
data = iris.data[:, [0, 2, 3]]
labels = iris.target
feature_names = ['sepal length (cm)', 'petal length (cm)', 'petal width (cm)']
```

```python
# Standardize the features
scaler = StandardScaler()
scaled_data = scaler.fit_transform(data)

# Perform K-Means clustering
kmeans = KMeans(n_clusters=3, random_state=42)
kmeans.fit(scaled_data)
clusters = kmeans.labels_

# Plot the clustering results in 3D
fig = plt.figure(figsize=(10, 8))
ax = fig.add_subplot(111, projection='3d')

# Define colors and markers
colors = ['blue', 'orange', 'purple']
markers = ['o', 's', 'D']

# Plot each cluster with different color and marker
for cluster in np.unique(clusters):
    ax.scatter(scaled_data[clusters == cluster, 0],
               scaled_data[clusters == cluster, 1],
               scaled_data[clusters == cluster, 2],
               c=colors[cluster],
               marker=markers[cluster],
               label=f'Cluster {cluster+1}',
               edgecolor='black')

# Plot centroids with a star marker
centroids = kmeans.cluster_centers_
for i, centroid in enumerate(centroids):
    ax.scatter(centroid[0], centroid[1], centroid[2],
               s=300,
               c='yellow',
               marker='*',
               edgecolor='black',
               linewidths=2,
               label=f'Centroid {i+1}')

ax.set_xlabel('Standardized Sepal Length (cm)')
ax.set_ylabel('Standardized Petal Length (cm)')
ax.set_zlabel('Standardized Petal Width (cm)')
ax.legend()
ax.set_title('K-Means Clustering of Iris Dataset (3D)')

# Save the plot to the specified file path
plt.savefig(output_file)

# Display a message confirming the plot has been saved
print(f"Plot has been saved as '{output_file}'")
```

In the provided code, the statement `clusters = kmeans.labels_` assigns the computed labels to the `clusters` variable, which is then used to color and group the data points in the plot based on their cluster membership.

The `kmeans.labels_` attribute returns an array of integer labels that denote the cluster each data point belongs to. This happens after fitting the K-means algorithm on the training dataset with the statement (`kmeans.fit(scaled_data)`). In essence, the statement `clusters = kmeans.labels_` assigns a cluster label to each data point in the dataset, showing which cluster the data point has been grouped into based on the clustering algorithm's results.

> Do not confuse labels with predictions. Although the statement `clusters = kmeans.labels_` assigns the cluster labels to each data point after training the K-means algorithm with the statement `kmeans.fit(scaled_data)`, it is not itself a predictor. Instead, it is an output of the K-means algorithm that tells you which cluster each data point belongs to. It doesn't predict cluster memberships for new, unseen data points. If you want to predict the cluster for new data points using a trained K-means model, you need to use the `kmeans.predict()` method of the KMeans class. More details will be provided in the next chapter.

To recap, the method `kmeans.fit()` trains the K-means model on the training data, whereas the attribute `kmeans.labels_` returns the cluster labels for the training data, and the method `kmeans.predict()` predicts the cluster labels for new, unseen data points.

Now that you understand how the code works, you can see the three clusters in Figure 4.17. The three-dimensional plot of the K-means clustering of the Iris dataset effectively illustrates the grouping of data points based on three standardized features: sepal length, petal length, and petal width. The plot uses distinct shapes to differentiate the three clusters, highlighting their spatial separation in the feature space. The centroids of each cluster are prominently displayed with larger yellow star markers, making them easily identifiable. This visualization provides a clear, intuitive representation of how the K-means algorithm has segmented the Iris dataset into three distinct groups, reflecting the natural clustering of the different Iris species.

To use the built-in K-means algorithm in Amazon SageMaker, you can follow these steps. First, set up an Amazon SageMaker session and specify the K-means algorithm container. Then, create a K-means estimator, specify the number of clusters, and fit the model on your data. Last, deploy the trained estimator to an endpoint to derive inference. The following snippet shows a brief example:

```
import sagemaker
from sagemaker import get_execution_role
from sklearn.preprocessing import StandardScaler

# Set up SageMaker session and role
sagemaker_session = sagemaker.Session()
role = get_execution_role()
```

156 Chapter 4 ▪ Model Selection

FIGURE 4.17 3D K-means clustering of Iris dataset.

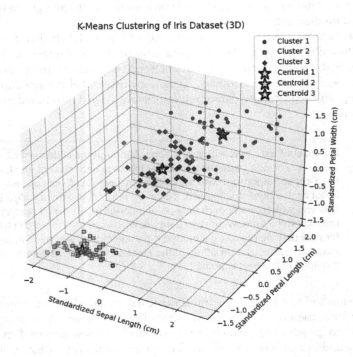

```
# Specify the K-Means algorithm container
container = sagemaker.image_uris.retrieve(
    'kmeans',
    sagemaker_session.boto_region_name
)

# Create KMeans estimator
kmeans = sagemaker.estimator.Estimator(
    container,
    role,
    instance_count=1,
    instance_type='ml.m4.xlarge',
    output_path='s3://your-bucket/path-to-output',
    sagemaker_session=sagemaker_session
)

# Specify the number of clusters
kmeans.set_hyperparameters(k=3)

# Fit the model on your data stored in S3
kmeans.fit({'train': 's3://your-bucket/path-to-train-data'})
```

Developing Models with Amazon SageMaker Built-in Algorithms

```
# Once trained, the model can be deployed to an endpoint for inference
predictor = kmeans.deploy(
    initial_instance_count=1,
    instance_type='ml.m4.xlarge'
)

# Use the predictor to make predictions on new data
new_data = [[5.1, 3.5, 1.4, 0.2], [6.2, 3.4, 5.4, 2.3]]
scaler = StandardScaler()
scaled_new_data = scaler.transform(new_data) # Ensure new data is standardized

# Make predictions
predicted_clusters = predictor.predict(scaled_new_data)
print(predicted_clusters)
```

Use Cases

K-means is best suited for scenarios where you have a clear idea of the number of clusters you expect to find in your dataset. This algorithm is highly effective for partitioning datasets into distinct, nonoverlapping groups based on feature similarity. It excels in scenarios with well-separated and spherical clusters in feature space. Applications such as customer segmentation, market basket analysis, image compression, and anomaly detection are ideal for K-means, as the algorithm efficiently handles large datasets and scales well with an increasing number of samples. When the input data is primarily numerical and relatively well-structured, K-means can provide insightful and actionable groupings.

Avoid using K-means if your data does not conform to the assumptions of spherical and equally sized clusters or if the clusters you aim to detect are of varying shapes and densities. K-means is sensitive to outliers, so if your data contains significant anomalies, these can skew the results and lead to poor clustering. Also, K-means requires a predefined number of clusters (k), which can be challenging to determine without prior knowledge of the data structure. If your dataset includes non-numerical features or if you require a more flexible clustering method that can handle arbitrary cluster shapes and densities, such as density-based spatial clustering of applications with noise (DBSCAN) or hierarchical clustering, K-means may not be the best choice.

Dimensionality Reduction

Dimensionality reduction algorithms are pivotal in unsupervised ML, helping to simplify complex datasets by reducing the number of features while retaining essential information. These techniques transform high-dimensional data into a lower-dimensional form, making it easier to visualize and analyze your data. Common algorithms include PCA, which identifies the directions (principal components) that maximize variance in the data, and t-distributed stochastic neighbor embedding (t-SNE), which focuses on preserving the local structure and relationships between data points. By reducing dimensionality, these algorithms help to uncover underlying patterns, facilitate data compression, and improve the efficiency of subsequent ML tasks.

158   Chapter 4 ▪ Model Selection

Amazon SageMaker offers PCA as a built-in algorithm for dimensionality reduction, enabling ML engineers and data scientists to effectively reduce the number of features in a dataset while preserving as much variability as possible, thereby enhancing the efficiency and performance of subsequent ML models.

Principal Component Analysis

PCA is a powerful dimensionality reduction technique widely used in ML and data analysis. It works by identifying the *principal components*, which are the directions in the data that explain the most variance. By transforming the original high-dimensional data into a new coordinate system defined by these principal components, PCA effectively reduces the number of features while preserving as much of the data's variability as possible. This makes it easier to visualize and analyze the data and also enhances the performance of subsequent ML algorithms by mitigating issues related to multicollinearity and overfitting.

With reference to the previous example, let's apply the PCA algorithm to the Iris dataset to reduce the dimensionality from four to three.

The following Python program uses the PCA algorithm to reduce the dimensionality of our dataset and then applies K-means clustering to group the datapoints in three clusters:

```python
import pandas as pd
import numpy as np
import matplotlib.pyplot as plt
from sklearn.datasets import load_iris
from sklearn.preprocessing import StandardScaler
from sklearn.decomposition import PCA
from sklearn.cluster import KMeans
from mpl_toolkits.mplot3d import Axes3D
import os

# Create the output directory if it doesn't exist
output_dir = './ch04/images'
os.makedirs(output_dir, exist_ok=True)

# Load the Iris dataset
iris = load_iris()
data = iris.data

# Scale the data
scaler = StandardScaler()
scaled_data = scaler.fit_transform(data)

# Apply PCA to reduce to 3 dimensions
pca_3d = PCA(n_components=3)
pca_data_3d = pca_3d.fit_transform(scaled_data)

# Apply K-Means clustering
kmeans = KMeans(n_clusters=3, random_state=42)
```

Developing Models with Amazon SageMaker Built-in Algorithms   **159**

```
kmeans.fit(pca_data_3d)
cluster_assignments_3d = kmeans.predict(pca_data_3d)
centroids_3d = kmeans.cluster_centers_

# Plotting the results in 3D
fig = plt.figure(figsize=(10, 8))
ax = fig.add_subplot(111, projection='3d')

# Define colors and markers
colors = ['blue', 'orange', 'purple']
markers = ['o', 's', 'D']

# Plot each cluster with different color and marker
for cluster in np.unique(cluster_assignments_3d):
    ax.scatter(pca_data_3d[cluster_assignments_3d == cluster, 0],
               pca_data_3d[cluster_assignments_3d == cluster, 1],
               pca_data_3d[cluster_assignments_3d == cluster, 2],
               c=colors[cluster],
               marker=markers[cluster],
               label=f'Cluster {cluster + 1}',
               edgecolor='black')

# Plot centroids with yellow stars and enumerate them
for i, centroid in enumerate(centroids_3d):
    ax.scatter(centroid[0], centroid[1], centroid[2],
               s=300, c='yellow', marker='*',
               edgecolor='black', label=f'Centroid {i + 1}')
    ax.text(centroid[0], centroid[1], centroid[2], f'C{i + 1}',
            color='black', fontsize=12, ha='center', va='center')

ax.set_xlabel('Principal Component 1')
ax.set_ylabel('Principal Component 2')
ax.set_zlabel('Principal Component 3')
ax.legend()
ax.set_title('3D K-Means Clustering of Iris Dataset Using PCA')

# Save the plot to the specified file path
plt.savefig(os.path.join(output_dir, 'pca_kmeans_iris_plot_3d.png'))
plt.close()
print(f"3D plot has been saved in '{output_dir}' as 'pca_kmeans_iris_
plot_3d.png'")
```

I ran this program in Amazon SageMaker Studio; Figure 4.18 displays the resulting image, illustrating the 3D K-means clustering of the Iris dataset with PCA-reduced dimensions and highlighted centroids.

The plot shows three distinct clusters, each represented by a different shape:

- Cluster 1: circles
- Cluster 2: squares
- Cluster 3: diamonds

FIGURE 4.18 3D K-means clustering of Iris dataset using PCA.

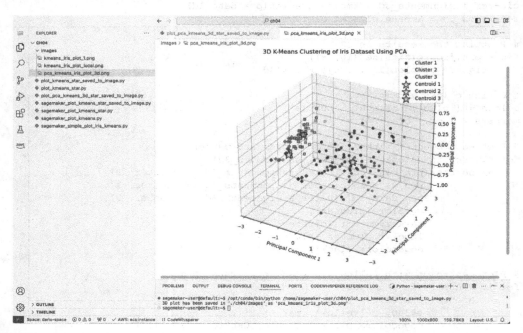

The axes of the 3D plot represent the three principal components (PC1, PC2, and PC3) derived from the PCA algorithm. These components capture the maximum variance in the dataset, effectively reducing its dimensionality while preserving its essential structure.

The centroids of each cluster are highlighted with stars and are enumerated as C1, C2, and C3. These centroids represent the central points of each cluster, providing a reference for the typical features of data points within each group.

The spatial separation of the clusters in the 3D plot demonstrates the effectiveness of PCA in reducing dimensionality and K-means in identifying distinct groups within the data. The clear distinction between clusters suggests that the features of the Iris flowers are well-represented by the chosen principal components.

Amazon SageMaker provides a highly scalable and efficient implementation of PCA, which can handle large datasets with ease. To use PCA in Amazon SageMaker, you start by creating a PCA estimator object, specifying the number of components you want to retain. You then fit the estimator to your dataset, which involves calculating the principal components and transforming the original data into the new lower-dimensional space. Amazon SageMaker's PCA algorithm supports both sparse and dense data formats, making it versatile for various types of data preprocessing tasks.

Developing Models with Amazon SageMaker Built-in Algorithms

Once the PCA model is trained, you can deploy it as an endpoint in Amazon SageMaker to transform new data on the fly, or you can use it in batch transformations for larger datasets. This enables seamless integration into your ML workflows, allowing you to preprocess data in real time or at scale. Additionally, Amazon SageMaker's integration with other AWS services like Amazon S3 for data storage and Amazon SageMaker Studio for development provides a comprehensive environment for developing, testing, and deploying PCA models. By leveraging Amazon SageMaker's built-in PCA algorithm, data scientists and ML engineers can efficiently reduce dimensionality, improve model performance, and streamline their data processing pipelines.

The following snippet in Python shows an example of how to use PCA with Amazon SageMaker:

```python
import pandas as pd
import boto3
import sagemaker
from sagemaker import get_execution_role
import os

# Initialize the SageMaker session
sagemaker_session = sagemaker.Session()

# Get the execution role
role = get_execution_role()

# Load the Iris dataset
from sklearn.datasets import load_iris
iris = load_iris()
df = pd.DataFrame(iris.data, columns=iris.feature_names)

# Save the DataFrame to a CSV file
data_csv = 'iris.csv'
df.to_csv(data_csv, index=False, header=False)

# Upload the CSV file to S3
s3_bucket = sagemaker_session.default_bucket()
s3_data_path = f's3://{s3_bucket}/pca/iris.csv'
boto3.Session().resource('s3').Bucket(s3_bucket).Object('pca/iris.csv').
upload_file(data_csv)

# Get the PCA container image URI
pca_image_uri = sagemaker.image_uris.retrieve(
    'pca',
    boto3.Session().region_name
)

# Create the PCA estimator
pca = sagemaker.estimator.Estimator(
```

Chapter 4 • Model Selection

```
    image_uri=pca_image_uri,
    role=role,
    instance_count=1,
    instance_type='ml.m4.xlarge',
    output_path=f's3://{s3_bucket}/pca/output'
)

# Set PCA hyperparameters
pca.set_hyperparameters(
    feature_dim=4,
    num_components=3,
    subtract_mean=True,
    algorithm_mode='regular'
)

# Fit the PCA model
pca.fit({'train': s3_data_path})

# Deploy the PCA model
pca_transformer = pca.transformer(
    instance_count=1,
    instance_type='ml.m4.xlarge',
    strategy='SingleRecord'
)

# Perform the transformation
transformed_output = pca_transformer.transform(
    data=s3_data_path,
    content_type='text/csv',
    split_type='Line'
)

transformed_output.wait()

# Download and view the transformed data
transformed_output_path = transformed_output.output_path
transformed_data = pd.read_csv(transformed_output_path + '/train.csv.out',
header=None)
print(transformed_data.head())
```

You will learn more about hyperparameter tuning, model deployment, and model monitoring in Chapters 5, 6, and 7, respectively.

Use Cases

PCA is highly useful in scenarios where data dimensionality needs to be reduced to improve analysis and modeling efficiency. It is particularly effective in dealing with high-dimensional datasets where multicollinearity (high correlation) among features is a concern. By transforming the data into a new set of orthogonal components, PCA helps in retaining the most significant variance while reducing the number of variables. Common use cases include image compression, where PCA reduces the number of pixels required to represent an image without significant loss of quality, and exploratory data analysis, where it helps in visualizing complex datasets by projecting them into lower-dimensional spaces. Additionally, PCA is used to preprocess data for ML models, enhancing performance by reducing noise and overfitting risks.

However, PCA should not be used indiscriminately. One limitation is that it assumes linear relationships between variables, which might not capture the complexity in data with nonlinear interactions. It's also not suitable for datasets where the variance is not an appropriate measure of importance, as PCA prioritizes features with higher variance, potentially discarding smaller yet crucial variances. Additionally, the interpretability of principal components can be challenging, as they are combinations of original features that may not have a clear, intuitive meaning. Therefore, although PCA is a powerful tool for dimensionality reduction, it is essential to consider the nature of your data and the specific requirements of your analysis before applying it.

Topic Modeling

Topic modeling is considered an unsupervised ML technique because it does not require labeled data to identify patterns or topics within a collection of documents. Unlike supervised learning, where models are trained on input - output pairs to predict specific outcomes, topic modeling algorithms like LDA and NTM explore the inherent structure of the data. They aim to discover the underlying topics that best represent the semantics of the documents, purely based on word co-occurrence patterns without any prior knowledge or annotations. This makes topic modeling highly valuable for exploring and understanding large, unstructured text datasets, enabling users to uncover hidden themes and insights without the need of prelabeled training data.

To draw an analogy, think of topic modeling as similar to clustering. Just as clustering algorithms group data points based on their similarity, topic modeling algorithms group documents based on their underlying topics. By recognizing patterns and relationships in the text, these algorithms can categorize documents into distinct topics, making it easier to manage and understand large volumes of textual data.

Amazon SageMaker offers LDA and NTM out of the box, enabling users to effortlessly implement and scale their topic modeling solutions without requiring prior expertise in deep learning.

Latent Dirichlet Allocation

LDA is a generative probabilistic model used for identifying topics within a large corpus of text. It assumes that each document is a mixture of topics, and each topic is a mixture of words. The name "Dirichlet" comes from the Dirichlet distribution, a type of probability distribution that is essential in LDA. A Dirichlet distribution is used to model the uncertainty about the probabilities of different topics within a document. It essentially provides a way to assign probabilities to the various topics in a document, ensuring that the sum of these probabilities is one. This distribution helps in determining the proportion of different topics in each document, allowing LDA to uncover the latent thematic structure of the text. The

164   Chapter 4 ▪ Model Selection

shape of the Dirichlet distribution is controlled by a set of parameters (called *concentration parameters*) that can be adjusted to influence how the probability mass is distributed across different topics. By iteratively updating the distributions of topics over documents and words over topics, LDA can identify meaningful topics that best represent the semantics of the text.

In AWS, LDA can be utilized efficiently through Amazon SageMaker, which offers a built-in LDA algorithm for topic modeling. To use LDA in Amazon SageMaker, you start by preparing your text data and uploading it to an Amazon S3 bucket (or Amazon EFS or Amazon FSx for Lustre). Next, you create an LDA estimator by specifying the number of topics and other hyperparameters. Amazon SageMaker takes care of the training process, leveraging its scalable infrastructure to handle large datasets and computationally intensive tasks. Once the model is trained, you can use it to transform new documents, providing insights into their topic distributions. This capability is particularly useful for applications such as document clustering, content recommendation, and information retrieval, where understanding the thematic structure of text is crucial. By integrating LDA into your AWS workflow, you can harness the power of topic modeling to enhance your data analysis and ML solutions.

Use Cases

LDA is highly effective in scenarios where understanding the thematic structure of a large corpus of text is critical. It excels in applications like document clustering, content recommendation, and information retrieval. For example, in a news aggregation service, LDA can help group articles by topics such as politics, sports, or technology, improving the user experience by enabling topic-based browsing. Similarly, in academic research, LDA can be used to analyze a vast number of research papers to discover prevalent topics and trends over time. By identifying the distribution of topics within each document, LDA allows businesses and researchers to extract insights from unstructured text data efficiently.

However, LDA has some limitations due to its assumption of Dirichlet-distributed topics, which may not capture more complex dependencies between words and topics. In such cases, NTM can come into play. NTM leverages neural networks to learn topic representations, allowing for greater flexibility and the ability to capture intricate patterns in the data. This makes NTM particularly effective for datasets with strong temporal or sequential dependencies or where the relationships between words and topics are not well-modeled by a Dirichlet distribution. By incorporating NTM into your AWS workflow, you can address some of LDA's shortcomings and enhance your ability to analyze and understand complex text data, ensuring more accurate and meaningful topic representations.

Neural Topic Model

NTM is an advanced approach to topic modeling that utilizes neural networks to learn more flexible and nuanced representations of topics compared to traditional methods like LDA. By leveraging the power of deep learning, NTM can capture complex patterns and dependencies in textual data, making it highly effective for extracting meaningful topics from large volumes of text. Unlike LDA, which relies on Dirichlet distributions to model the probability of topics within documents, NTM uses neural networks to automatically learn these distributions, providing greater adaptability to various types of text data. This results in more accurate and interpretable topics, which can be incredibly valuable for applications such as document clustering, content recommendation, and sentiment analysis.

NTM can be seamlessly implemented using Amazon SageMaker, which offers a built-in algorithm for NTM. To utilize NTM in Amazon SageMaker, you begin by preparing your text data and uploading it to an Amazon S3 bucket (or Amazon EFS or Amazon FSx for Lustre). Next, you create an NTM estimator in Amazon SageMaker by specifying the necessary hyperparameters and training configurations. Amazon SageMaker's scalable infrastructure handles the computational demands of training the NTM algorithm, making it suitable for large datasets. Once the model is trained, it can be used to transform new documents and generate topic distributions, providing valuable insights into the thematic structure of your text data. This capability allows businesses to efficiently analyze and understand their textual data, enabling them to make data-driven decisions and enhance their ML workflows. By integrating NTM into your AWS environment, you can leverage the strengths of neural networks to uncover deeper insights from complex textual data.

Use Cases

NTM is particularly useful in scenarios where traditional topic modeling methods like LDA fall short. For instance, NTM excels in handling large, complex datasets where the relationships between words and topics are intricate and not well-represented by Dirichlet distributions. Its ability to leverage deep learning allows it to capture more nuanced and flexible topic representations, making it ideal for applications such as sentiment analysis, customer feedback analysis, and thematic exploration in extensive text corpora. Additionally, NTM is well-suited for tasks that require understanding temporal or sequential dependencies in the text, providing more accurate and meaningful insights into the underlying thematic structure.

Nonetheless, NTM may not be the best choice for all use cases. When dealing with smaller datasets or situations where the computational resources are limited, the complexity and resource demands of the NTM algorithm might outweigh its benefits. In such cases, simpler models like LDA can be more efficient, cost-effective, and sufficient. Additionally, if the text data is highly structured or if the topics are already well-defined, the added flexibility of NTM might not offer significant advantages over traditional topic modeling methods. It's essential to consider the nature of the data and the specific requirements of the analysis to determine the most appropriate algorithm for the task at hand.

Anomaly Detection

Anomaly detection is an unsupervised ML approach because it identifies outliers or unusual patterns in data without requiring labeled examples of anomalies. This is particularly useful when labeled data is scarce or when anomalies are rare and unpredictable.

166 Chapter 4 • Model Selection

Amazon SageMaker offers Random Cut Forest (RCF and IP Insights as built-in algorithms for anomaly detection.

RCF is a powerful unsupervised anomaly detection algorithm that works by creating a forest of random decision trees to identify data points that deviate from the norm.

IP Insights learns usage patterns of IPv4 addresses to detect suspicious activities, such as unusual login attempts or resource creation from anomalous IP addresses.

Both algorithms are designed to operate without labeled data, making them ideal for real-time anomaly detection in various applications.

Random Cut Forest

The RCF algorithm works by constructing a forest of random decision trees. Each tree in the forest is built using a random sample of the training data, and anomalies are detected based on the depth at which data points fall within these trees. Data points that significantly alter the structure of the trees, resulting in unusually deep placements, are flagged as anomalies. This method is highly effective for identifying outliers in large datasets, such as detecting fraudulent transactions or network intrusions.

Like other ML algorithms, to implement RCF in Amazon SageMaker, you start by preparing your dataset and uploading it to an Amazon S3 bucket (or Amazon EFS or Amazon FSx for Lustre). Next, you create an RCF estimator in Amazon SageMaker by specifying hyperparameters such as the number of trees and the number of samples per tree. Amazon SageMaker handles the training process, leveraging its scalable infrastructure to efficiently build the RCF. Once the model is trained, you can deploy it to an Amazon SageMaker endpoint for real-time anomaly detection, allowing you to monitor and respond to anomalies as they occur.

Use Cases

RCF is particularly useful for detecting anomalies in large, high-dimensional datasets where traditional methods might struggle. It excels in applications like fraud detection, network security, and predictive maintenance. For example, in financial services, RCF can identify unusual transaction patterns that may indicate fraudulent activity. In network security, it can detect anomalies in traffic that suggest potential intrusions. Similarly, in industrial settings, RCF can monitor sensor data from machinery to detect early signs of failure (e.g., MTBF mean time between failure), helping to prevent costly breakdowns and downtime. Its ability to handle large volumes of data and uncover subtle, unexpected patterns makes it a powerful tool for real-time anomaly detection.

RCF is less effective when anomalies are already well-defined and labeled, as supervised learning algorithms can provide more precise results in such cases. Additionally, RCF might not perform well with very small datasets where the random sampling approach could miss important patterns. When the dataset is small or when labeled anomaly examples are available, other methods like supervised classification algorithms or simpler statistical techniques may be more appropriate. It's essential to consider the nature of the data and the specific requirements of the application to determine if RCF is the right fit.

IP Insights

The IP Insights algorithm is an unsupervised learning method that learns usage patterns of IPv4 addresses by associating them with entities such as user IDs or account numbers. It captures associations between IP addresses and entities, determining how likely it is that an entity would use a particular IP address.

IP Insights uses neural networks to learn latent vector representations for both entities and IP addresses, and it can generate embeddings that can be used in downstream ML tasks. When queried with an (entity, IPv4 address) pair, IP Insights returns a score indicating how anomalous the pattern is, making it useful for detecting suspicious activities like unusual login attempts or resource creation from anomalous IP addresses.

To implement IP Insights in Amazon SageMaker, you start by preparing your data in the form of (entity, IPv4 address) pairs and uploading it to an Amazon S3 bucket (or Amazon EFS or Amazon FSx for Lustre). Next, you create an IP Insights estimator in Amazon SageMaker, specifying hyperparameters such as the number of entity vectors and the size of embedding vectors. Amazon SageMaker handles the training process, and once the model is trained, you can deploy it to an Amazon SageMaker endpoint for real-time predictions or batch processing. This allows you to monitor and respond to anomalies as they occur, enhancing your security measures and operational efficiency.

Use Cases

IP Insights is best suited to detect anomalous behavior in scenarios where tracking the usage patterns of IP addresses is critical. It excels in applications like detecting fraudulent login attempts, unusual access patterns, and identifying compromised accounts. For instance, e-commerce platforms and online services can use IP Insights to monitor and flag suspicious login activities that deviate from normal user behavior enhancing security and preventing unauthorized access. Moreover, it can be utilized to safeguard resources by identifying and mitigating unusual patterns of resource creation or usage from anomalous IP addresses, helping to maintain the integrity and security of systems.

However, IP Insights may not be suitable for all scenarios. It is less effective in environments where IP addresses frequently change or where entities do not have consistent IP usage patterns, as the model relies on learning stable associations between entities and IP addresses. In such cases, traditional rule-based systems or other anomaly detection methods might be more appropriate. Furthermore, IP Insights might not perform well in contexts where labeled data is available and supervised learning approaches could provide more precise anomaly detection.

Textual Analysis Algorithms

Textual analysis refers to the process of using algorithms and ML techniques to understand, interpret, and derive meaningful information from text data. This can involve various tasks such as text classification, sentiment analysis, entity recognition, topic modeling, and summarization. The goal of textual analysis is to transform unstructured text into structured insights that can be used for decision-making, improving user experiences, and ultimately deriving inferences.

You already learned at the beginning of the chapter how Amazon Comprehend addresses textual analysis as a managed AI service. You also learned previously how the LDA and NTM algorithms, which are unsupervised ML techniques, play a significant role in textual analysis, specifically topic modeling. These algorithms automatically identify patterns and group related words into topics within large text datasets without needing labeled data.

In this section, we will focus on more advanced textual analysis techniques provided by Amazon SageMaker's built-in BlazingText and Sequence-to-Sequence algorithms.

BlazingText

BlazingText is an efficient and scalable algorithm provided by Amazon SageMaker for NLP tasks, specifically optimized for text classification and generating word embeddings using the Word2Vec model. BlazingText is designed to process large volumes of text data quickly, making it suitable for real-time applications and large datasets. This algorithm is particularly beneficial for tasks such as semantic similarity, sentiment analysis, and document classification, where understanding the relationships between words is crucial.

An *embedding* in the context of NLP and ML is a dense vector representation of data, typically words, that captures their meanings, syntactic properties, and relationships with other words. These embeddings are learned from data and are used to convert categorical data into continuous numerical data, which can then be processed by ML models. For example, in word embeddings, each word in a vocabulary is mapped to a high-dimensional vector space. Words with similar meanings or usages are placed close to each other in this space, allowing models to understand semantic similarity and relationships between words. Put differently, embeddings translate semantic similarity as perceived by humans to proximity in a vector space. Common embedding techniques include Word2Vec, GloVe, and FastText, which have significantly improved the performance of various NLP tasks such as text classification, sentiment analysis, and machine translation.

BlazingText operates by utilizing two main techniques: Word2Vec and text classification. The Word2Vec model creates dense vector representations of words, also known as *word embeddings*, by analyzing large text corpora and capturing the semantic and syntactic relationships between words. These word embeddings are then used to understand word similarities and analogies. For text classification, BlazingText employs efficient implementations of deep learning models that can categorize text into predefined classes based on the learned word embeddings. The algorithm leverages multithreading and hardware acceleration to speed up the training process, ensuring rapid and scalable performance.

Developing Models with Amazon SageMaker Built-in Algorithms 169

To use BlazingText in Amazon SageMaker, you start by preparing your text data and uploading it to an Amazon S3 bucket (or Amazon EFS or Amazon FSx for Lustre). Next, you create an estimator, specifying BlazingText as the algorithm, and configure the necessary hyperparameters for your training job. Once the estimator is set up, you launch the training job by pointing it to the location of your data in Amazon S3. After training is complete, you can deploy the model to an endpoint for real-time predictions or use it for batch inference. The following code in Python can be used as a reference:

```python
import sagemaker

# Initialize the SageMaker session
sagemaker_session = sagemaker.Session()
role = '<your-iam-role>'

# Get the BlazingText container image
container = sagemaker.image_uris.retrieve(
    'blazingtext', sagemaker_session.boto_region_name
)

# Create the BlazingText estimator
bt_estimator = sagemaker.estimator.Estimator(
    container,
    role,
    instance_count=1,
    instance_type='ml.c4.2xlarge',
    output_path='s3://<your-bucket>/output',
    sagemaker_session=sagemaker_session
)

# Set hyperparameters
bt_estimator.set_hyperparameters(
    mode='supervised',
    epochs=10,
    min_count=2,
    learning_rate=0.05
)

# Launch the training job
bt_estimator.fit({'train': 's3://<your-bucket>/train'})

# Deploy the model
predictor = bt_estimator.deploy(
    initial_instance_count=1,
    instance_type='ml.m4.xlarge'
)
```

Notice how you can specify the mode of operation of the estimator in the statement `bt_estimator.set_hyperparameters()`.

170 Chapter 4 ▪ Model Selection

This method takes a dictionary object as the only parameter, whose keys are defined in the Amazon SageMaker's documentation.

The hyperparameters for the BlazingText algorithm depend on which mode you use: Word2Vec (unsupervised) or Text Classification (supervised). For more information about this method, visit https://docs.aws.amazon.com/sagemaker/latest/dg/blazingtext_hyperparameters.html.

Use Cases

BlazingText is ideal for scenarios that require efficient and scalable text classification or the creation of word embeddings. It's particularly useful for applications involving large volumes of text data, such as processing customer reviews, social media analysis, and document categorization. The Word2Vec model within BlazingText is excellent for tasks like semantic similarity, word clustering, and building feature representations for downstream NLP tasks. Additionally, its speed and scalability make it suitable for real-time applications and large datasets, where quick processing and high performance are essential.

However, BlazingText may not be the best choice for more complex natural language understanding tasks that require context beyond word embeddings, such as deep contextual analysis or nuanced language generation. For tasks that involve understanding the context of sentences or paragraphs, like question answering or advanced conversational AI, FMs such as cohere. embed-english-v3 and cohere.embed-multilingual-v3 might be more appropriate due to their ability to capture contextual information more effectively. These FMs produce embeddings and are available in Amazon Bedrock. BlazingText is also less suitable for tasks that require extensive customization beyond text classification and word embeddings, where more specialized models or custom-built algorithms may offer better results.

Sequence-to-Sequence

The Sequence-to-Sequence (Seq2Seq) algorithm in Amazon SageMaker is a supervised learning algorithm designed for tasks where the input is a sequence of tokens (such as text or audio) and the output is another sequence of tokens. This makes it suitable for applications like machine translation (translating text from one language to another), text summarization (creating a concise summary of a longer text), and speech-to-text (converting spoken language into written text). Seq2Seq leverages advanced neural network architectures, including RNNs and convolutional neural networks (CNNs) with attention mechanisms, to effectively model and generate sequences.

Use Cases

The Seq2Seq algorithm is highly effective for tasks where the input and output are sequences, making it an excellent choice for applications like machine translation, text summarization, and question answering. For instance, in machine translation, Seq2Seq can translate text from one language to another by understanding the context of the input sequence and generating a corresponding sequence in the target language. Similarly, in text summarization, Seq2Seq models can distill long documents into concise summaries by identifying and retaining the most relevant information. Additionally, Seq2Seq is useful in chatbot development for generating coherent and contextually appropriate responses, making it a versatile tool for a wide range of NLP tasks that require sequence transformation or generation.

Nevertheless, Seq2Seq may not be the best fit for tasks that do not primarily involve sequence generation or transformation. For instance, if the goal is to perform simple text classification, such as identifying the sentiment of a tweet (positive or negative), other models like traditional classifiers or even CNNs might be more efficient and less resource-intensive. Similarly, tasks that require the analysis of static features, such as image classification and time-series prediction without the need for sequence output, are better suited for other specialized algorithms. In such cases, Seq2Seq's capabilities may be overkill and may not provide any additional benefits over simpler models designed for those specific tasks.

Image Processing Algorithms

Amazon SageMaker offers a suite of built-in algorithms designed to streamline various image processing tasks, leveraging advanced ML techniques to deliver high accuracy and efficiency. These include algorithms like Image Classification, which categorizes images into predefined classes; Object Detection, which identifies and locates objects within images; Semantic Segmentation, which classifies each pixel in an image to distinguish different objects; and Image Embeddings, which transforms images into fixed-size vectors for use in various downstream tasks. Each of these algorithms provides powerful tools for automating and enhancing image processing workflows, making them essential for developing sophisticated computer vision applications.

Image Classification

Image classification is a fundamental task in computer vision, where the goal is to assign a label or category to an input image. This process involves analyzing the content of the image and categorizing it into one of several predefined classes. For instance, in a dataset of animal photos, an image classification model can label each image as "cat," "dog," "bird," etc. Image classification is widely used in various applications such as medical imaging, autonomous driving, security surveillance, and many others, where accurate identification of objects within images is key.

Image classification is a supervised ML algorithm that leverages deep learning techniques, particularly CNNs, to process and analyze images. CNNs are designed to automatically and adaptively learn spatial hierarchies of features from images. The process involves several layers of convolutional operations, pooling, and fully connected layers, which work together to extract features and make predictions. During training, the model learns to recognize patterns and features within images by minimizing the classification error over a large dataset of labeled images. Once trained, the model can accurately predict the class of new, unseen images based on the features it has learned.

The Image Classification built-in algorithm comes in three "flavors": the first is implemented using the popular TensorFlow ML platform, the second using the PyTorch ML framework, and the third using the MXNet deep learning library.

To use Image Classification in Amazon SageMaker, you start by preparing your labeled dataset and uploading it to an Amazon S3 bucket (or Amazon EFS or Amazon FSx for Lustre). Next, you create an image classification model using an Amazon SageMaker estimator, specifying the algorithm and the necessary hyperparameters and pointing to your dataset. The estimator handles the training process, utilizing Amazon SageMaker's powerful infrastructure to efficiently train your model. Once training is complete, you can deploy the model as an endpoint for real-time predictions or batch processing. Amazon SageMaker also offers tools for model evaluation and monitoring to ensure your image classification model performs optimally. These tools will be discussed in the next chapter.

Use Cases

Image classification algorithms are ideal when you need to categorize images into specific classes based on their content. These algorithms are particularly useful in scenarios where accurate identification and labeling of images are required. For example, in medical imaging, they can be used to classify X-rays or MRI scans to detect diseases. In the retail industry, image classification can help in organizing products by identifying items in images. Moreover, these algorithms are valuable in security and surveillance systems to recognize faces, license plates, or other objects of interest. Overall, they are beneficial in any application where the goal is to automatically and accurately categorize visual data.

Image classification algorithms may not be suitable for tasks that require understanding the context or relationships between multiple objects within an image. For instance, if the goal is to detect and locate various objects in an image (object detection) or segment different regions (semantic segmentation), more specialized algorithms would be needed. Also, tasks that involve analyzing images to extract detailed, structured information, such as OCR, may require different approaches. Furthermore, in cases where the images lack clear distinctions between categories or where the primary objective is not classification but other forms of analysis, image classification algorithms might not be the most effective choice.

Object Detection

With object detection, the goal is not only to identify objects within an image but also to pinpoint their precise locations using bounding boxes. This dual capability of classification and localization is integral to applications such as autonomous driving, security systems intelligence, surveillance, reconnaissance, the retail sector, and many others. As a supervised learning algorithm, object detection requires labeled datasets for training, where each image includes detailed annotations indicating the objects and their locations.

The Object Detection algorithm in Amazon SageMaker employs sophisticated deep learning techniques, with popular architectures such as Single Shot MultiBox Detector (SSD), Region-based Convolutional Neural Networks (R-CNN), and You Only Look Once (YOLO). The SSD approach integrates a CNN pretrained for image classification tasks as its base network. Popular CNN architectures such as VGG-16 and ResNet-50 are often used as the backbone. The algorithm divides the input image into a grid and, for each grid cell, predicts multiple bounding boxes and the class probabilities for the objects within those boxes. During training, the model is fed a dataset of images along with their corresponding bounding box annotations and class labels. It learns to minimize the error between its predictions and the ground truth data, effectively refining its ability to detect and classify objects accurately. Amazon SageMaker's implementation of SSD also includes data augmentation techniques, like flipping, rescaling, and jittering, to enhance the model's robustness and avoid overfitting.

Just like other built-in algorithms, to utilize object detection in Amazon SageMaker, you begin by preparing and labeling your dataset, ensuring that each image contains annotations for the objects of interest. This labeled dataset is then uploaded to an Amazon S3 bucket (or Amazon EFS or Amazon FSx for Lustre). You can create an object detection model using an Amazon SageMaker estimator, specifying the algorithm (MXNet or TensorFlow) and the necessary hyperparameters and pointing to your dataset. The estimator manages the training process, leveraging Amazon SageMaker managed infrastructure to optimize the model based on your data. After training is complete, you can deploy the model as an endpoint for real-time predictions or batch processing.

Use Cases

Object detection is highly effective in scenarios where both the identification and precise localization of objects within images are critical. This makes it ideal for applications such as autonomous driving, where vehicles need to detect and track pedestrians, other cars, and obstacles to navigate safely. It is also valuable in security and surveillance systems, which rely on identifying potential threats or suspicious activities by recognizing and tracking objects like faces, vehicles, and bags in real time. In the retail sector, object detection can help manage inventory by automatically recognizing and counting products on shelves, as well as analyzing customer behavior by tracking their movements within the store. Additionally, it is used in medical imaging to locate and identify abnormalities or diseases in scans, aiding in diagnosis and treatment planning. In military applications, especially in intelligence, surveillance, and reconnaissance (ISR), object detection is crucial for identifying and tracking enemy vehicles, personnel, and equipment from aerial and ground surveillance images, enhancing situational awareness and decision-making on the battlefield.

Object detection may not be your best choice for tasks that require understanding the context or relationships between objects without needing precise localization. For instance, if the goal is simply to classify the overall content of an image, such as determining whether an

174 Chapter 4 ▪ Model Selection

image contains a cat or a dog, image classification algorithms are more appropriate. Similarly, for tasks that involve segmenting images into regions based on object boundaries, such as distinguishing between different tissue types in a medical scan, semantic segmentation algorithms would be more effective. Additionally, if the primary objective is to analyze static features or patterns in nonvisual data, such as text or time-series data, other specialized algorithms should be used. Object detection's strength lies in its ability to not only recognize objects but also provide their exact locations, which may be unnecessary for simpler classification or segmentation tasks.

Semantic Segmentation

Semantic segmentation is a powerful computer vision technique that involves labeling each pixel in an image with a class label from a predefined set of classes. Unlike object detection, which identifies objects and their bounding boxes, and image classification that analyzes only whole images, classifying them into one of multiple output categories, semantic segmentation provides a detailed understanding of the image by labeling every pixel according to its category. This makes it invaluable for applications that require precise localization and differentiation of objects within an image.

Semantic segmentation algorithms typically use deep learning models, particularly CNNs with specialized architectures like fully convolutional networks (FCNs), pyramid scene parsing (PSP), and DeepLabV3. These models start with a pretrained classification network, which is modified to output segmentation maps instead of class probabilities. The network processes the input image through multiple convolutional layers to extract features at various levels of abstraction. During training, the model learns to map these features to pixel-level labels using a loss function that measures the difference between predicted and true labels. Techniques like upsampling and skip connections are often employed to improve the spatial resolution of the output, ensuring that the segmentation map accurately represents the fine details and boundaries of objects within the image.

To use semantic segmentation in Amazon SageMaker, you first need to prepare and label your dataset, ensuring that each image has a corresponding segmentation mask that labels each pixel. This labeled dataset is then uploaded to an Amazon S3 bucket (or Amazon EFS, or Amazon FSx for Lustre). You can create a semantic segmentation model using an Amazon SageMaker estimator, specifying the algorithm (such as U-Net or DeepLab) and the necessary hyperparameters and pointing to your dataset. The estimator handles the training process, leveraging Amazon SageMaker's robust infrastructure to optimize the model based on your data. Once training is complete, you can deploy the model as an endpoint for real-time predictions or batch processing.

Use Cases

Semantic segmentation is best utilized in scenarios where a detailed understanding of the image is required, down to the pixel level. This makes it ideal for applications in medical imaging, such as segmenting different types of tissues, organs, or tumors in MRI or CT scans, which is crucial for accurate diagnosis and treatment planning. In autonomous driving, semantic segmentation is used to understand the environment by identifying and differentiating between various objects like roads, sidewalks, vehicles, and pedestrians. This detailed segmentation helps in safe navigation and decision-making. Additionally, in agricultural monitoring, semantic segmentation can be used to differentiate between crops and weeds, assess plant health, and monitor growth stages, aiding in efficient farming practices. This technique is also valuable in satellite imagery, where detailed maps are created to identify different land cover types, such as forests, urban areas, and water bodies for environmental monitoring and urban planning.

Semantic segmentation is not recommended for tasks that do not require pixel-level precision or where the primary objective is to simply classify an entire image or detect objects with bounding boxes. For example, if the goal is to categorize images into broad classes, such as identifying whether an image contains a cat or a dog, image classification algorithms are more appropriate. Similarly, for applications that need to locate and classify objects within an image, such as detecting faces or vehicles, object detection algorithms are better suited, as they provide bounding boxes around detected objects but do not require detailed pixel-level annotations. Additionally, semantic segmentation may be less effective in cases where the computational cost and complexity are prohibitive, or where there is limited labeled data available for training, as it requires a significant number of annotated images to achieve high accuracy.

Criteria for Model Selection

Choosing the right model for your ML problem involves considering several critical factors. This section outlines key criteria that will guide you in selecting the best model for your specific use case and includes examples of algorithms that fit each criterion.

Accuracy The primary goal of any ML model is to achieve high accuracy for the given task. Algorithms like XGBoost and SVMs are known for their high accuracy in various applications, including classification and regression.

Interpretability Interpretability is equally as important as accuracy, especially in domains where understanding the decision-making process is essential. Linear learner and logistic regression models are highly interpretable, providing clear insights into how predictions are made. Decision trees are also interpretable, as they visually map the decision process. These models balance accuracy with interpretability, ensuring that their decisions can be easily understood and trusted by stakeholders.

Scalability The ability of a model to handle increasing data volumes and complexity is critical for large-scale applications. Algorithms like Linear Learner and K-means clustering scale efficiently and can manage large datasets. Random Cut Forest is also scalable, making it suitable for anomaly detection in big data scenarios.

Latency and speed For real-time applications, the speed at which a model can provide predictions is crucial. Algorithms such as random forest offer quick inference times, making them ideal for scenarios where timely decisions are critical, like fraud detection and recommendation systems.

176   Chapter 4 ▪ Model Selection

Resource requirements   The computational resources required for training and inference can impact the feasibility of using certain models. Linear learners, k-NN, and PCA generally require fewer resources compared to deep neural networks. Assessing the resource requirements ensures that the models align with your available infrastructure and budget.

Data availability and quality   The availability and quality of data significantly influence model performance. Algorithms like LDA and BlazingText perform well with large textual datasets, and K-Means can work effectively with smaller datasets for clustering tasks. Ensuring high-quality data for training is critical for developing accurate and reliable models.

Regulatory and ethical considerations   In many industries, models must comply with regulatory requirements and ethical standards. Logistic regression and decision trees are often favored in regulated industries due to their transparency and ease of explanation. Ethical considerations are particularly important in fields like healthcare and finance, where the implications of model predictions can have significant consequences.

Cost   The cost of implementing and maintaining different models can vary widely. Models like linear learner and random forest are generally cost-effective, whereas deep learning models like CNNs may incur higher costs due to their computational demands. Considering the cost implications, including cloud resources and data labeling, is essential for long-term projects.

There is often a trade-off among these factors—for example, accuracy and interpretability, where complex models that achieve high accuracy may be difficult to understand, whereas simpler models with better interpretability may have lower accuracy. Your job as an AWS ML engineer is to balance these trade-offs to meet the specific needs and constraints of your ML problem, ensuring that the chosen model aligns with the business objectives and operational requirements. This involves continuously evaluating and adjusting the model based on new data and feedback to achieve the best possible performance while maintaining transparency and trust.

By considering these criteria and understanding which algorithms align with them, you'll be well-equipped to select the most appropriate model for your ML problem. This comprehensive approach ensures that your models are not only high-performing but also interpretable, scalable, and aligned with your specific requirements.

Summary

In this chapter, we explored various AWS AI services and Amazon SageMaker's built-in algorithms that can be leveraged for different ML use cases.

AWS AI services offer a range of prebuilt and pretrained ML models designed to simplify and accelerate the deployment of AI in your applications. These services include Amazon Rekognition for image and video analysis, Amazon Comprehend for NLP, Amazon Polly for text-to-speech conversion, Amazon Lex for building conversational interfaces, Amazon

Textract for extracting text and data from documents, Amazon Transcribe for converting speech to text, Amazon Translate for real-time translation, and Amazon Personalize for creating personalized user experiences. Amazon Bedrock, with the new Nova FMs, also provides robust capabilities for generative AI tasks, enhancing the flexibility and power of your AI applications. These AI services are fully managed, requiring minimal ML expertise, and are ideal for developers looking to integrate AI capabilities quickly into their applications.

For higher flexibility and more specialized ML tasks, Amazon SageMaker offers a wide range of built-in algorithms and support for popular frameworks like TensorFlow, PyTorch, and MXNet, empowering you to tailor your ML models to meet specific requirements and optimized performance.

We explored Amazon SageMaker's supervised ML algorithms, which are designed for tasks that use labeled data for training. Examples included Linear Learner for regression and classification, XGBoost for gradient boosting on decision trees, k-NN for classification and regression, and Factorization Machines for recommendation systems and large-scale classification tasks. These models learn from the input-output pairs in the training data to make predictions on new, unseen data.

We then learned built-in Amazon SageMaker's unsupervised ML algorithms, which are designed to uncover hidden patterns and structures within unlabeled data. These algorithms include K-Means for clustering similar data points into distinct groups, PCA for dimensionality reduction, LDA and NTM for topic modeling, and RCF and IP Insights for anomaly detection.

Later in the chapter, more advanced algorithms leveraging deep neural networks for textual analysis and image processing were introduced. These included built-in Amazon SageMaker algorithms like BlazingText for efficient word embeddings and text classification, Seq2Seq for sequence-to-sequence tasks such as machine translation and text summarization, Image Classification for categorizing images into predefined classes, Object Detection for identifying and locating multiple objects within an image, and Semantic Segmentation for pixel-level classification of image content. These deep learning models are designed to handle complex tasks with high accuracy, enabling robust AI solutions across various domains such as NLP, computer vision, and autonomous systems.

The chapter concluded with a curated list of criteria you need to consider in the selection of your model, including accuracy, interpretability, scalability, latency, resource requirements, data availability, regulatory, and cost.

Exam Essentials

Know the AWS AI services for vision. AWS offers two AI services tailored for vision-related tasks. Amazon Rekognition enables image and video analysis, allowing users to detect objects, faces, landmarks and text, as well as recognize celebrities and analyze

178 Chapter 4 ▪ Model Selection

sentiments. For document processing, Amazon Textract extracts text, tables, and other data from scanned documents, making it easier to digitize and manage document workflows efficiently.

Know the AWS AI services for speech and chatbots. AWS provides two AI services for speech-related tasks. Amazon Polly delivers text-to-speech capabilities, transforming written content into natural-sounding speech in multiple languages. Amazon Transcribe offers automatic speech recognition (ASR), converting audio recordings into accurate text transcriptions. Amazon Lex enables the creation of conversational interfaces, combining ASR and natural language understanding (NLU) to power chatbots and voice assistants.

Know the AWS AI services for language. AWS offers two AI services for language processing tasks. Amazon Comprehend enables natural language processing (NLP) by extracting insights from text, such as sentiment analysis, entity recognition, and key phrase extraction. Amazon Translate provides real-time and batch translation services, allowing for seamless multilingual communication.

Know the AWS AI services for generative AI. AWS offers Amazon Bedrock, with a large selection of foundation models (FMs) including the newly released Nova FMs. Amazon Bedrock provides a robust platform for creating and deploying generative AI applications, allowing developers to build sophisticated solutions like text generation, image synthesis, embeddings, and more. These services empower users to leverage state-of-the-art generative AI models with ease, enabling innovative and creative applications across various domains.

Know the difference between classification and regression algorithms. Classification algorithms are used to categorize data into distinct classes or labels, such as determining whether an email is spam. Regression algorithms, on the other hand, predict continuous numerical values, such as forecasting stock prices or estimating house values based on various features.

Know the linear learner algorithms provided by Amazon SageMaker. Amazon SageMaker provides linear learner algorithms for both classification and regression tasks. These include Linear Regression, Logistic Regression, and Support Vector Machines. These algorithms are highly interpretable, making them ideal for applications where understanding the contribution of each feature to the predictions is critical.

Know the k-NN algorithm and when to use it. The k-nearest neighbors algorithm is a simple yet powerful supervised ML algorithm for classification and regression tasks, where predictions are made based on the closest data points in the feature space. It is an Amazon SageMaker built-in algorithm, particularly useful when the decision boundary is complex and nonlinear, and when interpretability is important, as the reasoning behind each prediction is clear by examining the nearest neighbors. k-NN is best used with smaller datasets, due to its computational complexity, and in cases where you have a clear understanding of the data's structure and relationships.

Know the decision tree supervised algorithms provided by Amazon SageMaker and when to use them. Amazon SageMaker provides powerful decision-tree-based supervised algorithms like Random Forest and XGBoost. Random Forest is valuable for its ability to reduce overfitting and improve accuracy by creating an ensemble of decision trees and averaging their predictions, making it suitable for tasks that involve a large number of input features. XGBoost is known for its computational efficiency and performance, particularly with large datasets and complex models, and is often used for classification and regression tasks that require high predictive accuracy and speed.

Know the clustering algorithms provided by Amazon SageMaker. Amazon SageMaker provides the unsupervised K-Means algorithm for clustering, which is not be confused with the supervised k-NN algorithm intended for classification and regression tasks.

Know the dimensionality reduction algorithms provided by Amazon SageMaker. Amazon SageMaker provides the unsupervised Principal Component Analysis algorithm for dimensionality reduction, which is useful for reducing the number of features in a dataset while retaining as much variability as possible.

Know the topic modeling algorithms provided by Amazon SageMaker. Amazon SageMaker provides the unsupervised Latent Dirichlet Allocation and Neural Topic Model algorithms for topic modeling use cases, enabling users to discover hidden topics in large collections of textual data without the need for labeled data.

Know the anomaly detection algorithms provided by Amazon SageMaker. Amazon SageMaker provides the unsupervised Random Cut Forest and IP Insights algorithms for anomaly detection use cases, which are particularly useful for identifying unusual patterns or behaviors in data, such as detecting fraudulent activities or network intrusions.

Know the textual analysis algorithms provided by Amazon SageMaker. Amazon SageMaker provides the BlazingText and Sequence-to-Sequence algorithms for textual analysis use cases, enabling efficient handling of large-scale textual data and supporting various natural language processing tasks such as text classification, translation, and summarization.

Know the image processing algorithms provided by Amazon SageMaker. Amazon SageMaker provides the Image Classification, Object Detection, and Semantic Segmentation algorithms for image processing use cases, enabling developers to build, train, and deploy machine learning models that can analyze and understand visual data, such as recognizing objects, classifying images into categories, and segmenting images at the pixel level for detailed analysis.

Review Questions

1. Which AWS AI service would you use to analyze large volumes of unstructured text and extract insights such as entity recognition and sentiment analysis?
   A. Amazon Textract
   B. Amazon Lex
   C. Amazon Comprehend
   D. Amazon Polly

2. Which AWS AI service is specifically designed for generative AI applications, providing a robust platform for creating text, images, and other creative outputs?
   A. Amazon Rekognition
   B. Amazon Bedrock
   C. Amazon Translate
   D. Amazon Transcribe

3. For detecting objects and people in real-time video feeds, which AWS AI service would be most appropriate?
   A. Amazon Textract
   B. Amazon Lex
   C. Amazon Rekognition
   D. Amazon Comprehend

4. Which AWS service provides a highly efficient and scalable solution for dimensionality reduction in large datasets?
   A. Amazon Translate
   B. Amazon Polly
   C. Principal Component Analysis (PCA) on Amazon SageMaker
   D. K-Means on Amazon SageMaker

5. Which Amazon SageMaker algorithm is particularly useful for classification and regression tasks due to its efficiency and high performance?
   A. Random Forest
   B. XGBoost
   C. k-Nearest Neighbors
   D. Principal Component Analysis

Review Questions **181**

6. Which supervised ML algorithm provided by Amazon SageMaker is ideal for reducing overfitting by averaging multiple decision trees?

    A. Linear Learner

    B. BlazingText

    C. Random Forest

    D. Latent Dirichlet Allocation

7. For which type of tasks is Amazon SageMaker's Linear Learner algorithm particularly well-suited?

    A. Text classification

    B. Clustering

    C. Classification and regression

    D. Anomaly detection

8. Which algorithm would you use in Amazon SageMaker if you need highly interpretable results in a linear relationship model?

    A. Random Cut Forest

    B. Linear Learner

    C. Neural Topic Model

    D. DeepAR

9. Which Amazon SageMaker supervised ML algorithm is specifically designed for time series forecasting?

    A. IP Insights

    B. DeepAR

    C. Neural Topic Model

    D. Sequence-to-Sequence

10. Which supervised ML algorithm in Amazon SageMaker is known for boosting weak learners to create a strong predictive model?

    A. K-Means

    B. Latent Dirichlet Allocation

    C. XGBoost

    D. Random Cut Forest

11. For your ML problem you need an unsupervised, highly interpretable algorithm in Amazon SageMaker to reduce data dimensionality while preserving maximum variance. Which built-in algorithm would you use?

    A. K-Means

    B. Random Cut Forest

    C. Principal Component Analysis

    D. Neural Topic Model

Chapter 4 · Model Selection

12. For detecting rare events and anomalies with high accuracy in data streams, which unsupervised Amazon SageMaker algorithm would you choose?

    A. Latent Dirichlet Allocation

    B. IP Insights

    C. Random Cut Forest

    D. Factorization Machines

13. When you need to discover hidden topics in large text datasets with high interpretability and accuracy, which Amazon SageMaker algorithm would you select?

    A. K-Means

    B. Latent Dirichlet Allocation

    C. Principal Component Analysis

    D. Random Cut Forest

14. For accurately clustering large datasets into predefined groups based on feature similarity, which highly interpretable Amazon SageMaker algorithm would you use?

    A. Random Cut Forest

    B. Principal Component Analysis

    C. K-Means

    D. Neural Topic Model

15. Which Amazon SageMaker algorithm is known for its high accuracy and performance in large-scale text classification tasks, while also being cost-effective?

    A. BlazingText

    B. Sequence-to-Sequence

    C. Latent Dirichlet Allocation

    D. IP Insights

16. Identify the Amazon SageMaker algorithm that offers high performance and accuracy for text translation tasks, while also being cost-effective and interpretable.

    A. Random Cut Forest

    B. Sequence-to-Sequence

    C. BlazingText

    D. Principal Component Analysis

17. For high-accuracy identification and localization of multiple objects within an image, which Amazon SageMaker algorithm excels in performance and cost-efficiency?

    A. Image Classification

    B. Object Detection

    C. Semantic Segmentation

    D. Factorization Machines

18. Which Amazon SageMaker algorithm provides high accuracy and cost-effectiveness for classifying images into predefined categories, ensuring interpretability and performance?

    A. Latent Dirichlet Allocation

    B. Image Classification

    C. Object Detection

    D. IP Insights

19. Identify the Amazon SageMaker algorithm that allows for detailed pixel-level analysis of images, offering high accuracy and interpretability while being performance-efficient.

    A. Random Cut Forest

    B. Image Classification

    C. Semantic Segmentation

    D. BlazingText

20. Which Amazon SageMaker algorithm utilizes word embeddings for natural language processing tasks, balancing accuracy, cost-effectiveness, interpretability, and performance?

    A. Random Cut Forest

    B. Principal Component Analysis

    C. Latent Dirichlet Allocation

    D. BlazingText

Chapter 5

Model Training and Evaluation

THE AWS CERTIFIED MACHINE LEARNING (ML) ENGINEER ASSOCIATE EXAM OBJECTIVES COVERED IN THIS CHAPTER MAY INCLUDE, BUT ARE NOT LIMITED TO, THE FOLLOWING:

✔ **Domain 2: ML Model Development**
  - 2.2 Train and refine models
  - 2.3 Analyze model performance

Chapter 5 ▪ Model Training and Evaluation

In the machine learning (ML) lifecycle, the training phase is a critical step where the model learns from data to make accurate predictions. This phase involves feeding the model with a large dataset, allowing it to recognize patterns and relationships within the data. During this process, the model adjusts its parameters to minimize errors and improve its predictive accuracy. The success of this phase is fundamental to the overall performance of the model, as it sets the foundation for its ability to generalize and perform well on unseen data. Throughout this chapter, we will delve into the various techniques and best practices for training and evaluating ML models with Amazon SageMaker, ensuring that they are robust and effective.

Hyperparameter tuning (also known as *hyperparameter optimization*) is an essential aspect of optimizing the performance of a ML model. Unlike the parameters learned during training, hyperparameters are preset values that define the model's structure and learning process. These include, for example, learning rate, number of layers in a neural network, batch size, and regularization terms. Fine-tuning these hyperparameters can significantly impact the model's ability to generalize and avoid issues like overfitting or underfitting. Amazon SageMaker provides robust solutions for hyperparameter optimization, allowing ML engineers and data scientists to efficiently search for the best hyperparameter configurations. This chapter will explore various hyperparameter tuning techniques and demonstrate how to implement them using Amazon SageMaker to achieve optimal model performance.

Evaluating a model's performance is key to understanding its effectiveness and reliability. This involves using various metrics and evaluation methods to assess how well the model performs on a validation or test dataset. Metrics such as accuracy, precision, recall, F1 score, and area under curve-receiver operating characteristic (AUC-ROC) are commonly used for classification tasks, whereas metrics like mean squared error (MSE), mean absolute error (MAE), and R-squared are used for regression tasks. Amazon SageMaker offers a comprehensive suite of tools for model evaluation, enabling users to conduct thorough cross-validation, monitor performance, and fine-tune the model based on the insights gained. Throughout this chapter, we will cover different evaluation techniques and metrics, providing a detailed guide on how to assess and improve your model's performance using Amazon SageMaker.

This chapter will conclude with a dedicated section on evaluating Amazon Bedrock foundation models. We will explore how to assess pretrained foundation models, ensuring they meet the specific requirements of your use cases. By the end of this chapter, you will have a comprehensive understanding of the entire model training and evaluation processes, equipped with the knowledge to apply best practices and techniques in your ML projects.

Training

As illustrated in Figure 5.1, the training phase of the ML lifecycle happens after the selection of an algorithm that best suits your specific business problem at hand, taking into consideration factors such as data characteristics and the desired outcome.

During this phase, supervised ML algorithms are provided with labeled datasets, which consist of input features and their corresponding output labels. This allows the model to learn the relationship between the inputs and outputs by iteratively adjusting its parameters to minimize the prediction error. Conversely, unsupervised ML algorithms operate on

FIGURE 5.1 The model training phase in the machine learning lifecycle.

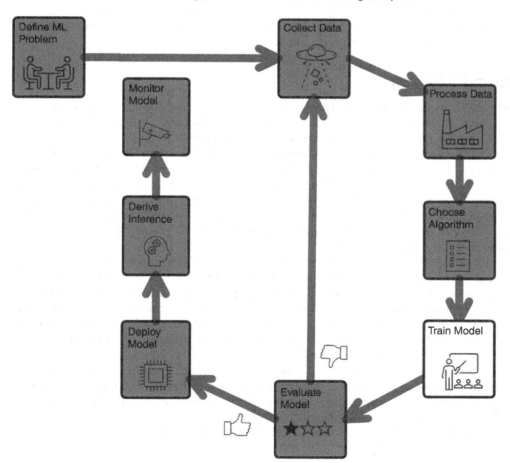

188 Chapter 5 ▪ Model Training and Evaluation

unlabeled datasets, aiming to uncover underlying patterns, clusters, or associations within the data without predefined labels.

The training process involves several steps, including data preprocessing, model initialization, and iterative parameter updates through optimization techniques. The goal is to find the optimal set of parameters that enable the model to generalize well to new, unseen data. This phase is crucial as it directly influences the model's ability to make accurate predictions or reveal meaningful insights from the data.

There are different approaches to model training, including local training, remote training, and distributed training. Local training involves running the training process on a local machine, providing the advantage of immediate feedback and easy debugging. Remote training utilizes cloud services, such as Amazon SageMaker, to leverage more powerful resources without being limited by local hardware constraints. Distributed training goes a step further by distributing the training workload across multiple machines or nodes, significantly speeding up the process and handling larger datasets more efficiently. Each approach has its own benefits and trade-offs, allowing ML engineers to choose the best method based on their specific needs and resources available.

Local Training

The development of an ML model is an iterative process, requiring continuous refinement and experimentation to achieve optimal results. Often, datasets are too large to fit into a host machine's memory, which significantly impacts experimentation.

This is where local training comes into play, allowing ML engineers to test the chosen algorithm with a subset of the data, controlling the training environment and facilitating rapid testing and adjustment of algorithms, feature combinations, and hyperparameters. This approach ensures a more efficient and effective model development cycle, enabling quick iteration and fine-tuning to enhance the model's predictive capabilities. For example, in the previous chapter, we locally trained various algorithms on the Iris dataset using the `sklearn` module of the Scikit-Learn library.

Although Amazon SageMaker provides a Jupyter Notebook interface for model development, we opted to use Python scripts instead. This choice was driven by the limitations of notebooks, which can scale up but not out, meaning they are not suitable for distributed training across multiple machines. Additionally, notebooks are challenging to version-control effectively compared to Python scripts, which can be easily managed and maintained using version control systems like Git. This ensures a more robust and scalable development process, facilitating collaboration and reproducibility.

Local training also offers the advantage of being able to package Python programs and their dependencies in containers. This approach ensures that the development environment is consistent across different machines and stages of the project, eliminating issues related to dependency management. By using containers, ML engineers can create a portable and reproducible setup, making it easier to share and deploy models in various environments.

Docker is the most commonly used container runtime for consuming ML algorithm container images in Amazon SageMaker, but it's not the only option. Because Amazon SageMaker leverages Amazon ECR to retrieve container images, you can use any container runtime that produces Open Container Initiative (OCI)–compliant images, as Amazon ECR supports the OCI standard. This standard allows for flexibility in choosing a container runtime like Containerd or CRI-O, although Docker is the most widely adopted and recommended approach. For more information, visit https://aws.amazon.com/about-aws/whats-new/2024/06/amazon-ecr-oci-image-distribution-version-1-1.

Moreover, containers streamline the process of scaling and deploying ML models. Once the model is trained locally and the dependencies are packaged in a container, it can be easily deployed and scaled to different environments, such as Amazon Elastic Kubernetes Service (EKS). This ensures that the model runs consistently regardless of the underlying infrastructure, enhancing the reliability and scalability of ML solutions. Local training, combined with containers, provides a powerful workflow for developing, testing, and deploying ML models efficiently.

Remote Training

After training your ML model locally on a small dataset for development and testing, the next step is to launch a training job on the entire dataset. This is where remote training becomes essential, as it allows you to leverage more powerful computational resources and handle larger datasets efficiently. Remote training ensures that your model is trained on the full dataset, enabling it to learn more comprehensive patterns and make better predictions.

Amazon SageMaker provides a convenient and powerful solution for remote training. Using the Amazon SageMaker Python SDK, you can easily launch a remote training job with just a few lines of code. The SDK simplifies the process of setting up and managing training jobs, making it easier for developers to focus on their models rather than the underlying infrastructure. With Amazon SageMaker, you can specify the type and number of instances you want to use, ensuring that your training job has the necessary resources to complete efficiently.

As a fully managed service, Amazon SageMaker takes care of provisioning, scaling, and managing the training instances for you. This eliminates the need to manually set up and maintain the infrastructure, saving time and reducing complexity. Amazon SageMaker handles everything from data loading and preprocessing to model training and evaluation, providing a seamless and scalable solution for ML workflows.

190 Chapter 5 ▪ Model Training and Evaluation

Here's an example of how to launch a remote training job using Amazon SageMaker's Python SDK. In this example, we create an `estimator` instance and use the `fit` method to start the training job:

```
import sagemaker
from sagemaker.estimator import Estimator

# Define the IAM role with necessary permissions
role = 'arn:aws:iam::your-account-id:role/SageMakerRole'

# Create the estimator instance
estimator = Estimator(
    image_uri='your-docker-image-uri',
    role=role,
    instance_count=1,
    instance_type='ml.m5.large',
    volume_size=50,   # Size in GB
    max_run=3600,     # Maximum training time in seconds
    hyperparameters={
        'epochs': 10,
        'batch_size': 32,
        'learning_rate': 0.001,
    }
)

# Launch the training job
estimator.fit({'train': 's3://your-bucket/train-data', 'validation':
's3://your-bucket/validation-data'})
```

In this example, we define the training job's configuration, including the Docker image URI, IAM role, instance type, and hyperparameters, which we'll cover in detail in the next sections. The `fit` method is then used to start the training job, pointing to the S3 buckets where the training and validation data are stored. With Amazon SageMaker, you can seamlessly transition from local development to scalable and reliable remote training, ensuring that your models are trained on the full dataset with the resources they need.

Distributed Training

Distributed training is essential for scaling ML models to handle large datasets and complex architectures efficiently. By distributing the training process across multiple machines, we can significantly reduce the time required to train models. There are two primary approaches to distributed training: *data parallel training* and *model parallel training*. Both methods aim to utilize computational resources more effectively, but they differ in how they distribute the workload.

Data parallel training involves splitting the dataset into smaller subsets, called *mini-batches*, and distributing these subsets across multiple devices. Each device processes its mini-batch independently, and the gradients calculated during the training are then aggregated and used to update the model parameters. This approach allows for parallel processing of data, leading to faster iterations. In the context of ML, an *iteration* refers to the process of updating the model parameters using one mini-batch, and an *epoch* represents a complete pass through the entire dataset. By leveraging data parallelism, we can achieve significant speed-ups in training time, especially for large datasets.

Model parallel training, on the other hand, divides the model itself across multiple devices. Each device is responsible for computing a specific part of the model's operations. This approach is particularly useful for very large models that cannot fit into the memory of a single device. By splitting the model, we can distribute the computational load and memory requirements, allowing us to train models that would otherwise be infeasible on a single device. Although model parallelism can be more complex to implement compared to data parallelism, it offers a solution for training cutting-edge models with millions or even billions of parameters.

In practice, combining data and model parallelism can yield even greater benefits. For instance, a large model can be split across multiple devices using model parallelism, and each segment can further utilize data parallelism to process mini-batches concurrently. This hybrid approach maximizes resource utilization and enables efficient training of state-of-the-art models on large-scale datasets. Distributed training, with its ability to handle both extensive data and complex models, is a cornerstone of modern ML, driving advancements in fields such as natural language processing, computer vision, and beyond.

Deciding whether to use data parallel training or model parallel training depends on various factors:

- If the dataset is large but the model fits comfortably in the memory of a single machine, data parallel training is the preferred choice. This allows for efficient processing of mini-batches across multiple machines.

- If the model is very large and cannot fit into the memory of a single machine (e.g., GPT-3 developed by OpenAI, which has 175 billion parameters), model parallel training is more suitable. This divides the model's operations across multiple machines, distributing the computational load.

- In cases where both the dataset is large and the model is complex, a combination of data and model parallel training can be employed. This hybrid approach ensures optimal utilization of resources and efficient training.

By considering the size of the dataset, the complexity of the model, and the available computational resources, your job as ML engineer is to choose the most appropriate distributed training method to achieve efficient and scalable model training.

Monitoring Training Jobs

As a fully managed service, Amazon SageMaker provides robust tools for monitoring and visualizing training metrics in real time. With its integration with Amazon CloudWatch, you can track various metrics such as training loss, accuracy, and resource utilization. These metrics can help you diagnose issues, fine-tune hyperparameters, and ensure that the model is learning effectively.

To start monitoring a training job, you can specify the metrics you want to track using the AWS Management Console or the Amazon SageMaker Python SDK. Once the training job begins, Amazon SageMaker automatically streams the specified metrics to Amazon CloudWatch, where you can visualize them as time-series curves. This real-time monitoring allows you to make informed decisions during the training process, such as adjusting hyperparameters or stopping a job if it's not performing as expected. The ability to access these metrics programmatically also enables automated workflows and integration with other monitoring tools.

Amazon EventBridge is another powerful service that can help you proactively respond to failed training jobs. By integrating Amazon EventBridge with your training workflows, you can set up rules and alarms to detect when a training job fails. For example, you can config-ure Amazon EventBridge to monitor CloudWatch metrics for failed training jobs and trigger automated responses, such as sending notifications to your team, restarting the training job, or even initiating a rollback to a previous model version. Amazon EventBridge also supports the use of dead-letter queues (DLQs) to capture failed events and retries. This ensures that you have a record of any issues and can take appropriate actions to address them.

In addition to real-time monitoring, Amazon SageMaker provides detailed logs and metrics after the training job completes. You can view graphs of the metrics in Amazon CloudWatch and retrieve the final metric values by calling the `DescribeTrainingJob` operation. This post-training analysis helps evaluate the model's performance and identify areas for improvement. By leveraging these monitoring tools, you can ensure that your training jobs are running efficiently and producing high-quality models.

Overall, monitoring training jobs in AWS with Amazon SageMaker, Amazon CloudWatch, and Amazon EventBridge provides a comprehensive solution for tracking and optimizing ML workflows. Whether you're optimizing hyperparameters, diagnosing issues, or evaluat-ing model performance, these tools offer the visibility and control needed to achieve success-ful training outcomes.

Debugging Training Jobs

Debugging training jobs in ML can be challenging due to the complexity and scale of modern models and datasets. Issues can arise at various stages, from data preprocessing to model convergence. Common challenges include identifying data quality problems, diagnos-ing nonconverging models, and managing resource bottlenecks. The large volume of data and the intricacy of the models add layers of difficulty, making it hard to pinpoint the root cause of issues. Additionally, the iterative nature of training, where models undergo numer-ous epochs and iterations, can hide the source of problems, requiring detailed logs and metrics to trace back the issue.

Amazon SageMaker Debugger offers powerful debugging and profiling functions that significantly enhance the training and troubleshooting process for ML models. One of the key features of Amazon SageMaker Debugger is its ability to automatically capture and save intermediate tensors and metrics during the training process. This allows ML engineers to inspect the internal states of the model at various points, making it easier to identify and diagnose issues such as vanishing gradients and improper data preprocessing. By providing detailed insights into the training dynamics, Amazon SageMaker Debugger helps ensure that models are trained effectively and efficiently.

Profiling is another crucial function provided by Amazon SageMaker Debugger. It enables ML engineers and operation teams to monitor and analyze the performance of their training jobs by capturing detailed system resource utilization metrics, such as CPU, GPU, memory, and network usage. With these profiling capabilities, users can identify performance bottlenecks and optimize their training jobs for better efficiency. Amazon SageMaker Debugger offers built-in rules to automatically detect common performance issues, and it provides visualizations and reports to help users understand and address these issues promptly. This proactive approach to profiling ensures that training resources are used optimally, reducing costs and improving training times.

Additionally, Amazon SageMaker Debugger supports the open-source library smdebug, which extends the debugging and profiling capabilities to custom and complex training workflows. This library allows users to define custom rules and save specific tensors, metrics, and other data during training. It integrates seamlessly with popular deep learning frameworks such as TensorFlow, PyTorch, and MXNet, providing a flexible and extensible solution for monitoring and debugging training jobs. By leveraging smdebug, ML engineers can create tailored debugging and profiling workflows that suit their unique requirements, further enhancing the effectiveness of their ML projects.

Hyperparameter Tuning

Model evaluation is a pivotal phase in the ML lifecycle. As illustrated in Figure 5.2, this phase takes place after the model has been trained using an algorithm that best fits your use case.

This phase is focused on evaluating the performance of your model to ensure it meets the success criteria stated in your ML problem. But *how do you evaluate the performance of your model?* The evaluation process involves calculating a range of metrics that are specifically selected to assess the model's predictive performance. These metrics, such as accuracy, precision, recall, and F1 score, provide insights into how well the model is performing on different aspects of the data. Accuracy measures the overall correctness of the model's predictions, whereas precision and recall provide a deeper understanding of the model's effectiveness in handling imbalanced datasets. The F1 score, which combines precision and recall, offers a balanced assessment of the model's performance, particularly in scenarios where class distribution is uneven.

Hyperparameter tuning plays a key role in this stage by optimizing these metrics to ensure the model can make accurate and reliable predictions. Hyperparameters are external settings

194 Chapter 5 ■ Model Training and Evaluation

FIGURE 5.2 The model evaluation phase in the machine learning lifecycle.

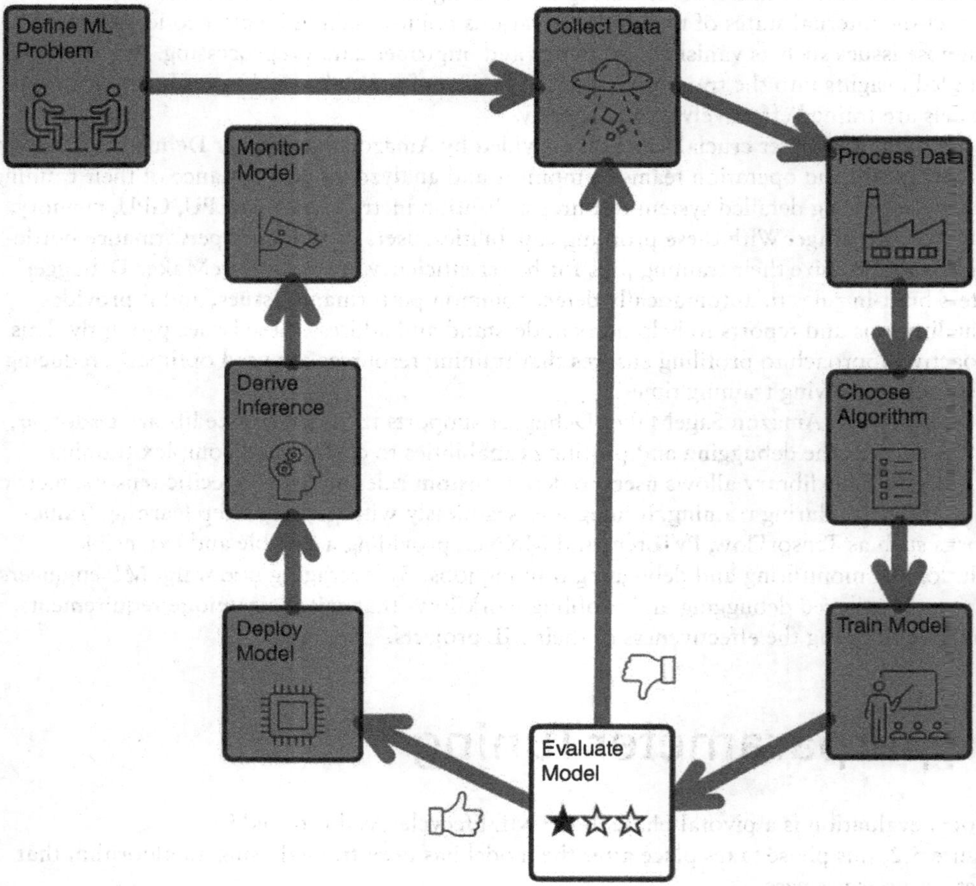

that control the behavior of the learning algorithm, such as the learning rate, batch size, and number of epochs. Unlike model parameters, which are learned and adjusted during training, hyperparameters need to be set *before the training begins*. By carefully tuning these hyperparameters, you can significantly improve the model's performance and its ability to generalize to new, unseen data. This process involves running multiple training jobs with different hyperparameter configurations and selecting the one that yields the best results based on the evaluation metrics.

Amazon SageMaker provides powerful tools to simplify hyperparameter tuning. With Amazon SageMaker, you can conduct this process manually or automatically using Amazon SageMaker AI Automatic Model Tuning (AMT). Manual tuning involves selecting different hyperparameter values, running multiple training jobs, and evaluating their performance to

Hyperparameter Tuning 195

identify the best combination. This approach can be time-consuming and resource-intensive. Alternatively, Amazon SageMaker AI AMT leverages optimization algorithms to automatically search for the best hyperparameters. It evaluates multiple configurations in parallel, significantly reducing the time and effort required for tuning. This automated approach ensures that the model achieves optimal performance with minimal manual intervention, allowing you to focus on other critical aspects of your ML project.

By leveraging these evaluation metrics and optimizing hyperparameters, you can ensure that your model meets the desired performance criteria and is well-equipped to make accurate predictions. This iterative process of evaluation and tuning is essential for developing robust and effective ML models that can reliably address the specific challenges of your use case. Whether you are using manual or automated methods, the goal remains the same: to refine your model until it meets the highest standards of accuracy and reliability.

Let's start this section by highlighting the difference between model parameters and hyperparameters and by learning what these are for the most common algorithms.

Model Parameters and Hyperparameters

In ML, the term *learning* means that the model gains knowledge (i.e., learns) from input data. But *what knowledge does the model learn?* For instance, in regression models like linear regression, it learns coefficients. In neural networks, it learns weights and biases. In K-means algorithms, it learns cluster centroids. These entities learned by the model during training are called *parameters* and are considered internal to the model because their values change during training, as the model learns to minimize the error between its predictions and the actual outcomes. More specifically, at the core of most ML algorithm implementations, there is an optimization technique whose primary goal is to minimize the loss function based on the training data. The loss function (or cost function) quantifies how well the model's predictions match the actual target values. It measures the "error" or "difference" between the predicted values and the true values. The optimization technique is an algorithm designed to adjust the model's internal parameters (such as weights in a neural network) to minimize the loss function. Common optimization techniques include gradient descent, stochastic gradient descent (SGD), and more advanced methods like adaptive moment estimation (Adam) and root mean square propagation (RMSprop), which are not in the scope of the exam.

On the other hand, there are other factors, known as *hyperparameters*, that cannot be estimated from the input training data and are independent of it. These hyperparameters must be set before the training process begins and remain constant during the training process. For this reason, they are considered external to the model. These include settings such as learning rate, batch size, and number of epochs. Unlike parameters, which are adjusted during training to minimize errors, hyperparameters require tuning to optimize the model's performance and ensure that it can generalize well to new data.

196   Chapter 5 ▪ Model Training and Evaluation

For the exam, it is important for you to know that model training and model evaluation should use different datasets to ensure that the model generalizes well to new, unseen data and produces accurate predictions.

The use of separate datasets for these two different phases is critical because evaluating the model on the training data can lead to overly optimistic results, as the model has already seen this data during training. The purpose of the validation dataset is to provide an unbiased evaluation of the model's ability to generalize to new, unseen data. By using a separate validation dataset, we can better understand how well the model performs in real-world scenarios and avoid overfitting, which occurs when the model learns the training data too well and fails to generalize to new data. This process helps in selecting the best model and tuning hyperparameters to achieve optimal performance.

With respect to the exam analogy we used in the "Data Splitting" section in Chapter 3, to accurately evaluate the student's performance, it is essential to assess them using a different set of questions than those they prepared with. Think about it: if the evaluation uses the same questions, the student's performance may appear better than it actually is, as they have become familiar with those specific questions. Similarly, evaluating a ML model on a separate validation dataset provides a more accurate assessment of its ability to generalize and perform well on new data.

These concepts are summarized in Figure 5.3, where model training and model evaluation are visually compared, highlighting the different use of parameters and hyperparameters in each phase, as well as training and validation datasets.

In the upcoming sections, we will cover in detail the most common hyperparameter tuning techniques and evaluation metrics. But before doing that, we need to level set on the concept of hyperparameter space.

Exploring the Hyperparameter Space with Amazon SageMaker AI Automatic Model Tuning

Hyperparameter space refers to the range of values that different hyperparameters can take in a ML model. Exploring this space is critical for identifying the best combination of hyperparameters that optimize the model's performance. As you learned in the previous section, hyperparameters are predefined settings that influence the training process but are not learned from the data. They include factors such as the learning rate, batch size, number of epochs, regularization parameters, and architecture-specific settings like the number of layers and units in a neural network.

Amazon SageMaker offers several tools to help navigate the hyperparameter space effectively. Amazon SageMaker AI AMT is a powerful tool that automates the process of hyperparameter tuning. It uses advanced optimization algorithms (covered in the upcoming sections), such as Bayesian optimization, random search, and grid search, to explore the hyperparameter space and find the best configurations. AMT allows you to define ranges for

FIGURE 5.3 Model training and evaluation.

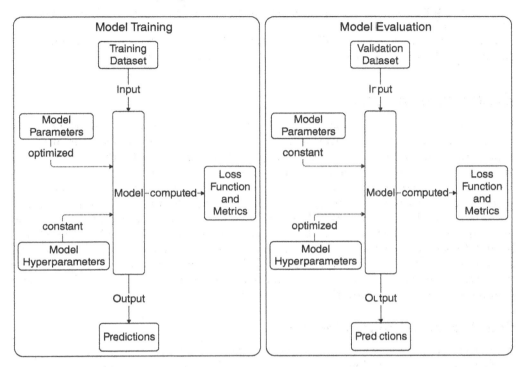

hyperparameters and automatically evaluates multiple combinations in parallel, significantly reducing the time and effort required for tuning.

Additionally, Amazon SageMaker hyperparameter tuning jobs provide a structured way to configure and launch hyperparameter tuning experiments. You can specify the hyperparameter ranges, objective metric, and resource limits for the tuning job. Amazon SageMaker also supports *warm starts*, which allow you to use the knowledge gained from previous tuning jobs to inform subsequent searches, making the optimization process more efficient.

Each Amazon SageMaker built-in algorithm comes with different types of hyperparameters. To view the list of hyperparameters for your chosen algorithm, visit https://docs.aws.amazon.com/sagemaker/latest/dg/algos.html. In the provided table, select the "Built-in algorithms" column and locate your algorithm. Click the link, and locate the hyperparameters section. For example, the DeepAR algorithm's hyperparameters are available at https://docs.aws.amazon.com/sagemaker/latest/dg/deepar_hyperparameters.html.

Chapter 5 ▪ Model Training and Evaluation

By leveraging these tools, you can systematically explore the hyperparameter space and identify the optimal settings for your ML model, leading to improved performance and better generalization to new data.

Later in the chapter, we will walk you through a deep-dive example on how to use Amazon SageMaker AI AMT to select the best model that fits a use case.

Evaluation Metrics

In the previous section, we introduced Amazon SageMaker AI AMT as a powerful tool to explore your model hyperparameter space in the search for the best combination of hyperparameters. You may wonder, how do you define what *optimal* really means? The answer lies in the evaluation metrics used to assess the performance of your ML model. Key metrics depend on the specific ML problem you are addressing, whether it is classification, regression, clustering, or another type. For classification problems, metrics such as accuracy, precision, recall, F1 score, and AUC-ROC are essential. In regression tasks, metrics like root mean squared error (RMSE), mean absolute percentage error (MAPE), and R-squared are pivotal. Clustering requires metrics like silhouette score and Davies-Bouldin index, which go beyond the scope of the exam. This section will cover the key metrics you need to know for the exam, providing a comprehensive understanding of how to evaluate and interpret your model's performance effectively.

Classification Problem Metrics

A commonly used approach to evaluate model performance for classification problems is a *confusion matrix*. A confusion matrix provides a detailed breakdown of how well a model predicts different classes, highlighting areas where the model might be making mistakes and allowing for targeted improvements. From the confusion matrix, we can derive key metrics such as accuracy, which measures overall correctness; precision, which indicates the accuracy of positive predictions; and recall (or sensitivity), which assesses the ability to identify true positives. The F1 score combines precision and recall into a single metric for balanced evaluation. Additionally, the AUC-ROC offers insight into the model's ability to distinguish between classes across various thresholds. Each of these metrics provides a unique perspective on the model's effectiveness.

Confusion Matrix

A confusion matrix provides a holistic view of the performance of a classification ML model. You can use a confusion matrix to determine the significance of an evaluation score.

For example, with a model that performs with an accuracy score of 90%, you would think the model performs very well. After all, 90% seems to be a high accuracy score, right? But what if you were to discover that although the model predicts all 90% data from one class, it completely fails to predict the remaining 10% data from another class? In this scenario, would you still believe the model was performing very well? This case would prove that a model with an accuracy score of 90% can still be wrong.

This is where a confusion matrix comes in handy. The key metrics associated with a confusion matrix are displayed in Figure 5.4—in the use case of binary classification—and are discussed in the following sections.

> For multiclass classification problems, the confusion matrix is a matrix with *N* rows and *N* columns. Each row represents the actual class (true label), and each column represents the class predicted by the model (predicted label). This matrix captures the counts of correct and incorrect classifications for each class. Mathematically, $N \times N = \{(a,b) \mid a \in N, b \in N\}$, where *N* is the number of classes, *a* is the actual class, and *b* is the predicted class.

Accuracy

In a classification problem, *accuracy* is the simplest form of evaluation score and is defined by the number of correctly predicted observations over the total number of observations.

FIGURE 5.4 Confusion matrix for a binary classification problem.

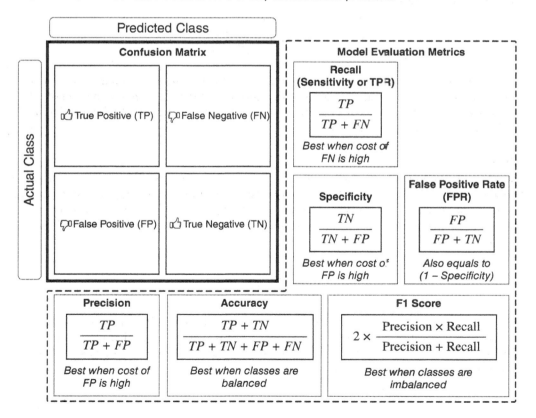

The following is the formula for calculating the accuracy of your classification model:

$$\text{Accuracy} = \frac{TP + TN}{TP + TN + FP + FN}$$

The accuracy score is considered a reliable metric for evaluating a model's performance *only when the dataset is balanced*, meaning all classes have roughly equal representation; if the dataset is imbalanced, accuracy can be misleading and other metrics like F1 score (discussed later in this section) are often preferred.

Precision

In a classification problem, *precision* is a metric that measures the accuracy of the positive predictions made by the model. It is defined as the ratio of true positives (*TP*) to the sum of true positives and false positives (*TP + FP*):

$$\text{Precision} = \frac{TP}{TP + FP}$$

In simpler terms, precision indicates how many of the instances predicted as positive by the model are actually positive. High precision means that the model has a low rate of false positives, making it particularly important in scenarios where the cost of false positives is high, such as in medical diagnoses.

Recall

In a classification problem, *recall* (also called *sensitivity* or *true positive rate* [TPR]) measures how well a model can identify *all* the positive instances within a dataset, essentially focusing on its ability to capture all relevant cases, even if it might include some false positives as well. It is defined as the ratio of true positives (*TP*) to the sum of true positives and false negatives (*TP + FN*):

$$\text{Recall} = \frac{TP}{TP + FN}$$

Put differently, recall indicates how many of the actual positive instances in the dataset are correctly identified by the model. High recall means that the model has a low rate of false negatives, making it particularly important in situations where missing positive cases is costly, such as in medical diagnoses or fraud detection.

Specificity

Specificity, also known as the true negative rate (TNR), is a metric in a confusion matrix that measures the proportion of actual negative instances that are correctly identified by the model. It provides insight into the model's ability to correctly classify negative cases.

The formula for specificity is as follows:

$$\text{Specificity} = \frac{TN}{TN + FP}$$

Specificity is key in scenarios where accurately identifying negative cases is important, such as in medical screening, where you want to avoid falsely diagnosing healthy individuals with a condition.

False Positive Rate

The false positive rate (FPR) in a confusion matrix measures the proportion of actual negative instances that are incorrectly classified as positive by the model. It provides insight into how often the model mistakenly identifies a negative instance as positive.

The formula for FPR is

$$\text{FPR} = \frac{FP}{FP + TN}$$

In simpler terms, the FPR tells you how often the model incorrectly predicts the positive class when it should have predicted the negative class. This metric is important for understanding how well the model is avoiding false alarms, especially in scenarios where false positives can have significant consequences, such as in spam detection or medical screening.

FPR and specificity are complements of each other: as FPR decreases, specificity increases, and vice versa. As a result of their respective definitions, FPR = 1 − Specificity.

F1 Score

In a classification problem, the *F1* score is a metric that combines precision and recall into a single number, providing a balanced measure of a model's performance. It is particularly useful when you need to balance the trade-off between precision (the accuracy of positive predictions) and recall (the ability to identify all positive instances).

The F1 score is calculated using the harmonic mean of precision and recall:

$$\text{F1 Score} = 2 \times \frac{\text{Precision} \times \text{Recall}}{\text{Precision} + \text{Recall}}$$

The F1 score gives you a single metric that takes both false positives and false negatives into account, making it especially valuable in situations where you need to strike a balance between these two aspects. A high F1 score indicates that the model has both high precision and high recall, ensuring that it performs well overall in classifying positive instances.

AUC-ROC

The AUC-ROC is a popular evaluation metric used in ML to assess the performance of binary classification models. The ROC curve plots the TPR against the FPR at various threshold settings. The AUC represents the area under this curve, providing a single value that summarizes the model's ability to distinguish between positive and negative classes. Although AUC-ROC is primarily used for binary classification problems, it can be generalized to multiclass classification through techniques such as one-vs.-rest (OvR) and one-vs.-one (OvO).

The ROC curve is essentially a probability curve that shows the trade-off between sensitivity (recall) and specificity (1 − FPR) for different threshold values. As you move along the ROC curve, you change the threshold for classifying a positive instance. This helps in understanding the model's performance across different decision boundaries and gives a comprehensive view of its behavior. The curve's shape indicates how well the model distinguishes between positive and negative classes.

An ideal AUC-ROC score is 1.0, which indicates perfect classification with no false positives or false negatives. In contrast, an AUC of 0.5 suggests that the model performs no better than random guessing, represented by the diagonal line in the ROC plot. Thus, the closer the AUC value is to 1.0, the better the model is at distinguishing between the positive and negative classes.

Let's demonstrate AUC-ROC with a simple example using Python. We'll use the Digits dataset and evaluate different models with varying hyperparameter configurations to show how the AUC-ROC score improves.

The Digits dataset is a popular benchmark in ML, consisting of 1,797 8 × 8-pixel grayscale images of handwritten digits (0–9). Each image is a 64-dimensional vector representing pixel intensities. This dataset is widely used for tasks like image classification and algorithm evaluation. For more details, visit https://scikit-learn.org/stable/modules/generated/sklearn.datasets.load_digits.html.

Given that AUC-ROC is designed primarily for binary classification problems and the Digits dataset involves a multiclass classification scenario with 10 classes (ranging from 0 to 9), it's necessary to transform this 10-class problem into a binary classification problem.

This example plots ROC curves for logistic regression, random forest, and XGBoost classifiers, comparing their performance in terms of true positive rate (sensitivity) versus false positive rate (1-specificity) across different threshold settings:

Hyperparameter Tuning 203

```python
import numpy as np
import matplotlib.pyplot as plt
from sklearn import datasets
from sklearn.model_selection import train_test_split
from sklearn.linear_model import LogisticRegression
from sklearn.ensemble import RandomForestClassifier
from xgboost import XGBClassifier
from sklearn.metrics import roc_curve, roc_auc_score
import os

# Load the Digits dataset
digits = datasets.load_digits()
X = digits.data
y = (digits.target == 1).astype(int)  # Convert to binary classification (class
1 vs. rest)

# Split the dataset into training and testing sets
X_train, X_test, y_train, y_test = train_test_split(X, y, test_size=0.3,
random_state=42)

# Initialize different models and hyperparameters
models = {
    'Logistic Regression': [
        LogisticRegression(C=1, solver='liblinear', random_state=42),
        LogisticRegression(C=0.1, solver='liblinear', random_state=42)
    ],
    'Random Forest': [
        RandomForestClassifier(n_estimators=50, max_depth=5, random_state=42),
        RandomForestClassifier(n_estimators=100, max_depth=7, random_state=42)
    ],
    'XGBoost': [
        XGBClassifier(n_estimators=50, max_depth=5, eval_metric='logloss',
random_state=42),
        XGBClassifier(n_estimators=100, max_depth=7, eval_netric='logloss',
random_state=42)
    ]
}

# Create directory if it doesn't exist
output_dir = './ch05/images'
os.makedirs(output_dir, exist_ok=True)

# Plot ROC curves
plt.figure(figsize=(10, 7))

for model_name, model_list in models.items():
    for model in model_list:
        model.fit(X_train, y_train)
        y_pred_prob = model.predict_proba(X_test)[:, 1]
        fpr, tpr, _ = roc_curve(y_test, y_pred_prob)
        auc = roc_auc_score(y_test, y_pred_prob)
```

Chapter 5 ▪ Model Training and Evaluation

```python
        label = f'{model_name} (n_estimators={getattr(model, "n_estimators",
"N/A")}, C={getattr(model, "C", "N/A")}, max_depth={getattr(model, "max_depth",
"N/A")}) (AUC = {auc:.2f})'
        plt.plot(fpr, tpr, label=label)

# Plot random guessing line
plt.plot([0, 1], [0, 1], linestyle='--', color='gray')

# Add labels and legend
plt.xlabel('False Positive Rate')
plt.ylabel('True Positive Rate')
plt.title('ROC Curve for Different Models and Hyperparameters (Digits
Dataset)')
plt.legend(loc='best')

# Save the plot instead of showing it
plt.savefig(os.path.join(output_dir, 'roc_curve_digits_dataset.png'))
plt.close()
```

The AUC-ROC plot in Figure 5.5 provides a clear comparison of the performance of logistic regression, random forest, and XGBoost classifiers in distinguishing "1" digits from the rest of the digits in the Digits dataset. By plotting the TPR (sensitivity) against the FPR (1 – Specificity) at various thresholds, we can visually assess each model's ability to correctly identify the "1" digits while minimizing false positives. The closer the ROC curve is to the top-left corner, the better the model is at differentiating between the positive and negative classes.

The AUC value quantifies this performance, with a higher AUC indicating superior classification capability. By comparing the AUC values for logistic regression, random forest, and XGBoost, we can determine which model performs best in classifying "1" digits. A model with a higher AUC is more effective at distinguishing the "1" digits from the rest, making it the preferable choice for this binary classification task.

Regression Problem Metrics

Unlike classification problems, where the goal is to categorize data points into discrete classes, regression problems aim to predict continuous values. In other words, whereas a classification model might predict whether an email is spam (a binary decision), a regression model might predict the price of a house given its features (a continuous value). This fundamental difference in the type of output necessitates different evaluation metrics for regression models.

When evaluating regression models, several key metrics are commonly used to assess performance. Some of these include MSE, RMSE, MAE, MAPE, and R-squared. These metrics help quantify the difference between the predicted values and the actual values, providing insights into the model's accuracy and reliability. Whereas classification metrics like accuracy, precision, recall, and AUC-ROC are geared toward evaluating the correctness of categorical predictions, regression metrics focus on the magnitude of the errors in

FIGURE 5.5 ROC curve comparison.

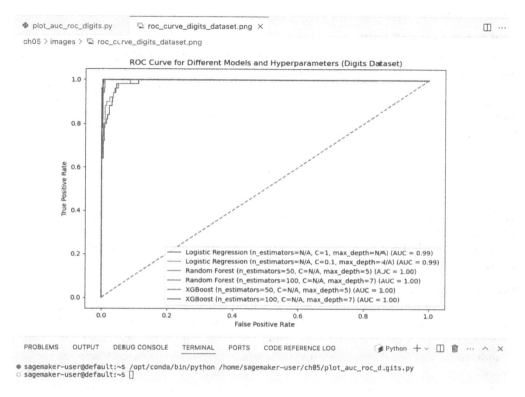

continuous predictions. These measures ensure that we can effectively gauge the quality and performance of regression models in predicting real-valued outcomes

In the following sections, we will explain the essential metrics you need to understand for the exam to evaluate the performance of ML regression models.

Mean Squared Error

MSE is a commonly used metric to evaluate the performance of regression models. It measures the average squared difference between the actual and predicted values, giving a sense of how close the predictions are to the actual values. The MSE is calculated by summing the squared differences between the actual (y_i) and predicted values $(\widehat{y}_i)$ and then dividing by the number of data points (n). The squaring of the differences ensures that both positive and negative errors contribute equally to the metric, and it penalizes larger errors more heavily. The formula for MSE is given by the following:

$$MSE = \frac{1}{n} \sum_{i=1}^{n} (y_i - \widehat{y}_i)^2$$

Chapter 5 • Model Training and Evaluation

MSE is a key metric for assessing the accuracy of regression models, with a lower MSE indicating better predictive performance.

Root Mean Squared Error

RMSE is another widely used metric for evaluating the performance of regression models. It is the square root of the MSE and provides an interpretable measure of the average error magnitude. RMSE is particularly useful because it retains the units of the original data, making it easier to understand the scale of the errors. By taking the square root of the MSE, RMSE gives a sense of how much prediction errors deviate from the true values on average. The formula for RMSE is given by the following:

$$RMSE = \sqrt{\frac{1}{n}\sum_{i=1}^{n}(y_i - \widehat{y}_i)^2}$$

where n is the number of data points, y_i denotes the actual value, and $\widehat{y}_i$ denotes the predicted value for the i-th data point.

Just like MSE, lower RMSE values indicate higher model accuracy, resulting in better model performance.

Mean Absolute Error

MAE measures the average magnitude of the errors in predictions, without considering their direction (positive or negative). MAE is calculated as the mean of the absolute differences between the actual values (y_i) and the predicted values ($\widehat{y}_i$). This metric is easy to understand and interpret, as it provides a straightforward measure of how far the predictions are from the actual values on average. Unlike metrics that square the errors, MAE treats all errors equally, which can be particularly useful in applications where large errors should not be excessively penalized. The formula for MAE is given by the following:

$$MAE = \frac{1}{n}\sum_{i=1}^{n}|y_i - \widehat{y}_i|$$

where n is the number of data points, y_i denotes the actual value, and $\widehat{y}_i$ denotes the predicted value for the i-th data point.

MAE is another essential metric for assessing model accuracy, with a lower MAE indicating better predictive performance.

Mean Absolute Percentage Error

MAPE is another popular metric for evaluating the accuracy of regression models, especially in cases where understanding the relative error is critical. MAPE calculates the average absolute percentage difference between the actual values and the predicted values, offering an intuitive understanding of prediction accuracy in percentage terms. This metric is particularly useful when dealing with data of varying scales, as it normalizes the error, making it easier to interpret the results. By expressing errors as percentages, MAPE allows for straightforward comparisons across different datasets and models. The formula for MAPE is given by the following:

$$\text{MAPE} = \frac{100}{n} \sum_{i=1}^{n} \left| \frac{y_i - \widehat{y}_i}{y_i} \right|$$

where n is the number of data points, y_i denotes the actual value, and $\widehat{y}_i$ denotes the predicted value for the i-th data point.

MAPE provides a percentage-based error, making it easier to understand and compare prediction performance across different contexts.

R-squared

The R-squared, also known as the *coefficient of determination*, is another key metric for evaluating regression models. It indicates the proportion of the variance in the dependent variable that is predictable from the independent variables. Essentially, R-squared measures the goodness of fit of the model. An R-squared value ranges from 0 to 1, where a value closer to 1 signifies that the model explains a large portion of the variance in the response variable, and a value closer to 0 indicates that the model fails to explain much of the variance. The formula for R-squared is as follows:

$$R^2 = 1 - \frac{\sum_{i=1}^{n} (y_i - \widehat{y}_i)^2}{\sum_{i=1}^{n} (y_i - \bar{y})^2}$$

where n is the number of data points, $\bar{y}$ denotes the mean of the actual values, y_i denotes the actual value, and $\widehat{y}_i$ denotes the predicted value for the i-th data point.

R-squared provides an intuitive measure of how well the regression model captures the underlying trend in the data.

When compared with the other regression evaluation metrics, R-squared differs from MSE, RMSE, MAE, and MAPE in that it provides a measure of the proportion of the variance in the dependent variable explained by the model. Whereas MSE, RMSE, MAE, and MAPE focus on quantifying the magnitude of prediction errors, R-squared offers an insight into the goodness of fit of the model. A higher R-squared value indicates that the model explains a larger portion of the variance in the data, making it a useful metric for understanding how well the model captures the underlying trend.

On the other hand, MSE, RMSE, MAE, and MAPE are error-based metrics that directly measure the accuracy of the predictions. MSE and RMSE penalize larger errors more heavily due to the squaring of differences, with RMSE providing an interpretable measure in the

Chapter 5 · Model Training and Evaluation

same units as the original data. MAE and MAPE, on the other hand, provide average error magnitudes, with MAPE expressing errors as percentages, facilitating comparison across different datasets and models. Each of these metrics offers unique insights into model performance, and the choice of metric depends on the specific evaluation needs and context of the problem.

Hyperparameter Tuning Techniques

Up until now, you've learned about hyperparameters and their role in shaping the structure of a model, as well as their distinction from the model's internal parameters, which are learned during training. You've also explored how Amazon SageMaker AI AMT can assist in finding the optimal combination of hyperparameters. Additionally, we've covered the key evaluation metrics for both classification and regression ML problems.

But with the vastness of the hyperparameter space, how can a ML engineer efficiently streamline the hyperparameter tuning process? It's essential to adopt the right approach to determine the best configuration of hyperparameters to achieve optimal model performance.

The high-level process of hyperparameter tuning involves several critical steps:

1. Visualizing the data and understanding the ML problem
2. Choosing the best algorithm
3. Splitting the dataset into training, validation, and test sets
4. Determining the list of hyperparameters and creating the hyperparameter space
5. Selecting and applying the most suitable tuning technique for discovering the optimal hyperparameter combination
6. Implementing cross-validation
7. Evaluating the model score
8. Repeating steps 5, 6, and 7 until the best possible model score is achieved

In the upcoming sections, we'll focus on step 5 in the aforementioned process. We will introduce several hyperparameter tuning techniques, including manual search, grid search, random search, Bayesian optimization, and multi-algorithm optimization. Each of these methods offers unique strategies for navigating the hyperparameter space and identifying the most effective set of hyperparameters for your ML models.

Manual Search

Manual search is a straightforward and intuitive method for tuning hyperparameters in ML models. This technique involves manually selecting and testing different hyperparameter values based on experience, domain knowledge, and intuition about the model and dataset. As you can imagine, this approach can be time-consuming and may not explore the hyperparameter space as thoroughly as automated methods. For these reasons, this method is generally not recommended for most use cases because the probability of achieving an optimized model is low, given the vastness of the hyperparameter space and the manual effort required. Manual search is often used as a starting point before applying more sophisticated hyperparameter tuning techniques.

Grid Search

Grid search is a hyperparameter tuning technique that involves an exhaustive search through a predefined set of hyperparameters. By systematically exploring all possible combinations within the specified grid, this method performs a brute-force approach to identify the optimal combination of hyperparameters for a ML model. The primary advantage of grid search is its ability to find the best hyperparameters by thoroughly evaluating every possible configuration, ensuring that no potential combination is overlooked. However, this approach can be extremely time-consuming and compute-intensive, especially when dealing with a large number of hyperparameters or an extensive ranges of values.

The computational burden of grid search grows when dealing with large datasets. The volume of data can exponentially increase the time and resources required to complete the search, making this method impractical in such scenarios. As the size and complexity of the dataset grow, the exhaustive nature of grid search can lead to significantly longer runtimes and higher computational costs, which may not be feasible for many projects. As a result, grid search is often more suitable for smaller datasets or use cases where computational resources are optimized.

Although grid search can identify the optimal hyperparameter combination, it also carries the risk of overfitting the model to the training data. Overfitting occurs when the model captures noise or random fluctuations in the training data rather than the underlying pattern, leading to poor generalization to new, unseen data. By thoroughly exploring all hyperparameter combinations, grid search may fine-tune the model excessively, resulting in a model that performs well on the training set but fails to generalize to the validation or test sets. As a result, it's essential to balance the thoroughness of grid search with the potential risks of overfitting, and to consider alternative tuning methods for more complex or larger datasets.

Random Search

As the name suggests, this technique randomly selects different combinations of hyperparameters and performs cross-validation on the dataset instead of searching the entire hyperparameter space. Random search is faster than grid search, but sometimes it can miss the best combination of hyperparameters due to the random nature of this approach.

Although it may still be compute-intensive and time-consuming for large datasets, random search is less prone to model overfitting than grid search.

Bayesian Search

Bayesian search is a sophisticated hyperparameter tuning technique that leverages the concept of "state" to remember the performance of previous searches. Unlike grid search and random search, which rely on brute-force or random exploration, Bayesian search uses probabilistic models to intelligently explore the hyperparameter space. By keeping track of past evaluations, Bayesian search continuously refines its probabilistic model of the objective function, typically using Gaussian processes or other surrogate models. This stateful approach allows the algorithm to make informed decisions about which hyperparameters to explore next, focusing on regions that are more likely to contain optimal hyperparameters.

The process begins with evaluating an initial set of hyperparameter values. Based on these evaluations, the Bayesian optimization algorithm updates its probabilistic model, predicting the performance of different hyperparameter combinations. This iterative process balances exploration (trying new regions) and exploitation (focusing on known promising areas) until a specified number of evaluations is reached or performance improvement plateaus. By incorporating prior knowledge and adapting its search strategy, Bayesian search can efficiently navigate complex hyperparameter landscapes.

One of the key advantages of Bayesian search is its efficiency in finding optimal hyperparameters, reducing the number of evaluations needed compared to exhaustive methods like grid search. However, careful implementation and parameterization of the optimization algorithm are essential. At the end of this chapter, we will provide a demonstration of Bayesian search with Amazon SageMaker AI AMT, showcasing how this technique can be applied in practice to achieve optimal model performance.

Multi-algorithm Optimization

Multi-algorithm optimization refers to the process of tuning hyperparameters for different ML algorithms to find the best solution for a given problem. This technique involves running multiple algorithms with various hyperparameter configurations and comparing their performance to identify the most suitable model. By leveraging the strengths of different algorithms, multi-algorithm optimization aims to achieve the highest possible performance for a ML problem.

We used this technique to generate the plot in Figure 5.5, which illustrates ROC curves for logistic regression, random forest, and XGBoost classifiers using a binary converted version of the Digits dataset.

This technique is particularly useful when you have a complex ML problem and are unsure which algorithm will perform best. For example, you might tune hyperparameters for a decision tree, a random forest, a support vector machine, and a neural network and then compare their results to determine which algorithm and hyperparameter combination yields the best outcome. Multi-algorithm optimization provides a comprehensive search across various models, offering a robust solution tailored to the specific needs and characteristics of the data and problem at hand.

Managing Bias and Variance Trade-off

Bias and variance are two reducible errors in ML. For accurate predictions by the ML model, low values of bias and variance are desired. However, you cannot achieve low bias and low variance simultaneously.

When bias is high, the model tends to oversimplify your ML problem, leading to underfitting. This means the model cannot capture the underlying patterns in the data, resulting in poor performance on both the training and validation datasets. High bias usually occurs when the model is too simple, such as a linear model trying to fit nonlinear data. Reducing bias involves increasing the model complexity, but this can lead to an increase in variance.

On the other hand, high variance occurs when the model is too complex, capturing noise and fluctuations in the training data rather than the underlying pattern. This results in overfitting, where the model performs well on the training data but poorly on new, unseen data. High variance is often observed in models with many parameters, such as deep neural networks. Reducing variance involves simplifying the model, but this can increase bias.

As you can see, there is a trade-off between bias and variance. This trade-off is illustrated in Figure 5.6 (numbers are shown for illustrative purposes). The key to managing bias and variance is finding the optimal model complexity that balances both errors. This is where hyperparameter tuning comes into play. By adjusting the model hyperparameters, we are tweaking the model complexity. As we discussed earlier, hyperparameters control various aspects of the model's structure and learning process, directly impacting its complexity and behavior.

When the bias of the model increases, the variance decreases. Conversely, when the bias of the model decreases, the variance increases.

FIGURE 5.6 Bias-variance trade-off.

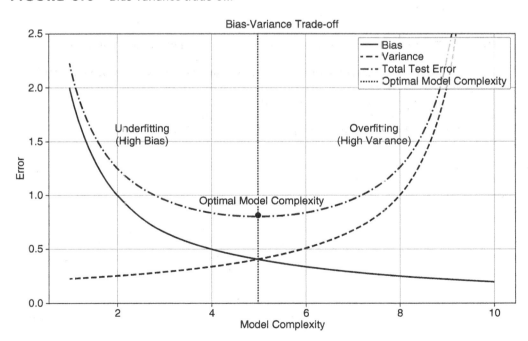

Remember, the goal of developing a ML model is always to perform well with new, unseen data. A low bias and high variance can make a model overfit the training dataset, whereas a model with high bias and low variance may underfit the dataset.

As a result, your job as an ML engineer is to discover the right balance between bias and variance while training and evaluating your model.

Addressing Overfitting and Underfitting

Addressing overfitting and underfitting in model training and evaluation is crucial for building robust ML models that generalize well to new data.

Underfitting

Underfitting occurs when a model is too simple to capture the underlying patterns in the data, as demonstrated by the dashed black line in the regression plot (degree 1 polynomial in Figure 5.7) and the classification plot (degree 1 polynomial in Figure 5.8). To address underfitting, we can increase the complexity of the model by incorporating more features, using higher-degree polynomials (if polynomial algorithms are being used), or selecting more sophisticated algorithms.

For example, the regression plot in Figure 5.7 better captures the data's true trend with the optimal fitting model (degree 5 polynomial), whereas the classification plot in Figure 5.8 more accurately separates the data points with the optimal fitting model (degree 3 polynomial).

FIGURE 5.7 Examples of overfitting and underfitting for polynomial regression.

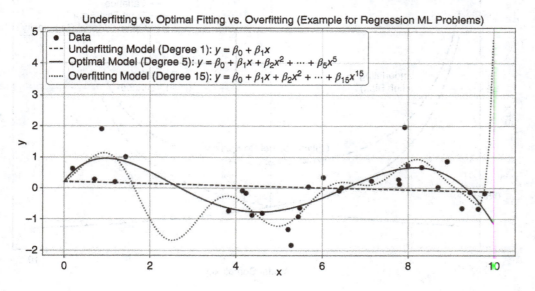

FIGURE 5.8 Examples of overfitting and underfitting for polynomial classification.

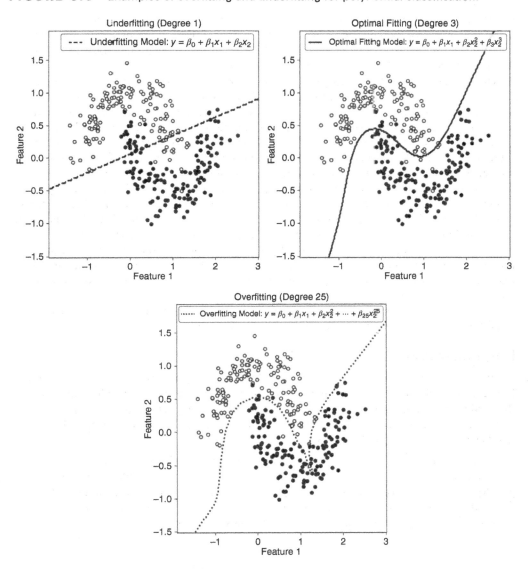

With respect to our exam analogy (introduced in the "Data Splitting" section of Chapter 3), underfitting is similar to a student skipping chapters from their study material, resulting in a lack of understanding and poor performance, as they have underfit the concepts needed to excel the exam.

Overfitting

Overfitting, on the other hand, occurs when a model is too complex and captures noise along with the underlying patterns, leading to poor generalization on new data. Put differently, when a model overlearns a dataset, to the extent of learning all the noise and errors in the dataset, the model has overfitted its training data.

This is illustrated by the dotted black line in the regression plot (degree 15 polynomial in Figure 5.7) and the classification plot (degree 25 polynomial in Figure 5.8). To address overfitting, techniques such as regularization (L1 or L2), pruning (in decision trees), and dropout (in neural networks) can be employed. Additionally, reducing the model's complexity by selecting a lower-degree polynomial or using fewer features can help prevent overfitting. For instance, the optimal fitting models in both regression and classification plots strike a balance between capturing the data's patterns without being overly complex.

Overfitting is similar to a student who prepares for an exam by studying with only a single source of information. Even though the student may feel fully prepared because they learned really well from the (only) study material, if the exam questions differ in content and scenarios from the study material, they may struggle to pass the exam. This is because they learned too well from the training material (e.g., they memorized the answers from the practice exams without truly understanding the concepts) and are unable to generalize to real-world scenarios that may happen while taking the actual exam or trying to solve an unseen problem at work.

For the exam, it is important you understand how regularization is an effective technique to address overfitting, which is covered in the next section.

Regularization

Regularization helps prevent your model from overfitting by adding a penalty term to the loss function, which the model aims to minimize during training. This penalty "discourages" the model from becoming too complex and fitting the training data too closely. There are different types of regularization techniques, including L1 regularization (LASSO), L2 regularization (Ridge), and Elastic Net:

L1 regularization (LASSO)   L1 regularization, also known as LASSO (least absolute shrinkage and selection operator), is commonly used in regression problems. It adds a penalty term λ to the loss function that is proportional to the sum of the absolute values of the model's coefficients. The formula for the loss function with L1 regularization in the context of linear regression can be written as follows:

$$L(w) = L_{original}(w) + \lambda \sum_{i=1}^{n} |w_i|$$

In the formula, $L(w)$ is the regularized loss function, $L_{original}(w)$ is the original loss function (e.g., MSE for regression), w_i are the model's coefficients, λ is the regularization parameter, and n is the number of coefficients.

The regularization parameter λ controls the strength of the regularization by scaling the penalty applied to the model's coefficients. When λ is small, the penalty is small, and the regularization effect is minimal, allowing the model to fit the training data more closely. When λ is large, the penalty is significant, forcing more coefficients to zero and resulting in a simpler, sparser model.

Sparsity refers to having a significant number of zero or near-zero values among the model's coefficients (internal parameters learned by the model during training). This means that the model relies on only a subset of the available features, effectively ignoring the rest.

L1 regularization encourages sparsity in the model's parameters, making it particularly useful for feature selection in regression problems. By driving some coefficients to zero, it effectively removes less relevant features, resulting in a simpler and more interpretable model.

Moreover, due to the nature of its penalty term, L1 regression is particularly robust (less sensitive) to outliers. This is because L1 regularization penalizes the absolute values of the coefficients, which don't amplify the effect of outliers as much as the squared term in L2 regularization—outliers typically result in large coefficients.

These characteristics of L1 regularization (driving sparsity and robustness to outliers) make it an ideal regularization technique to prevent your model from overfitting its training data. L1 regularization excels in scenarios when you have a high-dimensional dataset with many features and you want to focus on the most relevant ones while mitigating the influence of outliers that could skew the model's performance.

L2 regularization (Ridge)   L2 regularization, known as Ridge regression, is also used in regression problems. It adds a penalty term to the loss function that is proportional to the sum of the squared values of the model's coefficients. The formula for the loss function with L2 regularization in the context of linear regression can be written as follows:

$$L(w) = L_{original}(w) + \lambda \sum_{i=1}^{n} w_i^2$$

In the formula, $L(w)$ is the regularized loss function, $L_{original}(w)$ is the original loss function (e.g., MSE for regression), w_i are the model's coefficients, λ is the regularization parameter, and n is the number of coefficients.

In comparing L2 regularization with L1, the latter (L1) induces sparsity by driving many coefficients to zero, effectively performing feature selection and creating simpler models, whereas L2 regularization does not result in sparsity but instead shrinks coefficients evenly, maintaining all features. L1 is more robust to outliers due to its linear penalty on coefficients, whereas L2 is less robust because the squared penalty can disproportionately amplify the effect of outliers.

216 Chapter 5 ▪ Model Training and Evaluation

Elastic Net Elastic Net combines both L1 and L2 regularization and can be used in both regression and classification problems. The formula for the loss function with Elastic Net regularization can be written as follows:

$$L(w) = L_{original}(w) + \lambda_1 \sum_{i=1}^{n} |w_i| + \lambda_2 \sum_{i=1}^{n} w_i^2$$

In the formula, $L(w)$ is the regularized loss function, $L_{original}(w)$ is the original loss function (e.g., MSE for regression), w_i are the model's coefficients, λ_1 and λ_2 are the regularization parameters for L1 and L2 regularization, respectively, and n is the number of coefficients.

Elastic Net is particularly useful when dealing with datasets with highly correlated features (high multicollinearity). This is because Elastic Net regularization balances the trade-offs between L1 and L2 techniques, encouraging both sparsity and small coefficient values. This hybrid approach makes Elastic Net a versatile tool for preventing overfitting and ensuring robust model performance in both regression and classification tasks.

The comparison in Table 5.1 will help you determine the most appropriate regularization method for the exam.

TABLE 5.1 Regularization methods comparison.

Property	L1 (LASSO)	L2 (Ridge)	Elastic Net
Penalty term	$\lambda \sum_{i=1}^{n} |w_i|$	$\lambda \sum_{i=1}^{n} w_i^2$	$\lambda_1 \sum_{i=1}^{n} |w_i| + \lambda_2 \sum_{i=1}^{n} w_i^2$
Sparsity	Induces sparsity (many coefficients become zero)	Does not induce sparsity (all coefficients shrink)	Balance between sparsity and shrinkage
Feature selection	Effective for feature selection	Not effective for feature selection	Effective for feature selection with grouped features
Robustness to outliers	Robust to outliers due to linear penalty	Not robust to outliers due to squared penalty	Moderate robustness due to combined penalties
Use cases	High-dimensional data, feature selection	Regularization without feature elimination	High-dimensional data with high multicollinearity

Advanced Techniques

Evaluating model performance using techniques like *cross-validation* is essential for detecting and mitigating overfitting and underfitting. Cross-validation involves partitioning the entire dataset into training and evaluation datasets multiple times and averaging the results to ensure the model's robustness. By comparing performance metrics such as MSE for regression or accuracy for classification across different folds, you can determine whether the model is underfitting, overfitting, or performing optimally. The regression and classification plots we created in Figures 5.7 and 5.8 serve as visual clues, showing how models with varying degrees of polynomial complexity perform, helping in the understanding of these concepts. Just like a well-prepared student reviewing multiple sources and scenarios, cross-validation ensures the model is well-rounded and not biased toward a single source of training data. We'll cover cross-validation in detail in the upcoming section.

Finally, feature engineering and data augmentation can also play an important role in addressing overfitting and underfitting. For regression problems, transforming features, creating interaction terms, or scaling data can help models better capture the underlying relationships. In classification problems, techniques such as oversampling, undersampling, and adding synthetic data can enhance the model's ability to generalize, which is the ultimate goal of any ML model.

Model Performance Evaluation

Having covered hyperparameter tuning, it's important now to delve into the various methods used to evaluate the effectiveness and *generalizability* of your ML model. Generalizability and effectiveness are directly tied to the key performance indicators you learned in the "Evaluation Metrics" section earlier in the chapter.

Once you have selected the most suitable evaluation metrics for your model and the optimal set of hyperparameters, the next step is to ensure that your model performs *consistently* well on unseen data. This is where model evaluation methods come into play, providing a robust framework for assessing your model's performance and avoiding pitfalls like underfitting and overfitting.

Performance Evaluation Methods

Among the most widely used model evaluation methods are K-fold cross-validation, random train-test split, holdout set, and bootstrap. Each of these techniques offers a unique approach to partitioning data and evaluating model performance. K-fold cross-validation, for instance, divides the dataset into k subsets, systematically training and validating the model across different folds to ensure a comprehensive evaluation. The random train-test split method randomly allocates data into training and testing sets, offering a straightforward yet effective way to assess model accuracy. The holdout set

218   Chapter 5 ▪ Model Training and Evaluation

method reserves a portion of the dataset as a separate evaluation set, providing a final check on model performance after training. Finally, the bootstrap technique involves resampling the data with replacement, creating multiple training and testing sets to generate an ensemble of performance estimates. Understanding and employing these model evaluation methods is essential for validating your model's reliability and ensuring it performs well in real-world scenarios with new, unseen data.

K-Fold Cross-Validation

K-fold cross-validation is a robust technique used to assess the performance of a ML model and its ability to generalize to unseen data. In this method, the entire dataset is divided into k equal-sized subsets, or "folds." In the case of fourfold cross-validation, the dataset is split into four parts. Each fold acts as a unique segment of data that will be used for testing exactly once, and the remaining $k - 1$ folds are used for training the model. This approach ensures that every data point is used for both training and evaluation, providing a comprehensive assessment of the model's performance.

As illustrated in Figure 5.9, the process begins by designating the first fold as the evaluation (test) dataset and the remaining three folds as the training dataset. The model (referred to as Model 1 in Figure 5.9) is trained on the training dataset (step 1), learning its internal parameters from the provided data (step 2). Once trained, the model is then evaluated on the evaluation (test) fold (step 3), producing evaluation metrics such as accuracy, precision, and recall (step 4). These metrics provide insight into how well the model performs on this specific subset of data. This process is repeated for each of the four folds, with each fold serving as the evaluation (test) dataset once, and the remaining folds are used for training.

It is important to note that each fold uses its own model, which means that for each fold, the model is trained from scratch using the designated training data. As a result, each model learns its own internal parameters based on the specific training data for that fold. This approach ensures that the evaluation is not biased by a single model's peculiarities and provides a more accurate measure of the model's generalizability. Each iteration yields its own set of evaluation metrics, reflecting the model's performance on that particular fold.

After all folds have been used for evaluation, the results are aggregated to produce a comprehensive performance estimate. The average of the evaluation metrics across all folds gives a robust indication of the model's overall effectiveness and generalizability. At this point, a critical decision is made: whether the aggregated performance metrics meet the predefined criteria for acceptability. If the metrics are satisfactory, the model can be retrained on the entire dataset using the optimal hyperparameter configuration to create a final model ready for deployment—the topic of Chapter 6. If the metrics fall short of the criteria, further adjustments may be necessary, such as additional hyperparameter tuning or model refinement.

In addition to providing a holistic measurement of your model's overall performance K-fold cross-validation also helps reduce the risk of overfitting. This is because every data point is used for both training and evaluation. As a result, the model doesn't become too

FIGURE 5.9 K-fold cross-validation ($k = 4$).

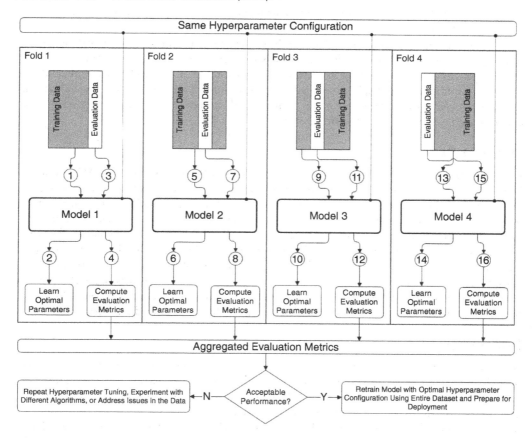

specialized to any single subset of the data, leading to a more accurate and dependable performance assessment.

By using K-fold cross-validation, you can confidently evaluate how well the model will perform on new, unseen data, ensuring that it is both reliable and capable of generalizing beyond the training dataset.

Random Train-Test Split

Random train-test split is a straightforward and widely used method for evaluating the performance of ML models. In this approach, the dataset is randomly divided into two subsets: a training dataset and a test dataset. The model is trained on the training dataset and then evaluated on the test dataset to assess its performance. This method is simple and quick to implement, providing a basic indication of how the model will perform on unseen

220   Chapter 5 ▪ Model Training and Evaluation

data. However, it has the limitation of potential variability in the evaluation results, depending on how the data is split, and may not provide a comprehensive assessment as more sophisticated methods.

In comparison, K-fold cross-validation offers a more robust and thorough evaluation of model performance because it is designed to ensure that every data point is used for both training and evaluation, resulting in a more reliable estimate of the model's generalizability. Whereas random train-test split gives a single performance estimate, K-fold cross-validation provides multiple performance estimates, which are then averaged to give a more stable and accurate measure of the model's effectiveness.

Holdout Set

Holdout set is another common method for evaluating the performance of ML models. In this approach, the dataset is split into three subsets: a training set, a validation set, and a test set. The model is trained on the training set and tuned using the validation set to optimize hyperparameters and improve performance. Finally, the model is evaluated on the test set to assess its generalizability to unseen data. This method ensures that the evaluation metrics are not biased by the tuning process. Although holdout set provides a clear separation between training, validation, and testing phases, just like random train-test split it has the limitation of potential variability in the results depending on how the data is split. Additionally, the evaluation is based on a single test set, which might not fully capture the model's performance on different data distributions.

Bootstrap

Bootstrap is a powerful resampling technique used to estimate the performance of ML models, particularly when the dataset is small or when it's essential to understand the variability of the model's performance. In this approach, multiple bootstrap samples are created by randomly sampling the dataset with replacement, meaning that some data points may be repeated and others may be excluded in each sample. The model is trained on each bootstrap sample and evaluated on the out-of-bag (OOB) data, which are the data points not included in the bootstrap sample. This process is repeated many times, and the performance metrics are averaged to provide an estimate of the model's generalizability. The bootstrap method is advantageous because it allows for the estimation of the variability and confidence intervals of the performance metrics, providing a more nuanced understanding of the model's robustness.

Whereas the bootstrap approach focuses on resampling with replacement and provides insights into the variability of the performance metrics, K-fold cross-validation systematically partitions the dataset and offers a more straightforward and stable estimate of the model's overall effectiveness.

Evaluating Foundation Models

Amazon Bedrock offers a variety of evaluation tools to help you assess the performance and effectiveness of foundation models (FMs) and knowledge bases. Some of the key evaluation tools available are briefly described in the upcoming sections.

Automatic Evaluations

These evaluations use predefined metrics such as accuracy, robustness, and toxicity to assess the performance of foundation models. You can bring your own custom datasets or use built-in, curated datasets to perform these evaluations. This method is quick and efficient, providing computed scores and metrics to help you evaluate the effectiveness of your models.

Human Evaluations

For more subjective or custom metrics, such as friendliness, style, and alignment to brand voice, Amazon Bedrock allows you to set up human evaluation workflows. You can either use your own workforce or have AWS manage the evaluations, providing ratings and preferences for specific metrics.

LLM-as-a-Judge

This evaluation method uses a large language model (LLM) as a judge to evaluate model outputs. You can provide custom prompt datasets and select metrics such as correctness, completeness, and harmfulness to assess the model's performance.

Programmatic Evaluations

These evaluations use traditional natural language algorithms and metrics like BERT score, F1, and exact matching techniques to evaluate model outputs. You can use built-in prompt datasets or bring your own datasets for these evaluations.

Knowledge Base Evaluations

For evaluating retrieval quality and end-to-end retrieval-augmented generation (RAG) workflows, Amazon Bedrock provides tools to assess the retrieval and generation capabilities of your knowledge bases. Metrics such as context relevance, context coverage, faithfulness, correctness, and completeness are used to ensure the quality of the retrieved and generated content.

Deep-Dive Model Tuning Example

In this example, we are going to train and evaluate the performance of the XGBoost algorithm against the Digits dataset using Amazon SageMaker AI AMT. The expected outcome is the optimal combination of hyperparameters by evaluating the performance of 20 models,

222 Chapter 5 ▪ Model Training and Evaluation

each with a different hyperparameter combination. We will use model accuracy as performance metric, and the results will be visually displayed in a plot.

I ran this Python program using the Code Editor feature of Amazon SageMaker Studio:

```python
import boto3
import sagemaker
from sagemaker import get_execution_role
from sagemaker.tuner import HyperparameterTuner, IntegerParameter,
ContinuousParameter
from sagemaker.inputs import TrainingInput
from sagemaker.analytics import HyperparameterTuningJobAnalytics
from sklearn.datasets import load_digits
from sklearn.model_selection import train_test_split
import pandas as pd
import os
import matplotlib.pyplot as plt

# Load the Digits dataset
digits = load_digits()
X = digits.data
y = digits.target

# Split the dataset
X_train, X_test, y_train, y_test = train_test_split(X, y, test_size=0.2,
random_state=42)

# Convert to DataFrame and ensure the target is the first column
train_data = pd.DataFrame(X_train)
train_data['target'] = y_train
train_data.insert(0, 'target', train_data.pop('target'))

val_data = pd.DataFrame(X_test)
val_data['target'] = y_test
val_data.insert(0, 'target', val_data.pop('target'))

# Create directories if they don't exist
data_dir = './ch05/data'
os.makedirs(data_dir, exist_ok=True)

# Save locally
train_data.to_csv(os.path.join(data_dir, 'train.csv'), index=False)
val_data.to_csv(os.path.join(data_dir, 'validation.csv'), index=False)

# Upload to S3
s3 = boto3.client('s3')
bucket_name = 'ch05-ml-hpo'
prefix = 'sagemaker/xgboost-digits'
s3.upload_file(os.path.join(data_dir, 'train.csv'), bucket_name,
f'{prefix}/train/train.csv')
s3.upload_file(os.path.join(data_dir, 'validation.csv'), bucket_name,
f'{prefix}/validation/validation.csv')
```

Deep-Dive Model Tuning Example

```python
# Define the role and session
role = get_execution_role()
session = sagemaker.Session()

# Define the XGBoost image
region = boto3.Session().region_name
xgb_image = sagemaker.image_uris.retrieve("xgboost", region, "1.2-1")

# Define the S3 paths for the input data
s3_train_data = f's3://{bucket_name}/{prefix}/train/train.csv'
s3_val_data = f's3://{bucket_name}/{prefix}/validation/validation.csv'

# Define the data channels
train_data = TrainingInput(s3_data=s3_train_data, content_type='csv')
val_data = TrainingInput(s3_data=s3_val_data, content_type='csv')

# Define the XGBoost estimator with required hyperparameters
xgb = sagemaker.estimator.Estimator(
    image_uri=xgb_image,
    role=role,
    instance_count=1,
    instance_type='ml.m5.large',
    output_path=f's3://{bucket_name}/{prefix}/output',
    sagemaker_session=session,
    hyperparameters={
        'objective': 'multi:softmax',  # Example for multi-class classification
        'num_class': 10,  # Number of classes in the Digits dataset
        'num_round': 100  # Default value; will be tuned
    }
)

# Define the hyperparameter ranges
hpt_ranges = {
    'alpha': ContinuousParameter(0.01, 0.5),
    'eta': ContinuousParameter(0.1, 0.5),
    'min_child_weight': ContinuousParameter(0.0, 2.0),
    'max_depth': IntegerParameter(1, 10)
}

# Define the hyperparameter tuner
tuner = HyperparameterTuner(
    estimator=xgb,
    base_tuning_job_name='bayesian',
    objective_metric_name='validation:accuracy',
    hyperparameter_ranges=hpt_ranges,
    strategy='Bayesian',
    max_jobs=20,  # Increase to 20 max jobs
    max_parallel_jobs=3,  # Number of parallel jobs
    objective_type='Maximize'
)
```

```python
# Launch the hyperparameter tuning job
tuner.fit({'train': train_data, 'validation': val_data})
tuner.wait()

# Get the best training job name
best_training_job_name = tuner.best_training_job()

# Retrieve the tuning results
tuning_job_name = tuner.latest_tuning_job.name
tuner_analytics = HyperparameterTuningJobAnalytics(tuning_job_name)
tuner_df = tuner_analytics.dataframe()

# Extract the best hyperparameters
if 'FinalHyperParameters' in tuner_df.columns:
    best_hyperparameters = tuner_df.loc[tuner_df['TrainingJobName'] ==
best_training_job_name, 'FinalHyperParameters'].values[0]
else:
    best_hyperparameters = tuner_df.loc[tuner_df['TrainingJobName'] ==
best_training_job_name].drop(['TrainingJobName', 'FinalObjectiveValue'],
axis=1).to_dict('records')[0]

# Print the best training job and hyperparameters
print(f"Best Training Job: {best_training_job_name}")
print("Best Hyperparameters:")
for key, value in best_hyperparameters.items():
    print(f"  {key}: {value}")

# Plot the tuning job results
plt.figure(figsize=(12, 8))
plt.scatter(tuner_df.index, tuner_df['FinalObjectiveValue'],
label='Tuning Jobs')
plt.scatter(tuner_df.loc[tuner_df['TrainingJobName'] ==
best_training_job_name].index,
            tuner_df.loc[tuner_df['TrainingJobName'] ==
best_training_job_name]['FinalObjectiveValue'],
            color='red', marker='*', s=200, label='Best Job')

plt.xlabel('Iteration')
plt.ylabel('Cross-Validation Accuracy')
plt.title('Hyperparameter Tuning Results')

# Display the best hyperparameters on the plot
best_hyperparameters_str = '\n'.join([f'{key}: {value}' for key, value in
best_hyperparameters.items()])
plt.figtext(0.5, -0.15, f'Best Hyperparameters:\n{best_hyperparameters_str}',
ha='center', va='top', fontsize=10, bbox=dict(facecolor='lightgrey',
alpha=0.5))

# Update legend position below the x-axis
plt.legend(loc='upper center', bbox_to_anchor=(0.5, -0.2), ncol=3)
```

Deep-Dive Model Tuning Example

```
# Save the plot as an image file
output_dir = './ch05/images'
os.makedirs(output_dir, exist_ok=True)
plt.savefig(os.path.join(output_dir, 'tuning_results.png'),
bbox_inches='tight')
```

Most of the steps are self-explanatory, so let's focus on the key aspects of training and evaluation.

As you learned at the beginning of the chapter, because we are using the Amazon SageMaker XGBoost built-in algorithm, we need to retrieve the XGBoost image URI for our specified region:

```
xgb_image = sagemaker.image_uris.retrieve("xgboost", region, "1.2-1")
```

Then, we need to define the input data channels: the sources where the algorithm should expect to find the training data and the evaluation data. The former will be used to train the model, and the latter will be used to tune its hyperparameters (model evaluation):

```
train_data = TrainingInput(s3_data=s3_train_data, content_type='csv')
val_data = TrainingInput(s3_data=s3_val_data, content_type='csv')
```

The XGBoost estimator in the provided code is used to train a model for multiclass classification on the Digits dataset:

```
xgb = sagemaker.estimator.Estimator(
    image_uri=xgb_image,
    role=role,
    instance_count=1,
    instance_type='ml.m5.large',
    output_path=f's3://{bucket_name}/{prefix}/output',
    sagemaker_session=session,
    hyperparameters={
        'objective': 'multi:softmax',  # Example for multi-class classification
        'num_class': 10,  # Number of classes in the Digits dataset
        'num_round': 100  # Default value; will be tuned
    }
)
```

In the instantiation of the xgb estimator, we pass the XGBoost image URI xgb_image, the IAM role being used for this session, the EC2 instance count 1, the instance type ml.m5.large, the S3 path where the artifacts generated after training will be stored, the session initiated by the boto3 (AWS SDK for Python) client, and finally the hyperparameters dictionary object. For more information about the Estimator signature, visit https://sagemaker.readthedocs.io/en/stable/api/training/estimators.html.

226 Chapter 5 ▪ Model Training and Evaluation

The `hyperparameters` dictionary object is specific to the XGBoost algorithm. For example, the `objective` key is set to the value `multi:softmax` to tell XGBoost to do multiclass classification using the `softmax` objective. Likewise, the key `num_class` specifies the number of classes (there are 10 classes in the Digits dataset), and the key `num_round` indicates the number of boosting rounds (iterations). For more information about the XGBoost hyperparameters, visit `https://docs.aws.amazon.com/sagemaker/latest/dg/xgboost-tuning.html`.

Upon defining the hyperparameter ranges dictionary object `hpt_ranges`—whose keys are also specific to the XGBoost algorithm—we are ready to optimize the hyperparameters using Bayesian optimization. This action is performed by creating a `tuner` object with this statement:

```
tuner = HyperparameterTuner(
    estimator=xgb,
    base_tuning_job_name='bayesian',
    objective_metric_name='validation:accuracy',
    hyperparameter_ranges=hpt_ranges,
    strategy='Bayesian',
    max_jobs=20,  # Increase to 20 max jobs
    max_parallel_jobs=3,  # Number of parallel jobs
    objective_type='Maximize'
)
```

and by fitting the tuner using the training dataset and the validation dataset:

```
tuner.fit({'train': train_data, 'validation': val_data})
```

Notice how the XGBoost hyperparameter `tuner` object is constructed by setting the `estimator` argument to the previously created `xgb` object, `validation:accuracy` as objective metric to be maximized, our hyperparameter ranges `hpt_ranges`, a Bayesian tuning strategy, and most importantly the maximum number of tuning and parallel jobs the tuner will utilize during the optimization process (respectively, 20 and 3). For more information about the `HyperparameterTuner` class, visit `https://sagemaker.readthedocs.io/en/stable/api/training/tuner.html`.

After the tuning job is complete, the best training job is identified:

```
best_training_job_name = tuner.best_training_job()
```

and the tuning results are analyzed to extract the best hyperparameter configuration. The results are finally visualized and plotted for better understanding.

Let's see this program in action! Figure 5.10 shows the program at runtime.

Deep-Dive Model Tuning Example   227

FIGURE 5.10   Running the program in Code Editor.

As a result of running this program, three new training jobs appear in the list of training jobs, as displayed in Figure 5.11. Why three? Because we set the maximum number of parallel jobs to three in the `tuner` object's constructor.

The program takes about 15 minutes to complete (45 seconds per job). It is always a good idea to proactively monitor the status of your training jobs in Amazon SageMaker Studio. Because we specified a maximum of 20 training jobs, 20 jobs are created in total.

> In the program, the training jobs will naturally terminate upon completion. This is because of how Amazon SageMaker handles training jobs. Once a training job is finished, Amazon SageMaker automatically shuts down the training instances, ensuring that we won't incur additional charges. However, to force the duration of a training job to a given amount of time, we could have set the `Estimator` argument `max_run` to a timeout in seconds. After this amount of time, Amazon SageMaker terminates the job regardless of its current status. Its default value is 86,400 seconds.

Upon successful completion, all jobs are marked with Completed status, as shown in Figure 5.12.

228 Chapter 5 ▪ Model Training and Evaluation

FIGURE 5.11 Training jobs start.

FIGURE 5.12 Training jobs completion.

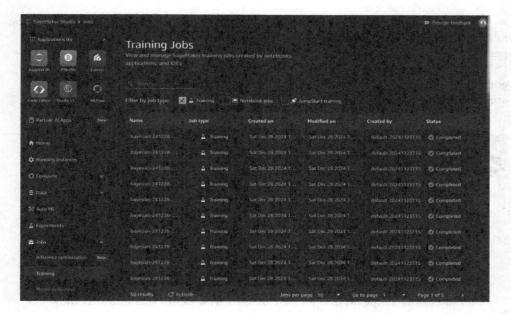

FIGURE 5.13 Tuning evaluation plot.

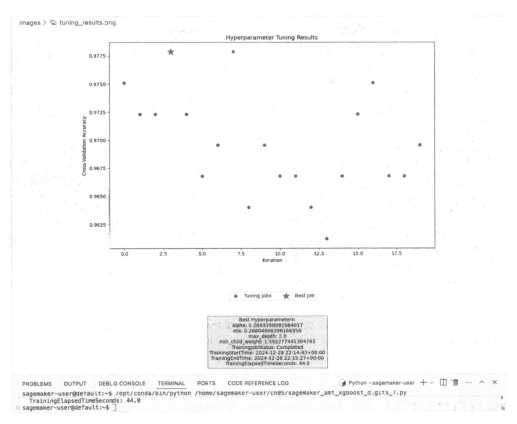

The expected outcome is the plot illustrated in Figure 5.13, which is saved in the images folder in the EFS file system attached to my Amazon SageMaker Studio instance.

As displayed in Figure 5.13, the fourth job from the left—marked with a star—is the best training job: i.e., the job with the maximum accuracy. Its hyperparameter combination is displayed in the bottom of the plot.

When you are done using Amazon SageMaker Studio, remember to stop your instance to avoid incurring in unwanted charges. Click the Stop button, as shown in Figure 5.14.

In this exercise, you learned how to use Amazon SageMaker AI AMT to optimize a XGBoost model using the Digits dataset. The program involved several steps: loading and splitting the dataset, saving the data locally and uploading it to an S3 bucket, defining the XGBoost estimator with required hyperparameters, and setting up a hyperparameter tuner with specified ranges for optimization. The tuner performed Bayesian optimization to find the best hyperparameter combination, and the program waited for

FIGURE 5.14 Stopping the Amazon SageMaker Studio instance.

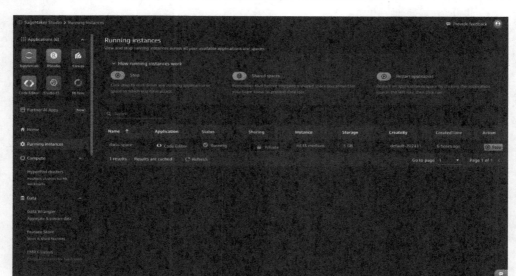

the tuning jobs to complete. After tuning, the best training job and hyperparameter combination were identified, and the tuning results were visualized and saved as an image.

Summary

In this chapter, we explored various facets of training ML models, including local, remote, and distributed training. We delved into monitoring and debugging techniques to ensure that model training runs smoothly and efficiently. These foundational concepts provide us with the necessary skills to manage and troubleshoot the training process, whether it's conducted on local machines or distributed across cloud resources.

The chapter then transitioned into hyperparameter tuning, differentiating between model parameters and hyperparameters and examining strategies for exploring the hyperparameter space using Amazon SageMaker AI AMT. Evaluation metrics were covered in detail, tailored to both classification and regression problems. We investigated various hyperparameter tuning techniques, including manual search, grid search, random search, Bayesian search, and multi-algorithm optimization. Additionally, we learned how to manage bias and variance tradeoff, as well as addressing overfitting and underfitting through regularization methods (L1, L2, Elastic Net).

Next, we focused on model performance evaluation, discussing various performance evaluation methods like K-fold cross-validation, random train–test, holdout set, and bootstrap. Each method was compared and contrasted, highlighting their strengths and limitations. These techniques are crucial for validating the model's performance and ensuring that it generalizes well to unseen data, which is the ultimate goal of any ML model.

We also provided insights into evaluating foundation models using Amazon Bedrock. We explored specific tools and methods for evaluating foundation models, including automatic evaluations, human evaluations, and knowledge base evaluations. This section emphasized the importance of a comprehensive evaluation framework to build and deploy generative AI applications with confidence and responsibility.

Finally, we concluded with a model tuning example, where we applied the concepts learned throughout the chapter. This practical example involved using Amazon SageMaker AI AMT configured with Bayesian optimization to perform hyperparameter tuning and model evaluation on the Digits dataset. By following the step-by-step instructions, we gained hands-on experience in optimizing ML models and evaluating their performance, reinforcing the theoretical knowledge acquired in the previous sections.

Exam Essentials

Know the difference between local, remote, and distributed training. Local training involves training a machine learning model on a single machine using its available resources. Remote training, on the other hand, runs the training process on a cloud service (e.g., Amazon SageMaker) or remote server, leveraging external compute resources without overloading the local system. Distributed training involves spreading the training workload across multiple machines or nodes, either locally or remotely, to handle larger datasets and reduce training time by parallelizing the computations.

Know the difference between model parameters and hyperparameters. Model parameters are the internal configurations that a machine learning model learns from the training data, such as the weights in a neural network or the coefficients in a linear regression model. These parameters are adjusted during the training process to minimize the error, also known as the loss function, and improve the model's performance. On the other hand, hyperparameters are external settings that control the overall behavior of the learning algorithm, such as the learning rate, the number of trees in a random forest, or the number of layers in a neural network. Hyperparameters are set *before* training begins and are typically tuned during evaluation through methods like grid search, random search, or Bayesian search to optimize the model's performance.

Know the main evaluation metrics for classification problems. For classification problems, the main evaluation metrics include accuracy, precision, recall, F1 score, and AUC-ROC. Accuracy measures the proportion of correctly classified instances out of the total instances. Precision evaluates the proportion of true positive predictions among all positive predictions, reflecting the quality of positive predictions. Recall (or sensitivity) measures the proportion of true positive predictions among all actual positives, indicating the model's ability to identify positive instances. The F1 score is the harmonic mean of precision and recall, providing a balanced measure that considers both false positives and false negatives. Area under the curve–receiver operating characteristic assesses the model's ability to discriminate between classes by plotting the true positive rate against the false positive rate across different threshold settings.

Know the main evaluation metrics for regression problems. For regression problems, the main evaluation metrics include mean squared error (MSE), root mean squared error (RMSE), mean absolute error (MAE), mean absolute percentage error (MAPE), and R-squared (R^2). MSE calculates the average of the squared differences between predicted and actual values, highlighting significant discrepancies. RMSE, the square root of MSE, provides error metrics in the same units as the target variable, making it easier to interpret. MAE measures the average magnitude of the absolute errors, offering a straightforward interpretation of prediction accuracy. MAPE provides a percentage-based evaluation of errors, useful for comparing models across different datasets. R^2 indicates the proportion of variance in the target variable predictable from the features, with values closer to 1 implying better model performance.

Know the difference between Bayesian search and other hyperparameter tuning techniques. Bayesian search is a hyperparameter optimization (HPO) technique that uses Bayesian inference to model the relationship between hyperparameters and the objective function, guiding the search for optimal hyperparameters based on prior knowledge and past evaluations. The objective function is a metric or measure that the optimization process aims to maximize or minimize, such as accuracy, loss, or other performance metrics. Unlike other HPO techniques such as grid search, which exhaustively searches a predefined space, or random search, which samples hyperparameters randomly, Bayesian search intelligently selects the next set of hyperparameters to evaluate by predicting their performance, thereby improving efficiency and often requiring fewer evaluations to find the best configuration. This makes Bayesian search particularly effective for complex models with large hyperparameter spaces. We used Bayesian search in our deep dive example to efficiently optimize our XGBoost model on the Digits dataset with Amazon SageMaker AI Automatic Model Tuning.

Understand the difference between underfitting and overfitting as well as the methods to address them. Underfitting occurs when a model is too simple to capture the underlying patterns in the data, resulting in poor performance on both the training and test datasets. Overfitting, on the other hand, happens when a model is too complex and captures noise or random fluctuations in the training data, leading to excellent performance on the training dataset but poor generalization to new, unseen data. To address underfitting, we can increase the model's complexity by adding more features, using a more sophisticated algorithm, or extending the training duration. To overcome overfitting, techniques such as K-fold cross-validation, pruning, regularization (e.g., L1, L2, Elastic Net), and data augmentation can be employed. These methods help strike a balance between model complexity and generalization, improving overall performance.

Understand the use of K-fold cross-validation and its benefits. K-fold cross-validation involves partitioning the dataset into k equally-sized folds or subsets. The model is then trained on $k - 1$ folds and tested on the remaining fold. This process is repeated k times, each time using a different fold as the test set, and the results are averaged to provide a comprehensive evaluation of the model's performance. This approach helps mitigate the bias and variance issues associated with a single train-test split by ensuring that every data point is used for both training and validation. Compared to methods like a single-holdout validation or random train-test split, K-fold cross-validation provides a more accurate and reliable assessment of the model's ability to generalize to unseen data, making it particularly useful for small or imbalanced datasets.

234 Chapter 5 ▪ Model Training and Evaluation

Review Questions

1. Which technique effectively combines the benefits of L1 and L2 regularization to control model complexity and improve generalization?

   A. LASSO regularization.

   B. Ridge regularization.

   C. Elastic Net regularization.

   D. It's not possible to combine the benefits of L1 and L2

2. What is a key advantage of Bayesian optimization over grid search in hyperparameter tuning?

   A. Bayesian optimization requires more hyperparameter evaluations.

   B. Bayesian optimization does not require prior evaluations.

   C. Bayesian optimization selects hyperparameters randomly.

   D. Bayesian optimization predicts the performance of hyperparameters to efficiently guide the search.

3. In the context of hyperparameter tuning, what is the primary goal of the objective function?

   A. To maximize the number of hyperparameters

   B. To minimize the computational cost

   C. To evaluate and optimize model performance

   D. To determine the model architecture

4. Which evaluation metric should be used to assess the performance of a regression model when comparing errors on different datasets with varying scales?

   A. Mean absolute error (MAE)

   B. Mean squared error (MSE)

   C. Root mean squared error (RMSE)

   D. Mean absolute percentage error (MAPE)

5. When using K-fold cross-validation, what is the primary benefit of stratifying the folds in classification problems?

   A. To increase the complexity of the model

   B. To ensure that each fold is representative of the overall class distribution

   C. To reduce the number of folds

   D. To maximize the training time

6. Which of the following scenarios indicates that a model is overfitting the training data?

A. High training accuracy and high test accuracy

B. Low training accuracy and high test accuracy

C. High training accuracy and low test accuracy

D. Low training accuracy and low test accuracy

7. What is a potential drawback of using random search for hyperparameter tuning compared to Bayesian search?

A. Random search always finds the best hyperparameters.

B. Random search is less efficient in searching large hyperparameter spaces.

C. Random search requires prior evaluations.

D. Random search is deterministic.

8. How does regularization help in addressing the issue of overfitting in machine learning models?

A. By increasing the model's complexity

B. By adding a penalty to the loss function to constrain model parameters

C. By removing training data

D. By increasing the number of training epochs

9. Which of the following is a common method to monitor and debug distributed training jobs in Amazon SageMaker?

A. Using Jupyter Notebooks

B. Enabling Spot Instances

C. Implementing Amazon SageMaker Debugger

D. Disabling Auto Scaling

10. In model evaluation, what does a high AUC-ROC score indicate for a classification model?

A. The model has a high number of false positives.

B. The model has a strong ability to discriminate between classes.

C. The model is likely overfitting the training data.

D. The model has a high number of false negatives.

Chapter 6

Model Deployment and Orchestration

THE AWS CERTIFIED MACHINE LEARNING (ML) ENGINEER ASSOCIATE EXAM OBJECTIVES COVERED IN THIS CHAPTER MAY INCLUDE, BUT ARE NOT LIMITED TO, THE FOLLOWING:

✔ **Domain 3: Deployment and Orchestration of ML Workflows**
- 3.1 Select deployment infrastructure based on existing architecture and requirements
- 3.2 Create and script infrastructure based on existing architecture and requirements
- 3.3 Use automated orchestration tools to set up continuous integration and continuous delivery (CI/CD) pipelines

AWS Model Deployment Services

In the previous chapter, you learned how to train and how to evaluate the performance of your model. You learned different training approaches to ensure that your chosen model has sufficient amounts of data to learn patterns and relationships between features and labels for supervised ML problems, as well as how it can uncover hidden structures and patterns in unsupervised ML problems.

Now, it's time to move forward and explore how to deploy these models effectively. Model deployment is the integration of your model and all its resources into a production environment so it can be used to generate predictions, or *inferences*.

In this chapter, we will delve into the *Deploy Model* and *Derive Inference* phases, as illustrated in Figure 6.1. These phases are essential for delivering the insights and predictions your model is capable of.

Throughout the chapter we will use the term "ML app" to denote the application responsible for producing inferences in response to inference requests. This application will receive inference requests as input, will pass this data to the model, and will eventually return inference responses upon receiving an output from the model.

I used the term *eventually* to indicate that the response produced by the ML app (after consuming the model) will be returned to the requestor "one way or the other." This may happen immediately (in real time), in near real time (with a few seconds delay), or after an undetermined period of time. In the last scenario, the processing of the inferences usually occurs in batches, because the requestor does not expect an immediate response. As a result, the period it takes for the ML app to return inferences depends on—among other factors—the batch size (how many inference requests are being batched?) and the amount of data for each inference request, also referred to as the *payload*.

Depending on your specific use case, you may choose to leverage Amazon AI Services that use pretrained models and obtain inferences by invoking directly their APIs, or you may choose to expose your model with an endpoint provided by Amazon SageMaker, now referred to as Amazon SageMaker AI.

Either way, it is critical that the deployment approach you pursue complies with well-architected best practices. This means ensuring that your organization's teams support efficient development and workload management, protecting your identities, data, infrastructure, and applications with robust security measures and maintaining the expected levels of

FIGURE 6.1 The machine learning lifecycle.

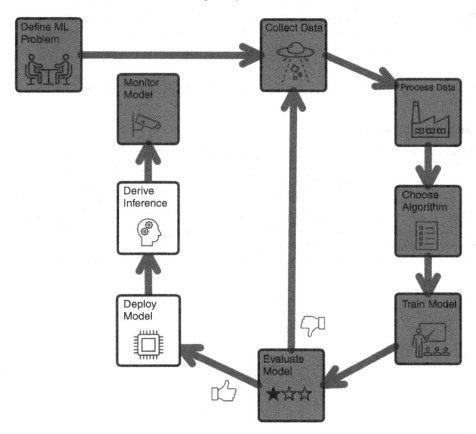

reliability metrics. Additionally, it's essential to use resources efficiently to meet system requirements, minimize costs by avoiding unnecessary expenses, and adopt sustainable practices to reduce your environmental impact. By adhering to these principles of operational excellence, security, reliability, performance efficiency, cost optimization, and sustainability, you can build a performant, robust, secure, and cost-effective model deployment that aligns with your organizational goals and environmental responsibilities.

Let's start the chapter with deployment techniques for Amazon AI services.

Deploying AI Services

Although Amazon SageMaker AI is often used to build, train, and deploy custom ML models, it also integrates seamlessly with several fully managed AI services provided by AWS. As you learned in Chapter 4, these services offer pretrained models that can be easily incorporated into your applications via API calls.

> For the exam, it's important to know that these pretrained models are hosted in managed AWS accounts owned by the respective services, so there is limited access to them. These models are exposed for consumption in the form of API calls.

This section explores how these AI services can be effectively deployed with your ML applications.

Amazon Rekognition

Amazon Rekognition offers pretrained models for image and video analysis. Deploying Amazon Rekognition involves making API calls to the service to analyze images and videos for objects, faces, text, and scenes. Amazon SageMaker AI can be used to orchestrate these API calls within your ML workflows, ensuring seamless integration with your applications. The orchestration aspect is a key requirement of the exam and will be covered in detail at the end of this chapter. This approach allows for scalable image and video processing without needing direct access to the underlying models.

The following snippet provides an example of how to use Amazon Rekognition:

```
import boto3

client = boto3.client('rekognition')

response = client.detect_labels(
    Image={'S3Object': {'Bucket': 'your-bucket-name', 'Name': 'your-image.jpg'}},
    MaxLabels=10,
    MinConfidence=75
)

for label in response['Labels']:
    print(f"Label: {label['Name']}, Confidence: {label['Confidence']}")
```

To get started with Amazon Rekognition using Python, you'll first need to set up your environment by installing and configuring the AWS SDK for Python, known as boto3. Amazon SageMaker Studio Code Editor comes with boto3 preinstalled.

Once your environment is ready, import the boto3 library, and create a client for the Rekognition service using the statement client = boto3.client('rekognition'). Next, prepare your data by uploading the images or videos you want to analyze to an Amazon S3 bucket. With your data in place, you can call the detect_labels API method to analyze the images and identify objects, scenes, and activities. The Image parameter specifies the S3 bucket and file name, whereas the MaxLabels and MinConfidence parameters define the maximum number of labels to return and the minimum confidence level for the detected labels. The API call returns a response object, which includes the identified labels and their corresponding confidence scores (response['Labels']), which you can print or use in your application for further processing. With the provided code you learned how to use Amazon Rekognition to analyze an image stored in an S3 bucket and print the detected labels and their confidence scores.

For more information, visit

```
https://docs.aws.amazon.com/rekognition/latest/APIReference/
Welcome.html.
```

Amazon Textract

Amazon Textract provides pretrained models for extracting text and data from scanned documents. To use Amazon Textract, create a client using the statement `client = boto3.client('textract')`. Key methods include `analyze_document`, `detect_document_text`, and `get_document_analysis` for processing documents. Here's an example of using the `analyze_document` method:

```
import boto3

client = boto3.client('textract')

response = client.analyze_document(
    Document={'S3Object': {'Bucket': 'your-bucket-name', 'Name': 'your-
document.pdf'}},
    FeatureTypes=['TABLES', 'FORMS']
)

for block in response['Blocks']:
    if block['BlockType'] == 'LINE':
        print(block['Text'])
```

For more information, visit:

```
https://docs.aws.amazon.com/textract/latest/dg/API_Reference.html.
```

Amazon Polly

Amazon Polly converts text into lifelike speech using pretrained models. To use Amazon Polly, create a client using the statement `client = boto3.client('polly')`. Key methods include `synthesize_speech`, `describe_voices`, and `list_lexicons` for generating speech. Here's an example of using the `synthesize_speech` method:

```
import boto3

client = boto3.client('polly')

response = client.synthesize_speech(
    Text='Hello, world!',
    OutputFormat='mp3',
```

242 Chapter 6 ▪ Model Deployment and Orchestration

```
    VoiceId='Joanna'
)

with open('speech.mp3', 'wb') as file:
    file.write(response['AudioStream'].read())
```

For more information, visit

`https://docs.aws.amazon.com/polly/latest/dg/API_Reference.html`.

Amazon Transcribe

Amazon Transcribe offers pretrained models for speech-to-text conversion. To use Amazon Transcribe, create a client using the statement `client = boto3.client('transcribe')`. Key methods include `start_transcription_job`, `get_transcription_job`, and `list_transcription_jobs` for managing transcription tasks. Here's an example of using the `start_transcription_job` method:

```
import boto3

client = boto3.client('transcribe')

response = client.start_transcription_job(
    TranscriptionJobName='TranscriptionJob',
    Media={'MediaFileUri': 's3://your-bucket-name/your-audio-file.mp3'},
    MediaFormat='mp3',
    LanguageCode='en-US'
)

# Wait for the job to complete and retrieve the transcript
while True:
    status =
client.get_transcription_job(TranscriptionJobName='TranscriptionJob')
    if status['TranscriptionJob']['TranscriptionJobStatus'] in ['COMPLETED'
'FAILED']:
        break

print(status['TranscriptionJob']['Transcript']['TranscriptFileUri'])
```

For more information, visit

`https://docs.aws.amazon.com/transcribe/latest/APIReference/Welcome.html`.

Amazon Comprehend

Amazon Comprehend offers pretrained models for natural language processing tasks such as sentiment analysis, entity recognition, and key phrase extraction. To use Amazon Comprehend, create a client using the statement `client = boto3.client('comprehend')`. Key methods

AWS Model Deployment Services **243**

include `detect_sentiment`, `detect_entities`, and `detect_key_phrases` for analyzing text. Here's an example of using the `detect_sentiment` method:

```
import boto3

client = boto3.client('comprehend')

response = client.detect_sentiment(
    Text='I love using Amazon Comprehend!',
    LanguageCode='en'
)

print(f"Sentiment: {response['Sentiment']}, Score:
{response['SentimentScore']}")
```

For more information, visit

https://docs.aws.amazon.com/comprehend/latest/APIReference/welcome.html.

Amazon Lex

Amazon Lex provides pretrained models for building conversational interfaces using voice and text. To use Amazon Lex, create a client using the statement `client = boto3.client('lexv2-runtime')`. A key method is `recognize_text` for managing interactions with your chatbot. Here's an example of using the `recognize_text` method:

```
import boto3

client = boto3.client('lexv2-runtime')

response = client.recognize_text(
    botId='YourBotId',
    botAliasId='YourBotAliasId',
    localeId='en_US',
    sessionId='User123',
    text='I would like to book a flight'
)

print(f"Bot Response: {response['messages'][0]['content']}")
```

For more information, visit

https://docs.aws.amazon.com/lexv2/latest/APIReference/welcome.html.

Amazon Personalize

Amazon Personalize offers pretrained models for creating individualized recommendations. To use Amazon Personalize, create a client using the statement `client = boto3`.

244　Chapter 6 ▪ Model Deployment and Orchestration

`client('personalize')`. Key methods include `get_recommendations`, `get_personalized_ranking`, and `create_campaign` for managing recommendation tasks. Here's an example of using the `get_recommendations` method:

```
import boto3

client = boto3.client('personalize')

response = client.get_recommendations(
    campaignArn='your-campaign-arn',
    userId='User123'
)

for item in response['itemList']:
    print(f"Recommended Item: {item['itemId']}, Score: {item['score']}")
```

For more information, visit

`https://docs.aws.amazon.com/personalize/latest/dg/API_Reference.html`.

Amazon Bedrock

Amazon Bedrock provides a secure and scalable framework for deploying and managing foundation models (FMs). To derive inference using Amazon Bedrock models, you can create a client using the statement `client = boto3.client('bedrock-runtime')`. Amazon Bedrock enables two primary approaches for deploying models: using agents and the Converse API.

Using Agents

Agents in Amazon Bedrock act as intermediaries between your application and the foundation model. They allow you to define specific tasks, behaviors, and interactions, providing a comprehensive framework for managing and orchestrating various types of models. The process involves creating an agent, configuring it with the tasks it will perform, and creating an alias for the agent to interact with your application. This approach is ideal for complex workflows and tasks that require extensive management and orchestration.

Using the Converse API

On the other hand, the Converse API is designed specifically for conversational interactions. It provides a direct way to manage text-based interactions by sending input text to the model and receiving responses. The Converse API is well-suited for use cases such as chatbots, virtual assistants, and customer service applications where conversational AI is the primary requirement. Here's an example of using the Converse API:

```
import boto3

# Create a Bedrock client
client = boto3.client('bedrock-runtime')
```

```
# Invoke the Converse API

response = client.converse(
    modelId='your-model-id'',    # Replace with your model ID
    messages=[{
        'role': 'user',
        'content':[
            {
                'text': 'Create a list of ten bestselling books about Calculus'
            }
        ]
    }]
)

print(f"Model Response: {response['output']['message']['content'][0]['text']}")
```

This snippet demonstrates how to create an Amazon Bedrock client, invoke the Converse API with the input text, and print the model's response. The Converse API provides a streamlined approach for conversational interactions, making it a suitable alternative for scenarios where agents might be too complex.

For more information on using Amazon Bedrock's boto3 API, you can refer to the Amazon Bedrock User Guide: https://docs.aws.amazon.com/bedrock/latest/user guide/getting-started-api.html.

Deploying Your Model

In the previous section, you learned how to deploy AI services provided by AWS. In this section, we will explore a more customized approach tailored to your specific use case, where you have built and fine-tuned your own model and now it's ready for deployment. The deployment phase is critical as it ensures that your ML model is accessible and can deliver predictions on new data in real time or batch mode. Amazon SageMaker AI offers robust and flexible deployment options that cater to various requirements, ranging from fully managed services to more customizable, self-managed solutions.

Managed model deployments in Amazon SageMaker AI provide a streamlined and hassle-free way to deploy your models. With managed endpoints, Amazon SageMaker AI takes care of all the underlying infrastructure, including provisioning, scaling, and load balancing, ensuring high availability and fault tolerance. This approach allows you to focus on your application's logic and performance without worrying about the operational aspects of deploying and maintaining your model. Managed deployments are ideal for production environments where reliability and scalability are paramount.

Unmanaged model deployments offer greater flexibility and control over the deployment process. By leveraging Amazon SageMaker AI's powerful SDKs and APIs, you can deploy your models on custom infrastructure that fits your unique needs. This approach is suitable for scenarios where you require specific configurations, custom networking setups, or

246 Chapter 6 ▪ Model Deployment and Orchestration

integration with existing systems. Unmanaged deployments give you the freedom to optimize resource allocation and cost while maintaining full control over the deployment lifecycle.

Choosing the right infrastructure (type and size) to support your deployments depends on several key criteria: scalability, ease of management, customization needs, security, and cost considerations. Managed deployments are ideal for applications requiring high availability and effortless scaling, as they offload the operational burden to Amazon SageMaker AI. This option is best for teams looking for a hassle-free, production-ready solution. Conversely, unmanaged deployments offer greater flexibility and control, making them suitable for complex configurations or integration with existing systems. This approach allows for fine-tuned resource allocation and cost optimization. Evaluating these criteria will help determine the most suitable deployment strategy for your specific use case.

Infrastructure Selection Considerations

Because the main purpose of deploying your model is to derive inferences, it is important to understand the computational aspects of inference and how they are different from training.

Inference is the phase where a trained model is utilized to make predictions on testing samples, involving a forward pass similar to the one used during training to generate predictions. However, unlike training, inference does not include a backward pass to calculate errors or update the model's weights (or other internal parameters) to minimize the loss function.

As a result, there are some important differences between inferencing and training that you need to know for the exam. This understanding will help you select the most suitable infrastructure for each use case. Table 6.1 summarizes these differences.

In short, training infrastructure in ML is designed for high computational power to handle extensive data processing and model optimization, whereas inferencing infrastructure prioritizes low latency and efficiency for real-time or batch prediction tasks.

TABLE 6.1 Inference and Training Comparison.

Inference compute	Training compute
Runs on single real-time endpoints (except batch inference)	Requires high parallelism with large batch processing for higher throughput
Less compute	More compute
Less memory	More memory
Runs ubiquitously (on devices at the edge and in the cloud)	Runs in the cloud
Runs all the time	Runs as needed (trains once, retrain infrequently)
Integrated into ML app stack	Standalone

Managed Model Deployments

Hosting a model in Amazon SageMaker AI, known as *managed model deployments*, offers numerous benefits that streamline the ML deployment process. By using Amazon SageMaker AI, you leverage the power of AWS to manage the underlying infrastructure, enabling you to focus more on developing and refining your models rather than handling the complexities of deployment. Amazon SageMaker AI provides a robust, scalable, and secure environment that ensures that your models can handle varying workloads and deliver reliable inferences. The service handles infrastructure provisioning, scaling, load balancing, and health monitoring, significantly reducing operational overhead.

Amazon SageMaker AI's managed model deployment options are highlighted in Figure 6.2 and include Batch Inference, Asynchronous Inference, Serverless Inference, and Real-time Inference.

Each of these deployment types caters to different use cases, providing flexibility and efficiency based on your ML problem's unique requirements. With managed endpoints, you benefit from automatic scaling and integration with other AWS services, such as Identity and Access Management (IAM) for secure access control and Amazon CloudWatch for monitoring and logging. Amazon SageMaker AI's seamless integration with the AWS ecosystem ensures that your models are not only robust but also compliant with best practices in security, performance, and cost optimization in accordance with the pillars of the AWS Well-Architected Framework.

An essential aspect of all Amazon SageMaker AI's model deployment options is the reliance on containers. Containers encapsulate the model and its dependencies, ensuring a consistent environment across different stages of the ML lifecycle. This approach provides flexibility and portability, enabling seamless transitions from development to production.

FIGURE 6.2 Amazon SageMaker AI managed model deployment types.

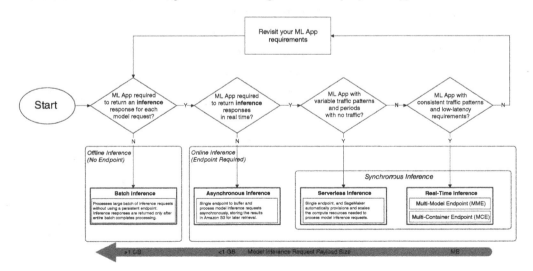

Additionally, the trained and evaluated model artifacts, typically saved as model.tar.gz, play a crucial role in deployments. This artifact contains the model parameters and any other necessary files required for inference. When you deploy a model in Amazon SageMaker AI, the service decompresses this artifact in the preconfigured instances to make the model ready to serve inference requests. This process ensures that all components of the model are intact and can be accessed efficiently during inference.

Now, let's dive into the specifics of each deployment method.

Real-Time Inference

Real-time inference in Amazon SageMaker AI is designed to provide instant predictions for incoming inference requests. This deployment approach is best suited for applications that require low-latency responses in the form of small payloads, such as fraud detection, recommendation systems, and interactive applications.

For real-time inference, Amazon SageMaker AI uses a trained model artifact from Amazon S3 and an inference container from Amazon Elastic Container Registry (ECR) with multiple, auto-scalable instances (Figure 6.3).

Here is how real-time inference works at a high level.

Decompressing the model artifact. When you deploy a model for real-time inference, the first step performed by Amazon SageMaker AI is to decompress the model artifact. This artifact is a compressed file (usually a tar.gz file) that contains the serialized model and any other necessary files (such as learned parameters during training, configuration files or scripts) that were output by the training job. As shown in Figure 6.3, Amazon SageMaker AI retrieves this artifact from the specified S3 bucket.

FIGURE 6.3 Real-time inference architecture.

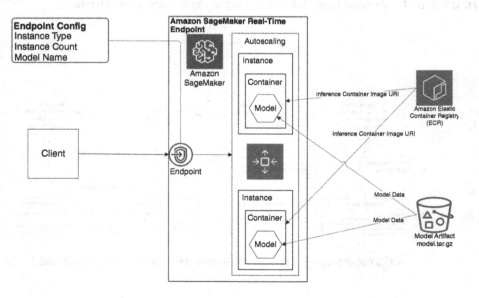

Serving the model. Next, the model is loaded and served by a framework-specific container. Amazon SageMaker AI supports various ML frameworks like TensorFlow, PyTorch, and many built-in algorithms, as you learned in Chapter 4. The serving container includes the necessary libraries to deserialize the model and make it ready for predictions. Amazon SageMaker AI accesses your selected algorithm/framework's container image from Amazon ECR and uses this image to create a container. The model is now running in a container runtime (Docker) hosted on an instance (or multiple instances based on incoming traffic) managed by Amazon SageMaker AI. In Figure 6.3, the model is represented as an hexagon and is running and waiting to serve inference requests.

Endpoint configuration. Amazon SageMaker AI creates an endpoint configuration, which includes details such as the instance type (e.g., `ml.m5.large`), the instance count, and the model to be deployed. This configuration allows Amazon SageMaker AI to manage the resources required to serve the model and handle incoming requests. The endpoint configuration can be customized based on the performance and scalability requirements of your deployment. Figure 6.3 shows some of the properties you can set when you create an endpoint configuration.

HTTPS endpoint. Once the endpoint configuration is ready, Amazon SageMaker AI creates an HTTPS endpoint. This endpoint is a unique URL that clients can use to send real-time inference requests to the model. The endpoint uses HTTPS for secure communication, ensuring that data sent between the client and the server is encrypted and secure.

Autoscaling and load balancing (optional). For real-time inference, you can optionally enable autoscaling to automatically adjust the number of instances based on incoming traffic. Amazon SageMaker AI integrates with AWS Application Auto Scaling, allowing the endpoint to elastically scale in or out based on predefined policies or real-time metrics. Application load balancing distributes incoming requests across all available instances, ensuring efficient balancing of traffic.

Monitoring and logging. Amazon SageMaker AI provides monitoring and logging capabilities to track the performance and health of the endpoint. You can view metrics such as invocation count, latency, and error rate in Amazon CloudWatch. Logs are captured and can be reviewed to debug issues or analyze the performance of the model.

Invoking the endpoint. Clients can now make real-time predictions by sending HTTPS POST requests to the endpoint. These requests include the input data, and the response contains the model's prediction. The serving container processes the input data, runs it through the model, and passes the response to the ML app, which returns the predictions to the client.

Before delving into other managed model deployment types, the exam requires you to know the different "flavors" of real-time inference deployments available with Amazon SageMaker AI. These are multi-model endpoints (MMEs) and multi-container endpoints (MCEs).

Multi-model Endpoints

MMEs offer an efficient and cost-effective solution for deploying multiple ML models on a single endpoint. With MMEs, different models share the same container image, optimizing resource usage and reducing the costs associated with managing separate endpoints for each

FIGURE 6.4 MME architecture.

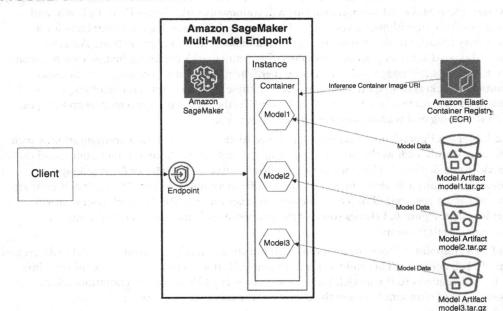

model. This setup is particularly advantageous for scenarios where you have numerous models that are infrequently used, as it allows you to dynamically load and unload models as needed. By leveraging a shared serving infrastructure, MMEs simplify model management while ensuring high performance, scalability, and reliability. This architecture, as illustrated in Figure 6.4, showcases a single endpoint with a shared container image, three models stored in Amazon S3, and efficient handling of inference requests by dynamically loading the required model into memory.

However, MMEs do have their limitations. One key limitation is that all models deployed on an MME must use the same container image, which includes the same framework and runtime environment. This requirement can be restrictive if you need to deploy models that rely on different frameworks or dependencies. Additionally, although MMEs provide isolated memory spaces for each model, the models still share the same container runtime, which may lead to resource contention in high-demand scenarios. It's important to carefully manage the loading and unloading of models to ensure optimal performance and avoid latency issues. Despite these limitations, MMS remain a powerful and flexible solution for deploying multiple ML models efficiently and cost-effectively. The architecture in Figure 6.4 highlights the key components of this deployment, ensuring a seamless and scalable inference experience.

Multi-container Endpoints

MCEs allow you to deploy containers with different frameworks, overcoming the limitation of MMEs where all models must use the same container image. As of the writing of this

FIGURE 6.5 MCE architecture with container direct invocation.

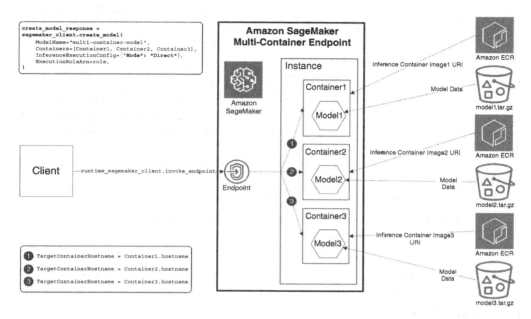

book, MCEs allow you to deploy up to 15 containers on a single endpoint. The containers can be run in a sequence (*serial invocation*) or individually (*direct invocation*). With direct invocation, each container can be accessed independently to improve endpoint utilization and optimize costs. By running multiple containers on the same EC2 instance, MCEs streamline resource utilization and simplify the deployment of complex inference pipelines.

The architecture in Figure 6.5 illustrates an MCE configured with direct invocation. The figure shows how you would create an MCE model with the CreateModel API.

The CreateModel API is a RESTful API that you can call directly to create a model in Amazon SageMaker AI. You provide the necessary information, such as the model name, container details, and execution role, in a structured request format. To learn more, visit https://docs.aws.amazon.com/sagemaker/latest/APIReference/API_CreateModel.html.

Notice how we define a "polymorphic" model by specifying which form (container) it can use. In our example, the model can be built from three distinct container images: Container1, Contaner2, and Container3. These could be, for example, the container image URIs for Scikit-Learn, TensorFlow, and PyTorch. With a direct invocation mode the three models are consumed by your ML app individually.

252 Chapter 6 ▪ Model Deployment and Orchestration

When the client calls the ML app requesting inference, it can select one of the three models by specifying which target container hostname to use. This selection can be accomplished with the `invoke_endpoint` API from the SageMaker Runtime client. For more details, visit `https://boto3.amazonaws.com/v1/documentation/api/latest/reference/services/sagemaker-runtime.html`.

Just like MMEs, your containers are hosted in the same EC2 instance, resulting in potential resource contention. This can lead to performance issues if the containers require substantial computational resources. Despite this limitation, MCEs provide a powerful and versatile solution for deploying sophisticated ML workflows, leveraging the modularity and flexibility of containerization to enhance the scalability and efficiency of your inference deployments.

For the exam, be aware of some of the most common MCE use cases, including the following:

- Hosting models across different frameworks
- Hosting models from the same framework with different ML algorithms
- A/B testing

If you need to deploy a complex ML workflow involving multiple models or preprocessing steps, each potentially requiring different frameworks and dependencies, then MCEs are a valid option to consider.

Serverless Inference

With serverless inference, you no longer have to guess how many instances you need and what instance type are best suited for your ML models. Amazon SageMaker AI serverless inference automatically provisions and scales the necessary compute resources based on your model's workload. Because Amazon SageMaker AI manages your model endpoint's infrastructure based on inference demand, you are charged only for the instances used to respond to inference requests. This flexibility ensures that your application can handle varying amounts of traffic without the need for manual intervention, providing a seamless and cost-effective solution for deploying ML models.

Figure 6.6 illustrates the serverless inference architecture.

The process begins by configuring the memory size and maximum concurrency for your serverless endpoint. These parameters help Amazon SageMaker AI allocate the appropriate compute resources to meet your ML app's performance requirements. When an inference request is made, Amazon SageMaker AI dynamically scales the compute capacity to match the demand (*scale-out*), ensuring that your model can handle bursts of traffic while maintaining low latency. Conversely, when inference requests are completed, this architecture reduces the compute resources (*scale-in*), deprovisioning the excess capacity to minimize costs. This elastic compute behavior is symbolized in Figure 6.6 with downward chevrons (scale-out) and upward chevrons (scale-in). This serverless architecture eliminates the need to preallocate resources, reducing costs when your model is idle or experiencing low traffic.

AWS Model Deployment Services

FIGURE 6.6 Serverless Inference architecture.

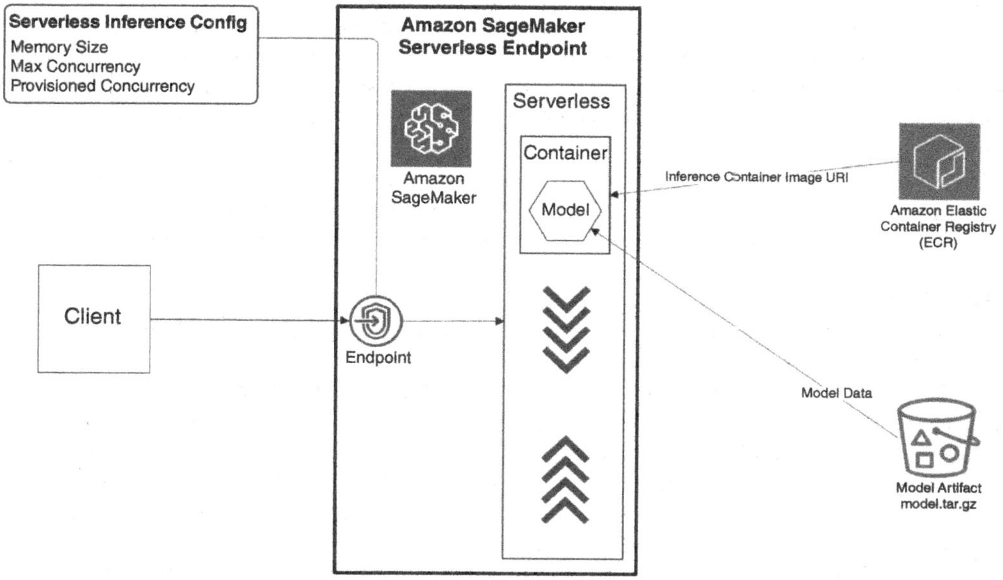

> *Max concurrency* refers to the maximum number of concurrent requests that can be processed by your serverless endpoint at any given time. By setting this parameter, you define the upper limit of simultaneous requests the endpoint can handle, which helps manage traffic spikes and ensures consistent performance. *Provisioned concurrency*, on the other hand, ensures that a specified number of execution environments are always ready to handle requests, reducing latency and providing a more predictable response time.

Another advantage of serverless inference is its seamless integration with Amazon SageMaker AI's model deployment pipeline. Once your model is trained and tuned, you can easily deploy it using the serverless inference configuration. This involves specifying the model artifacts (such as model.tar.gz) and the serving container image URI. Similarly to real-time inference, Amazon SageMaker AI takes care of downloading and decompressing the model files, initializing the model, and exposing an API endpoint for inference requests. This automated process simplifies deployment and ensures that your model is ready to serve predictions without manual setup.

By leveraging a serverless infrastructure, you can focus on building and optimizing your models rather than managing the underlying infrastructure. Serverless inference is

254   Chapter 6 ▪ Model Deployment and Orchestration

particularly suited for applications with variable or unpredictable traffic patterns, enabling efficient resource utilization and cost management.

At the end of the chapter, you will be walked through a deep-dive demonstration of how serverless inference works with the Amazon SageMaker Python SDK. Specifically, we will use an instance of the `ServerlessInferenceConfig` class to programmatically create a serverless endpoint exposing the best XGBoost model for the Digits dataset we tuned at the end of Chapter 5.

To learn more about the `ServerlessInferenceConfig` class, visit `https://sagemaker.readthedocs.io/en/stable/api/inference/serverless.html#sagemaker.serverless.serverless_inference_config.ServerlessInferenceConfig`.

Asynchronous Inference

Asynchronous inference is another managed model deployment designed to handle large-scale, long-running tasks that do not require an immediate response. Unlike real-time endpoints that process requests and return results within a short timeframe, asynchronous inference allows you to submit inference requests and process them at a later time. This means that requests can be queued and processed as resources become available, making it ideal for scenarios where inference latency is not a critical factor. Asynchronous inference helps manage and balance your workload effectively, ensuring that large volumes of data can be processed without overwhelming your infrastructure.

The workflow for Amazon SageMaker AI asynchronous inference is straightforward. You start by creating an asynchronous inference endpoint, similar to a real-time endpoint, and then submit your inference requests to this endpoint. Each request is stored in an Amazon S3 bucket, and Amazon SageMaker AI retrieves the requests from the bucket for processing. Once the inference is completed, the results are stored back in the Amazon S3 bucket, and you can retrieve them at your convenience. You can optionally choose to receive success or error notifications with Amazon SNS. This decoupled architecture allows for efficient handling of large datasets and long-running inference tasks without the constraints of real-time processing.

Asynchronous inference is best suited for use cases where inference tasks are resource-intensive and time-consuming and can tolerate delayed responses. Examples include processing large image datasets, running complex ML models, and performing extensive data transformations.

Batch Inference

As the volume and payload of your inference requests increase, a well-architected solution to generate inference at scale becomes essential. Amazon SageMaker AI batch inference is designed to address this challenge by allowing you to process large datasets in bulk. Unlike real-time endpoints, which cater to immediate predictions, batch inference is tailored for scenarios where low-latency responses are not a priority. By leveraging batch inference, you can efficiently handle extensive workloads, ensuring that your ML models can process significant amounts of data without compromising performance. It's important to highlight that batch transform jobs do not require endpoints; instead, they operate by processing data in bulk and storing the results in specified locations.

The process begins with creating a batch transform job, where you specify the input data location, the model to be used, and the output data location. Amazon SageMaker AI then processes the input data in parallel, utilizing its scalable infrastructure to optimize resource usage. Once the batch transform job is completed, the results are stored in the specified output location, allowing you to retrieve and analyze them at your convenience. Similarly to asynchronous inference, this decoupled architecture ensures that batch inference tasks can be managed effectively, minimizing the need for continuous monitoring and intervention.

Amazon SageMaker AI batch inference is particularly well-suited for use cases where large volumes of data need to be processed simultaneously and the immediacy of the model predictions is not critical. Examples include offline analytics, data preprocessing, and periodic model updates. It is also ideal for generating predictions for entire datasets, such as scoring customer data for marketing campaigns or analyzing sensor data for predictive maintenance.

Unmanaged Model Deployments

With AWS, you don't have to deploy your models with Amazon SageMaker AI. Although Amazon SageMaker AI offers a robust and fully managed solution for model deployment, providing numerous benefits such as automatic scaling, built-in algorithms, and simplified model training and deployment processes, it may not always be the best fit for every scenario. Unmanaged model deployments are referred to as a method where you, as the user, take on the responsibility for managing all the deployment infrastructure. This approach offers greater flexibility and control compared to fully managed services like Amazon SageMaker AI, but it also involves the trade-off of taking on the cost and complexity of managing the deployment infrastructure yourself.

Unmanaged deployments grant you greater control and customization over your environment, allowing for specific hardware configurations, custom software dependencies, and specialized network settings. This level of granularity is ideal for users who need to tailor their deployment setups extensively. Additionally, unmanaged deployments can lead to cost optimizations, as you have the flexibility to fine-tune instance types, utilize spot instances, and manage scaling policies manually, potentially providing significant cost savings. However, it is important to recognize that this control comes with the responsibility of maintaining and managing the infrastructure, which can introduce additional complexity and overhead.

Beyond control and cost, other factors such as complex workflows and integration needs, data residency, compute residency requirements, and compliance or regulatory considerations also drive the choice for unmanaged deployments. For instance, when deploying models in environments with strict data residency requirements or industry-specific regulations like GDPR and HIPAA, having full control over the infrastructure ensures that you can implement custom security measures and meet all necessary legal standards. In such cases, AWS compute services like Amazon EC2, ECS, EKS, and Lambda offer the flexibility and control needed to address these specific demands for your model deployments.

In the upcoming sections, you will learn how each of these AWS compute services can be used to deploy your ML models in AWS.

Amazon Elastic Compute Cloud (EC2)

Amazon EC2 provides scalable compute capacity in the cloud, allowing users to launch virtual servers and manage their own infrastructure. For unmanaged model deployments, EC2 instances can be used to host ML models, providing full control over the environment, including the operating system, network configuration, and security settings. This flexibility is ideal for users who need to customize their deployment setup extensively. By leveraging EC2, you can choose the instance types that best fit your workload requirements, ensuring optimal performance and cost efficiency.

When selecting EC2 instance types, it's important to consider whether your workload would benefit more from CPU or GPU resources.

CPUs are generally suitable for traditional ML workloads, data preprocessing, and applications that do not require intensive parallel processing. They are best suited for the early phases of the ML lifecycle, such as data cleaning, feature engineering, and model inference tasks that do not demand heavy computational power.

GPUs are highly efficient for deep learning tasks, image processing, and other compute-intensive operations that can take advantage of parallel processing capabilities. They are particularly beneficial during the training and evaluation phases of the ML lifecycle, where large datasets and complex algorithms require substantial computational resources to reduce training time and improve model accuracy.

> Whereas training a deep learning model often necessitates a high-powered GPU instance due to the heavy computational load, performing inferences (applying the trained model to new data) typically requires significantly less processing power and can often be done on a less powerful GPU or even a CPU, depending on the application and desired latency. As a result, deploying these deep learning models on a full-sized GPU may lead to underutilization and unnecessary costs.

Table 6.2 can help you select the appropriate EC2 instance types for different ML inference tasks. Because the cost varies by region and other factors, the provided figures are approximations. Keep in mind that although model training typically demands high memory consumption due to the large datasets processed during the learning phase, inference primarily focuses on achieving high throughput and low latency, meaning quick responses to new data with minimal delay.

> For the exam, be aware of how AWS Inferentia EC2 instance types (Inf1, Inf2) deliver high performance at the lowest cost for your deep learning (DL) and generative AI inference applications. More advanced inference capabilities on these compute architectures are enabled by the newly developed AWS Neuron SDK, which integrates natively with popular frameworks, such as PyTorch and TensorFlow, so that you can continue to use your existing code and workflows and run on AWS Inferentia chips. For more information, visit https://aws.amazon.com/ec2/instance-types/inf2.

TABLE 6.2 Inference-Based EC2 Instance Types.

Instance type	Use case	Key features	Approximate cost	GPU-based	Compute architecture
t2 (burstable performance)	Development, testing, basic inference	Low-cost, burstable CPU performance	Low	No	x86–64 (64-bit)
c5 (general purpose)	Versatile ML workloads, basic inference	Balanced CPU, memory, and network resources	Moderate	No	x86–64 (64-bit)
m5 (general purpose)	Mixed workloads, basic inference	Balanced CPU, memory, and network resources	Moderate	No	x86–64 (64-bit)
Inf1 (inferentia)	High-performance, cost-effective inference	Powered by AWS Inferentia chips	Moderate	No	AWS Inferentia
Inf2 (inferentia)	High-performance, cost-effective inference	Powered by second-generation AWS Inferentia chips	Moderate	No	AWS Inferentia
g4dn (GPU optimized)	Deep learning inference	NVIDIA GPUs, cost-effective	High	Yes	NVIDIA T4 Tensor Core GPUs
g5 (GPU optimized)	Deep learning inference	Higher-performance NVIDIA GPUs	High	Yes	NVIDIA A10G Tensor Core GPUs
g6 (GPU optimized)	Deep learning inference	NVIDIA L4 Tensor Core GPUs	High	Yes	NVIDIA L4 Tensor Core GPUs
p4 (compute optimized)	High-performance inference	Higher-performance NVIDIA GPUs	Highest	Yes	NVIDIA A100 Tensor Core GPUs
p5 (compute optimized)	High-performance inference	Higher-performance NVIDIA GPUs	Highest	Yes	NVIDIA H100 Tensor Core GPUs

(*Continued*)

TABLE 6.2 (Continued)

Instance type	Use case	Key features	Approximate cost	GPU-based	Compute architecture
Trn1	High-performance AI training and inference (LLMs and generative AI)	Powered by AWS Trainium chips	Highest	No	AWS Trainium
Trn2	High-performance AI training and inference (LLMs and generative AI)	Powered by AWS Trainium2 chips	Highest	No	AWS Trainium2

Amazon Elastic Container Service

Amazon ECS is another powerful option for unmanaged model deployments. Amazon ECS allows you to run and manage containerized applications, making it well-suited for deploying ML models in a flexible and scalable manner. With Amazon ECS, you can define and manage your containerized model deployment using task definitions, which specify the necessary Docker container images, resources, and networking settings. One of the key advantages of using Amazon ECS for unmanaged model deployment is the ability to utilize both EC2 and AWS Fargate launch types. The EC2 launch type allows for granular control over the underlying infrastructure, enabling you to optimize performance and cost by selecting specific instance types. On the other hand, the AWS Fargate launch type abstracts away the infrastructure management, providing a serverless experience where you focus only on running your containerized models. This flexibility makes Amazon ECS an attractive choice for a variety of deployment scenarios.

In addition to flexibility, Amazon ECS offers robust integration with other AWS services, enhancing the overall deployment experience. For instance, Amazon ECS integrates seamlessly with Amazon CloudWatch for monitoring container performance, AWS Identity and Access Management (IAM) for security and access control, and Amazon EFS for persistent storage. By leveraging these integrations, you can build a comprehensive deployment pipeline that includes logging, monitoring, and scaling. Furthermore, Amazon ECS provides support for service discovery, allowing your containerized applications to easily communicate with each other within the same network. This feature is particularly useful for microservices architectures where different components of your ML application need to interact seamlessly. Overall, Amazon ECS offers a powerful, flexible, and integrated platform for unmanaged model deployments, enabling you to efficiently run and manage your ML models at scale.

Amazon Elastic Kubernetes Service

Amazon Elastic Kubernetes Service (Amazon EKS) leverages the power of Kubernetes, a leading open-source container orchestration platform, for unmanaged model deployments. By utilizing Amazon EKS, you can efficiently deploy, manage, and scale containerized ML models with Kubernetes-native tools and APIs. Amazon EKS automates critical aspects of setting up and maintaining a Kubernetes control plane, providing high availability, security, and performance, which allows you to concentrate on running your ML workloads. Additionally, Amazon EKS integrates seamlessly with other AWS services, such as Amazon S3 for data storage, AWS IAM for secure access control, and Amazon CloudWatch for monitoring and logging.

Moreover, Amazon EKS offers unparalleled flexibility and control, allowing you to leverage Kubernetes' full capabilities for your ML deployments. With support for Kubernetes add-ons and third-party tools, you can enhance your deployment environment with advanced features like service meshes, logging, and monitoring solutions. Amazon EKS enables you to take advantage of essential Kubernetes features such as autoscaling, rolling updates, and self-healing, ensuring that your models are running optimally at all times. This flexibility is beneficial for organizations with existing Kubernetes infrastructure or expertise, as it provides a consistent deployment experience whether operating on-premises or in the cloud. Overall, Amazon EKS delivers a robust and scalable platform for deploying and managing ML models, making it another valuable choice for organizations looking to harness the full potential of Kubernetes.

AWS Lambda

AWS Lambda offers a serverless computing model that is well-suited for deploying ML models, especially when you need to run inference at scale without managing the underlying infrastructure. With AWS Lambda, you can package your ML model as a Lambda function and deploy it to automatically scale in response to incoming requests. This pay-as-you-go model ensures that you pay only for the compute time consumed by your model, making it a cost-effective solution for running inference tasks. Lambda functions can be triggered by various AWS services such as API Gateway, S3, or DynamoDB, allowing you to build a seamless and integrated deployment pipeline for your ML applications.

One of the significant advantages of using AWS Lambda for unmanaged model deployment is its ability to handle highly variable workloads with ease. Lambda automatically scales up and down based on the number of requests, ensuring that your model can handle sudden spikes in demand without manual intervention. This is particularly beneficial for applications with unpredictable traffic patterns or seasonal variations. Additionally, Lambda's integration with Amazon CloudWatch provides robust monitoring and logging capabilities, enabling you to track the performance and health of your deployed models. You can set up alarms and notifications to stay informed about any issues or anomalies, ensuring that your models are always running optimally.

Finally, AWS Lambda supports a variety of programming languages, including Python, which is widely used for ML. This flexibility allows you to use familiar tools and

Chapter 6 ▪ Model Deployment and Orchestration

frameworks to develop and deploy your models. You can also leverage AWS Lambda Layers to manage dependencies and share common code across multiple functions, simplifying the deployment process. Lambda's stateless nature means that each invocation of the function is independent, ensuring consistent performance and reliability. By combining AWS Lambda with other AWS services like S3 for model storage and API Gateway for creating RESTful APIs, you can build a scalable, cost-effective, and fully managed deployment solution for your ML models.

Optimizing ML Models for Edge Devices

Optimizing ML models for edge devices involves several strategies to ensure efficient performance and resource utilization. Amazon SageMaker Neo is a powerful service designed specifically for this purpose, enabling developers to optimize and deploy ML models on various edge devices with ease. Amazon SageMaker Neo compiles and tunes models to run efficiently on specific hardware and software configurations, making it ideal for edge deployment.

With Amazon SageMaker Neo, you can optimize models for a wide range of edge devices, including those powered by ARM, Intel, Nvidia, and other processors. This service supports popular frameworks such as TensorFlow, TensorFlow-Lite, PyTorch, and the Open Neural Network Exchange (ONNX) standard format, providing flexibility and compatibility with different development workflows. Amazon SageMaker Neo automatically applies techniques like quantization, compression, and pruning to reduce the size and complexity of ML models, ensuring that they run efficiently on resource-constrained devices.

The process begins by training your ML model (in the cloud using Amazon SageMaker or somewhere else). Once the model is trained, you can use Amazon SageMaker Neo to compile and optimize it for your target edge device. Amazon SageMaker Neo creates a binary file that is highly optimized for the target hardware, allowing for faster and more efficient inference. This approach not only reduces latency but also conserves energy, making it suitable for low-power edge devices.

To continuously monitor and update ML models deployed on edge devices, Amazon SageMaker Neo provides tools for over-the-air (OTA) updates. This ensures that models remain up to date and maintain high accuracy over time without requiring physical access to the devices. With Amazon SageMaker Neo you can create responsive, secure, and robust AI applications that deliver exceptional user experiences on edge devices.

You can see the list of supported edge devices, cloud instances, and framework versions by visiting https://docs.aws.amazon.com/sagemaker/latest/dg/neo-supported-devices-edge.html.

The following snippet shows an example of exporting a pretrained TensorFlow model, uploading it to S3, and creating an Amazon SageMaker Neo compilation job to optimize it for an iPhone using Apple Core ML:

```
import tensorflow as tf
import boto3
from sagemaker import get_execution_role, Session
```

```python
# Step 1: Export the Pre-trained Model
# Load your pre-trained model
model = tf.keras.models.load_model('path_to_your_model.h5')

# Save the model in the SavedModel format
model.save('saved_model_path')

# Step 2: Upload the Model to S3
s3 = boto3.client('s3')
s3.upload_file('saved_model_path', 'your-bucket', 'saved_model_path')

# Step 3: Create a SageMaker Neo Compilation Job
# Initialize SageMaker session
sagemaker_session = Session()

# Get the execution role
role = get_execution_role()

# Define the S3 bucket paths
input_model_path = 's3://your-bucket/saved_model_path'
output_model_path = 's3://your-bucket/compiled-model'

# Create a Neo compilation job
sagemaker_client = boto3.client('sagemaker')

response = sagemaker_client.create_compilation_job(
    CompilationJobName='MyCompilationJob',
    RoleArn=role,
    InputConfig={
        'S3Uri': input_model_path,
        'DataInputConfig': '{"input": [1, 224, 224, 3]}',
        'Framework': 'TENSORFLOW'
    },
    OutputConfig={
        'S3OutputLocation': output_model_path,
        'TargetDevice': 'ml_coreml'  # Target device for iPhone
    },
    StoppingCondition={
        'MaxRuntimeInSeconds': 3600
    }
)

# Wait for the compilation job to complete
sagemaker_client.get_waiter('compilation_job_completed_or_stopped').wait(
    CompilationJobName='MyCompilationJob'
)

# Check the status of the compilation job
status = sagemaker_client.describe_compilation_job(
    CompilationJobName='MyCompilationJob'
)['CompilationJobStatus']
print(f'Compilation job status: {status}')
```

Advanced Model Deployment Techniques

Amazon SageMaker AI offers advanced deployment techniques to ensure that your ML models perform optimally and reliably in production. With Amazon Application Auto Scaling, you can automatically scale your SageMaker endpoints based on predefined metrics, ensuring efficient resource utilization and cost management during variable traffic loads. Deployment strategies such as Blue/Green deployments and testing strategies like canary, shadow, and A/B testing allow for seamless and reliable transitions to new model versions with minimal disruption. These techniques will be described in the following sections, providing a comprehensive framework for deploying ML models effectively using Amazon SageMaker AI.

Autoscaling Endpoints

Autoscaling Amazon SageMaker AI endpoints ensures that your deployed ML models can handle varying levels of traffic efficiently by scaling horizontally (scale-in, scale-out) the instances responsible for serving incoming inference requests. Amazon Application Auto Scaling allows you to automatically adjust the number of instance replicas for your Amazon SageMaker AI endpoints based on predefined metrics, such as CPU utilization or request count. This helps in maintaining optimal performance while keeping costs under control. To begin with, you need to configure your endpoint with an autoscaling policy using the `application-autoscaling` boto3 client.

First, let's create an autoscaling policy for a real-time endpoint. To do so, you need to define two components:

- A *scaling target*: Sets the boundaries for scaling (e.g., minimum 1 instance, maximum 10 instances)

- A *scaling policy*: Specifies the metric to monitor (e.g., `SageMakerVariant InvocationsPerInstance` or `CPUUtilization`), the target value for this metric, and the conditions under which to scale in or out

Here's a simple example in Python to illustrate this:

```
import boto3

client = boto3.client('application-autoscaling')

# Register a scalable target
response = client.register_scalable_target(
    ServiceNamespace='sagemaker',
    ResourceId='endpoint/your-endpoint-name/variant/AllTraffic',
    ScalableDimension='sagemaker:variant:DesiredInstanceCount',
    MinCapacity=1,
```

```
    MaxCapacity=10
)

# Create a scaling policy
response = client.put_scaling_policy(
    PolicyName='ScalingPolicy',
    ServiceNamespace='sagemaker',
    ResourceId='endpoint/your-endpoint-name/variant/AllTraffic',
    ScalableDimension='sagemaker:variant:DesiredInstanceCount',
    PolicyType='TargetTrackingScaling',
    TargetTrackingScalingPolicyConfiguration={
        'TargetValue': 70.0,  # Target number of endpoint invocations
per instance
            'PredefinedMetricSpecification': {
                'PredefinedMetricType': 'SageMakerVariantInvocationsPerInstance',
            },
            'ScaleInCooldown': 300,
            'ScaleOutCooldown': 300
    }
)
```

In this example, autoscaling is triggered based on the number of invocations (requests) per instance for your Amazon SageMaker AI endpoint. Specifically, the scaling policy is set to maintain an average of 70 invocations per instance. If the average number of invocations per instance goes above 70, the policy will automatically add more instances (scale out) to handle the increased load. Conversely, if the average number of invocations per instance drops below 70, the policy will reduce the number of instances (scale in) to optimize resource usage. This "elastic" behavior ensures that your real-time inference endpoint can dynamically adapt to changing traffic levels, maintaining performance and efficiency.

The `ScaleInCooldown` and `ScaleOutCooldown` parameters define the cool down period in seconds for scaling in and scaling out actions, respectively. In this case, both are set to 300 seconds (5 minutes). When a scaling action is triggered, such as adding more instances (scaling out) or reducing instances (scaling in), the cooldown period ensures that no further scaling actions of the same type can be taken until the cooldown period has elapsed. This helps prevent rapid and excessive scaling actions in response to short-term fluctuations in traffic, ensuring that the system has sufficient time to stabilize before considering another scaling adjustment.

Let's look at another example where we scale based on CPU utilization. We can modify the scaling policy to use a custom metric, such as average CPU utilization. Here's how you can achieve this:

```
import boto3

client = boto3.client('application-autoscaling')

# Register a scalable target
response = client.register_scalable_target(
    ServiceNamespace='sagemaker',
```

```
    ResourceId='endpoint/your-endpoint-name/variant/AllTraffic',
    ScalableDimension='sagemaker:variant:DesiredInstanceCount',
    MinCapacity=1,
    MaxCapacity=10
)

# Create a scaling policy
response = client.put_scaling_policy(
    PolicyName='CPUScalingPolicy',
    ServiceNamespace='sagemaker',
    ResourceId='endpoint/your-endpoint-name/variant/AllTraffic',
    ScalableDimension='sagemaker:variant:DesiredInstanceCount',
    PolicyType='TargetTrackingScaling',
    TargetTrackingScalingPolicyConfiguration={
        'TargetValue': 50.0,  # Target average CPU utilization
        'CustomizedMetricSpecification': {
            'MetricName': 'CPUUtilization',
            'Namespace': 'AWS/SageMaker',
            'Dimensions': [{'Name': 'EndpointName', 'Value': 'your-endpoint-name'}],
            'Statistic': 'Average',
            'Unit': 'Percent'
        },
        'ScaleInCooldown': 300,
        'ScaleOutCooldown': 300
    }
)
```

In this second example, autoscaling is triggered based on the average CPU utilization of the instances running the Amazon SageMaker AI endpoint. The scaling policy is set to maintain an average CPU utilization of 50%. If the average CPU usage across the instances exceeds 50%, the policy will automatically add more instances (scale out) to handle the increased load. Conversely, if the average CPU usage drops below 50%, the policy will reduce the number of instances (scale in) to optimize resource usage. The cooldown periods ensure that these scaling actions are not triggered too frequently, allowing the system to stabilize before making further adjustments.

These two programs demonstrate the use of Amazon Application Auto Scaling—*Target Tracking* autoscaling, specifically—to "elastically" adjust the number of instances for your Amazon SageMaker AI endpoints, ensuring optimal performance, reliability, and cost efficiency.

For the exam, be aware of other types of autoscaling, such as *step scaling* and *scheduled scaling*. Step scaling adjusts the number of instances (resources) based on predefined steps that you define in response to a target threshold triggering event (e.g., the lower bound, the upper bound and the amount by which to scale). Scheduled scaling adjusts the number of instances (resources) based on a set schedule.

Amazon Application Auto Scaling is fully supported by MMEs and MCEs. In the latter use case (MCEs), use caution. If you want to configure automatic scaling for an MCE using the `InvocationsPerInstance` metric, make sure the model in each container exhibits similar CPU utilization and latency on each inference request. This is best practice because if traffic to the MCE shifts from a low-CPU-utilization model to a high-CPU-utilization model, but the overall volume of invocations remains the same, the endpoint will not scale out. This will result in an insufficient number of instances to handle all the requests to the high CPU utilization model.

Notice how both examples denote the real-time inference endpoint with the `ResourceId` variable, whose value is set to `endpoint/your-endpoint-name/variant/AllTraffic`. The term *variant* refers to different versions or configurations of the model deployed to the same Amazon SageMaker endpoint. This concept allows for multiple variants within the same endpoint, each potentially having different instance types, counts, or even different model versions. By specifying the suffix `variant/AllTraffic`, we apply the autoscaling policy to all the traffic directed to the endpoint. You can also define specific named variants (e.g., `variant/VersionA`), enabling you to manage and scale different model versions independently. This flexibility is especially useful for tasks such as Blue/Green deployments, shadow testing, or canary testing when deploying new model updates, which will be discussed in the next section.

Deployment and Testing Strategies

A key aspect of any deployment strategy is to minimize downtime to the consumers of your models (or applications). To avoid disrupting service for users while updating to a new, or an improved, model, you can take advantage of Amazon SageMaker AI's *production variants* feature.

This feature comes really handy if you consider how frequently a ML model gets updated and continuously evaluated for performance. A new version of a model may be created as a result of training on more recent data, hyperparameter tuning (with Amazon SageMaker AI AMT, for example), improving feature selection, or using better instances and inference containers. You can leverage production variants to compare your models and choose the best-performing candidate to respond to inference requests.

With Amazon SageMaker AI multivariant endpoints, you can distribute endpoint invocation requests across multiple production variants by providing the traffic distribution for each variant, or you can invoke a specific variant directly for each request. In this section, we look at these methods for deploying and testing ML models.

Blue/Green Deployment

Blue/Green deployment is a strategy that reduces the risk and downtime associated with deploying new versions of a model. In Amazon SageMaker AI, this approach can be effectively implemented by leveraging the production variant concept you just learned, which allows seamless traffic shifting between different model versions or configurations. By carefully controlling the traffic flow, you can ensure that users experience minimal disruption while you validate the performance and stability of the new model version.

Before going into more details, let's level set on a few terms you need to know for the exam and constitute the basis of this strategy. In the Blue/Green deployment strategy, the *blue fleet* refers to the compute infrastructure where the existing model version is serving live traffic. The *green fleet*, on the other hand, is the compute infrastructure that hosts the new model version you want to deploy. The goal is to shift traffic from the blue fleet to the green fleet in a controlled manner, ensuring that the new model performs well under real-world conditions before fully replacing the old one. By using this approach, you can minimize downtime and mitigate the risk of introducing issues with the new deployment.

Before fully transitioning to the new model, the new model version undergoes rigorous testing and validation to ensure its performance and reliability. During this interval—referred to as the *baking period*—the new model (deployed on the green fleet) is monitored while serving live traffic. This will ensure that it performs as expected, in accordance to performance metrics you established. Once the green fleet starts receiving live traffic, the baking period begins. To accomplish this, CloudWatch alarms must be properly configured to continuously monitor key performance metrics and the behavior of the new model. The baking period allows you to detect any issues early and address them before directing more traffic to the new model. This additional validation step is essential to maintaining service quality and minimizing the risk of disruptions.

The term *traffic shifting mode* denotes the pattern of ingress traffic you want your Amazon SageMaker AI endpoint to use while distributing inference requests between the blue fleet and the green fleet.

Last, *auto-rollbacks* indicate the Amazon CloudWatch alarms Amazon SageMaker AI uses to monitor how the new version of your model performs on the (containers hosted on the) green fleet.

Remember, Amazon CloudWatch alarms are required to implement the Blue/Green deployment strategy.

In the next three sections, the three traffic-shifting modes you need to know for the exam are explained: namely, All At Once, Canary, and Linear.

All at Once

When implementing *All At Once* traffic shifting, Amazon SageMaker AI directs 100% of the traffic to the new fleet (green fleet). As soon as the green fleet starts serving traffic, the baking period begins. This period is a predetermined interval during which Amazon CloudWatch alarms monitor the green fleet's performance. If no alarms are triggered during this time, Amazon SageMaker AI removes the old fleet (blue fleet). However, if any alarms are activated, an automatic rollback is initiated, redirecting 100% of the traffic back to the blue fleet.

Figure 6.7 illustrates the All At Once traffic-shifting mode.

Advanced Model Deployment Techniques

FIGURE 6.7 Blue/Green deployment with All At Once traffic-shifting mode.

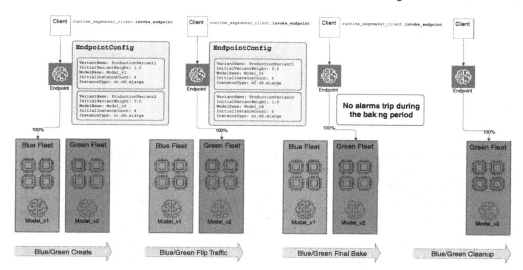

In Figure 6.7, we want to deploy a new version of our model named Model_v2. In the beginning the current version of the model, Model_v1, is serving live production traffic. Ingress traffic is initiated by an Amazon SageMaker AI client, which uses the invoke_endpoint boto3 API to get inferences from Model_v1 hosted in the blue fleet. To learn more about this API, visit https://boto3.amazonaws.com/v1/documentation/api/1.35 9/reference/services/sagemaker-runtime/client/invoke_endpoint.html.

As you can see in Figure 6.7, the endpoint has a configuration that contains two production variants, the first one for Model_v1 and the second one for Model_v2. This is the Blue/Green Create step in the process.

Then we change the traffic pattern by redirecting all live traffic to Model_v2. This is when the baking period begins. To implement this step, we use the update_endpoint boto3 API with the following snippet:

```
import boto3
client = boto3.client("sagemaker")

response = client.update_endpoint(
    EndpointName="<your-endpoint-name>",
    EndpointConfigName="<your-config-name>",
    DeploymentConfig={
        "BlueGreenUpdatePolicy": {
            "TrafficRoutingConfiguration": {
                "Type": "ALL_AT_ONCE"
            },
            "TerminationWaitInSeconds": 600,
```

Chapter 6 ▪ Model Deployment and Orchestration

```
        "MaximumExecutionTimeoutInSeconds": 1800
    },
    "AutoRollbackConfiguration": {
        "Alarms": [
            {
                "AlarmName": "<your-cw-alarm>"
            },
        ]
    }
}
)
```

In the snippet, the parameter `MaximumExecutionTimeoutInSeconds` sets the maximum amount of time that the deployment can run before it times out (30 minutes in this example). The parameter `TerminationWaitInSeconds` tells Amazon SageMaker AI to wait for the specified amount of time (in seconds) after your green fleet is fully active before terminating the instances in the blue fleet. In this example, Amazon SageMaker AI waits for 10 minutes after the final baking period before terminating the blue fleet.

For a detailed syntax of the `update_endpoint` API call, visit `https://boto3.amazonaws.com/v1/documentation/api/latest/reference/services/sagemaker/client/update_endpoint.html`.

The effect of the `update_endpoint` API call is the new endpoint configuration shown in the middle of Figure 6.7.

In the best-case scenario, no alarms are triggered during the baking period, resulting in a termination of the blue fleet. Otherwise, an auto-rollback initiates, and 100% of the traffic shifts back to the blue fleet.

Canary

In a Canary deployment with Amazon SageMaker AI, the traffic shifting is more gradual compared to the All At Once approach. Initially, a small portion of the traffic deemed feasible is directed to the new fleet (green fleet), and the majority continues to be directed to the old fleet (blue fleet). This initial phase is called the "canary test." If the new fleet performs well during the canary test without triggering any Amazon CloudWatch alarms, traffic is gradually increased to the new fleet in additional steps until it reaches 100%. This method allows for closer monitoring of the new version in a production environment and reduces the risk of introducing issues by catching potential problems early with a smaller subset of users.

The approach to implement a Canary deployment programmatically is similar to the All At Once, as shown in the following snippet:

```
import boto3
client = boto3.client("sagemaker")

response = client.update_endpoint(
    EndpointName="<your-endpoint-name>",
    EndpointConfigName="<your-config-name>",
```

Advanced Model Deployment Techniques

```
DeploymentConfig={
    "BlueGreenUpdatePolicy": {
        "TrafficRoutingConfiguration": {
            "Type": "CANARY",
            "CanarySize": {
                "Type": "CAPACITY_PERCENT",
                "Value": 30
            },
            "WaitIntervalInSeconds": 600
        },
        "TerminationWaitInSeconds": 600,
        "MaximumExecutionTimeoutInSeconds": 1800
    },
    "AutoRollbackConfiguration": {
        "Alarms": [
            {
                "AlarmName": "<your-cw-alarm>"
            }
        ]
    }
}
)
```

The update_endpoint API allows you to set the Type parameter of the TrafficRoutingConfiguration dictionary to the value CANARY. The Value parameter of the CanarySize dictionary sets the percentage of your green fleet you want to use as the canary. In the example, we configured the endpoint to shift 30% of the ingress traffic to the green fleet. We could have chosen to direct traffic to the green fleet based on INSTANCE_COUNT instead of CAPACITY_PERCENT, which is another valid option for Type.

The canary size should be equal to or less than 50% of the green fleet's capacity.

The WaitIntervalInSeconds parameter denotes the duration (in seconds) of the canary baking period. In the preceding example, Amazon SageMaker AI waits for 10 minutes after the canary shift and then completes the second and final traffic shift.

When comparing Canary with All At Once, it is important to remember that the All At Once approach shifts 100% of the traffic to the green fleet in a single step as soon as the deployment starts. Although this method is faster, it carries higher risk because any undetected issues in the new fleet can affect all users immediately. All At Once relies heavily on extensive predeployment testing and a robust rollback plan, as the entire user base is exposed to the new version immediately.

As a result, the key difference between the two approaches lies in the risk management and traffic transition speed. Canary deployments provide a safer, more controlled rollout by gradually increasing traffic and monitoring each phase for stability, whereas All At Once

270   Chapter 6 ▪ Model Deployment and Orchestration

deployments prioritize speed and immediate transition but come with higher risks. Choosing between these methods depends on your application's tolerance for risk and the criticality of ensuring seamless, uninterrupted user experience.

Linear

The linear Blue/Green deployment option provides the most granular control over traffic shifting. Instead of deploying your green fleet in one step (All At Once) or in two steps (Canary), linear traffic shifting gradually directs traffic from the blue fleet to the green fleet in small, equal increments over a specified period.

Just like Canary traffic shifting, you can choose the increment size by specifying the number of instances or the percentage (10–50%) of the green fleet's capacity to activate during each phase.

For each phase of the deployment, you define a baking period where your preconfigured Amazon CloudWatch alarms monitor the green fleet's metrics. If the baking period concludes without any alarms being triggered, the green fleet continues to receive a greater share of traffic as the process moves to the next phase. Should any alarms go off during any of these baking periods, all the endpoint traffic will immediately revert to the blue fleet.

The following example shows how to implement the linear traffic-shifting pattern using the `update_endpoint` API:

```
import boto3
client = boto3.client("sagemaker")

response = client.update_endpoint(
    EndpointName="<your-endpoint-name>",
    EndpointConfigName="<your-config-name>",
    DeploymentConfig={
        "BlueGreenUpdatePolicy": {
            "TrafficRoutingConfiguration": {
                "Type": "LINEAR",
                "LinearStepSize": {
                    "Type": "CAPACITY_PERCENT",
                    "Value": 20
                },
                "WaitIntervalInSeconds": 300
            },
            "TerminationWaitInSeconds": 300,
            "MaximumExecutionTimeoutInSeconds": 3600
        },
        "AutoRollbackConfiguration": {
            "Alarms": [
                {
                    "AlarmName": "<your-cw-alarm>"
                }
            ]
        }
    }
)
```

The approach is similar to the Canary deployment. The `TrafficRoutingConfiguration` dictionary allows you to set a `Type` parameter with a value `LINEAR` and a corresponding configuration `LinearStepSize` where you can specify how to incrementally route more traffic to the green fleet. In our example, at each step we will direct live traffic to the green fleet in 20% increments (the parameter `CAPACITY_PERCENT` is set to 20). `INSTANCE_COUNT` can also be used as an alternative way to direct traffic to the green fleet. With linear traffic-shifting mode, as the name suggests, the amount of inference traffic routed to the green fleet increases in a linear fashion.

Notice how we also define a baking period for each step by assigning the value 300 to the `WaitIntervalInSeconds` parameter. In the example, Amazon SageMaker AI waits for 5 minutes between each traffic shift. If no alarms are triggered within 5 minutes, Amazon SageMaker directs 20% more traffic to the green fleet until 100% of traffic is sent to the new model. Upon completion—assuming no alarms are triggered—Amazon SageMaker AI waits for another 5 minutes (`TerminationWaitInSeconds` is set to 300) and finally terminates all the instances in the blue fleet. If an alarm is triggered in any of the five steps (0–20, 20–40, 40–60, 60–80, 80–100), Amazon SageMaker AI rolls back 100% of the endpoint traffic to the blue fleet.

The linear deployment offers the highest level of risk reduction during your model deployment process at the expense of potentially longer deployment times. This approach is perfect for critical deployments where stability and minimizing risk are essential, ensuring a smooth transition with ongoing monitoring and the ability to roll back if any issues arise.

Orchestrating ML Workflows

You have learned so far how to ingest the data to train your ML models; engineer the relevant features; choose a suitable algorithm; train, refine, and optimize your model; and finally deploy it. These foundational steps are crucial in the ML lifecycle and set the stage for building robust and efficient models that can drive impactful insights and decisions.

However, orchestrating these steps manually can be time-consuming and prone to errors. This is where Amazon SageMaker AI's comprehensive suite of tools comes into play, providing an integrated environment to streamline and automate the entire ML workflow. By leveraging Amazon SageMaker AI, you can seamlessly manage data preprocessing tasks, engineer your features, and train, evaluate and deploy your model, all within a cohesive platform that enhances productivity and reduces complexity.

One of the standout features in this ecosystem is *Amazon SageMaker Pipelines*. This powerful tool enables the design, deployment, and management of end-to-end ML workflows with ease. Amazon SageMaker Pipelines comes with its own SDK, allowing you to define and visualize your workflows programmatically, ensuring consistency and repeatability, which are both key characteristics of modern ML operations.

In the upcoming sections you will learn Amazon SageMaker Pipelines' main capabilities you need to know for the exam.

Introducing Amazon SageMaker Pipelines

In the rapidly evolving world of ML, operationalizing ML models—often referred to as *MLOps*—has become a cornerstone of successful AI-driven projects. MLOps bridges the gap between ML model development and production, ensuring seamless integration, deployment, monitoring, and maintenance of models.

Amazon SageMaker Pipelines is a powerful tool that embodies the principles of MLOps, enabling data scientists and ML engineers to automate and orchestrate their workflows efficiently. The term *orchestration* refers to the automation and management of the end-to-end ML lifecycle. Amazon SageMaker Pipelines serves as a core tool in this orchestration process by offering a structured framework to define, schedule, and monitor ML workflows. This systematic approach ensures reliability and reduces the time to market for your ML models.

Amazon SageMaker Pipelines offers several key advantages over other AWS workflow solutions.

First, your ML pipelines operate on autoscaling serverless infrastructure. With Amazon SageMaker Pipelines there's no need to manage the underlying orchestration infrastructure. This allows you to concentrate on core ML tasks. Amazon SageMaker AI automatically provisions, scales, and shuts down the pipeline orchestration compute resources according to your ML workload demands.

Second, your ML pipelines can be created and managed through your preferred interface: visual editor, SDK, APIs, or JSON. You can easily drag and drop the various ML steps to design your pipelines using the Amazon SageMaker Studio visual interface.

To learn how to use the Amazon SageMaker Pipeline Python SDK, visit https://sagemaker.readthedocs.io/en/stable/workflows/pipelines/index.html.

Last, your ML pipelines can be seamlessly integrated with all Amazon SageMaker AI features and other AWS services to automate data processing, model training, fine-tuning, evaluation, deployment, and monitoring jobs. Because they operate in a serverless environment, you only pay for your SageMaker Studio instance and the underlying jobs that are orchestrated by Amazon SageMaker Pipelines.

Before seeing Amazon SageMaker Pipelines in action, let's level set on a few constructs that are key to MLOps: namely, code repository, continuous integration/continuous deployment (CI/CD), and Orchestration.

Code Repository and Version Control

A code repository, often referred to simply as a *repo*, is a storage location for software code and related files. It's a central place where developers can store, share, and manage their codebase. Code repositories can be hosted on platforms like GitHub, GitLab, and Bitbucket, which provide tools and services to facilitate collaborative development. These platforms enable multiple developers to work on the same codebase concurrently, track changes, and contribute to the project seamlessly. In the context of ML with Amazon SageMaker Pipelines, a code repository plays a crucial role in organizing scripts, notebooks, and other artifacts required for building, training, and deploying models. It ensures that all team members have access to different versions of the code, fostering collaboration and maintaining consistency across the development process.

Version control, on the other hand, is a system that tracks changes to files over time. It allows developers to manage multiple versions of code, collaborate effectively, and maintain a history of changes. Git is one of the most widely used version control systems, and it operates by creating snapshots of the code at various points in time, known as *commits*. Each commit records a set of changes made to the codebase, along with metadata such as the author's information and a timestamp. Version control systems enable developers to revert to previous versions of the code, compare changes between different commits, and merge contributions from multiple team members. In the context of Amazon SageMaker Pipelines, version control is essential for managing the iterative nature of ML development. It ensures that any modifications to data preprocessing scripts, model training code, or deployment configurations are tracked and can be reviewed or rolled back if necessary. This level of control enhances collaboration, improves the reliability of the pipeline, and ensures that the ML workflow remains repeatable and transparent.

Introducing Amazon SageMaker Model Registry

Because a model artifact is the result of training and fine-tuning ML algorithms on data, it's critical to manage and track these artifacts effectively throughout their lifecycle. Amazon SageMaker Model Registry is a fully managed service that helps you catalog, organize, and manage your ML models. It allows you to keep track of different versions of a model, from initial development through production deployment. Amazon SageMaker Model Registry provides a centralized repository to store and manage models, enabling you to track metadata, performance metrics, and the history of each model version. This is particularly useful in collaborative environments where multiple data scientists and ML engineers work on the same project. Amazon SageMaker Model Registry ensures that everyone has access to the latest versions of the models, and it supports governance and compliance by providing an audit trail of changes and deployments.

Using Amazon SageMaker Model Registry, you can automate the process of registering, tracking, and deploying models. It integrates seamlessly with Amazon SageMaker Pipelines, making it easier to automate model versioning and lifecycle management within your ML workflows. By incorporating the Model Registry into your Amazon SageMaker Pipelines, you can ensure that your models are version-controlled, repeatable, and easily retrievable for future use. This improves the efficiency and reliability of your MLOps, allowing you to focus on building and deploying high-quality models.

CI/CD

A CI/CD pipeline is a crucial component of modern software development practices, enabling teams to automate the process of integrating code changes, building applications, running tests, and deploying to production environments. AWS offers a suite of services to support CI/CD workflows, ensuring seamless and efficient software delivery. AWS CodeArtifact is a fully managed artifact repository service that makes it easy for organizations to securely store, publish, and share software packages. AWS CodeBuild is a fully managed build service that compiles source code, runs tests, and produces software packages that are ready for deployment. AWS CodeDeploy automates the deployment of applications to a variety of compute services such as Amazon EC2, AWS Lambda, and on-premises servers. Finally, AWS CodePipeline is a continuous integration and continuous delivery service for fast and reliable application updates, enabling you to model, visualize, and automate the steps required to release your software.

Because modern infrastructure is virtualized, managing and provisioning computing resources through manual processes becomes impractical and prone to errors. This is where *infrastructure as code (IaC)* comes into play, allowing you to define and manage your infrastructure using machine-readable configuration files in a declarative manner. AWS CloudFormation and Terraform are two popular IaC tools that enable you to automate the setup and management of your infrastructure. AWS CloudFormation provides a common language for you to describe and provision all the infrastructure resources in your cloud environment. Using AWS CloudFormation, you can use a simple text file (in JSON or YAML format) to model and provision, in an automated and secure manner, all the resources needed for your applications across all regions and accounts. Terraform, developed by HashiCorp, is an open-source IaC tool that allows you to build, change, and version infrastructure safely and efficiently. It provides a consistent CLI workflow to manage hundreds of cloud services. Both tools ensure that your infrastructure setup is repeatable, consistent, and version-controlled, just like application code. However, AWS CloudFormation and Terraform require developers to use specific configuration languages, which can be restrictive. These tools utilize JSON, YAML, and HashiCorp Configuration Language (HCL), limiting the choice of programming languages for defining infrastructure. Many developers prefer to use the language they are more comfortable with, such as JavaScript or Python. This is where AWS Cloud Development Kit (AWS CDK) comes into play. With AWS CDK, developers can create IaC with JavaScript, TypeScript, Python, Java, C#, and Go. Figure 6.8 illustrates how these services fit into the CI/CD pipeline and IaC landscape.

MLOps Orchestration

Orchestration tools are key in automating and managing complex ML workflows. MLOps integrates the principles of DevOps into ML ensuring continuous integration, delivery, and deployment of ML models.

For the exam, in addition to Amazon SageMaker Pipelines—which was already introduced—you need to be aware of other options: namely, AWS Step Functions and

FIGURE 6.8 CI/CD pipeline.

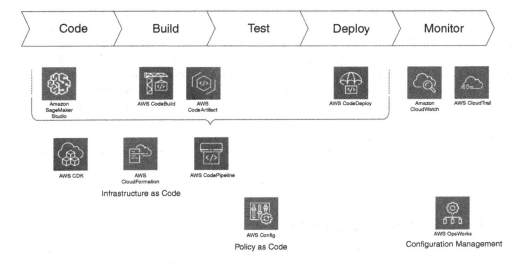

Amazon Managed Workflows for Apache Airflow. AWS Step Functions is a powerful orchestration service that enables you to coordinate multiple AWS services into serverless workflows, making it easier to build and monitor automated processes. Amazon Managed Workflows for Apache Airflow is another key orchestration service that simplifies the setup and operation of Apache Airflow, allowing you to programmatically author, schedule, and monitor workflows. These tools are essential for managing the various stages of the ML pipeline, from data preprocessing and feature engineering to model training, evaluation, and deployment. Let's now review these two orchestration tools in more detail.

AWS Step Functions

AWS Step Functions is a serverless orchestration service that allows you to coordinate multiple AWS services into scalable workflows. By using AWS Step Functions, you can design and run complex workflows that are composed of individual tasks, each representing a step in the process. The service provides a visual interface to build workflows, making it easier to monitor and manage the execution of each step. In the context of MLOps with Amazon SageMaker AI, AWS Step Functions can orchestrate the entire ML lifecycle, from data preprocessing and feature engineering to model training, tuning, and deployment. You can define state machines that capture the sequence of tasks, and AWS Step Functions ensures that each step is executed in the correct order and handles errors gracefully. Additionally, AWS Step Functions supports large-scale parallel workflows, enabling concurrent executions of your data-intensive ML tasks. This orchestration capability simplifies the management of ML pipelines, improves repeatability, and enhances the overall efficiency of ML operations.

Amazon Managed Workflows for Apache Airflow

Amazon Managed Workflows for Apache Airflow (MWAA) is a managed service that simplifies the setup and operation of Apache Airflow, an open-source workflow orchestration platform. Airflow allows you to programmatically author, schedule, and monitor workflows, making it ideal for managing complex data pipelines. With MWAA, AWS handles the provisioning, scaling, and maintenance of Airflow environments, allowing you to focus on building and managing workflows without the overhead of infrastructure management. MWAA integrates seamlessly with other AWS services, such as S3, Redshift, and Elastic Map Reduce (EMR), enabling you to create highly scalable and reliable data workflows. In the context of MLOps, MWAA can be used to orchestrate the various stages of the ML pipeline, including data extraction, transformation, loading (ETL), model training, evaluation, and deployment. By leveraging MWAA, organizations can ensure that their data workflows are efficient, consistent, and resilient, providing a robust foundation for their ML operations.

Choosing an Orchestration Tool

When selecting an orchestration tool for ML workflows in AWS, it's important to consider the complexity of your workflows and your team's familiarity with the tools.

AWS Step Functions is a serverless, easy-to-use orchestration service that integrates seamlessly with other AWS services. It is ideal for orchestrating end-to-end ML pipelines, providing a visual interface for designing and monitoring workflows. It is well-suited for teams seeking simplicity and minimal operational overhead.

MWAA caters to more customizable and flexible orchestration needs. It supports complex workflows and offers a rich plugin ecosystem, making it perfect for data engineering tasks and for teams familiar with Apache Airflow. MWAA handles the provisioning, scaling, and maintenance of Airflow environments, allowing you to focus on workflow management.

Amazon SageMaker Pipelines is specifically designed for ML workflows. It provides built-in orchestration capabilities that allow ML engineers and data scientists to define, visualize, and automate end-to-end ML processes. Amazon SageMaker Pipelines seamlessly integrates with other Amazon SageMaker services, making it an excellent choice for managing the entire ML lifecycle, from data preprocessing and feature engineering to model training, tuning, and deployment.

The choice between AWS Step Functions, Amazon MWAA, and Amazon SageMaker Pipelines ultimately depends on your specific use case. AWS Step Functions and Amazon MWAA offer general-purpose orchestration for a variety of workflows, whereas Amazon SageMaker Pipelines is tailored specifically for ML ensuring seamless integration with the entire Amazon SageMaker ecosystem.

Figure 6.9 summarizes the repository and orchestration services you just learned to help streamline your ML workflows and ensure efficient, repeatable operations.

In the upcoming sections, we will focus our attention on Amazon SageMaker Pipelines, which is the a key requirement for the exam.

FIGURE 6.9 Repository and orchestration services.

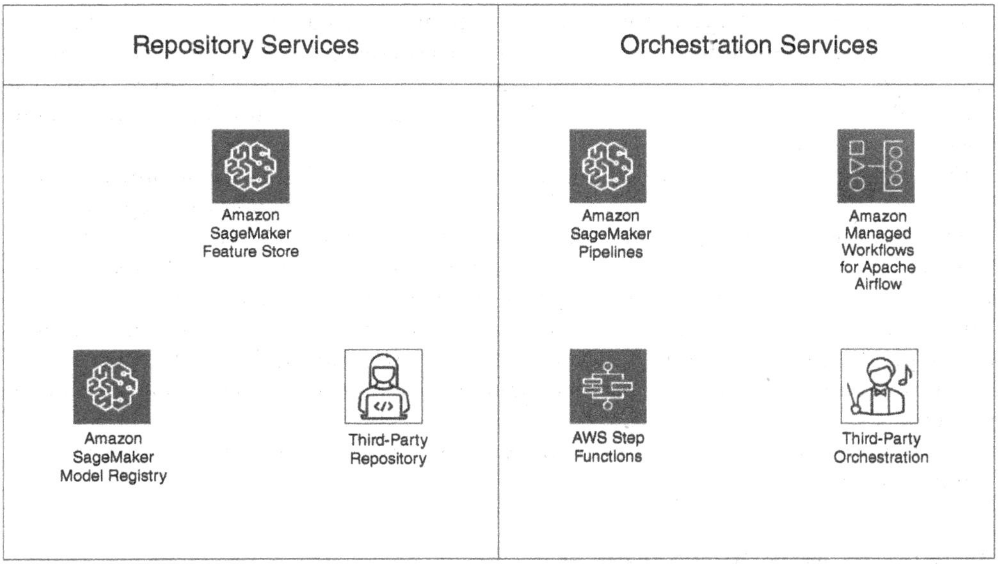

Repository Services		Orchestration Services	
Amazon SageMaker Feature Store		Amazon SageMaker Pipelines	Amazon Managed Workflows for Apache Airflow
Amazon SageMaker Model Registry	Third-Party Repository	AWS Step Functions	Third-Party Orchestration

Automating Model Building and Deployment

Automating model building and deployment using Amazon SageMaker Pipelines involves creating a sequence of well-defined steps that form your ML workflow. This automation ensures that each phase of the ML process is executed efficiently, consistently, and reliably. One of the significant benefits provided by Amazon SageMaker Pipelines is *repeatability*. Amazon SageMaker Pipelines can help you transform manual tasks into streamlined, repeatable processes, resulting in workflows that can be reliably re-created and produce consistent results. This repeatability aspect is critical for validating models, conducting experiments, and ensuring that the results can be replicated by different team members or over time. This is particularly helpful if you consider the iterative nature of the ML lifecycle. Additionally, this approach allows data scientists and ML engineers to focus on more critical, high-value activities, enhancing productivity and reducing the chances of human error, leading to more robust and reliable models. Think of each step in the pipeline as a LEGO block. Just as LEGO blocks are assembled to create a complex structure, each step in the ML workflow is like a block that contributes to building a complete and functional ML pipeline.

The first step in automating model building and deployment is to identify and define the critical components of your ML workflow. These components typically include data preprocessing, feature engineering, model training, evaluation, and deployment. Each of these components is represented as a separate step in the pipeline. For example, the data preprocessing step involves cleaning and transforming raw data into a format suitable for model training, and the feature engineering step focuses on creating new features or modifying existing ones to improve model performance. This modular approach ensures that each step is independently developed and optimized, which can significantly improve the overall efficiency of the workflow.

Once the individual steps are defined, they are combined into a single pipeline using the Amazon SageMaker `Pipeline` object. This pipeline ensures that the steps are executed in the correct sequence, with each step being completed before the next one begins. Additionally, triggers and schedules can be set up to automate the execution of the pipeline, ensuring that it runs at regular intervals or in response to specific events. This automation not only saves time but also ensures that the models are continuously updated and refined as new data becomes available. Ultimately, this leads to better-performing models that can adapt to changing data patterns and deliver more accurate predictions.

The following sections describe how to design and implement a simple pipeline to deploy a model.

Define the Workflow Steps

You start by identifying the critical components of your ML workflow:

- **Data preprocessing**: Cleaning and transforming raw data
- **Feature engineering**: Enhancing data to improve model accuracy
- **Model training**: Using algorithms to build the model
- **Model evaluation**: Assessing model performance
- **Model deployment**: Deploying the trained model to production

Each of these components will be mapped to individual steps in the pipeline.

Create and Configure Pipeline Steps

The Amazon SageMaker Pipeline Python SDK provides classes for each step in the pipeline, so you don't have to "reinvent the wheel." This makes it easy to define and configure each component of the workflow:

- `ProcessingStep`: For data preprocessing tasks
- `TransformStep`: For feature engineering tasks
- `TrainingStep`: For training the model
- `ModelStep`: For deploying the model

Orchestrating ML Workflows   **279**

For example, you can start by creating a pipeline session:

```python
from sagemaker.workflow.pipeline_context import PipelineSession

# Create a PipelineSession
pipeline_session = PipelineSession()
```

Define the processing step:

```python
from sagemaker.processing import ScriptProcessor
from sagemaker.workflow.steps import ProcessingStep

# Define the data preprocessing step
processor = ScriptProcessor(
    image_uri='your_image_uri',
    role='your_iam_role',
    instance_count=1,
    instance_type='ml.m5.large',
    sagemaker_session=pipeline_session
)

processing_step = ProcessingStep(
    name="DataPreprocessing",
    processor=processor,
    inputs=[...],
    outputs=[...],
    code="preprocessing_script.py"
)
```

Define the feature engineering step:

```python
from sagemaker.transformer import Transformer
from sagemaker.workflow.steps import TransformStep

# Define the feature engineering step
transformer = Transformer(
    model_name='your_model_name',
    instance_count=1,
    instance_type='ml.m5.large',
    output_path='s3://your-bucket/transform-output',
    sagemaker_session=pipeline_session
)

feature_engineering_step = TransformStep(
    name="FeatureEngineering",
    transformer=transformer,
    inputs={
```

Chapter 6 ▪ Model Deployment and Orchestration

```python
        'data': 's3://your-bucket/processed-data'
    }
)
# Add dependency to ensure feature engineering step runs after processing step
feature_engineering_step.add_depends_on([processing_step])
```

Define the training step:

```python
from sagemaker.estimator import Estimator
from sagemaker.workflow.steps import TrainingStep

# Define the model training step
estimator = Estimator(
    image_uri='your_image_uri',
    role='your_iam_role',
    instance_count=1,
    instance_type='ml.m5.large',
    hyperparameters={'max_depth': 5, 'eta': 0.2},
    sagemaker_session=pipeline_session
)

training_step = TrainingStep(
    name="ModelTraining",
    estimator=estimator,
    inputs={
        'train': 's3://your-bucket/train-data',
        'validation': 's3://your-bucket/validation-data'
    }
)
# Add dependency to ensure training step runs after feature engineering step
training_step.add_depends_on([feature_engineering_step])
```

Define the deployment step:

```python
from sagemaker.model import Model
from sagemaker.workflow.steps import ModelStep

# Define the model deployment step
model = Model(
    model_data='s3://your-bucket/model.tar.gz',
    role='your_iam_role',
    entry_point='inference_script.py',
    sagemaker_session=pipeline_session
)

model_step = ModelStep(
    name="ModelDeployment",
    model=model,
    inputs=[...],
```

```
    outputs=[...]
)
# Add dependency to ensure deployment step runs after training step
model_step.add_depends_on([training_step])
```

Define the Pipeline

Once all the steps are defined, you can put them all together into a single pipeline using the Amazon SageMaker Pipeline object. This process ensures that the steps are executed in the correct sequence, with each step being completed before the next one begins. By composing each step into a unified pipeline, you create a seamless and automated workflow that is both efficient and reliable. Moreover, Amazon SageMaker Pipelines offers built-in error-handling capabilities. If an error occurs in any step of the pipeline, the process can be halted, and notifications can be sent to alert the relevant team members. This ensures that errors are promptly addressed, maintaining the integrity of the workflow:

```
from sagemaker.workflow.pipeline import Pipeline

# Define the pipeline by putting all the steps together
pipeline = Pipeline(
    name="MyMLPipeline",
    steps=[processing_step, feature_engineering_step, training_step,
model_step]
)
```

Set Up Triggers and Schedules

You can now automate the pipeline execution by setting up triggers and schedules. For example, you can use Amazon EventBridge to trigger the pipeline based on specific events. The following snippet shows you how you can create an EventBridge rule to trigger MyMLPipeline when a new object is uploaded to an S3 bucket:

```
import boto3

# Create an EventBridge client
client = boto3.client('events')

# Create an EventBridge rule
response = client.put_rule(
    Name='MyMLPipelineRule',
    EventPattern='{\n    "source": ["aws.s3"],\n    "detail-type": ["AWS API
Call via CloudTrail"],\n    "detail": {\n        "eventSource":
["s3.amazonaws.com"],\n        "eventName": ["PutObject"]\n    }\n}',
    State='ENABLED',
    Description='Rule to trigger MyMLPipeline when a new object is uploaded to
S3'
)
```

```
# Add targets to the rule
response = client.put_targets(
    Rule='MyMLPipelineRule',
    Targets=[
        {
            'Id': '1',
            'Arn': 'arn:aws:states:us-east-
1:123456789012:stateMachine:MyMLPipeline'
        }
    ]
)
```

Execute the Pipeline

Alternatively, you can manually start the pipeline execution using the Amazon SageMaker SDK. Steps within the pipeline can also be executed concurrently if they do not have dependencies on each other, allowing for more efficient processing and reduced overall runtime:

```
pipeline.start()
```

Key Considerations

When using Amazon SageMaker Pipelines, scalability is a significant advantage as it automatically manages and scales the required infrastructure, ensuring that your ML workflows perform efficiently and reliably. However, it is your responsibility—as an ML engineer—to implement robust monitoring and logging to keep track of pipeline performance and troubleshoot any issues that may arise. This integration helps maintain the health of your pipelines and ensures smooth operations. Error handling is another crucial aspect to consider. Amazon SageMaker Pipelines offers built-in error-handling capabilities, which halt the process if an error occurs in any step, and notifications are sent to alert relevant team members. This ensures that errors are promptly addressed, maintaining the integrity of the workflow.

Concurrency is also a vital consideration in Amazon SageMaker Pipelines. Steps within the pipeline can be executed concurrently if they do not have dependencies on each other, optimizing processing time and efficiency. This concurrent execution allows for more efficient use of resources and reduced overall runtime. By automating these key aspects—scalability, monitoring, error handling, and concurrency—you can ensure that your ML processes are not only effective but also resilient and adaptable to changing demands.

Deep Dive Model Deployment Example

In this section, we will extend the model tuning deep-dive example in Chapter 5 by exposing the best model with a serverless inference endpoint. We are also going to test the deployed endpoint by creating a simple inference request and by letting the serverless endpoint generate a prediction based on the request.

Deep Dive Model Deployment Example

For the sake of simplicity, cost, and time, we are going to use 3 jobs (instead of 20) to select the best model: i.e., the model with the maximum accuracy.

As a quick reminder, the deep-dive example at the end of Chapter 5 was intended to evaluate the performance of the XGBoost algorithm against the Digits dataset using Amazon SageMaker AI Automatic Model Tuning (AMT) with Bayesian optimization strategy.

The expected outcome of this example is a functioning model deployment in the form of a serverless inference endpoint that can receive inference requests and generate accurate predictions. The inference requests are CSV representations of handwritten digits, which are then processed by the deployed model to predict the corresponding digit class.

I ran this Python program using the Code Editor feature of Amazon SageMaker Studio:

```python
import boto3
import sagemaker
import json
from sagemaker import get_execution_role
from sagemaker.tuner import HyperparameterTuner, IntegerParameter,
ContinuousParameter
from sagemaker.inputs import TrainingInput
from sagemaker.analytics import HyperparameterTuningJobAnalytics
from sagemaker.serverless import ServerlessInferenceConfig
from sagemaker.model import Model
from sagemaker.predictor import Predictor
from sagemaker.serializers import CSVSerializer
from sagemaker.deserializers import JSONDeserializer
from sklearn.datasets import load_digits
from sklearn.model_selection import train_test_split
import pandas as pd
import os
import numpy as np
import matplotlib.pyplot as plt

# Load the Digits dataset
digits = load_digits()
X = digits.data
y = digits.target

# Split the dataset
X_train, X_test, y_train, y_test = train_test_split(X, y, test_size=0.2,
random_state=42)

# Convert to DataFrame and ensure the target is the first column
train_data = pd.DataFrame(X_train)
train_data['target'] = y_train
train_data.insert(0, 'target', train_data.pop('target'))

val_data = pd.DataFrame(X_test)
val_data['target'] = y_test
val_data.insert(0, 'target', val_data.pop('target'))
```

Chapter 6 • Model Deployment and Orchestration

```python
# Create directories if they don't exist
data_dir = './ch06/data'
os.makedirs(data_dir, exist_ok=True)

# Save locally
train_data.to_csv(os.path.join(data_dir, 'train.csv'), index=False)
val_data.to_csv(os.path.join(data_dir, 'validation.csv'), index=False)

# Upload to S3
s3 = boto3.client('s3')
bucket_name = 'ch05-ml-hpo'
prefix = 'sagemaker/xgboost-digits'
s3.upload_file(os.path.join(data_dir, 'train.csv'), bucket_name, f'{prefix}/
train/train.csv')
s3.upload_file(os.path.join(data_dir, 'validation.csv'), bucket_name,
f'{prefix}/validation/validation.csv')

# Define the role and session
role = get_execution_role()
session = sagemaker.Session()

# Define the XGBoost image
region = boto3.Session().region_name
xgb_image = sagemaker.image_uris.retrieve("xgboost", region, "1.2-1")

# Define the S3 paths for the input data
s3_train_data = f's3://{bucket_name}/{prefix}/train/train.csv'
s3_val_data = f's3://{bucket_name}/{prefix}/validation/validation.csv'

# Define the data channels
train_data = TrainingInput(s3_data=s3_train_data, content_type='csv')
val_data = TrainingInput(s3_data=s3_val_data, content_type='csv')

# Define the XGBoost estimator with required hyperparameters
xgb = sagemaker.estimator.Estimator(
    image_uri=xgb_image,
    role=role,
    instance_count=1,
    instance_type='ml.m5.large',
    output_path=f's3://{bucket_name}/{prefix}/output',
    sagemaker_session=session,
    hyperparameters={
        'objective': 'multi:softmax',  # Example for multi-class classification
        'num_class': 10,  # Number of classes in the Digits dataset
        'num_round': 100  # Default value; will be tuned
    }
)

# Define the hyperparameter ranges
hpt_ranges = {
    'alpha': ContinuousParameter(0.01, 0.5),
```

Deep Dive Model Deployment Example

```python
    'eta': ContinuousParameter(0.1, 0.5),
    'min_child_weight': ContinuousParameter(0.0, 2.0),
    'max_depth': IntegerParameter(1, 10)
}

# Define the hyperparameter tuner
tuner = HyperparameterTuner(
    estimator=xgb,
    base_tuning_job_name='bayesian',
    objective_metric_name='validation:accuracy',
    hyperparameter_ranges=hpt_ranges,
    strategy='Bayesian',
    max_jobs=3,  # Reduced from 20 to 3 max jobs
    max_parallel_jobs=3,  # Number of parallel jobs
    objective_type='Maximize'
)

# Launch the hyperparameter tuning job
tuner.fit({'train': train_data, 'validation': val_data})
tuner.wait()

# Get the best training job name
best_training_job_name = tuner.best_training_job()

# Retrieve the tuning results
tuning_job_name = tuner.latest_tuning_job.name
tuner_analytics = HyperparameterTuningJobAnalytics(tuning_job_name)
tuner_df = tuner_analytics.dataframe()

# Extract the best hyperparameters
if 'FinalHyperParameters' in tuner_df.columns:
    best_hyperparameters = tuner_df.loc[tuner_df['TrainingJobName'] == best_
training_job_name, 'FinalHyperParameters'].values[0]
else:
    best_hyperparameters = tuner_df.loc[tuner_df['TrainingJobName'] == best_
training_job_name].drop(['TrainingJobName', 'FinalObjectiveValue'], axis=1).
to_dict('records')[0]

# Print the best training job and hyperparameters
print(f"Best Training Job: {best_training_job_name}")
print("Best Hyperparameters:")
for key, value in best_hyperparameters.items():
    print(f"  {key}: {value}")

# Plot the tuning job results
plt.figure(figsize=(12, 8))
plt.scatter(tuner_df.index, tuner_df['FinalObjectiveValue'],
label='Tuning Jobs')
plt.scatter(tuner_df.loc[tuner_df['TrainingJobName'] ==
best_training_job_name].index,
```

Chapter 6 ▪ Model Deployment and Orchestration

```python
            tuner_df.loc[tuner_df['TrainingJobName'] ==
best_training_job_name]['FinalObjectiveValue'],
            color='red', marker='*', s=200, label='Best Job')

plt.xlabel('Iteration')
plt.ylabel('Cross-Validation Accuracy')
plt.title('Hyperparameter Tuning Results')

# Display the best hyperparameters on the plot
best_hyperparameters_str = '\n'.join([f'{key}: {value}' for key, value in
best_hyperparameters.items()])
plt.figtext(0.5, -0.15, f'Best Hyperparameters:\n{best_hyperparameters_str}',
ha='center', va='top', fontsize=10, bbox=dict(facecolor='lightgrey',
alpha=0.5))

# Update legend position below the x-axis
plt.legend(loc='upper center', bbox_to_anchor=(0.5, -0.2), ncol=3)

# Save the plot as an image file
output_dir = './ch06/images'
os.makedirs(output_dir, exist_ok=True)
plt.savefig(os.path.join(output_dir, 'tuning_results.png'),
bbox_inches='tight')
plt.close()

# Create a serverless inference configuration
serverless_config = ServerlessInferenceConfig(
    memory_size_in_mb=2048,
    max_concurrency=5
)

# Define the custom predictor class (if you have one)
class CustomPredictor(Predictor):
    def __init__(self, *args, **kwargs):
        super().__init__(*args, **kwargs)
        # You can add custom initialization code here

# Retrieve the best model from the hyperparameter tuning job
best_model = Model(
    image_uri=xgb_image,

    model_data=f's3://{bucket_name}/{prefix}/output/{best_training_job_name}/
output/model.tar.gz',
    role=role,
    sagemaker_session=session,
    predictor_cls=CustomPredictor  # Specify the custom predictor class
)

# Deploy the best model as a serverless endpoint with a unique endpoint name
try:
    predictor = best_model.deploy(
        serverless_inference_config=serverless_config,
```

```
        endpoint_name='xgboost-digits-serverless-endpoint-dario',   # Use a
unique endpoint name
        serializer=CSVSerializer(),  # Specify CSV serializer
        deserializer=JSONDeserializer()  # Optional: Specify a deserializer
    )
    print(f"Successfully deployed serverless endpoint: {predictor.
endpoint_name}")
except Exception as e:
    print("Failed to deploy serverless endpoint")
    print(e)
    predictor = None


# Example inference
if predictor is not None:
    test_sample = X_test[0].reshape(1, -1)
    test_sample_csv = ','.join(map(str, test_sample.flatten()))  # Convert
numpy array to CSV-encoded string
    result = predictor.predict(test_sample_csv)
    print('Prediction for the first test sample:', result)
else:
    print("Cannot perform inference because the predictor object is None")


# Plot and save the test sample image without extra data points
plt.figure(figsize=(4, 4))
image_sample = X_test[0].reshape(8, 8)
output_image_path = os.path.join(output_dir, 'test_sample_image.png')
plt.imshow(image_sample, cmap='gray')
plt.title(f"Test sample label (actual digit): {y_test[0]}")
plt.axis('off')   # Turn off the axis
plt.savefig(output_image_path)
plt.close()

print(f"Test sample image saved to: {output_image_path}")
```

Because we already covered in Chapter 5 the model tuning aspects of the program, let's focus now on how this program deploys the best model.

The deployment phase involves several key steps to ensure that the model can handle inference requests efficiently. Initially, the program sets up a serverless inference configuration object ServerlessInferenceConfig, specifying critical parameters such as memory size and maximum concurrency to optimize resource allocation. This configuration helps Amazon SageMaker AI manage the computational resources needed to serve inference requests dynamically, without requiring dedicated instances.

The best trained model, saved as model.tar.gz in an S3 bucket, is then retrieved for deployment. The Model object is created, specifying the S3 path to the model.tar.gz artifact file and the XGBoost container image URI. This container (xgboost:1.2-1) is designed to work seamlessly with the serialized model format, ensuring compatibility and ease of deployment.

When the deploy method of the Model object is called, Amazon SageMaker orchestrates the deployment process. The container starts up and downloads the model artifacts file model.tar.gz, decompressing it automatically. The decompressed files are placed in the appropriate directories within the container, and the XGBoost model is loaded into memory, ready to serve inference requests. This automation ensures that the model is correctly initialized and available for predictions.

To handle inference requests, the endpoint expects input in CSV format, which is ensured by using a CSVSerializer for input data and a JSONDeserializer for output data. A unique endpoint name is assigned to avoid conflicts, and the CustomPredictor class is used to manage interactions with the endpoint. The endpoint exposes an API that processes CSV representations of hand-written digits, performs predictions, and returns the results.

The program concludes by performing an example inference using the deployed endpoint. A test sample is converted to a CSV-encoded string and sent to the endpoint. The predicted digit class is then returned and displayed, as displayed in Figure 6.10.

FIGURE 6.10 Prediction from the serverless inference endpoint.

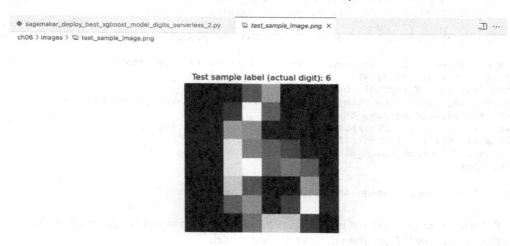

FIGURE 6.11 Serverless inference endpoint summary.

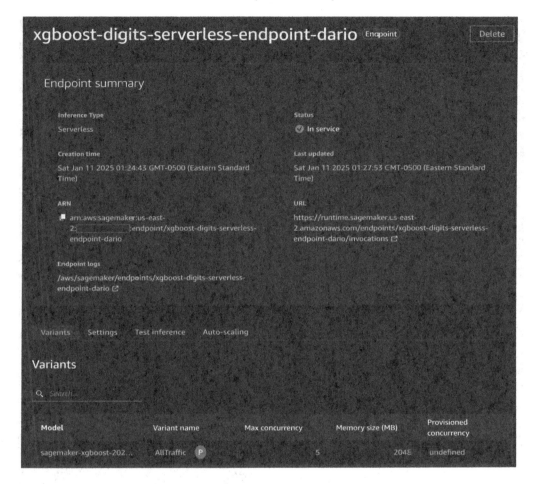

As you can see, the model correctly predicted the test sample, which is a CSV-representation of the digit 6.

Figure 6.11 displays the serverless endpoint.

Notice at the bottom of Figure 6.11 the endpoint model, the variant, the max concurrency, and the memory size we set up programmatically in the code. Because its status is "In service," the endpoint is ready to serve inference requests at the specified URL.

Amazon SageMaker Studio allows you to test your endpoint directly from the UI. In Figure 6.12, you can see the result of testing the endpoint by sending the CSV-encoded string of the test sample.

FIGURE 6.12 Test inference.

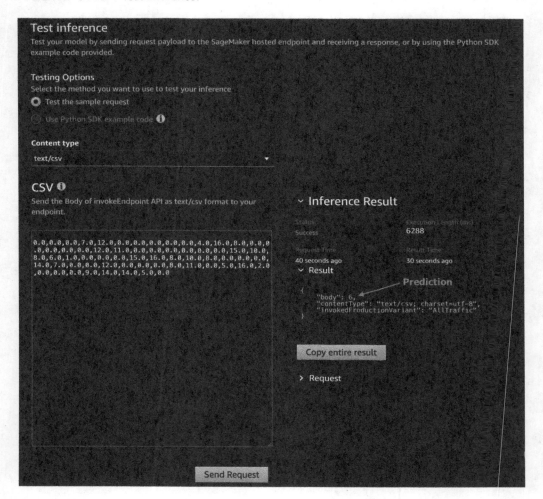

Last, if you are curious to see the model's hyperparameters and why it was chosen by the Bayesian strategy during the tuning process, I have included the plot in Figure 6.13.

You just learned how to programmatically deploy a model to a serverless inference endpoint. This deployment process, leveraging the power of Amazon SageMaker AI's managed containers and serverless infrastructure, ensures efficient and scalable handling of inference requests without the need for manual resource management.

FIGURE 6.13 Model selection.

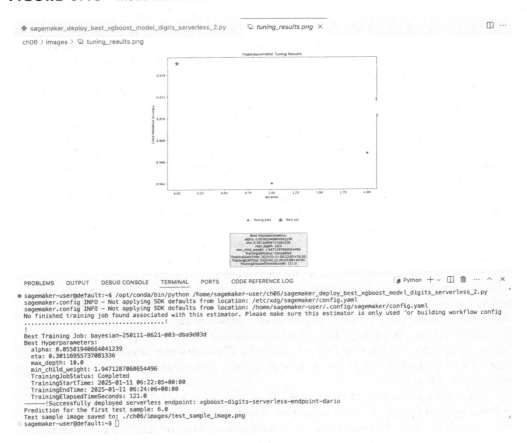

Summary

In this chapter, you learned how to make the models you carefully developed and refined ready to work. If your use case is a good fit for AWS AI services, AWS provides a suite of fully managed AI services that can be easily incorporated into applications through API calls. These services include Amazon Rekognition, Textract, Polly, Transcribe, Translate, Comprehend, Lex, and Personalize, which offer pretrained models for various tasks. Because these models are hosted in managed AWS accounts, users have limited access to the underlying models; however, these pretrained models can be easily consumed, allowing for rapid integration and deployment without the need for complex model management. Additionally, you learned how Amazon Bedrock requires a different approach to deploying models by using the concept of agents and the Converse API, which act as intermediaries between your application and the foundation models, offering both comprehensive orchestration and streamlined conversational interactions. This initial step sets the foundation for leveraging AI capabilities effectively in AWS.

Building on the ease of using AWS AI services, Amazon SageMaker AI offers several deployment options to manage and host ML models. These options include real-time inference for low-latency predictions, serverless inference for automatic scaling (as demonstrated in the deep-dive exercise), asynchronous inference for handling large payloads and long processing times, and batch inference for processing large datasets in bulk. Each deployment method is designed to cater to specific use cases, ensuring flexibility and scalability in model deployment.

Although Amazon SageMaker AI provides robust managed deployment options, there are scenarios where unmanaged model deployments are more suitable. This involves deploying models on alternative compute platforms, such as Amazon EC2 instances, Amazon EKS clusters, AWS Lambda functions, and even on-premises servers. Although this approach requires more manual effort for infrastructure setup, scaling, and maintenance, it offers greater control and customization over the deployment environment.

To further enhance model performance and deployment efficiency, Amazon SageMaker Neo can be used to optimize models for various hardware platforms, reducing latency and improving performance. Advanced deployment techniques, such as autoscaling and Blue/ Green deployments (including All At Once, Canary, and Linear strategies), enable safe and controlled updates to models as they get deployed. These methods ensure continuous improvement and robust deployment strategies, making the deployment process more resilient and efficient.

Finally, you learned how orchestrating ML workflows is essential for managing the end-to-end ML lifecycle. Amazon SageMaker Pipelines provides a powerful way to automate workflows from data preparation to model deployment. Moreover, services like Amazon Managed Workflows for Apache Airflow and AWS Step Functions can be integrated to enhance orchestration capabilities, allowing for complex workflows and conditional logic. This orchestration ensures that ML processes are streamlined, repeatable, and maintainable, ultimately accelerating model deployment and improving operational efficiency.

Exam Essentials

Know the difference between inference infrastructure and training infrastructure. Inference infrastructure generally requires significantly less compute and memory than training infrastructure because inference only involves applying a pretrained model to new data, whereas training involves the computationally intensive process of learning and optimizing the model parameters from a large dataset.

Know Amazon SageMaker AI's managed deployment options. Amazon SageMaker AI offers four managed deployment options to cater to diverse use cases. Real-time inference provides low-latency endpoints for immediate predictions, perfect for interactive applications. Serverless inference automatically scales resources based on traffic, ideal for applications with intermittent or unpredictable patterns. Asynchronous inference handles large payloads and long processing times efficiently, making it suitable for heavy workloads. Batch inference processes large datasets in bulk, ideal for non-real-time predictions. These options ensure flexibility, scalability, and efficiency, allowing you to choose the best approach for your specific use case.

Know when to use multi-model endpoints (MMEs) vs. multi-container endpoints (MCEs). Use MMEs to host multiple models within the same container on a single endpoint when you have many models with low traffic volume and want to save on costs by sharing resources. Use MCEs to host different models in separate containers on a single endpoint when each model has distinct dependencies and resource requirements and you need better isolation and scalability for independent updates.

Know when to use CPU- vs. GPU-powered infrastructure. Use GPU-powered infrastructure for compute-intensive jobs to train deep learning models with large amounts of data. Use CPU-powered infrastructure for tasks that don't require the massive parallel processing capabilities of GPUs. These tasks include preprocessing data, performing feature engineering, running smaller training jobs, and handling inference tasks where the computational demands are lower.

Know the autoscaling metrics for Amazon SageMaker AI endpoints. Autoscaling metrics include `InvocationsPerInstance`, which measures the average number of invocations per instance per minute; `CPUUtilization`, tracking the percentage of CPU usage; `Latency`, measuring the time taken to process requests; and `GPUUtilization`, which measures the percentage of GPU usage. These metrics help create scaling policies to automatically adjust the number of instances, ensuring optimal performance and cost-efficiency.

Know when to use All At Once, Canary, and Linear traffic-shifting patterns with Blue/Green deployments. Use the All At Once traffic-shifting pattern for Blue/Green deployments when you have high confidence in the new version of your model and want a quick transition. Choose the Canary pattern when you want to minimize risk by gradually shifting a small portion of traffic (Canary) to the new version and monitoring its performance before a full rollout. Choose the Linear pattern for a controlled, step-by-step traffic shift, providing the most balanced approach that allows for incremental monitoring and adjustments.

Know the different ML workflow orchestration services available with AWS and when to use them. AWS offers several ML workflow orchestration services to streamline and manage ML pipelines: Amazon SageMaker Pipelines for automating end-to-end ML workflows, perfect for managing the entire ML lifecycle; AWS Step Functions for coordinating complex workflows with multiple steps, ideal for integrating with other AWS services and handling error recovery; and Amazon Managed Workflows for Apache Airflow (MWAA) for managing Apache Airflow workflows in a fully managed environment, suitable for orchestrating complex workflows like ETL jobs or ML pipelines with minimal operational overhead.

Review Questions

1. Which instance type should you select for an Amazon SageMaker AI multi-model endpoint hosting several deep learning models trained on large datasets to optimize cost and performance?

    A. t2.medium

    B. m5.xlarge

    C. p3.8xlarge

    D. c5.4xlarge

2. When configuring an Amazon SageMaker AI endpoint, under what circumstances would you choose a managed deployment over an unmanaged deployment?

    A. When you require full control over the deployment infrastructure

    B. When you need seamless scalability and managed resource allocation

    C. When deploying models on non-AWS environments

    D. When you need to customize the deployment setup extensively

3. Which traffic shifting pattern is most appropriate for deploying a critical model update with minimum risk and thorough performance monitoring before full rollout?

    A. All At Once

    B. Linear

    C. Canary

    D. Partial

4. What is the primary advantage of using Amazon SageMaker Neo for model deployment in an IoT environment?

    A. To reduce the cost of training models

    B. To ensure high accuracy of predictions

    C. To optimize models for diverse hardware, enabling efficient edge deployments

    D. To improve data preprocessing speed

5. Which Amazon SageMaker AI orchestration service would you use to automate end-to-end machine learning workflows with minimal manual intervention?

    A. Amazon SageMaker Pipelines

    B. Amazon Managed Workflows for Apache Airflow (MWAA)

    C. AWS Step Functions

    D. Amazon SageMaker Clarify

6. Which EC2 instance type should you choose for an inference workload that requires high throughput and low latency using custom-built machine learning models?

   A. t3.medium

   B. r5.4xlarge

   C. g4dn.xlarge

   D. inf1.2xlarge

7. When should you select Amazon SageMaker Serverless Inference as a managed deployment option?

   A. When you need low-latency real-time predictions

   B. When you have intermittent or unpredictable traffic patterns

   C. When you require high-throughput batch processing

   D. When you need to run inference on large payloads with long processing times

8. When should you choose AWS Step Functions over Amazon SageMaker Pipelines and MWAA for ML workflow orchestration?

   A. When you need to automate simple ETL tasks

   B. When you require a managed service to orchestrate complex ML workflows with conditional branching and error handling

   C. When you need to use prebuilt templates for ML projects

   D. When you need to perform bias detection and explain model predictions

9. What are the key functionalities provided by the Amazon SageMaker Model Registry, and when should you use it in a continuous integration/continuous delivery (CI/CD) pipeline?

   A. It provides model monitoring and bias detection capabilities; use it to continuously monitor model performance in production.

   B. It offers model versioning, approval workflows, and deployment automation; use it to manage and deploy models efficiently in a CI/CD pipeline.

   C. It simplifies data preprocessing and feature engineering; use it to prepare datasets for training.

   D. It integrates with AWS Step Functions for orchestrating complex ML workflows; use it to coordinate multiple ML tasks.

10. When should you use the Amazon Bedrock Converse API in Amazon SageMaker AI?

    A. For managing and deploying machine learning models

    B. For automated real-time natural language understanding and generation tasks

    C. For conducting data preprocessing and feature engineering

    D. For optimizing models for various hardware platforms

Chapter 7

Model Monitoring and Cost Optimization

THE AWS CERTIFIED MACHINE LEARNING (ML) ENGINEER ASSOCIATE EXAM OBJECTIVES COVERED IN THIS CHAPTER MAY INCLUDE, BUT ARE NOT LIMITED TO, THE FOLLOWING:

✓ **Domain 4: ML Solution Monitoring, Maintenance, and Security**
   - 4.1 Monitor model inference
   - 4.2 Monitor and optimize infrastructure and costs

Monitoring Model Inference

Machine learning (ML) models are usually trained and evaluated using historical data. However, real-world data may (and should) be different from training data so that models can generalize well to new, unseen data. This is particularly true as models age over time and the distributions of data change as a result of entropy, leading to potential shifts in the underlying patterns and relationships within the data. As these changes accumulate, the model's assumptions about the data may become less accurate, resulting in a gradual decrease in the model's performance and prediction quality. This gradual decrease in the model's performance is referred to as model *drift*. A drift can significantly impact your model's prediction quality.

An effective way to address this problem is to continuously monitor your model and retrain it as needed. Continuous monitoring ensures that your model adapts to evolving data distributions and maintains its effectiveness. This step is illustrated in the ninth and last phase of the ML lifecycle, i.e., Monitor Model, as shown in Figure 7.1.

Model monitoring is a key phase in the ML lifecycle whose main focus is to maintain the reliability, availability, and performance of your newly deployed ML model.

In this chapter, you will learn the techniques and services provided by AWS to monitor the inferences produced by your model, and the infrastructure that your model utilizes to generate them.

The exam also requires that you are well-versed in the guiding principles that are relevant to monitoring. Understanding how to instrument your ML solution with a robust monitoring framework is essential for ensuring the ongoing performance, reliability, and security of your models. This involves setting up appropriate metrics, alerts, and dashboards to keep track of various aspects of your ML solution, such as model accuracy, latency, resource utilization, and data drift.

It's even more important to understand the rationale behind these monitoring practices. This means knowing why each metric matters and how it can impact the overall performance and health of your ML application. For instance, monitoring model accuracy helps you detect when the model's performance is degrading, whereas tracking resource utilization allows you to optimize costs and prevent system overloads.

FIGURE 7.1 The model monitoring phase in the machine learning lifecycle.

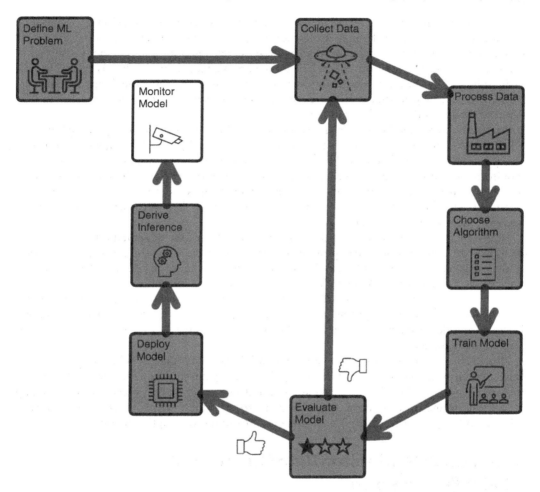

The rationale behind these monitoring practices is formalized in a collection of best practices referred to as the Machine Learning Well-Architected Lens. This framework provides detailed guidance on how to "well-architect" your ML solution in alignment with the six pillars of the AWS Well-Architected Framework: operational excellence, security, reliability, performance efficiency, cost optimization, and sustainability.

By following these best practices, you can ensure that your ML solutions are not only robust and efficient but also adaptable to changing conditions and aligned with business objectives.

Drifts in Models

As mentioned earlier, drift in ML models is a phenomenon where the model's performance degrades over time due to changes in the underlying data. These changes can occur for various reasons, such as evolving user behavior, seasonal trends, or external factors. In the context of Amazon SageMaker AI, understanding and managing model drift is critical to maintaining the accuracy and reliability of your deployed models. As models age and the real-world data they encounter begins to differ from the training data, it becomes essential to detect and address these drifts promptly.

Amazon SageMaker AI provides powerful tools to help monitor and detect model drift. One of the key services in this regard is Amazon SageMaker Model Monitor, which allows you to continuously track the quality of your ML models in production. By setting up monitoring schedules, you can automatically capture data from your endpoints, analyze it for signs of drift, and generate alerts when significant changes are detected. This proactive approach helps ensure that your models remain aligned with the current data distributions and continue to deliver accurate predictions.

There are different types of drift that you might encounter, including data drift, model drift, bias drift, and feature attribution drift. Data drift occurs when the statistical properties of the input data change over time, whereas model drift happens when the model's performance metrics deteriorate. Bias drift is related to changes in the fairness of the model's predictions, and feature attribution drift occurs when the importance of input features shifts. By monitoring these various forms of drift, you can gain a comprehensive understanding of how your models are behaving in real-world scenarios and take necessary actions to mitigate any negative impacts.

To effectively manage model drift and maintain high performance, it's important to implement robust techniques for monitoring data quality and model performance. In the next sections, we will explore these techniques in detail, covering best practices for setting up monitoring frameworks, selecting appropriate metrics, and leveraging Amazon SageMaker AI's capabilities to ensure that your models continue to perform optimally over time.

Techniques to Monitor Data Quality and Model Performance

Amazon SageMaker Model Monitor is designed to oversee the quality of ML models deployed in production within Amazon SageMaker AI. With Model Monitor, you have several options for setting up monitoring:

- Continuous monitoring with a real-time endpoint
- Continuous monitoring with a batch transform job that runs at regular intervals
- Scheduled monitoring for asynchronous batch transform jobs

Amazon SageMaker Model Monitor allows you to set up Amazon CloudWatch alarms that notify you of any drifts in data or model quality. Early and proactive detection of these drifts enables you to take corrective actions, such as retraining models, auditing upstream systems, or fixing quality issues, without the need for manual monitoring or implementing additional tools. You can utilize prebuilt monitoring capabilities, which require no coding, or you have the flexibility to code custom analysis for more tailored monitoring.

Amazon SageMaker Model Monitor provides the following monitoring types:

- **Data quality:** Monitors drift in data quality
- **Model quality:** Monitors drift in model quality metrics, such as accuracy
- **Bias drift for models in production:** Monitors bias in your model's predictions
- **Feature attribution drift for models in production:** Monitors drift in feature attribution

The last two types of monitoring—bias drift and feature attribution drift—can be considered part of overall model quality monitoring. The former (bias drift) monitors changes in the fairness of your model's predictions over time. Because maintaining fairness is a crucial aspect of a model's quality and ethical deployment, monitoring for bias drift is essential for ensuring that the model continues to perform equitably across different groups. The latter (feature attribution) monitors shifts in the importance of input features. If the relevance of certain features changes over time, it can affect your model's decision-making process, ultimately impacting its performance and quality. Keeping an eye on feature attribution drift helps ensure that your model remains accurate and reliable.

Figure 7.2 illustrates how data quality and model quality fit in the overall monitoring process with Amazon SageMaker AI.

Data quality monitoring involves creating a *baseline* of the input data during model training and continuously comparing incoming data to this baseline. If there are changes in the incoming data, a drift is detected.

You can also spot drift through model quality monitoring, which means checking actual outcomes (labels) against predictions. For instance, if you forecast daily sales, you can compare the predicted sales figures to the actual sales the next day. Some use cases might need extra effort to gather real outcomes. For example, when recommending products, you might need to survey a group of customers to see how well the recommendations match their preferences.

As you learned in Chapter 3, Amazon SageMaker Clarify provides insights into the model's predictions by showing the importance of different input features, which is often referred to as feature attribution. This helps you understand the reasoning behind the model's decisions and can reveal any biases or unexpected patterns in the data. For example, if a model is used for predicting loan approvals, Amazon SageMaker Clarify can show which input features (such as credit score, income level, or employment history) most influenced the model's decision for a specific prediction.

If feature attribution changes between retrained models, a drift has occurred. Evaluating drift involves monitoring data, detecting changes, and triggering actions when needed. You can set up rules and thresholds in Amazon CloudWatch to receive notifications about drifts and automatically take corrective actions to address them.

Figure 7.3 shows a logical architecture for real-time model monitoring with data sources for training and production on the left, monitoring components (data quality and model quality) in the middle, and observed findings on the right. A similar architecture can be

302 Chapter 7 ■ Model Monitoring and Cost Optimization

FIGURE 7.2 Monitoring process.

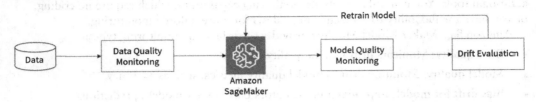

FIGURE 7.3 Monitoring architecture for real-time inference.

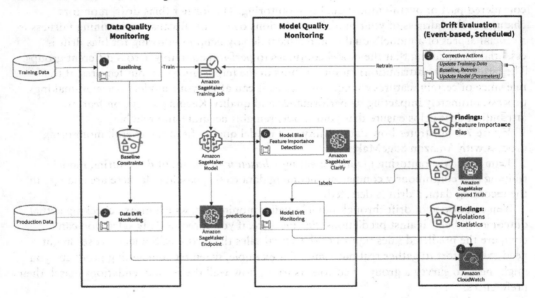

created for batch inference. You can use Amazon SageMaker Data Wrangler to clean and prepare your input data for ML tasks. The features you create for your models can be stored in the Amazon SageMaker Feature Store, which is a fully managed repository designed to store, update, retrieve, and share ML features. These services were detailed in Chapter 3 as well. Think of the architecture illustrated in Figure 7.3 as a lower-level view of the model monitoring process described in Figure 7.2. The next section will describe this process in detail.

Monitoring Workflow

The rectangular boxes in Figure 7.3 show the tasks for detecting data and model drift. You can include these tasks in your ML workflow using Amazon SageMaker Pipelines. The drift observation data—denoted as *findings*—can be captured in tabular format, such as comma-separated values or Parquet, on Amazon S3 and analyzed with Amazon Athena and Amazon QuickSight.

Let's see how the overall monitoring process works. First, you need to enable Amazon SageMaker model monitoring. For a real-time endpoint, you have to enable the endpoint to capture data from incoming requests to a deployed ML model, and the resulting model predictions. For a batch transform job, you have to enable data capture of the batch transform inputs and outputs.

The workflow starts with the baselining task (step 1 in Figure 7.3), which uses Amazon SageMaker Model Monitor to define a data profile from your training data and stores it in Amazon S3 as a collection of constraints.

The baseline job computes metrics and creates constraints for the metrics. For example, the recall score for the model shouldn't decrease to less than 0.8, or tne precision score shouldn't fall below 0.9. Real-time (or batch) predictions from your model are later compared to the constraints and are reported as violations if they are outside the constrained values. The baseline job runs before training or retraining the model.

The data drift monitoring task (step 2) continually analyzes the input data and compares it to a baseline created in step 1. The results are then logged in Amazon CloudWatch (step 4). For example, you can monitor metrics such as the mean, median, and standard deviation of feature values or the rate of missing values in your input data. When Amazon CloudWatch detects that these metrics deviate significantly from the established baseline, it can trigger alerts, enabling you to take timely corrective actions. The data drift monitoring task operates on its own computational resources using Deequ (an open-source tool implemented on top of Apache Spark), ensuring that it doesn't slow down your ML inference process and can scale with the data size. You can adjust how often this task runs to control costs, based on how quickly you expect the data to change.

The model drift monitoring task (step 3) compares the predictions your model produces with ground truth labels to measure the quality of the model. For this to work, you periodically label data captured by your endpoint (or batch transform) job and upload it to Amazon S3. You then specify the location of your labels as a parameter when you create the monitoring job. Just like the data drift monitoring task, the model drift monitoring task logs the results of the comparison in Amazon CloudWatch (step 4) and reports any violations in a designated bucket in Amazon S3.

Amazon CloudWatch is a monitoring and observability service that manages logs, events, and alarms. With Amazon CloudWatch, you can define rules to respond to deviations in data drift or model performance. By leveraging its integration with Amazon Simple Notification Service (SNS), you can set up alarms to notify users via email or SMS. As a result of these events, Amazon CloudWatch can also automatically trigger the ML model retraining process (step 5).

For the exam, make sure you know the difference between logs, events, and alarms.

Logs are detailed records of events that occur within your applications, systems, or services, which can be used for troubleshooting and analysis.

Events are specific occurrences or changes in the state of your resources that you want to monitor and act on, such as a system failure or a change in configuration.

Alarms are notifications triggered by specified thresholds or conditions, such as those defined by baseline constraints in the data drift monitoring task. When these thresholds are crossed, alarms alert you of potential issues and can initiate automated actions in response, such as updating training data, updating your model hyperparameters, baselining, and retraining your model (step 5).

You just learned the main techniques to monitor data quality and model performance. In the next section, a detailed coverage of the design principles relevant to monitoring will be provided. This knowledge is not only a requirement for the exam but also instrumental in ensuring that your ML models remain accurate, reliable, and effective in real-world applications.

Design Principles for Monitoring

Given the criticality of the monitoring phase for being focused on *live* observations of your model performance (and its underlying infrastructure) in a production environment, the exam requires that you—as an AWS ML engineer—know well the guiding principles that help you design and build a robust, efficient, and sustainable monitoring framework for your newly deployed ML models.

Figure 7.4 summarizes the guiding principles that are relevant to monitoring from the Machine Learning Well-Architected Lens.

> **NOTE** To learn more about the Machine Learning Well-Architected Lens, visit: https://docs.aws.amazon.com/wellarchitected/latest/machine-learning-lens/best-practices-by-ml-lifecycle-phase.html.

Let's break these principles down by pillar and examine the main theme for each and what you need to do to implement them.

Operational Excellence Pillar

Operational excellence (OE) means making sure we build software the right way while always providing a great experience for our customers. The OE pillar includes best practices for organizing our teams, designing our work, running it effectively on a large scale, making it adaptive to changes, and continuously improving it over time.

The OE pillar is formalized by the two following principles.

MLOE-15: Enable Model Observability and Tracking

When it comes to ML, a well-architected application must include a framework that enables your team to proactively observe vital performance metrics of your model. These may include, for example, metrics that measure the operational health of the compute instances hosting the endpoint and the health of endpoint responses for real-time inference.

Monitoring Model Inference   305

FIGURE 7.4   Monitoring guiding principles.

ML Phase	Pillar	Principle
Monitoring	Operational excellence	MLOE-15: Enable model observability and tracking
		MLOE-16: Synchronize architecture and configuration, and check for skew across environments
	Security	MLSEC-12: Restrict access to intended legitimate consumers
		MLSEC-13: Monitor human interactions with data for anomalous activity
	Reliability	MLREL-12: Allow automatic scaling of the model endpoint
		MLREL-13: Ensure a recoverable endpoint with a managed version control strategy
	Performance efficiency	MLPER-13: Evaluate model explainability
		MLPER-14: Evaluate data drift
		MLPER-15: Monitor, detect, and handle model performance degradation
		MLPER-16: Establish an automated re-training framework
		MLPER-17: Review for updated data/features for retraining
		MLPER-18: Include human-in-the-loop monitoring
	Cost optimization	MLCOST-27: Monitor usage and cost by ML activity
		MLCOST-28: Monitor Return on Investment for ML models
		MLCOST-29: Monitor endpoint usage and right-size the instance fleet
	Sustainability	MLSUS-15: Measure material efficiency
		MLSUS-16: Retrain only when necessary

Implementation

This principle can be implemented by incorporating in your solution the following services/ capabilities:

- **Amazon SageMaker Model Monitor** to continually monitor the quality of Amazon SageMaker ML models in production and compare with the results from training
- **Amazon CloudWatch** to gather and analyze usage statistics for your ML models
- **Amazon SageMaker Model Dashboard** to view, search, and explore your models in a centralized portal
- **Amazon SageMaker Clarify** to discover bias that can emerge during model training or when the model is in production
- **Amazon SageMaker ML Lineage Tracking** to keep a history of model discovery experiments
- **Amazon SageMaker Model Cards** to simplify model information gathering such as business requirements, key decisions, and observations during model development and evaluation
- **Amazon SageMaker Automated Validation** to compare the performance of new models against production models, using the same real-world inference request data in real time

MLOE-16: Synchronize Architecture and Configuration, and Check for Skew Across Environments

This principle is focused on ensuring that all systems and configurations are identical across the development and deployment phases.

Implementation

This principle can be implemented by incorporating in your solution the following services/ capabilities:

- **Amazon CloudFormation** to provision the necessary resources quickly and consistently with infrastructure as code (IaC)
- **Amazon SageMaker Model Monitor** to continuously monitor the quality of your models in production and compare them with the results from training

Security Pillar

The security pillar—as the name suggests—aims at building the necessary security guardrails to protect all components of your ML applications, including identities (users and roles), infrastructure (compute and network resources), the ML application built to serve your model, and, most importantly, your data. Remember, the data is not just limited to training, validation, and test data, but also includes the model artifacts (`model.tar.gz`) where parameters and configurations are stored. Chapter 8 will cover the security pillar extensively.

The security pillar is formalized by the two following principles.

MLSEC-12: Restrict Access to Intended Legitimate Consumers

This principle is about enforcing the *least privilege principle* for all consumers of your model endpoint.

Implementation

This principle can be implemented by treating inference endpoints as you would any other HTTPS API. This means implementing network controls, such as restricting access to specific IP ranges, and bot control. Also, the HTTPS requests for these API calls should be signed so that the requestor identity can be verified and the requested data is protected in transit.

MLSEC-13: Monitor Human Interactions with Data for Anomalous Activity

This principle aims at reducing the attack surface of your model endpoint.

Implementation

This principle can be implemented by instrumenting your ML application with the following services/configurations:

- **Enabling data access logging** to better track events in response to your model endpoint inference requests
- **Amazon Macie** to classify and protect your Amazon S3 sensitive data in accordance with its sensitivity level
- **Amazon GuardDuty** to monitor for malicious and unauthorized activities, including unauthorized access to AWS accounts, workloads, and data stored in Amazon S3

Reliability Pillar

The reliability pillar focuses on the ability of your ML application to perform its intended function correctly and consistently when it's expected to. By *correctly*, we mean your ML application should fulfill all the business requirements it was designed to do. By *consistently*, we mean your ML application should always perform in a satisfactory way from a user standpoint. As a result, performance metrics need to be defined with specific thresholds (lower and upper bounds) to indicate acceptable performance, e.g., uptime, latency, and so on.

> To learn more about site reliability engineering (SRE), visit https://aws.amazon.com/what-is/sre.

The reliability pillar is formalized by the following two principles.

MLREL-12: Allow Automatic Scaling of the Model Endpoint

This principle ensures the automatic scaling of model endpoints, resulting in reliable and elastic processing of predictions to meet changing workload inference demands.

Implementation

As you learned in Chapter 6, this principle can be implemented by Amazon SageMaker Auto Scaling Endpoints with techniques like target tracking, step scaling or scheduled scaling, and Amazon EC2 Auto Scaling.

MLREL-13: Ensure a Recoverable Endpoint with a Managed Version Control Strategy

This principle is about designing your model inference endpoint to be fault-tolerant. For this to happen, you need to make sure all the endpoint components "behind the scenes" are fault-tolerant. After all, "A chain is as strong as its weakest link."

Implementation

As illustrated in Figures 6.3 and 6.6 in the previous chapter, the components that make up a real-time inference endpoint include the endpoint instances, the endpoint configurations, the inference container images, your model artifacts, and so on. As a result, this principle is implemented by leveraging the following capabilities/services:

- **Amazon SageMaker Pipelines and Projects** to automate the full ML workflow, including recovery from failures

- **AWS CloudFormation** (or other IaC tools) to programmatically (re)build the infrastructure your ML application operates on

- **Amazon ECR** to securely store the inference container images your model uses during training and evaluation

Performance Efficiency Pillar

The performance efficiency pillar focuses on the optimization of cloud computing resources to achieve the necessary performance levels for your ML applications, while also ensuring that this efficiency is adaptive to fluctuating demand and evolving technologies. Put differently, this pillar is about using the right cloud resources at the right time to meet your ML application needs without overspending or underperforming.

The last statement highlights the different constraints this pillar is aiming to meet. As a result, there are several trade-offs you, as an ML engineer, you will need to consider. The following principles will help you choose which ones and how.

MLPER-13: Evaluate Model Explainability

This principle emphasizes the importance of assessing how well your model's predictions can be understood and explained in human terms, considering both business needs and compliance requirements when evaluating model performance. Essentially, it means evaluating whether your model's decisions are transparent and justifiable as a result of the trade-off between explainability and model complexity.

Implementation

This principle is implemented by leveraging Amazon SageMaker Clarify to explain model results. As you learned in Chapter 3, Amazon SageMaker Clarify helps improve your models by detecting potential bias and helping explain the predictions that models make. The fairness and explainability functions provided by Amazon SageMaker Clarify help you build less biased and more understandable and balanced ML models.

MLPER-14: Evaluate Data Drift

This principle refers to a specific benchmark test within the MLPerf suite designed to assess how well your model can detect and handle *data drift*: i.e., significant changes in the distribution of input data over time that can negatively impact your model's accuracy when applied to new, unseen data.

> MLPerf is a benchmark suite developed by MLCommons—a consortium of AI leaders from academia, research labs, and industry—that provides standardized tests to evaluate the performance of ML hardware, software, and services. To learn more, visit https://mlcommons.org.

Implementation

This principle is implemented by using the following services:

- **Amazon SageMaker Model Monitor** to maintain high-quality ML models by detecting model and concept drift in real time
- **Amazon SageMaker Clarify** to help identify potential bias in your ML models

MLPER-15: Monitor, Detect, and Handle Model Performance Degradation

This principle focuses on continuously monitoring your deployed models to identify and address any decline in their performance over time. This includes detecting issues like data drift, concept drift, and model bias and taking necessary actions like retraining or updating the model when performance degradation is detected. Essentially, it's a process to ensure that your model remains accurate and reliable in real-world applications.

Implementation

This principle is implemented by using the following services:

- **Amazon SageMaker Model Monitor** to continually monitor the quality of your models in production
- **Amazon SageMaker Auto Scaling** to dynamically adjust underlying compute resources supporting an endpoint based on demand

MLPER-16: Establish an Automated Retraining Framework

This principle advocates for setting up an automated system to regularly retrain your ML models. This system is intended to keep your models updated with changing data patterns and to maintain optimal performance over time by automatically triggering retraining when necessary based on monitored metrics like data drift or performance degradation.

Implementation

This principle is implemented by using the following services:

- **Amazon SageMaker Model Monitor** to continually monitor the quality of your models in production and trigger retraining when a specific event occurs, e.g., data drifts beyond a defined threshold

- **Amazon SageMaker Pipelines** or **AWS Step Functions** to enable orchestration using step creation and management.

MLPER-17: Review for Updated Data/Features for Retraining

This principle focuses on establishing a framework to periodically review and update the data and features used for retraining ML models. The goal is to ensure that the model remains accurate and relevant over time by incorporating new data and features that may have emerged since the initial training. This involves running data exploration and feature engineering at predetermined intervals based on data volatility and availability.

Implementation

This principle is implemented by leveraging Amazon SageMaker Data Wrangler, which is the fastest and easiest way to prepare data for your models, as you learned in Chapter 3.

MLPER-18: Include Human-in-the-loop Monitoring

This principle emphasizes the importance of incorporating human oversight into the monitoring of ML models. This involves having human reviewers evaluate the model's inferences, especially for low-confidence predictions or random samples. By comparing human-labeled results with the model's predictions, you can identify and address any performance degradation.

Implementation

This principle is implemented by leveraging Amazon Augmented AI (A2I) to get human review of low-confidence predictions or random prediction samples.

Cost Optimization Pillar

The cost optimization pillar focuses on designing, building, and operating ML applications that achieve the necessary business functionality while minimizing costs, essentially producing the most accurate inferences for the least amount of money spent.

The cost optimization pillar is formalized by the following three principles.

MLCOST-27: Monitor Usage and Cost by ML Activity

This principle relies on the concept of *tagging* your ML resources. Tagging allows you to effectively manage, identify, and organize your cloud infrastructure by attaching metadata (key-value pairs) to individual resources. By tagging your ML resources, you can easily group them based on purpose, owner, environment, or any other relevant criteria, which in turn facilitates easy searching, filtering, and cost analysis. This is particularly helpful when associating costs with specific activities like retraining and hosting through dedicated tags.

> Resource tagging is a key capability of FinOps, which is a set of practices for optimizing cloud costs. To learn more, visit https://docs.aws.amazon.com/whitepapers/latest/tagging-best-practices/tags-for-cost-allocation-and-financial-management.html.

Implementation

This principle is implemented by using the following services/capabilities:

- **AWS tagging** to selectively group your ML resources by purpose (e.g., ML phase), owner, environment, and other relevant metadata
- **AWS Budgets** to keep track of cost

MLCOST-28: Monitor Return on Investment for ML Models

This principle emphasizes the importance of establishing a reporting capability to track the value delivered by a ML model once it's deployed into production.

The goal is to compare the value delivered by the model against its ongoing runtime costs. This involves measuring key performance indicators (KPIs) relevant to the business outcomes the model aims to achieve. These KPIs should be clearly defined in the first phase of the ML lifecycle: i.e., "Define ML Problem," as shown in Figure 7.5.

Defining KPIs early ensures that the objectives and success criteria for the ML project are clear from the beginning, guiding the subsequent phases effectively. For example, if the model is used to support customer acquisition, you would track how many new customers are acquired in a given period of time, as well as their spending when the model's prediction is used compared to a baseline.

Effective reporting helps you take appropriate actions based on the return on investment (ROI). If the ROI is positive, you might consider scaling the model to similar challenges. If the ROI is negative, you might look into remedial actions such as optimizing model latency with serverless inference, or reducing runtime costs.

Implementation

This principle is implemented by using a reporting tool such as Amazon QuickSight to develop business focused reports showing the value delivered by using the model in terms of business KPIs.

312 Chapter 7 • Model Monitoring and Cost Optimization

FIGURE 7.5 The machine learning lifecycle.

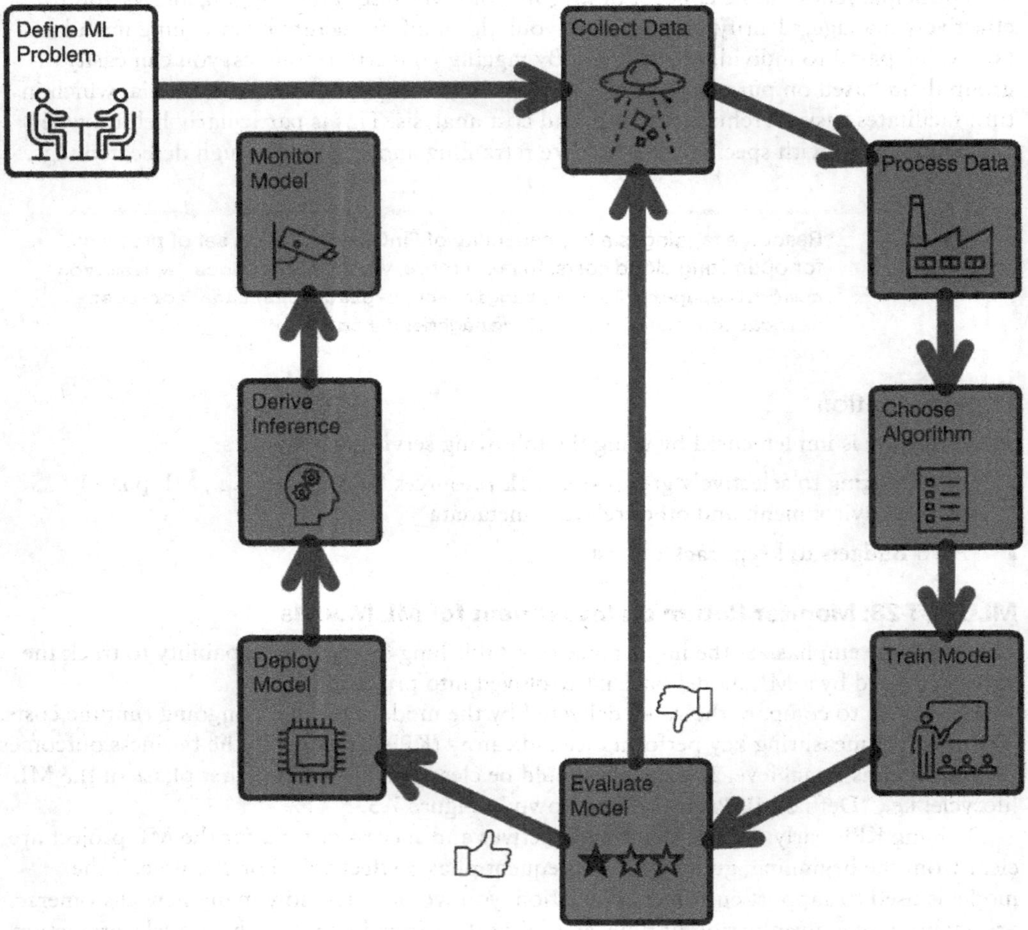

MLCOST-29: Monitor Endpoint Usage and Right-size the Instance Fleet

This principle focuses on efficient use of compute resources to run your models in production. For example, instrument your ML solution to monitor your endpoint usage and to elastically (scale-in, scale-out) scale your instances based on the workload demand.

Implementation

This principle is implemented by using the following services/strategies:

- **Amazon CloudWatch** to monitor your model Amazon SageMaker endpoints

- **Amazon SageMaker Auto Scaling** to dynamically adjust underlying compute resources supporting an endpoint based on demand
- Designing and developing a *Frugal Architecture* for your overall ML solution

Frugal Architecture is a design philosophy that treats cost and sustainability as critical nonfunctional requirements alongside other factors like security, compliance, and performance. This concept was introduced by Dr. Werner Vogels (CTO of Amazon) at re:Invent 2023. For example, in use cases where you need fast access to large datasets of training data, you may consider using Amazon FSx for Lustre, as you learned in Chapter 2. This principle guides you to deploy Amazon FSx for Lustre and Amazon SageMaker AI in the same Availability Zone to minimize egress costs. To learn more, visit https://aws.amazon.com/blogs/architecture/achieving-frugal-architecture-using-the-aws-well-architected-framework-guidance.

Sustainability Pillar

The sustainability pillar aims at reducing environmental impacts, especially energy consumption, to improve efficiency and to allow for responsible use of resources. This pillar emphasizes the importance of sustainable practices to lessen the carbon footprint, conserve resources, and ensure long-term environmental health.

Given the massive computational power needed to train and fine-tune foundation models like GPT-3, which has 175 billion parameters, this pillar becomes critical in shaping the architecture of your ML solution.

The sustainability pillar is formalized by the following two principles.

MLSUS-15: Measure Material Efficiency

This principle focuses on assessing how efficiently a ML workload utilizes its provisioned resources per unit of work done, essentially measuring the "material efficiency" of a system. The provided guidance allows users to benchmark and identify areas for improvement to minimize resource consumption while maintaining performance.

Implementation

This principle is implemented by the following strategies:

- **Define provisioned resources per unit of work as one of your KPIs** to normalize your sustainability KPIs and compare the performance over time.
- **Define a baseline for your workload material efficiency** to establish a reference point and track improvements over time as they implement optimization strategies.
- **Estimate improvements** to quantify the ROI from your optimization strategies.

MLSUS-16: Retrain Only When Necessary

As mentioned in Chapter 6 when we compared the computational needs between training and inferencing, training is an expensive process. This principle advises that you should only retrain your ML models when absolutely needed, instead of retraining them on a fixed schedule or too frequently. This can be achieved by actively monitoring their performance in production and only triggering retraining when a significant model drift is detected.

Implementation

This principle is implemented by the following services/strategies:

- **Defining KPIs for your ML problem with your business stakeholders:** for example, a minimum acceptable accuracy and a maximum acceptable error

- **Amazon SageMaker Model Monitor** to continually monitor the quality of your models in production and trigger retraining only when data drifts beyond a defined threshold are detected

- **Amazon SageMaker Pipelines** or **AWS Step Functions** to automate your retraining pipelines

Monitoring Infrastructure and Cost

In the first part of this chapter, you learned how to monitor all aspects of your machine learning model's ability to derive inference, ensuring that it remains accurate and reliable over time. However, model performance is just one piece of the puzzle. Equally important is the infrastructure that supports your model and the associated costs. Effective monitoring of your ML infrastructure and costs is critical for maintaining optimal performance and achieving cost efficiency.

AWS provides a suite of tools to help you monitor your ML infrastructure. These tools allow you to track key metrics such as CPU and memory utilization, disk I/O, network throughput, and instance health. By keeping an eye on these metrics, you can ensure that your infrastructure is performing efficiently, and you can quickly identify and address any issues that arise. In addition to Amazon CloudWatch for setting up alarms and notifications, you can leverage AWS X-Ray for tracing and debugging your ML distributed application, Amazon GuardDuty for continuous security monitoring, Amazon Inspector for automated security assessments, and several others.

Cost management is another critical aspect of monitoring ML infrastructure. AWS cost optimization services, like AWS Cost Explorer, AWS Trusted Advisor, and AWS Budgets, can help you gain insights into your spending patterns and forecast future costs. Additionally, Amazon SageMaker Savings Plan offers a flexible pricing model that can help you save significantly on your ML workloads. By committing to a consistent amount of usage over one or three years, you can benefit from lower costs compared to on-demand pricing. Setting up cost and usage alerts allows you to avoid unexpected expenses and make informed decisions about resource allocation. By leveraging these AWS services, you can achieve a balanced approach to monitoring both the performance and cost of your ML infrastructure, ensuring sustainable and cost-effective operations. Let's start by reviewing the monitoring and observability services you need to know for the exam.

Monitoring and Observability Services

Monitoring and observability services are essential for ensuring the performance, reliability, and security of ML workloads in AWS. These services play a crucial role in enabling Site Reliability Engineering (SRE) practices, which focus on maintaining the scalability and stability of applications through automated operations and proactive monitoring. We briefly introduced the concept of SRE while discussing the reliability pillar in the Machine Learning Well-Architected Lens. In the context of ML, SRE ensures that ML models and their supporting infrastructure consistently produce accurate inferences. Moreover, these services also contribute to OE by streamlining monitoring and troubleshooting processes, thus enabling efficient management of ML infrastructure. They aid in cost optimization by providing insights that help you allocate resources more effectively and avoid unnecessary expenses. Additionally, by promoting efficient resource usage, these services support sustainability efforts. As a result, when you are instrumenting your ML workloads with a robust monitoring and observability framework, you are effectively well-architecting your ML solution.

To achieve the aforementioned SRE goals, AWS offers a suite of monitoring and observability services that can be tailored for various use cases, including ML workloads. These services include Amazon CloudWatch Logs Insights for log analytics, AWS X-Ray for tracing and debugging your ML distributed applications, Amazon GuardDuty for continuous threat detection, Amazon Inspector for automated security assessments, and AWS Security Hub for unified security management. By leveraging these AWS services, SRE teams can gain comprehensive insights into system behavior, detect and respond to anomalies, maintain compliance with security standards, and ensure seamless and efficient operations in Amazon SageMaker AI.

For the exam, you need to know what these services do and when you should use them based on the specifics of your ML use case.

Amazon CloudWatch Logs Insights

With Amazon CloudWatch Logs Insights, you can dynamically search and analyze large volumes of log data within Amazon CloudWatch Logs. With its extensive query language support, you can efficiently perform root-cause analysis and streamline incident and problem management tasks.

Amazon CloudWatch Logs Insights supports three query languages:

- A purpose-built **Logs Insights query language** (**Logs Insights QL**) with a few simple but powerful commands
- **OpenSearch Service Piped Processing Language (PPL)**, which enables you to analyze your logs using a set of commands delimited by pipes (|)
- **OpenSearch Service Structured Query Language (SQL)**, which enables you to analyze your logs using a SQL-like declarative syntax

Moreover, this service offers the following features to further simplify and accelerate the discovery of insights from your ML applications' logs and events:

- **Automatic discovery of log fields** from services like Amazon Route 53, AWS Lambda, AWS CloudTrail, and Amazon VPC
- Creating **field indexes** to reduce costs and speed results, especially for queries of large number of log groups or log events
- **Encrypting query results** with AWS Key Management Service to secure your log sensitive data
- **Detection and analysis of patterns**
- **Saving queries** and **adding queries to dashboards** to simplify your log analysis experience

Use Cases

In the context of ML, Amazon CloudWatch Logs Insights is best suited for the following use cases:

- **Training job monitoring:** By analyzing logs from Amazon SageMaker training jobs, you can identify any issues or inefficiencies in the training process, such as resource bottlenecks or data inconsistencies.
- **Endpoint monitoring:** For real-time endpoints, Amazon CloudWatch Logs Insights helps you track request logs and diagnose issues with model inferences.
- **Batch transform monitoring:** By querying logs from batch transform jobs, you can troubleshoot errors and ensure that the batch processing is running smoothly.

Amazon EventBridge

Amazon EventBridge is a serverless event bus service that makes it easy to connect applications using data from various sources. It allows you to create *event-driven architectures* by routing events from supported sources to various AWS services and custom targets.

> Event-driven architecture is a design approach for creating loosely coupled software systems that interact by generating and reacting to events. This architecture style enhances agility and enables the development of reliable, scalable applications. To learn more, visit
> https://aws.amazon.com/event-driven-architecture.

For ML workloads, Amazon EventBridge can play a pivotal role in orchestrating workflows (to supplement other orchestration services such as Amazon SageMaker Pipelines, AWS Step Functions, and others), triggering actions based on events, and ensuring seamless communication between different components of the ML pipeline. By integrating with various AWS services, Amazon EventBridge provides best-in-class monitoring and observability capabilities, ensuring that your ML workloads are efficient, reliable, and secure.

One of the key strengths of Amazon EventBridge is its ability to integrate with a wide range of AWS services, providing a unified platform for event-driven processing. For ML workloads, Amazon EventBridge can be integrated with services like AWS Lambda, AWS Step Functions, and Amazon SageMaker AI to automate and streamline various aspects of the ML lifecycle. For example, Amazon EventBridge can trigger Lambda functions in response to specific events, such as the completion of a training job or the detection of an anomaly in model performance. This enables you to automate actions like data preprocessing, model deployment, and retraining, ensuring that your ML workflows are responsive and adaptive to changing conditions.

Amazon EventBridge also supports integration with other monitoring and observability services like Amazon CloudWatch, AWS X-Ray, and AWS Security Hub. By routing events to Amazon CloudWatch, you can create custom metrics, dashboards, and alarms to monitor the performance and health of your ML workloads. AWS X-Ray can be used to trace and analyze the flow of events through your ML pipeline, providing detailed insights into dependencies, latencies, and potential bottlenecks. AWS Security Hub can consolidate security findings and alerts from various sources, allowing you to respond to security incidents in a coordinated and efficient manner. These integrations ensure that you have comprehensive visibility into your ML environment and can proactively address any issues that arise.

Use Cases

In terms of use cases, Amazon EventBridge offers numerous possibilities for enhancing the monitoring and observability instrumentation of your ML workloads. For instance, you can use Amazon EventBridge to automate the retraining of models based on predefined triggers, such as the accumulation of new training data or the detection of model drift. Amazon EventBridge can also be used to orchestrate complex ML pipelines by coordinating the execution of different steps, such as data preprocessing, feature engineering, model training, and deployment. Additionally, you can set up event-driven notifications to alert stakeholders about the status of ML jobs, performance metrics, and potential issues, ensuring timely intervention and collaboration. With Amazon EventBridge, you can build robust, scalable, and responsive ML workflows that deliver accurate and reliable inferences.

AWS CloudTrail

AWS CloudTrail is a service that enables auditing, compliance, and operational and risk management of your AWS accounts. As the name suggests, AWS CloudTrail provides a

318 Chapter 7 ▪ Model Monitoring and Cost Optimization

detailed audit trail of actions taken by users, roles, and services. For ML workloads, AWS CloudTrail is instrumental in maintaining the integrity and security of your ML environment. It allows you to track changes and actions across your Amazon SageMaker AI instances, ensuring that you have a clear record of who did what and when, which is essential for debugging, auditing, and compliance purposes.

AWS CloudTrail logs provide detailed information on actions taken, such as creating, updating, and deleting Amazon SageMaker AI resources such as training jobs, endpoints, instances, and others. By analyzing these logs, you can identify unusual or unauthorized activities, ensuring that your ML environment remains secure and compliant with organizational policies and regulatory requirements. The traceability provided by CloudTrail is crucial for understanding the sequence of events and actions taken within your ML infrastructure.

Use Cases

AWS CloudTrail offers several benefits for ML workloads. For example, AWS CloudTrail logs can be used to monitor the access and usage patterns of your Amazon SageMaker AI resources, helping you detect and respond to potential security threats. Additionally, the audit trail provided by AWS CloudTrail is invaluable for compliance purposes, as it allows you to demonstrate adherence to data governance and security standards. Furthermore, AWS CloudTrail can be integrated with Amazon CloudWatch to create alarms that notify you of specific activities or anomalies, enabling proactive monitoring and response. With its auditing and traceability capabilities, AWS CloudTrail can assist in ensuring your ML workloads are secure, compliant, and efficiently managed.

AWS X-Ray

AWS X-Ray is a comprehensive tracing service that collects detailed data on requests made to your application, including those within your ML workflows. It provides a suite of tools that enable you to view, filter, and analyze this data, allowing you to identify issues and discover optimization opportunities. With AWS X-Ray, you gain visibility into the entire lifecycle of a request, from the initial request through the various stages of processing and response.

For ML workloads in Amazon SageMaker AI, AWS X-Ray offers granular insights not only into the request and its response but also into the calls your application makes to downstream AWS resources, microservices, databases, and web APIs. This detailed tracing helps you understand the performance and behavior of your ML models, pinpoint bottlenecks, and troubleshoot errors effectively.

Additionally, X-Ray's visual representation of service maps allows you to see how different services within your ML architecture interact, making it easier to identify and address any interdependencies and performance issues. This holistic view is critical for maintaining the reliability and efficiency of your ML workflows.

Use Cases

AWS X-Ray is best suited for the following ML use cases:

- **Model deployment tracing:** AWS X-Ray allows you to trace the interactions between various components in your Amazon SageMaker AI deployment, such as data preprocessing, model inference, and post-processing. This helps you identify and optimize any stages causing latency.

- **Inference request tracing:** When an inference request is made to your Amazon SageMaker AI endpoint, AWS X-Ray captures the detailed flow, helping you diagnose issues related to model serving and response times.

- **End-to-end pipeline tracing:** For complex ML pipelines that involve multiple steps and services, AWS X-Ray visualizes the entire workflow, enabling you to see how different services interact and identify any interdependencies or performance issues.

Amazon GuardDuty

Amazon GuardDuty is a threat detection service that provides continuous monitoring, analysis, and processing of AWS data sources and logs within your environment.

By leveraging threat intelligence feeds—including lists of malicious IP addresses, domains, file hashes, and ML models—Amazon GuardDuty identifies suspicious and potentially malicious activities in your AWS environment, including your AWS accounts, your data, and your AWS resources.

Amazon GuardDuty produces a detailed findings report that you can use to automate responses. Although Amazon GuardDuty itself does not directly perform threat remediation, it integrates seamlessly with other AWS services to enable automated responses to security threats. Some services you can use to automate responses using Amazon GuardDuty findings are as follows:

- AWS Lambda
- Amazon CloudWatch Events
- AWS Security Hub
- Amazon EventBridge

These integrations help protect your ML workloads by ensuring that potential security threats are detected and responded to quickly, minimizing the risk of data breaches, data exfiltration, or unauthorized access to your Amazon SageMaker AI environment.

Use Cases

Amazon GuardDuty is best suited for the following ML use cases:

- **Data protection:** Amazon GuardDuty can detect unusual data access patterns or attempts to exfiltrate data from your Amazon SageMaker notebooks or storage, helping to protect your valuable training data and model artifacts.

320   Chapter 7 • Model Monitoring and Cost Optimization

- **Endpoint security:** For real-time endpoints, Amazon GuardDuty can monitor API calls and detect any suspicious activity, such as unauthorized access attempts or abnormal request patterns.
- **Compliance:** Amazon GuardDuty helps ensure that your Amazon SageMaker AI workloads comply with security best practices and regulatory requirements by continuously monitoring for potential threats and vulnerabilities.
- **Resource integrity:** Amazon GuardDuty can detect compromised instances or abnormal behavior in the underlying infrastructure supporting your Amazon SageMaker AI workloads, ensuring the integrity and reliability of your ML environment.

Amazon Inspector

Amazon Inspector is an automated vulnerability management service that evaluates the security and compliance of your AWS applications, including those supporting ML workloads. Amazon Inspector scans your AWS resources, such as Amazon EC2 instances and container images, for vulnerabilities, network exposures, and deviations from best practices. For ML workloads, this means ensuring that the infrastructure supporting your Amazon SageMaker AI environments is secure and up to date. By identifying security risks in your compute resources and containerized environments, Amazon Inspector helps maintain the integrity and reliability of your ML models and workflows.

One of the key differences between Amazon Inspector and Amazon GuardDuty lies in their focus areas and functionalities. Whereas Amazon GuardDuty specializes in continuous threat detection and monitoring, providing real-time alerts for suspicious activities and potential security threats, Amazon Inspector focuses on vulnerability management and compliance. Amazon Inspector conducts periodic assessments to detect known vulnerabilities, such as unpatched software, weak configurations, and outdated dependencies, in your ML infrastructure. This proactive approach ensures that your Amazon SageMaker AI workloads run on secure and compliant resources, minimizing the risk of exploitation due to vulnerabilities.

Use Cases

For ML use cases, Amazon Inspector provides several benefits that complement the capabilities of Amazon GuardDuty. Amazon Inspector's assessments help identify and remediate security weaknesses in the underlying infrastructure, ensuring that the compute environments used for training and inference are secure. This is particularly important for maintaining the confidentiality and integrity of training data, model artifacts, and inference results. By integrating Amazon Inspector with other AWS services like AWS Lambda and AWS Systems Manager, you can automate the remediation of identified vulnerabilities, ensuring continuous security and compliance for your ML workloads. Together with Amazon GuardDuty, Amazon Inspector provides a comprehensive security strategy, covering both real-time threat detection and ongoing vulnerability management for your ML environment.

AWS Security Hub

AWS Security Hub is a centralized cloud security posture management (CSPM) service that provides comprehensive insights into your security state across your AWS environment. It aggregates, organizes, and prioritizes security findings from multiple AWS services, enabling you to monitor and manage security issues from a single location. For ML workloads, AWS Security Hub plays a key role in ensuring that your ML models and supporting infrastructure adhere to security best practices. By integrating with services like Amazon GuardDuty, Amazon Inspector, and others, AWS Security Hub provides a holistic view of your security landscape, helping you maintain a robust and secure ML environment.

One of the primary ways AWS Security Hub strengthens the security posture of your ML workloads is by leveraging the continuous threat detection capabilities provided by Amazon GuardDuty. Amazon GuardDuty monitors for suspicious activities and potential security threats, such as unauthorized access attempts and unusual data access patterns. AWS Security Hub consolidates these findings, providing you with a centralized and prioritized view of potential threats. This integration allows you to quickly identify and respond to security incidents that could impact your Amazon SageMaker AI environments, ensuring the protection of your training data, model artifacts, and inference results.

In addition to Amazon GuardDuty, AWS Security Hub also integrates with Amazon Inspector to enhance the security of your ML workloads. Amazon Inspector performs automated security assessments, identifying vulnerabilities and deviations from best practices in your compute resources and containerized environments. AWS Security Hub aggregates these findings and provides actionable insights to help you remediate identified security issues. By continuously monitoring for vulnerabilities and integrating with AWS Security Hub, Amazon Inspector ensures that your Amazon SageMaker AI infrastructure remains secure and compliant, reducing the risk of exploitation due to unpatched software or misconfigurations.

AWS Security Hub further strengthens your ML security posture by integrating with other AWS security services, such as AWS Config and AWS IAM Access Analyzer. AWS Config continuously monitors and records your AWS resource configurations, enabling you to track configuration changes and ensure compliance with security policies. AWS IAM Access Analyzer helps you identify and mitigate excessive or unintended access permissions. AWS Security Hub consolidates findings from these services as well, offering a comprehensive view of your security posture and enabling you to take proactive measures to safeguard your ML workloads. By leveraging these integrations, AWS Security Hub provides a unified and efficient approach to managing the security of your ML environment, ensuring that your models and data remain protected from potential threats.

Use Cases

For ML use cases, AWS Security Hub offers several specific benefits. It helps safeguard the confidentiality and integrity of your training data by monitoring access patterns and alerting you to unauthorized access attempts. Additionally, AWS Security Hub ensures the

322   Chapter 7 ▪ Model Monitoring and Cost Optimization

security and compliance of your Amazon SageMaker AI environments by continuously assessing configurations and identifying deviations from best practices. Inference endpoints are also protected through the integration of Amazon GuardDuty and Amazon Inspector, which detect and respond to potential threats and vulnerabilities. With a centralized view of your security posture and automated responses, AWS Security Hub ensures that your ML workloads remain secure, resilient, and compliant, allowing you to focus on developing and optimizing your models without compromising on security and observability.

Cost Tracking and Optimization Services

AWS offers a range of cost tracking and optimization services that are particularly beneficial for ML workloads. AWS Cost Explorer provides detailed insights into your spending patterns, allowing you to identify trends and allocate costs effectively. With AWS Cost and Usage Reports, you can gain comprehensive visibility into your AWS usage and costs, helping you make informed decisions about resource allocation and budgeting. Additionally, AWS Budgets allows you to set custom budgets and receive alerts when your spending exceeds predefined thresholds, ensuring that you stay within your financial limits.

For ML workloads, Amazon SageMaker AI includes built-in cost optimization features. Amazon SageMaker AI's Model Monitoring and Autopilot capabilities can help reduce costs by optimizing model training and deployment processes. With Spot Instances and Saving Plans, you can further reduce expenses for non-critical tasks and predictable workloads. These services, combined with effective tagging strategies and automated policy enforcement, enable you to track, manage, and optimize costs throughout the ML lifecycle, ensuring efficient and cost-effective use of AWS resources.

AWS Cost Explorer

AWS Cost Explorer is a powerful tool that allows you to visualize, understand, and manage your AWS costs and usage over time. For ML workloads, AWS Cost Explorer provides detailed insights into your spending patterns related to Amazon SageMaker AI and other ML services. By breaking down costs by various dimensions such as service, usage type, and time period, you can identify trends and anomalies in your ML expenses. This level of visibility helps you allocate resources more effectively, ensuring that your ML projects stay within budget. AWS Cost Explorer's forecasting capabilities enable you to predict future spending based on historical data, allowing you to plan and budget for upcoming ML initiatives with greater accuracy.

Moreover, AWS Cost Explorer excels in tracking and optimizing costs associated with different stages of the ML lifecycle. For example, you can use AWS Cost Explorer to monitor the costs of data preprocessing, model training, and inference separately, helping you identify areas where cost optimization is needed. By analyzing usage patterns, you can determine if you are over-provisioning resources or if there are opportunities to leverage cost-saving options such as Spot Instances or Reserved Instances.

Finally, Cost Explorer's integration with AWS Budgets allows you to set custom budgets and receive alerts when your ML spending exceeds predefined thresholds, ensuring proactive cost management. With these capabilities, AWS Cost Explorer empowers you to make informed decisions and optimize the cost-efficiency of your ML workloads.

AWS Cost and Usage Reports

AWS Cost and Usage Reports (CUR) provides the most granular level of billing data, delivering comprehensive insights into your AWS costs and usage. Unlike AWS Cost Explorer, which offers a more user-friendly and visual interface for cost analysis, CUR gives you raw data that can be used for in-depth analysis and custom reporting. For ML work-loads, this detailed data enables you to break down costs associated with various stages of the ML lifecycle, such as data preprocessing, model training, and inference. With CUR, you can gain a deeper understanding of your spending patterns and identify cost drivers specific to your ML projects. Reports are typically generated daily and can be customized to be delivered to an Amazon S3 bucket, making it easy to access and analyze the data.

A notable distinction between AWS Cost Explorer and AWS CUR lies in the level of detail and flexibility they offer. Cost Explorer provides an intuitive interface for visualizing and exploring your costs, making it easy to identify trends and anomalies. It is ideal for high-level cost management and budgeting. In contrast, CUR delivers raw billing data in the form of report files, which can be ingested into data analytics tools like Amazon QuickSight or third-party applications. The report files include numerous columns, providing detailed information on resource usage, cost allocation, and pricing. This allows for custom analysis and reporting, enabling you to create tailored dashboards and reports that meet your specific ML cost management needs. The granularity of CUR data makes it particularly valuable for detailed cost optimization and financial accountability.

For ML use cases, AWS CUR offer several advantages. By analyzing CUR data, you can monitor the costs of different stages of your ML workflows, helping you identify inefficien-cies and opportunities for optimization. For example, you can track the usage and costs of your Amazon SageMaker AI instances, identify underutilized resources, and make data-driven decisions to optimize your ML infrastructure. Additionally, CUR can help you allocate costs to different ML projects or teams, ensuring accurate cost attribution and better financial management. By leveraging the detailed insights provided by AWS CUR, including the specific columns and granularity of data, you can optimize the cost-efficiency of your ML workloads and maintain control over your AWS spending.

AWS Trusted Advisor

AWS Trusted Advisor is a service that provides real-time guidance to help you provision your resources following AWS best practices. For ML workloads, Trusted Advisor is invaluable in ensuring that your AWS environment is optimized for performance, security, and cost-effectiveness. The service offers insights across five categories: cost optimization, performance, security, fault tolerance, and service limits. For example, AWS Trusted Advisor can help you identify underutilized Amazon SageMaker AI instances, suggesting

324 Chapter 7 ▪ Model Monitoring and Cost Optimization

opportunities to downsize or terminate instances to save costs. Additionally, it can highlight security best practices, such as ensuring that your ML data stored in Amazon S3 is encrypted and that your IAM policies follow the principle of least privilege.

Trusted Advisor's recommendations are particularly beneficial for managing the complexities of ML workloads. By continuously monitoring your AWS resources, AWS Trusted Advisor helps ensure that your ML infrastructure remains compliant with best practices and is configured for optimal performance. This includes identifying opportunities to improve the efficiency of data preprocessing, model training, and inference tasks. For instance, AWS Trusted Advisor might recommend enabling auto-scaling for your Amazon SageMaker AI endpoints to handle varying loads efficiently, or it may suggest optimizing your storage configurations to enhance data access speeds. With the insights provided by AWS Trusted Advisor, you can maintain a secure, efficient, and cost-effective ML environment, allowing you to focus on developing and deploying high-quality ML models.

AWS Budgets

AWS Budgets is a powerful service that allows you to set custom cost and usage budgets for your AWS resources, helping you monitor and control your spending effectively. For ML workloads, AWS Budgets can be particularly beneficial in managing the costs associated with various stages of the ML lifecycle, such as data preprocessing, model training, and inference. By setting specific budgets for different ML projects or teams, you can ensure that your spending aligns with your financial goals and prevent unexpected cost overruns. Additionally, AWS Budgets allows you to receive alerts via email or SMS when your actual or forecasted spending exceeds predefined thresholds, enabling proactive cost management and timely intervention.

In the context of ML workloads, AWS Budgets provides several advantages. For instance, you can create cost allocation tags to categorize your ML resources by project, department, or any other relevant criteria. This allows you to track and allocate costs accurately, ensuring that each ML project stays within its budget. AWS Budgets also integrates with AWS Cost Explorer, enabling you to visualize your budget performance and make data-driven decisions to optimize your ML infrastructure. By leveraging AWS Budgets, you can maintain control over your ML spending, allocate resources efficiently, and ensure the financial sustainability of your ML initiatives.

Pricing Models

AWS offers several pricing models for compute infrastructure, each designed to provide flexibility and cost-efficiency based on different usage patterns and needs. For ML workloads, selecting the right pricing model is crucial for managing costs while ensuring optimal performance. The primary pricing models include On-Demand Instances, Reserved Instances, Savings Plans, Spot Instances, and Dedicated Hosts. These models offer varying levels of commitment, cost savings, and flexibility, making it possible to tailor your ML infrastructure to specific project requirements and budget constraints.

On-Demand Instances are charged on a pay-as-you-go model, making them ideal for unpredictable ML workloads that require flexibility without long-term commitments. They

Monitoring Infrastructure and Cost **325**

allow you to pay for compute capacity by the hour or second, depending on the instance type. *Reserved Instances*, on the other hand, provide significant cost savings for steady-state and predictable workloads by committing to a specific capacity for one or three years. *Savings Plans* offer a more flexible alternative to Reserved Instances, allowing you to commit to a specific amount of usage (measured in $/hour) for one or three years. At the time of writing this book, there are three different savings plans: Compute (applies to Amazon EC2, AWS Lambda, and AWS Fargate usage), EC2 Instance, and Amazon SageMaker Savings Plans. *Spot Instances* enable you to bid for unused EC2 capacity at a lower price, making them suitable for flexible, fault-tolerant ML tasks such as batch processing and data preprocessing. *Dedicated Hosts* provide physical servers dedicated to your use, ensuring compliance and security for sensitive ML workloads.

Table 7.1 summarizes these AWS pricing models, highlighting how each model works, its most suitable use cases, and tenancy (whether the infrastructure is shared with other AWS

TABLE 7.1 AWS Pricing Models for Compute Infrastructure.

Pricing Model	How It Works	Tenancy	Use Cases and ML Relevance
On-Demand	Pay for compute time used, no long-term commitment	Shared	Ideal for unpredictable workloads and exploratory data analysis. Suitable for ad hoc model training and testing new algorithms.
Reserved Instances	Commit to capacity for 1 or 3 years at a discount	Shared/Dedicated	Best for steady-state, predictable workloads. Cost-effective for long-term ML projects and production environments.
Savings Plans	Commit to a specific dollar/hour usage for one or three years for lower prices	Shared/Dedicated	Suitable for workloads with predictable usage. Reduces costs for continuous training and inference tasks.
Spot Instances	Bid for unused capacity at lower prices: can be interrupted	Shared	Ideal for flexible, fault-tolerant applications. Useful for noncritical ML tasks like batch processing and data preprocessing.
Dedicated Hosts	Pay for a physical server dedicated to your use	Dedicated	Best for regulatory requirements needing physical isolation. Ensures compliance and security for sensitive ML workloads.

customers or dedicated to your AWS account). This table serves as a useful reference for understanding the different pricing options available for ML compute infrastructure.

The variety of different pricing models offered by AWS can help you optimize costs to meet your budgets, ensure efficient resource utilization, and maintain the performance and security of your ML environment.

Amazon SageMaker Savings Plan

Amazon SageMaker Savings Plans is applicable only to Amazon SageMaker AI instance usage.

Amazon SageMaker Savings Plans offer a flexible and cost-effective pricing model for ML workloads. You commit to a consistent amount of usage (measured in dollars/hour) for a one- or three-year term and benefit from significant cost savings—up to 64% compared to On-Demand pricing. These savings plans automatically apply to eligible Amazon SageMaker AI instance usage, including Amazon SageMaker Studio Notebook, Amazon SageMaker On-Demand Notebook, Amazon SageMaker Processing, Amazon SageMaker Data Wrangler, Amazon SageMaker Training, Amazon SageMaker Real-Time Inference, and Amazon SageMaker Batch Transform. This flexibility allows you to switch instance types or regions without losing the savings, making it easier to manage costs while optimizing your ML infrastructure.

In addition to cost savings, Amazon SageMaker Savings Plans provide the most flexibility among AWS Savings Plans. You can change your usage from one instance type to another or move workloads across different regions while still benefiting from the committed Savings Plan rate. For example, you can switch from a CPU instance `ml.c5.xlarge` running in US East (Ohio) to a `inf1.2xlarge` instance in US West (Oregon) for inference workloads at any time, and continue to pay the Savings Plan price. This adaptability ensures that you can efficiently manage your ML projects without worrying about unexpected cost spikes, making it an ideal choice for organizations looking to optimize their ML investments.

Summary

In this chapter, we covered the essential aspects of monitoring ML model inference and infrastructure. Monitoring model inference is crucial to ensure the accuracy and reliability of ML models. We discussed the importance of identifying and addressing drift in models, which occurs when the performance of a model degrades over time due to changes in the underlying data patterns. By comparing the model's predictions with actual outcomes, discrepancies can be detected and corrective actions, such as retraining the model with updated data, can be taken to maintain its performance.

We also explored the significance of monitoring data quality and model performance. Ensuring that input data is accurate, complete, and consistent is vital for reliable predictions. Tracking key performance metrics, such as accuracy, precision, recall, and F1 score, allows for evaluation of the model's performance and the identification of any deviations. Regular assessment of data quality and performance metrics enables timely intervention and continuous improvement of the model. We emphasized the importance of adhering to design principles for monitoring, such as setting up automated alerts for performance degradation, ensuring transparency and interpretability of monitoring processes, and integrating monitoring tools with existing workflows.

In addition, we highlighted the need for monitoring the infrastructure supporting ML workloads to ensure optimal performance and cost-efficiency. Monitoring and observability services like Amazon CloudWatch and AWS X-Ray provide real-time visibility into the health and performance of the infrastructure. These tools track resource usage, detect anomalies, and offer insights into system performance, allowing for quick identification and resolution of issues. Effective monitoring ensures that ML workloads run smoothly and efficiently, minimizing downtime and maximizing productivity.

Finally, we delved into cost tracking and optimization services, which are essential for managing the expenses associated with ML workloads. AWS provides tools like AWS Cost Explorer, AWS Cost and Usage Reports, and AWS Budgets to help monitor and control costs. These services offer detailed insights into spending patterns, enabling the identification of areas for cost optimization. For instance, leveraging Spot Instances or Savings Plans can significantly reduce expenses without compromising performance. Moreover, considering the sustainability pillar, you learned how designing frugal architectures can enable sustainability for ML workloads. Frugal architectures make cost a non-functional requirement, meaning that cost-efficiency is built into the design and operation of the system. This involves optimizing resource usage and reducing waste, which not only lowers costs but also minimizes the environmental impact of ML projects. By effectively tracking and optimizing costs while incorporating sustainable practices, you can ensure the financial and environmental sustainability of your ML projects and allocate resources efficiently.

Exam Essentials

Know the types of model monitoring provided by Amazon SageMaker Model Monitor. There are four types of model monitoring. The first is data quality monitoring, which checks for anomalies in the input data. The second is model quality monitoring, which tracks performance metrics like accuracy and precision. The third is bias drift monitoring, which ensures that the model remains unbiased. The fourth is feature attribution drift monitoring, which observes changes in the importance of features.

Know when baselining is performed in the monitoring workflow. Baselining is performed at the very beginning of model development, before training any complex models, to

328 Chapter 7 ▪ Model Monitoring and Cost Optimization

establish a reference point against which the performance of more advanced models can be measured and compared.

Know the services that detect data quality monitoring. Amazon SageMaker Model Monitor uses the constraints in the model baseline to detect data drift such as the standard deviation of feature values or the rate of missing values in your input data. When Amazon CloudWatch detects that these metrics deviate significantly from the established baseline, it can trigger alerts, enabling you to take timely corrective actions. Additionally, Amazon SageMaker Data Wrangler can be used to simplify data preparation and profiling, whereas Amazon SageMaker Feature Store can store and maintain consistent feature availability. Together, these services provide robust data quality monitoring throughout the ML lifecycle.

Know the services that detect model quality monitoring. Amazon SageMaker Model Monitor continuously tracks your model's key performance metrics and alerts you of any deviations, ensuring that model performance remains high. Amazon SageMaker Clarify detects bias and explains model predictions, ensuring fairness and transparency. Amazon CloudWatch monitors custom metrics related to model performance and sets up alarms for significant changes that can trigger corrective actions, such as updating training data, updating the model's parameters, and retraining the model. Together, these services provide robust model quality monitoring throughout the ML lifecycle.

Know the pillars of the Machine Learning Well-Architected Lens specific to the Monitoring ML lifecycle phase. The pillars of the Machine Learning Well-Architected Lens specific to the Monitoring ML lifecycle phase are operational excellence, security, reliability, performance efficiency, cost optimization, and sustainability

Know the difference between Amazon CloudWatch and Amazon EventBridge. Amazon CloudWatch focuses on monitoring and managing AWS resources by collecting metrics, logs, and events and providing actionable insights with alarms. Amazon EventBridge, on the other hand, is an event bus that routes events from various sources to targets, enabling event-driven architectures. In summary, Amazon CloudWatch is primarily for monitoring, whereas Amazon EventBridge is for routing and reacting to events across your AWS environment.

Know the AWS services to track and optimize cost. AWS Cost Explorer provides a comprehensive view of your AWS spending and usage, allowing you to analyze and forecast costs with visualizations and custom reports. You can set custom budgets and receive alerts with AWS Budgets, ensuring you stay within your defined spending limits. AWS Trusted Advisor offers best practice recommendations to optimize your AWS resources, improve performance, and reduce costs. For detailed billing data, AWS Cost and Usage Report (CUR) delivers insights into your spending patterns over time. Lastly, AWS Savings Plans provide discounted pricing by committing to a consistent usage level over a one- or three-year term, helping you save money on your AWS costs.

Review Questions

1. What is a critical impact of not addressing model drift in a production environment?

   A. Increased computational efficiency

   B. Accurate long-term predictions

   C. Potential regulatory compliance issues and degradation of decision-making accuracy

   D. Improved model interpretability

2. Which AWS service provides continuous monitoring for detecting anomalies in real-time data and comparing it against baselines?

   A. AWS Glue

   B. AWS Step Functions

   C. Amazon SageMaker Model Monitor

   D. AWS CodePipeline

3. To ensure that ML models maintain high performance, which set of advanced metrics should be regularly tracked and analyzed?

   A. Mean absolute error (MAE), root mean squared error (RMSE), and receiver operating characteristic (ROC) curve

   B. Average network latency, CPU utilization, and disk I/O rates

   C. Total number of API requests, latency spikes, and throughput

   D. Volume of data ingress, egress, and storage capacity

4. What is a key consequence of failing to monitor the quality of data input for machine learning models?

   A. Enhanced model scalability

   B. Reduced need for feature engineering

   C. Introduction of biases and inaccuracies in model predictions

   D. Increased model training speed

5. Which aspects of infrastructure should be prioritized for monitoring to support large-scale ML deployments?

   A. Application load balancing, user authentication processes, and API gateway endpoints

   B. Network latency, resource utilization metrics, and system anomaly detection

   C. Interface design consistency, session state management, and cache invalidation

   D. User experience feedback loops, front-end load times, and graphical rendering

330 Chapter 7 ▪ Model Monitoring and Cost Optimization

6. How does Amazon CloudWatch contribute to maintaining the performance and reliability of ML infrastructure?

   A. Provides automated code deployment pipelines

   B. Offers real-time visibility into system health, enabling prompt anomaly detection and resource usage tracking

   C. Manages serverless function scaling and memory allocation

   D. Facilitates infrastructure as code (IaC) provisioning and version control

7. For optimizing costs in ML workloads, which strategy combines predictive analysis and alert mechanisms to avoid unexpected expenses?

   A. Implementing cross-region replication

   B. Setting up cost and usage dashboards with AWS Cost Explorer

   C. Utilizing enhanced monitoring for server instance performance

   D. Enabling automated backup and recovery solutions

8. What is a significant advantage of using AWS Savings Plans specifically for predictable and sustained ML workload patterns?

   A. Unlimited API call capacity

   B. Flexibility in choosing data storage types

   C. Substantial cost reductions for long-term consistent usage across multiple AWS services

   D. Access to dedicated cloud infrastructure

9. Why is real-time monitoring of model inference critical in dynamic production environments?

   A. To maintain accurate prediction capabilities despite variations in input data over time

   B. To minimize the latency of user interface components

   C. To automate the training dataset generation process

   D. To ensure the consistency of version control systems

10. Which AWS service is integral for orchestrating complex workflows and automating multi-step processes in an ML pipeline?

   A. Amazon GuardDuty

   B. AWS Step Functions

   C. Amazon CloudWatch

   D. Amazon EventBridge

Chapter 8

Model Security

THE AWS CERTIFIED MACHINE LEARNING (ML) ENGINEER ASSOCIATE EXAM OBJECTIVES COVERED IN THIS CHAPTER MAY INCLUDE, BUT ARE NOT LIMITED TO, THE FOLLOWING:

- ✔ **Domain 4: ML Solution Monitoring, Maintenance, and Security**
  - 4.3 Secure AWS resources

Security Design Principles

In the last chapter of this guide, a key aspect of your ML solution will be examined, i.e., security. As you have learned since Chapter 1, security is a pillar of the AWS Well-Architected Framework, and it should be taken into consideration in any phase of the ML lifecycle. This way of thinking security is referred to as *security by design*, which can be generalized to any phase of the software development lifecycle, not just machine learning.

AWS offers a broad spectrum of services that you can use to design and build a robust security-by-design architecture for your ML workloads.

In this section, we will introduce the security design principles that can help you decide which AWS services suit best the components of your ML solution. Any solution you design, architect, and build in AWS should tie back to one (or a collection) of these principles.

Implement a Strong Identity Foundation

AWS offers several services to help you implement a strong security identity foundation for your ML workloads. These services are all centered around AWS Identity and Access Management (IAM), which allows you to securely control access to AWS services and resources. You can create and manage users and groups and use permissions to allow or deny their access to AWS resources.

It all starts by implementing the *least privilege principle* and enforcing separation of duties with appropriate authorization for each interaction with AWS resources.

The least privilege principle dictates that any identity (users, applications, and systems) should be granted only the minimal level of access necessary to perform its functions. By limiting permissions, the risk of malicious activity or accidental misuse is significantly reduced. This approach enhances security by ensuring that if credentials are compromised, the potential impact is minimized.

The *separation of duties principle* involves dividing responsibilities among multiple identities or systems to prevent malicious activities, errors, and unauthorized actions. By ensuring that no single entity has control over all critical operations, this principle introduces checks and balances that enhance oversight and security. This approach reduces the risk of insider threats and ensures greater accountability within an organization.

Later in the chapter, you will learn how to implement these principles for your ML workloads.

Apply Security at All Layers

The application of security at all layers embodies the *defense-in-depth principle*, which is a security strategy that employs multiple layers of security controls to protect your workload's identities, infrastructure, and data. By implementing several layers of defense, this approach ensures that if one layer fails, others will continue to provide protection. This comprehensive strategy helps to delay and mitigate potential security breaches, providing more time for detection and response.

Figure 8.1 illustrates how you can implement this principle for a web application exposed to the internet:

- **Amazon CloudFront:** Acts as the content delivery network (CDN) at the edge, distributing content globally and providing distributed denial-of-service (DDoS) protection
- **AWS Web Application Firewall (WAF):** Protects the application from common web exploits and attacks at the edge
- **Application load balancer (ALB):** Distributes incoming traffic across multiple targets, such as EC2 instances or containers
- **Network access control list (NACL):** Provides subnet-level firewall control, allowing or denying traffic based on specified rules
- **Security Group:** Acts as a virtual firewall for controlling inbound and outbound traffic at the resource level

The list can continue, for example, with services like Amazon GuardDuty for threat detection, AWS Key Management Service (KMS) for data encryption, and Amazon Inspector

FIGURE 8.1 Defense-in-depth principle.

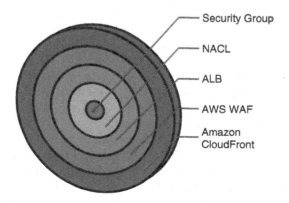

for continuous scanning of EC2 instances and container images for software vulnerabilities and unintended network exposure.

Enable Traceability

The *enable traceability* security principle originates from the nonrepudiation principle, which ensures that actions and transactions cannot be denied after they have taken place. Nonrepudiation provides proof of the integrity and origin of data, guaranteeing that it has not been tampered with. This foundational principle forms the basis for *traceability*, which is essential for accountability and forensic analysis in any security framework.

To learn more about nonrepudiation, visit https://csrc.nist.gov/glossary/term/non_repudiation.

Enabling traceability involves logging and monitoring actions within your AWS environment to maintain an accurate and comprehensive record of activities. This principle ensures that every action taken by users, applications, and systems is recorded and can be traced back to its origin. By enabling traceability, organizations can detect and respond to security incidents more effectively, as they have detailed information about what occurred and who was responsible. AWS provides several services and tools to facilitate traceability, such as AWS CloudTrail and Amazon CloudWatch.

As you learned in Chapter 7, AWS CloudTrail enables auditing, compliance, and operational and risk management of your AWS accounts. As a result, this service is a key enabler of traceability, as it records API calls made within your AWS environment. AWS CloudTrail logs provide a detailed history of AWS API calls, including information about the requestor, the time of the request, and the actions performed. This helps organizations monitor and audit their AWS resources, detect unusual activities, and investigate security incidents. Additionally, integrating CloudTrail with Amazon S3 allows you to store and analyze these logs for long-term retention and forensic analysis.

AWS Config is also instrumental in traceability, monitoring, and recording changes to your resource configurations to ensure compliance and facilitate auditing. For ML workloads, ensuring traceability also includes monitoring model training and inference activities.

Amazon GuardDuty complements this by providing threat detection and monitoring for malicious activity and unauthorized behavior within your AWS environment. It uses ML, anomaly detection, and integrated threat intelligence to identify potential security threats, ensuring your ML workloads and data are protected.

Amazon CloudWatch complements AWS CloudTrail by providing real-time monitoring and alerting capabilities. Amazon CloudWatch collects and tracks metrics, collects log files, and sets alarms to help you gain visibility into your AWS resources and applications. By analyzing Amazon CloudWatch logs and metrics, you can identify patterns, detect anomalies, and respond to potential security threats. Together, AWS CloudTrail, AWS

Security Design Principles

Config, and Amazon CloudWatch enable comprehensive traceability, empowering organizations to maintain a security and compliance posture in their AWS environments.

Additionally, Amazon EventBridge can be used to centralize events from various sources into a single location for processing, providing more traceability and enabling automated responses to specific events. By integrating Amazon EventBridge with your ML workflows, you can ensure that all relevant events are captured, monitored, and acted on, enhancing the overall security and traceability of your ML workloads.

Protect Your Data (At Rest, In Use, and In Transit)

Data protection is critical for ensuring the *confidentiality, integrity,* and *availability* of your data. These essential characteristics of your data are referred to as the *CIA Triad*, and they constitute the three key tenets of any information security strategy. This principle applies to all forms of data storage and processing, but it is particularly important for ML workloads, where large volumes of sensitive data are often handled. By implementing robust security measures at every stage of the ML lifecycle, you can safeguard your data from unauthorized access, tampering, and breaches.

To protect your data at rest, which refers to data stored on disks or other storage devices, AWS offers several services. AWS KMS is a powerful tool that enables you to create and manage cryptographic keys used to encrypt your data. Native AWS KMS integration with storage services like Amazon S3, Amazon EBS, Amazon RDS, Amazon DynamoDB, and many others ensures that your data is encrypted at rest, providing a strong layer of protection.

> As you learned in Chapter 2, Amazon S3, Amazon EFS, and Amazon FSx for Lustre are natively integrated with Amazon SageMaker AI. These storage services encrypt your data at rest by default, meaning all data stored on S3 or the file system is encrypted before being written, without any additional configuration required from the user.

Additionally, AWS Secrets Manager leverages AWS KMS to encrypt and store sensitive information, such as database credentials and API keys, further enhancing data security.

Data in use refers to data being actively processed or accessed by applications. To protect data in use, AWS provides services such as AWS Nitro Enclaves, which create isolated compute environments for processing highly sensitive data. AWS Nitro Enclaves use hardware-based security measures to ensure that data remains secure while in use. Moreover, you can leverage AWS IAM to control access to data and resources, ensuring that only authorized users and applications can interact with your ML workloads.

Protecting data in transit, or data being transmitted over networks, is equally important. AWS offers AWS Certificate Manager (ACM) to help you provision, manage, and deploy SSL/TLS certificates, which are essential for encrypting data in transit. You can use ACM

336   Chapter 8 ▪ Model Security

with services like Amazon CloudFront, Elastic Load Balancing (ELB), and Amazon API Gateway to ensure that data is encrypted as it travels between different points, preventing unauthorized access and eavesdropping.

By implementing these services, you can create a comprehensive security strategy that protects your data at every stage, ensuring confidentiality, integrity, and availability for your ML workloads.

Automate Security Processes

Automating security processes through *Policy-as-Code* is a robust and modern approach to maintaining and enforcing security controls in a consistent and scalable manner. As the name suggests, Policy-as-Code involves defining security policies and configurations as code, which can be version-controlled, tested, and deployed just like application code. This approach ensures that security policies are automatically applied and enforced across your environment, reducing the risk of human error and enabling rapid response to security threats. Services like AWS Config and AWS IAM let you automate the management and enforcement of security policies, ensuring that your infrastructure and your identities remain compliant with organizational and regulatory requirements.

Integrating Policy-as-Code into MLOps pipelines further enhances the security posture of your ML workloads throughout the entire ML lifecycle. As you learned in Chapter 6, MLOps pipelines automate the process of building, training, tuning, and deploying ML models, and by incorporating Policy-as-Code, you can ensure that security controls are applied at every stage. For example, you can use AWS CodePipeline and AWS CodeBuild to automate the deployment of ML models, while simultaneously applying security policies defined in code. This ensures that ML models are deployed in a secure manner, with appropriate access controls, encryption, and monitoring in place.

Automated security processes also enable continuous monitoring and compliance (i.e., traceability) for your ML workloads. By integrating services like Amazon GuardDuty and AWS Security Hub into your MLOps pipelines, you can continuously monitor your ML environment for security threats and compliance violations. These services provide real-time alerts and insights, allowing you to quickly detect and respond to potential security issues. When you combine these services with AWS Lambda, Amazon CloudWatch, and Amazon EventBridge, you can automate remediation actions based on predefined security policies, strengthening the security and resilience of your ML workloads. This holistic approach ensures that security is an integral part of your ML workflows in accordance with the security-by-design paradigm, providing robust protection against evolving threats.

Prepare for Security Events

When security incidents happen, having a solid response plan for your ML workloads is essential. Amazon Detective is a powerful tool that simplifies security investigations by automatically collecting log data from your AWS resources, including AWS CloudTrail and Amazon GuardDuty. It uses ML, statistical analysis, and graph theory to build a connected dataset, helping you quickly and efficiently investigate potential security threats. Amazon Detective can be integrated with your incident management policies and response simulations to ensure that your ML workloads are well-protected and resilient against security incidents.

Securing AWS Services

Securing AWS services is paramount for safeguarding your organization's data, applications, and infrastructure in the cloud. A systematic and methodical approach to security ensures comprehensive protection across all aspects of the AWS environment. The foundation of this approach begins with securing identities. Identity and access management are critical because they determine who has access to your resources and what actions they can perform. AWS IAM plays a pivotal role in this process. By creating and managing users, groups, and roles, organizations can assign granular permissions that control access to AWS resources. As a result, securing identities with multifactor authentication (MFA) and adhering to the least privilege principle strengthen your organization's security posture, reducing the risk of unauthorized access and potential breaches.

Following the establishment of robust identity management, the next step is to secure the infrastructure where your ML workloads operate. AWS offers several services to help achieve this, such as Amazon Virtual Private Cloud (VPC) for network isolation, network access control lists (NACLs), and security groups for controlling inbound and outbound traffic. These services ensure that only authorized traffic can access your AWS resources. Additionally, encrypting data at rest is a crucial aspect of securing infrastructure. These measures collectively fortify the infrastructure against unauthorized access and data breaches.

Securing data is another critical component of your security strategy. Protecting data at rest, in transit, and in use is essential to maintaining its confidentiality, integrity, and availability. AWS provides comprehensive solutions for data security, including encryption with AWS KMS, access controls, and continuous monitoring. For ML workloads, additional considerations are necessary to safeguard the data used for training and inference. Amazon SageMaker AI offers built-in security features that ensure data protection throughout the ML lifecycle. These features include encryption, fine-grained access controls, and real-time monitoring to detect and mitigate potential threats.

Securing your ML workflows involves more than just data protection. It encompasses the entire ML pipeline, from data ingestion and preprocessing to model training and deployment. By integrating security controls into each stage of the ML pipeline, organizations can ensure that their ML workloads are resilient against various security threats.

Finally, ensuring compliance with organizational and regulatory requirements is a critical aspect of a comprehensive security strategy. AWS offers several services to help organizations maintain compliance, including AWS Config, AWS Security Hub, and AWS Artifact.

338 Chapter 8 ▪ Model Security

AWS Config continuously monitors and records resource configurations, enabling organizations to assess and audit their compliance status. AWS Security Hub provides a centralized view of the security posture, aggregating and prioritizing security findings from multiple AWS services and third-party products. AWS Artifact provides on-demand downloads of auditor-issued reports, certifications, accreditations, and other third-party attestations for AWS managed services. These include reports on compliance with International Organization for Standardization (ISO) standards, Payment Card Industry (PCI) security standards, and System and Organization Controls (SOC). By leveraging these services, organizations can ensure that their AWS environment complies with security standards and best practices, ultimately providing a robust and secure foundation for their cloud-based operations.

Securing Identities with IAM

AWS IAM is a web service that helps you securely control access to AWS resources. With IAM, you can manage permissions that control which AWS resources users can access. You use IAM to control who is authenticated (signed in) and authorized (has permissions) to use resources. IAM provides the infrastructure necessary to control authentication and authorization for your AWS accounts.

With AWS, the term *principal* denotes a person or an application authenticated using an IAM user or an IAM role. Access management is often referred to as *authorization*. You manage access in AWS by creating policies and attaching them to IAM identities (IAM users, IAM groups, or IAM roles) or AWS resources.

Although the exam is focused on machine learning, you—as an ML engineer—are required to know how to secure all the components of your ML workflows. In the next sections, we will explore each aspect in more detail, beginning with identities, which are the entry point to your ML workloads.

Identities

An IAM *identity* is a representation of a human user or a programmatic workload that can be authenticated and authorized to perform actions within AWS accounts. Each identity can be linked to one or more *policies* that define the actions it can take, the AWS resources it can use, and the conditions under which these actions are allowed.

With AWS, IAM identities can be *IAM users*, *IAM groups*, or *IAM roles*. You can utilize AWS IAM Identity Center to create and manage identities and their access to AWS resources. With AWS IAM Identity Center, you can also manage *permission sets*, which automatically generate the necessary IAM roles to grant access to resources.

Identities don't have to be created in AWS. You have the option to federate existing identities from external identity providers, such as Microsoft Entra ID, Okta, and Cisco Duo, allowing them to assume IAM roles for accessing AWS resources. This method enables seamless integration with external identity providers.

Securing AWS Services

Do not confuse AWS accounts and AWS identities. An AWS account acts as a container for all your cloud resources, whereas an AWS identity refers to an entity within that account, like an IAM user, IAM group, or IAM role, which is assigned specific permissions to access those resources. AWS Identity and Access Management (IAM) is the service that manages identities and access.

Let's now review the different types of identities in AWS.

IAM Users

An IAM user is an entity that you create in your AWS account. The IAM user represents the human user or workload who uses this entity to interact with AWS resources. An IAM user consists of a name and credentials.

It is best practice to require human users to access AWS through federation with an identity provider, using temporary credentials. This approach is preferred over using IAM users with long-term credentials.

When you create an IAM user, AWS IAM Identity Center creates the following objects:

Friendly name This is the name you used when you created the IAM user and is displayed in the top-right corner when you access your AWS account with this IAM user using the AWS Management Console.

Amazon Resource Name (ARN) This is the ARN for your IAM user and is used to uniquely identify your IAM user across all of AWS. For example, you could use an ARN to specify the IAM user as a `Principal` in an IAM policy that allows the user to write to an Amazon S3 bucket. An ARN for an IAM user might look like this:

```
arn:aws:iam::123456789012:user/Dario
```

Unique identifier This ID is returned only when you use the API, Tools for Windows PowerShell, or AWS CLI to create the IAM user; you do not see this ID in the console.

Each IAM user is associated with one and only one AWS account. Because IAM users are defined within your AWS account, they don't need to have a payment method on file with AWS. Any AWS activity performed by IAM users in your account is billed to your account.

IAM Roles

An IAM role is another type of IAM identity that you can create in your AWS account. Just like an IAM user, an IAM role comes with specific permission policies that define what actions it is allowed to perform and what resources it is allowed to access in AWS. However unlike an IAM user, a role is designed to be *assumed* by anyone who needs it, rather than being tied to a single identity.

> Think of an IAM role as a persona, which an IAM user can impersonate on an as-needed basis.

Additionally, a role does not have long-term credentials, such as passwords or access keys. Instead, when you assume a role, it provides you with temporary security credentials for the duration of your role session. This is actually a good thing because short-term credentials limit the attack surface of your ML workload by timeboxing the permissions granted by the assumed IAM role.

An ARN for an IAM role might look like this:

`arn:aws:sts::123456789012:assumed-role/Accounting-Role/Mario`

> Notice how an IAM role's ARN uses the `sts` string instead of the `iam` string to indicate that IAM roles consume the AWS Security Token Service to request temporary, limited-privilege credentials for users.

IAM roles can be assumed by the following:

- An IAM user in the same AWS account or another AWS account
- IAM roles in the same AWS account
- Service principals (IAM principals that represents an AWS service)
- An external user authenticated by an identity provider (IdP)

Amazon SageMaker Role Manager

Amazon SageMaker Role Manager provides suggested permissions for a number of ML personas, including the Data Scientist persona, MLOps persona, and SageMaker AI Compute persona.

Each persona has suggested permissions in the form of selected ML activities and their associate permissions, as shown in Table 8.1.

Data Scientist persona   Use this persona to configure permissions to perform general ML development and experimentation in a SageMaker AI environment. This persona includes the following preselected ML activities:

- Run Studio Classic Applications
- Manage ML Jobs
- Manage Models

Securing AWS Services   **341**

- Manage AWS Glue Tables
- SageMaker Canvas AI Services
- SageMaker Canvas MLOps
- SageMaker Canvas Kendra Access
- Use MLflow
- Access required to AWS Services for MLflow
- Run Studio EMR Serverless Applications

MLOps persona   Choose this persona to configure permissions for operational activities. This persona includes the following preselected ML activities:
- Run Studio Classic Applications
- Manage Models
- Manage Pipelines
- Search and visualize experiments
- Amazon S3 Full Access

SageMaker AI Compute persona   This persona includes the following preselected ML activity:
- Access Required AWS Services

TABLE 8.1   ML Predefined Permissions.

ML Activity	Description
Access Required AWS Services	Permissions to access Amazon S3, Amazon ECR, Amazon CloudWatch, and Amazon EC2. Required for execution roles for jobs and endpoints.
Run Studio Classic Applications	Permissions to operate within a Studio Classic environment. Required for domain and user profile execution roles.
Manage ML Jobs	Permissions to audit, query lineage, and visualize experiments.
Manage Models	Permissions to manage SageMaker AI jobs across their lifecycles.
Manage Pipelines	Permissions to manage SageMaker pipelines and pipeline executions.

(*Continued*)

342 Chapter 8 ▪ Model Security

TABLE 8.1 (Continued)

ML Activity	Description
Search and visualize experiments	Permissions to audit, query lineage, and visualize SageMaker AI experiments.
Manage Model Monitoring	Permissions to manage monitoring schedules for SageMaker AI Model Monitor.
Amazon S3 Full Access	Permissions to perform all Amazon S3 operations.
Amazon S3 Bucket Access	Permissions to perform operations on specified Amazon S3 buckets.
Query Athena Workgroups	Permissions to run and manage Amazon Athena queries.
Manage AWS Glue Tables	Permissions to create and manage AWS Glue tables for SageMaker AI Feature Store and Data Wrangler.
SageMaker Canvas Core Access	Permissions to perform experimentation in SageMaker Canvas (i.e., basic data prep, model build, validation).
SageMaker Canvas Data Preparation (powered by Data Wrangler)	Permissions to perform end-to-end data preparation in SageMaker Canvas (i.e., aggregate, transform, and analyze data; create and schedule data preparation jobs on large datasets).
SageMaker Canvas AI Services	Permissions to access ready-to-use models from Amazon Bedrock, Amazon Textract, Amazon Rekognition, and Amazon Comprehend. Additionally, user can fine-tune foundation models from Amazon Bedrock and Amazon SageMaker JumpStart.
SageMaker Canvas MLOps	Permission for SageMaker Canvas users to directly deploy model to endpoint.
SageMaker Canvas Kendra Access	Permission for SageMaker Canvas to access Amazon Kendra for enterprise document search. The permission is only given to your selected index names in Amazon Kendra.
Use MLflow	Permissions to manage experiments, runs, and models in MLflow.

ML Activity	Description
Manage MLflow Tracking Servers	Permissions to manage, start, and stop MLflow Tracking Servers.
Access required to AWS Services for MLflow	Permissions for MLflow Tracking Servers to access S3, Secrets Manager, and Model Registry.
Run Studio EMR Serverless Applications	Permissions to Create and Manage EMR Serverless Applications on Amazon SageMaker Studio.

IAM Groups

You can manage the permissions of multiple IAM users by using IAM groups. With IAM groups, you can assign specific permissions to all members within the group. For example, you can create an ML-Trainers group with permissions specifically tailored for ML tasks, such as creating training jobs in Amazon SageMaker AI. Any user added to this group will automatically inherit those permissions. If a new ML engineer joins your organization and needs the ability to create training jobs, you can simply add them to the ML-Trainers group. Similarly, if an employee's job changes, you can update their permissions by moving them between groups without individually editing their permissions.

Just like IAM users and IAM roles, you can also attach policies to IAM groups, ensuring that all members receive the permissions defined in the policy. For instance, the ML-Trainers group could have a policy that grants the sagemaker:CreateTrainingJob permission. However, it's important to note that IAM groups cannot be identified as principals in a policy because IAM groups are related to permissions, not authentication. Principals are authenticated IAM entities and are represented by individual IAM users or IAM roles.

Now that you understand the concept of identity, you may wonder how AWS knows that a given IAM user/role/group is allowed to perform an action (e.g., write) on a specific AWS resource (e.g., an Amazon S3 bucket). This is where the concept of *access policy* comes into play, which will be covered in the next section.

Access Policies

Access policies (or simply policies) constitute the key component of authorization in AWS. A policy in AWS is an object that specifies the permissions for an identity or resource it is associated with. When a principal (such as an IAM user or IAM role) makes a request upon successful authentication, AWS evaluates the policies associated with its identity to determine whether the request should be allowed or denied. The outcome of this evaluation is referred to as the *effect* of the policy, and its values are *allow* or *deny*. The permissions outlined in the

344 Chapter 8 ▪ Model Security

policy are referred to as the *action* and govern what the principal is allowed to perform on the AWS resource specified in the policy. A policy may also have a *condition*, which specifies the condition under which the policy is in effect.

Most of these policies are stored as JSON documents in AWS.

The policies you need to know for the exam are outlined in the upcoming sections. For more information about access policies, visit https://docs.aws.amazon.com/IAM/latest/UserGuide/access_policies.html#access_policy-types.

Identity-Based Policies

Identity-based policies are JSON documents that control what actions an identity (IAM users, IAM groups, and IAM roles) can perform, on which AWS resources, and under what conditions. The following example shows a JSON policy that allows the IAM user to perform all Amazon DynamoDB actions (dynamodb:*) on the Vehicles table (table/Vehicles) in the 123456789012 account within the us-east-1 Region:

```
{
  "Version": "2012-10-17",
  "Statement": {
    "Effect": "Allow",
    "Action": "dynamodb:*",
    "Resource": "arn:aws:dynamodb:us-east-1:123456789012:table/Vehicles"
  }
}
```

Upon attaching this policy to your IAM user, the user will have permission to perform all actions on the Vehicles table in your DynamoDB instance. Typically, IAM users have multiple policies that collectively define their overall permissions.

Actions or resources not explicitly permitted by a policy are denied by default. For instance, if the previous policy is the only one attached to an IAM user, they can perform DynamoDB actions on the Vehicles table but cannot interact with other tables. Similarly the user is restricted from performing actions in Amazon EC2, Amazon S3, or any other AWS service, as the policy does not grant permissions for these services.

Resource-based Policies

Resource-based policies are JSON documents that you attach to an AWS resource instead of an AWS identity. These policies grant the specified principal permission to perform specific actions on that resource and defines under what conditions these apply.

The following JSON document is an example of an AWS resource-based policy for an S3 bucket that grants the principal arn:aws:iam::123456789012:user/Dario permissions to write to a bucket your-unique-bucket-name:

```
{
    "Version": "2012-10-17",
    "Statement": [
```

```
        {
            "Effect": "Allow",
            "Principal": {
                "AWS": "arn:aws:iam::123456789012:user/Dario"
            },
            "Action": "s3:PutObject",
            "Resource": "arn:aws:s3:::your-unique-bucket-name/*"
        }
    ]
}
```

In this policy:

- The `Effect` is set to `Allow`, which means the action is permitted.
- The `Principal` specifies the IAM user Dario with the ARN `arn:aws:iam::123456789012:user/Dario`.
- The `Action` is `s3:PutObject`, which allows the user to write objects to the bucket.
- The `Resource` specifies the ARN of the bucket and includes the wildcard (*) to allow writing to any object within the bucket.

Replace `your-unique-bucket-name` with the actual name of your S3 bucket.

> **Note:** Not all AWS resources support resource-based policies. To learn more, visit https://docs.aws.amazon.com/IAM/latest/UserGuide/reference_aws-services-that-work-with-iam.html#all_svcs.

Permission Boundaries

A permissions boundary is an advanced IAM feature that defines the maximum permissions an identity-based policy can grant to an IAM identity. When a permissions boundary is set for an IAM identity, the entity can only perform actions that are permitted by both its identity-based policies and the permissions boundary.

The following JSON document is an example of a permission boundary policy that limits the IAM user Dario to only use DynamoDB, S3, and CloudWatch services:

```
{
    "Version": "2012-10-17",
    "Statement": [
        {
            "Effect": "Allow",
            "Action": [
                "dynamodb:*",
                "s3:*",
                "cloudwatch:*"
            ],
```

```
            "Resource": "*"
        }
    ]
}
```

When you attach this permission boundary policy to the IAM user Dario, it limits the user's permissions but does not provide permissions on its own. In this example, the policy sets the maximum permissions of Dario as all operations in Amazon DynamoDB, Amazon S3, and Amazon CloudWatch. Dario can never perform operations in any other service, including IAM, even if he has a permissions policy that allows it.

Service Control Policies

If your AWS account is part of a large organization with multiple accounts designed to fulfill different business functions, you have the ability to implement Service Control Policies (SCPs) as a consistent way to manage permissions across your entire organization.

> AWS Organizations is a service that allows you to centrally manage and govern multiple AWS accounts within your organization. It enables you to consolidate billing, apply SCPs for fine-grained control over account permissions, and automate account provisioning and management. You should use AWS Organizations when you need to manage multiple accounts for your business, ensuring consistent security and compliance across all accounts. AWS Control Tower extends the capabilities of AWS Organizations by providing a preconfigured, secure, and compliant multi-account environment. It offers automated account setup (Account Factory), centralized security, and governance best practices, making it easier to manage and govern multi-account AWS environments. To learn more, visit https://docs.aws.amazon.com/controltower/latest/userguide/what-is-control-tower.html.

SCPs are powerful tools that allow you to define the maximum permissions for IAM users and roles within the accounts of your organization or organizational units (OUs). These JSON policies act as guardrails that set the boundaries for what actions can and cannot be performed, providing an additional layer of control, security, and compliance. For example, to enforce an organization policy that only allows EC2 instances to be created in a specific region for accounts within a designated OU, you would create an SCP that explicitly denies the ec2:RunInstances action for any region other than the designated one, applying this SCP to the relevant OU within your AWS organization. By using SCPs, you can ensure that only approved actions are allowed, thereby reducing the risk of accidental or malicious activities.

Furthermore, SCPs can be applied to all principals within the member accounts, including the AWS account root user. This means that even if a user has permissions granted through other policies, an explicit deny in an SCP will override any allows, effectively restricting their actions. SCPs are particularly useful for enforcing compliance and governance across large and complex organizations. By centrally managing permissions, you can streamline security operations and maintain consistent policies across all accounts, ensuring that your AWS environment remains secure and well-regulated.

To learn more about SCPs, visit https://docs.aws.amazon.com/organizations/latest/userguide/orgs_manage_policies_scps.html.

Securing Infrastructure and Data

Securing infrastructure in AWS is essential for protecting sensitive data and ensuring the integrity of ML workflows. One of the fundamental components of AWS security is the Virtual Private Cloud (VPC), which provides network isolation by creating a logically isolated section of the AWS cloud where you can launch AWS resources in a virtual network that you define. VPCs enable you to control the network settings, such as IP address ranges, subnets, route tables, and gateways, providing a secure environment for your ML infrastructure.

Network Isolation with VPCs

A VPC is the cornerstone of network isolation in AWS. Upon creating a VPC, you can launch AWS resources such as Amazon SageMaker notebooks, training jobs, and inference endpoints within a logically isolated network. This isolation allows you to define your IP address ranges, create subnets, and configure route tables, ensuring that your ML resources are securely segmented from other parts of the AWS network and external networks.

Within a VPC, NACLs serve as *stateless* firewalls that control inbound and outbound traffic at the subnet level. Stateless means that information about previously sent or received traffic is not saved. NACLs allow you to define rules that explicitly permit or deny traffic based on IP addresses, protocols, and ports. This additional layer of security is aligned with the defense-in-depth principle and helps protect your ML infrastructure from unauthorized access and potential threats.

You can associate a NACL with multiple subnets. However, a subnet can be associated with only one NACL at a time.

Security groups act as *stateful* firewalls for your ML instances, controlling inbound and outbound traffic at the instance level. Stateful means that information about previously sent or received traffic is saved. As a result, if a security group allows incoming traffic on port 443 to an EC2 instance, responses are automatically returned regardless of outbound security group rules. Security groups can be attached to various AWS resources, such as Amazon EC2 instances, Amazon RDS instances, Amazon Elastic Load Balancers (ELBs), and Amazon SageMaker notebooks. By defining security group rules, you can specify which traffic is allowed to reach your ML resources. These rules can also be based on IP addresses, protocols, and ports, ensuring that only authorized traffic can access your ML infrastructure. A key feature of security groups is the ability to reference other security groups or defined prefix lists as a source in rules. This allows you to manage access to groups of resources without needing to know their specific IP addresses, as in the case of an ELB with dynamically assigned IPs.

> You can associate multiple security groups with a single EC2 instance, effectively allowing you to manage inbound and outbound traffic with granular control by combining the rules from each security group.

Private Connectivity

Private connectivity options, such as *VPC interface endpoints* and *gateway endpoints*, further enhance the security of your ML infrastructure by enabling private connections to AWS services without traversing the public internet. VPC interface endpoints use AWS PrivateLink to create private connections to AWS services, such as Amazon S3 and Amazon SageMaker AI, within your VPC. However, AWS PrivateLink is not limited to private connectivity to AWS services. With this service, you can also create private connections to user-defined services across different VPCs and AWS accounts, enabling secure sharing of services without exposing traffic to the public internet. This approach reduces the risk of data exposure and improves data security by ensuring that traffic remains within the AWS network. Similarly, VPC gateway endpoints provide private connectivity to AWS services that are accessible via the AWS Management Console, API, and CLI, such as Amazon S3 and Amazon DynamoDB. By using gateway endpoints, you can ensure that data traffic between your VPC and these services is secure and private.

Data Protection

In addition to network and security isolation, it is crucial to implement encryption for data at rest, in use, and in transit to protect sensitive ML data. AWS KMS allows you to create and manage cryptographic keys that can be used to encrypt data stored in various AWS services, such as Amazon S3, Amazon RDS, and Amazon EBS. Additionally, AWS provides SSL/TLS encryption for data in transit, ensuring that data remains secure while being transferred between your ML infrastructure and other AWS services or external systems.

ACM further simplifies the process of provisioning, managing, and deploying SSL/TLS certificates for your websites and applications. You can use ACM to easily obtain and renew certificates and ensure secure communication between your ML infrastructure and users or other systems. Implementing encryption helps maintain the confidentiality and integrity of your ML data, preventing unauthorized access and tampering.

Monitoring and Auditing

Monitoring and auditing are also vital components of securing ML infrastructure in AWS. As you learned in Chapter 7, AWS provides several services, such as AWS CloudTrail and Amazon CloudWatch, to help you monitor and log activities within your VPC and ML infrastructure. AWS CloudTrail enables you to track API calls and user activities, providing a detailed audit trail that can be used for compliance and security analysis. Amazon CloudWatch allows you to collect and monitor metrics, set alarms, and gain insights into the performance and health of your ML infrastructure. With these monitoring and auditing tools, you can proactively detect and respond to security incidents, ensuring the ongoing protection and integrity of your ML workflows.

Ensuring Compliance

Amazon SageMaker AI is designed to meet a variety of industry standards and regulatory requirements, making it a suitable choice for organizations with stringent compliance needs. In the United States, Amazon SageMaker AI supports compliance with the Health Insurance Portability and Accountability Act (HIPAA), which is essential for handling sensitive healthcare data. This ensures that organizations in the healthcare sector can securely manage and analyze patient information while adhering to HIPAA's stringent privacy and security rules.

Another key compliance framework supported by Amazon SageMaker AI is the Payment Card Industry Data Security Standard (PCI DSS). This standard is critical for organizations that handle payment card information, as it sets requirements for securing cardholder data. By adhering to PCI DSS, organizations can ensure that their ML workflows involving payment data are secure and compliant with industry standards.

Moreover, Amazon SageMaker AI complies with ISO 27001, an international standard for information security management systems. This certification demonstrates that Amazon SageMaker AI follows best practices for managing information security, including risk assessment, management, and continuous improvement. Compliance with ISO 27001 ensures that organizations can trust Amazon SageMaker AI to protect their data and maintain robust security measures.

In addition to these frameworks, Amazon SageMaker AI supports compliance with several other regulatory standards, including SOC 1, SOC 2, SOC 3, FedRAMP, GDPR, and others. This wide range of compliance certifications makes Amazon SageMaker AI a versatile and secure platform for various industries, ensuring that organizations can meet their regulatory obligations while leveraging advanced ML capabilities.

You can leverage AWS Artifact to obtain third-party attestations and reports that validate your compliance status with respect to the aforementioned frameworks.

For more details on the compliance frameworks supported by Amazon SageMaker AI, you can visit the Compliance validation for Amazon SageMaker AI page at `https://docs.aws.amazon.com/sagemaker/latest/dg/sagemaker-compliance.html`.

350   Chapter 8 ▪ Model Security

For security compliance best practices, visit the Security Best Practices for Amazon SageMaker AI page at https://docs.aws.amazon.com/config/latest/developerguide/security-best-practices-for-SageMaker.html.

Summary

In this chapter, you learned about the importance of securing ML models with Amazon SageMaker AI and the various aspects involved in achieving this. Securing ML models requires a holistic approach that leverages a security-by-design strategy, which is founded on security design principles such as least privilege, separation of duties, and defense in depth. These principles ensure that users and applications have only the necessary permissions, multiple layers of security are implemented, and security controls are integrated into the architecture from the outset.

Managing identities and access control is crucial for securing ML resources in Amazon SageMaker AI. AWS IAM allows you to create and manage policies that define permissions for users, groups, and roles, ensuring that only authorized users can access specific Amazon SageMaker AI resources. Implementing MFA adds an extra layer of security, and creating permission boundaries and SCPs helps enforce organizational security policies and restrict access to critical resources. This ensures that your ML identities are managed securely and effectively.

Securing the infrastructure supporting ML workflows involves implementing network isolation and using appropriate security controls. VPCs provide network isolation, whereas NACLs and security groups act as firewalls controlling traffic at the subnet and instance levels. Private connectivity options, such as VPC interface endpoints and gateway endpoints, enable secure connections to AWS services without exposing data to the public internet. Monitoring and logging services like AWS CloudTrail and Amazon CloudWatch help you track and audit network activities, ensuring that potential security incidents are promptly detected and addressed.

Lastly, protecting data and ensuring compliance are critical aspects of securing ML models and workflows. AWS KMS allows you to create and manage cryptographic keys for encrypting data at rest, whereas SSL/TLS encryption ensures data in transit remains secure. ACM simplifies the process of provisioning, managing, and deploying SSL/TLS certificates. Amazon SageMaker AI supports various compliance frameworks, including HIPAA, PCI DSS, ISO 27001, SOC 1, SOC 2, SOC 3, FedRAMP, and GDPR, ensuring that your ML environment adheres to relevant industry standards and data residency regulations. By addressing each of these areas, you can build a secure and compliant ML infrastructure with Amazon SageMaker AI, protecting your models, infrastructure, and data from potential threats and vulnerabilities.

Exam Essentials

Know the difference between IAM users, IAM roles, and IAM groups. An IAM user is an AWS identity that represents an individual person or service that interacts with AWS resources. IAM users have long-term credentials like passwords or access keys. IAM roles are identities that can be assumed by IAM users or other roles and use temporary security tokens for access. This makes them ideal for granting temporary permissions to identities such as applications or users that need to assume different sets of permissions. Lastly, IAM groups are identities representing collections of IAM users that share common permissions.

Know the elements of an AWS access policy. An AWS access policy is a JSON document that defines permissions for an IAM identity (IAM user, IAM group, or IAM role) or an AWS resource. The main elements of an access policy include Version, which specifies the policy language version; Statement, which contains one or more individual permissions; Effect, which can be either Allow or Deny to grant or restrict access; Action, which specifies the API operations allowed or denied; Resource, which specifies the AWS resources to which the actions apply; and Condition, which optionally specifies the conditions under which the policy is in effect. Together, these elements outline what actions are permitted or denied for specified resources under defined conditions.

Know the different access policy types. Identity-based policies are attached directly to IAM users, IAM groups, or IAM roles and define what actions they can perform on which resources. Resource-based policies are attached to AWS resources like Amazon S3 buckets and specify who can access those resources and what actions they can take. Permissions boundaries are advanced policies that set the maximum permissions an identity-based policy can grant to an IAM user or IAM role. Service Control Policies (SCPs) are used within AWS Organizations to manage permissions across all accounts and organizational units, defining what actions can be performed by the accounts' users and roles.

Know what Amazon SageMaker Role Manager is. Amazon SageMaker Role Manager is a tool that simplifies the creation and management of IAM roles tailored for ML workflows. It allows ML administrators to define persona-based roles with predefined permissions for common ML activities. Personas include Data Scientist, MLOps, and SageMaker AI Compute. With Amazon SageMaker Role Manager, you can ensure least privilege access, granting only the necessary permissions for specific tasks. This helps streamline security management and ensures that different users have appropriate access levels for their roles within Amazon SageMaker AI.

Know the difference between NACLs and security groups. Network access control lists are stateless firewalls that control traffic at the subnet level, allowing or denying traffic based on IP address, protocol, and port. With NACLs, both inbound and outbound rules must be defined. Security groups, on the other hand, are stateful firewalls that control traffic at the

352 Chapter 8 ▪ Model Security

instance level, allowing traffic based on IP address, protocol, and port. Due to their stateful nature, security groups always return traffic automatically.

Know the ways to implement private connectivity in a VPC. Private connectivity in an AWS VPC can be implemented using VPC endpoints, which enable secure, private connections between your VPC and supported AWS services without traversing the public Internet. There are two types of VPC endpoints: interface endpoints and gateway endpoints. Interface endpoints use AWS PrivateLink to provide private access to services such as Amazon S3, Amazon SageMaker AI, and Amazon EC2 through an elastic network interface within your VPC. Gateway endpoints provide private connectivity to services like Amazon S3 and Amazon DynamoDB by adding route entries to your VPC route tables. By using these endpoints, you can ensure that your data traffic remains secure and private within the AWS network.

Review Questions

1. What is the main difference between IAM roles and IAM users when it comes to access credentials?

   A. IAM users have temporary security credentials, and IAM roles have long-term credentials.

   B. IAM roles provide temporary security credentials, and IAM users have long-term credentials.

   C. Both IAM roles and users have long-term security credentials.

   D. Both IAM roles and users have temporary security credentials.

2. Which AWS service allows you to monitor compliance with internal policies and regulatory standards in Amazon SageMaker AI?

   A. Amazon GuardDuty

   B. AWS Config

   C. AWS CloudTrail

   D. Amazon Inspector

3. What key distinction separates security groups from network access control lists (NACLs)?

   A. Security groups operate at the instance level and are stateless, whereas NACLs operate at the subnet level and are stateful.

   B. Security groups operate at the subnet level and are stateless, whereas NACLs operate at the instance level and are stateful.

   C. Security groups operate at the instance level and are stateful, whereas NACLs operate at the subnet level and are stateless.

   D. Security groups operate at the subnet level and are stateful, whereas NACLs operate at the instance level and are stateless.

4. Which personas are predefined using Amazon SageMaker Role Manager?

   A. Data Scientist and MLOps

   B. System Administrator and Network Engineer

   C. Financial Analyst and HR Manager

   D. Marketing Specialist and Sales Representative

5. What is a key benefit of using AWS PrivateLink for secure communication between VPCs and AWS services?

   A. It enables Internet access to AWS services.

   B. It creates public endpoints for AWS services.

   C. It provides private connectivity without exposing data to the public Internet.

   D. It manages network traffic within a VPC.

354 Chapter 8 ▪ Model Security

6. How do Service Control Policies (SCPs) enhance security within an AWS Organization?
   A. By providing detailed logs of API calls
   B. By enforcing maximum permissions for member accounts
   C. By encrypting data at rest
   D. By monitoring traffic within the VPC

7. Which AWS service helps enforce compliance for training data residency requirements in a machine learning application within a multi-account environment?
   A. AWS CloudTrail with identity-based policies
   B. AWS Config with resource-based policies
   C. AWS Control Tower with Service Control Policies
   D. Amazon CloudWatch with Access Control Lists

8. What is the role of AWS KMS in securing machine learning data in Amazon SageMaker AI?
   A. To generate detailed audit logs of API calls
   B. To monitor the performance of ML models
   C. To create and manage cryptographic keys for data encryption
   D. To control traffic between subnets and instances

9. Which AWS service is primarily used for tracking and logging API calls and activities for security and compliance auditing?
   A. AWS Shield
   B. AWS CloudTrail
   C. AWS CloudFormation
   D. Amazon CloudWatch

10. Which security strategy emphasizes incorporating security considerations from the initial stages of design and development?
   A. Defense in depth
   B. Least privilege
   C. Security by design
   D. Multifactor authentication (MFA)

Appendix A

Answers to the Review Questions

Chapter 1: Introduction to Machine Learning

1. D. PDF format is generally considered an example of unstructured data rather than semi-structured data. This is because although a PDF may contain text, its structure is not easily parsed by machines, making it difficult to extract meaningful data without specialized tools. NoSQL, JSON, and XML are all examples of semi-structured data because they have a flexible schema and can contain both structured and unstructured information. Therefore, answers A, B, C are incorrect.

2. D. A model must always be trained before evaluating its performance. During training, the model learns patterns and relationships within the data, adjusting its parameters to minimize error and improve its predictions. Gradient descent is an optimization technique to minimize the loss function, and not a phase in the ML lifecycle. Derive inference and deploy model occur after evaluate model. Therefore, answers A, B, C are incorrect.

3. D. Features are the inputs to an ML algorithm. Target variables are the desired output. Weights and biases are parameters that the algorithm adjusts during training to optimize its predictions based on the data. As a result, answers A, B, C are incorrect.

4. B. Gradient descent is not a type of ML algorithm. Gradient descent is an optimization technique to reduce the loss function during the training process by iteratively adjusting the model's parameters in the direction that minimizes the loss, ultimately improving the model's performance. Supervised, unsupervised, and reinforcement learning are all types of ML algorithms. Therefore, answers A, C, D are incorrect.

5. B. The model is the part that makes predictions based on learned patterns from data, whereas the algorithm is the set of instructions that defines how the model learns those patterns from the training data; essentially, the model is the output, and the algorithm is the process used to create it. Answers A, C, D are incorrect.

6. B. A hyperparameter is set before the training process begins, unlike model parameters, which are learned during training based on the data. The variable that holds the final output of the model is the target variable. A hyperparameter is not a metric. Answers A, C, D are incorrect.

7. B. In a neural network, activation functions are specifically used to introduce nonlinearity into the model, allowing it to learn complex patterns and relationships in data that a purely linear model could not capture. Answers A, C, D are incorrect.

8. B. In a neural network, backpropagation is a technique used to update the weights and biases of each neuron by calculating the error and adjusting the parameters in the opposite direction to minimize the overall error during the learning process. Answers A, C, D are incorrect.

9. B. Recurrent neural networks (RNNs) are best suited for processing sequential data, like time series or text, because their design allows them to maintain a "memory" of previous inputs within a sequence, making them ideal for tasks where the order of data elements matters significantly. Answers A, C, D are incorrect.

Chapter 2: Data Ingestion and Storage   **357**

10. B. Deep learning primarily relies on neural networks with multiple layers to automatically extract features from data, whereas machine learning often requires manual feature engineering where humans explicitly select and design relevant features from the data. Deep learning algorithms are particularly well-suited for image and speech recognition tasks due to their ability to learn complex patterns from large datasets, making them highly effective at identifying features within images and audio signals. Answers A, C, D are incorrect.

Chapter 2: Data Ingestion and Storage

1. B. Amazon S3 is the best option to store unprocessed data from IoT devices. Amazon S3 is centralized, cost-effective, highly available (99.99%), and highly durable (99.999999999%). Even though Amazon EFS is natively supported by Amazon SageMaker, it is less cost-effective than Amazon S3. Amazon DynamoDB and Amazon RDS are not natively supported as storage options for Amazon SageMaker. Answers A, C, D are incorrect.

2. A. Amazon S3 is the most cost-effective storage option, and Amazon Athena allows you to query data stored in Amazon S3 using SQL. Answers B, C, D are incorrect.

3. B. With Amazon Managed Service for Apache Flink, you can interactively query data streams, which is one of the requirements in the use case. Answers A, C, D are incorrect.

4. D. To handle large volumes of customer data and efficiently retrieve it for analysis and insights, Amazon Redshift is an excellent choice. Furthermore, Amazon Redshift offers fast query performance through columnar storage and parallel query execution. Given the requirements, answers A, B, C are incorrect.

5. A. Amazon Data Firehose makes it easy to reliably load streaming data into data lakes. It handles the ingestion and delivery of the data with minimal operational overhead. Amazon Managed Service for Apache Flink allows you to process and analyze streaming data in real time and supports the RANDOM_CUT_FOREST function, which is specifically designed for anomaly detection. Answers B, C, D are incorrect.

6. C. Amazon Data Firehose offers a pay-as-you-go pricing model, and the direct streaming ingestion reduces the need for additional infrastructure or intermediate processing steps. Amazon Redshift Streaming Ingestion allows you to ingest streaming data directly into your Amazon Redshift cluster, enabling near real-time analytics, which is a requirement in the use case. It also eliminates the need for intermediate data storage and batch processing, thus reducing latency and simplifying the data pipeline. Answers A, B, D are incorrect.

7. A. Amazon Kinesis Data Streams is designed for real-time data streaming and can handle high throughput with low latency, making it suitable for near real-time data ingestion. As a fully managed ETL service, AWS Glue allows you to efficiently transform the incoming CSV data into Apache Parquet format. Finally, AWS Glue integrates seamlessly with Amazon S3, allowing you to save the transformed Parquet data directly into your S3 bucket. Answers B, C, D are incorrect.

8. A. Amazon Managed Service for Apache Flink supports the query and processing of streaming data with low latency, making it suitable for gaining real-time insights. Apache Flink has built-in support for GZIP compression, making it ideal for handling GZIP compressed data records. AWS Lambda functions can be used to trigger further processing or actions based on the results of the real-time analytics performed by Apache Flink. Answers B, C, D are incorrect.

9. C. Amazon FSx for Lustre is specifically designed for high-performance computing (HPC) and can provide the high throughput and low latency required for training large-scale machine learning models like the one described in the use case. Answers A, B, D are incorrect.

10. C. Amazon S3 offers the most cost-effective storage solution, natively integrated with Amazon SageMaker. Additionally, it is designed to handle virtually unlimited amounts of data, making it ideal for large-scale IoT analytics projects. Answers, A, B, D are incorrect.

Chapter 3: Data Transformation and Feature Engineering

1. A. One-hot encoding is specifically designed to transform categorical features into a numerical format that can be used in machine learning models. It converts categorical features into a numerical format by creating separate binary columns for each unique category, where a 1 denotes the presence of that category for a given data point and a 0 denotes its absence. Feature scaling, feature extraction, and date formatting do not transform categorical features into numerical values. Answers B, C, D are incorrect.

2. A. One-hot encoding creates a new binary column for each unique category in the original column, assigning a 1 to the rows that belong to that category and a 0 to the others. This is ideal for representing categorical data where the categories are mutually exclusive and have no inherent order, like in the simple use case in the question. Answers B, C, D are incorrect.

3. B. Multiple imputations is the best-suited solution for handling missing values in a dataset to ensure that it does not misrepresent the data and reduce model reliability. Although Amazon SageMaker Clarify is useful for detecting bias and explaining model predictions, it is not specifically designed for imputing missing values. Dropping the feature may lead to loss of valuable information and reduce the predictive power of the model. Recollecting data can be time-consuming and costly. It may not always be feasible, especially for large datasets. Answers A, C, D are incorrect.

4. A. Using normalization ensures that your dataset's features are scaled to a uniform range, enhancing the model's predictive capability by preventing any single feature from dominating the learning process. Standardization scales the features to have a mean of 0 and a standard deviation of 1, which is useful for algorithms that assume a Gaussian distribution. However, it might not always reduce the influence of features with larger values as effectively as

Chapter 3: Data Transformation and Feature Engineering   359

normalization. Binning is used to convert continuous features into categorical bins, which is not suitable for scaling numerical values to reduce their influence. One-hot encoding is used to transform categorical features into numerical values and is not applicable for scaling numerical features. Answers B, C, D are incorrect.

5. D. Using feature hashing ensures that your high-cardinality categorical features are efficiently transformed and managed, making it a practical and cost-effective solution for your dataset. Label encoding assigns a unique numerical value to each category, which can introduce ordinal relationships and may not be suitable for high-cardinality features. Lag features are used for time series data and are not relevant for handling high-cardinality categorical features. Binary encoding reduces the dimensionality compared to one-hot encoding but is not as efficient as feature hashing for very high-cardinality features. Answers A, B, C are incorrect.

6. D. By using Amazon SageMaker JumpStart, you can leverage advanced prebuilt models and transfer learning techniques to re-engineer the features in your image dataset, ultimately improving the model's performance in recognizing cars. Tokenization is typically used for processing text data, not for image data. Lag features are relevant for time series data and do not apply to image data. Binning is used to convert continuous features into categorical bins, which is not suitable for image data transformation. Answers A, B, C are incorrect.

7. C. Using word embeddings ensures that your textual data is effectively transformed into numerical vectors, capturing the semantic meaning and improving the performance of your NLP models. One-hot encoding creates binary vectors that indicate the presence of a word but does not capture the semantic relationships between words. Tokenization is the process of splitting text into individual words or tokens, which is a preliminary step in text processing but does not convert words into numerical vectors. Normalization is used to standardize numerical values within a specific range, but it is not applicable for converting textual data into numerical vectors that capture semantic meaning. Answers A, B, D are incorrect.

8. B. Using data augmentation ensures that your machine learning dataset is balanced, helping the model to learn effectively from all classes and improving its predictive performance. Data encoding is used to transform categorical features into numerical values but does not address class imbalance. Feature scaling is used to normalize or standardize numerical features but does not help in handling class imbalance. Data splitting involves dividing the dataset into training and testing sets, which is essential for model evaluation but does not address class imbalance either. Answers A, C, D are incorrect.

9. B. Amazon SageMaker Ground Truth offers tools for automatic labeling, manual labeling, and a combination of both. Additionally, it integrates seamlessly with Amazon SageMaker and other AWS services, allowing you to use labeled data to train and validate your machine learning models. Amazon Comprehend is not specifically designed for data labeling. Amazon Rekognition does not provide data labeling capabilities either. Amazon SageMaker Clarify helps detect bias and explain predictions made by your machine learning models but is not a data labeling service. Answers A, C, D are incorrect.

10. C. By using separate datasets for training and validation, you can ensure that the model does not simply memorize the training data but learns to generalize to new, unseen data. The validation

Appendix A ▪ Answers to the Review Questions

set helps in tuning hyperparameters and making adjustments to prevent overfitting. The test dataset is used to evaluate the final model's performance. Because the test data is not seen during training or validation, it provides an unbiased assessment of how well the model is likely to perform on new data. Although splitting the dataset can lead to a more accurate model by preventing overfitting, the primary purpose is to evaluate performance and generalization. Ensuring diverse data is important but not the primary reason for splitting datasets. Splitting datasets does not necessarily simplify data processing. Answers A, B, D are incorrect.

Chapter 4: Model Selection

1. C. Using Amazon Comprehend ensures that you can effectively analyze unstructured text and extract valuable insights for your applications. Amazon Textract is designed for extracting text and data from scanned documents, such as forms and tables, but does not offer entity recognition or sentiment analysis. Amazon Lex is used for building conversational interfaces such as chatbots and does not provide text analysis capabilities. Amazon Polly is a text-to-speech service that converts text into lifelike speech and is not designed for text analysis. Answers A, B, D are incorrect.

2. B. Using Amazon Bedrock ensures that you have a robust and scalable platform for creating generative AI applications, enabling you to innovate and build creative outputs effectively. Amazon Rekognition is designed for image and video analysis, such as object detection and facial recognition, but it is not specifically for generative AI. Amazon Translate is a service for language translation and does not provide generative AI capabilities. Amazon Transcribe is used for converting speech to text and is not designed for generative AI applications either. Answers A, C, D are incorrect.

3. C. Amazon Rekognition provides the necessary tools and capabilities to detect objects and people in real-time video feeds effectively. None of the other options (Amazon Textract, Amazon Lex, and Amazon Comprehend) are suitable for real-time video analysis. Answers A, B, D are incorrect.

4. C. PCA is a widely used algorithm for dimensionality reduction that transforms high-dimensional data into a lower-dimensional space while preserving as much variability as possible. PCA is available in Amazon SageMaker as a built-in algorithm. Amazon Translate and Amazon Polly are not designed to reduce datasets dimensionality. K-means is an Amazon SageMaker built-in algorithm designed for clustering, but not specifically for dimensionality reduction. Answers A, B, D are incorrect.

5. B. XGBoost (Extreme Gradient Boosting) ensures that you have a high-performance and efficient algorithm for your classification and regression tasks in Amazon SageMaker. Random Forest is also a powerful algorithm for classification and regression, but it may not be as efficient or high-performing as XGBoost in many scenarios. K-NN is a simple and effective algorithm, but it can be computationally expensive and less efficient with large datasets compared to XGBoost. PCA is a dimensionality reduction technique and is not used for classification or regression tasks. Answers A, C, D are incorrect.

Chapter 4: Model Selection **361**

6. C. Random Forest is an ensemble learning method that creates multiple decision trees and averages their predictions. This process helps in reducing the variance of the model and minimizes the risk of overfitting. Linear Learner is used for linear regression and classification tasks but does not involve averaging multiple decision trees. BlazingText is designed for natural language processing tasks, such as text classification and word embedding, and is not related to decision trees. LDA is an unsupervised learning algorithm used for topic modeling and does not involve decision trees or reducing overfitting. Answers A, B, D are incorrect.

7. C. Linear Learner is an Amazon SageMaker built-in algorithm that can handle both binary and multiclass classification tasks as well as regression tasks, making it versatile for various machine learning applications. Although Linear Learner can be used for text classification, it is not specifically designed for NLP tasks. Clustering involves grouping similar data points and is typically handled by unsupervised learning algorithms like K-Means, not by the Linear Learner algorithm. Anomaly detection often requires specialized algorithms designed to identify outliers, such as Random Cut Forest, rather than linear models. Answers A, B, D are incorrect.

8. B. Linear Learner provides straightforward and interpretable models, making it easy to understand the relationship between input features and the target variable. Random Cut Forest (unsupervised learning) is used for anomaly detection, not for modeling linear relationships. Neural Topic Model (NTM) is used for topic modeling (unsupervised learning) and is not designed for linear relationship models. DeepAR is used for time series forecasting (supervised learning with recurrent neural networks) and does not specifically address linear relationships or provide highly interpretable results. As a result, answers A, C, D are incorrect.

9. B. DeepAR is a powerful algorithm designed specifically for forecasting time series data. It uses recurrent neural networks (RNNs) to predict future values based on historical data. IP Insights is used for identifying anomalous behavior in IP address usage, not for time series forecasting. NTM is designed for topic modeling and is not applicable to time series forecasting. Although Sequence-to-Sequence models can be used for time series forecasting, they are generally more complex and less specialized for this task compared to DeepAR. Answers A, C, D are incorrect.

10. C. XGBoost combines the predictions of multiple weak learners (usually decision trees) to create a strong predictive model. It focuses on the errors made by previous models and corrects them iteratively. K-Means is an unsupervised learning algorithm used for clustering and does not involve boosting weak learners. LDA is an unsupervised learning algorithm used for topic modeling and is not related to boosting weak learners. Random Cut Forest is used for anomaly detection and does not involve boosting weak learners. As a result, answers A, B, D are incorrect.

11. C. Principal Component Analysis (PCA) in Amazon SageMaker ensures that you can effectively reduce the dimensionality of your dataset while preserving the maximum amount of variance, resulting in a more manageable and interpretable dataset for further analysis. K-Means is a clustering algorithm and is not designed for dimensionality reduction. Random Cut Forest is used for anomaly detection and does not perform dimensionality reduction. NTM is used for topic modeling and is not relevant for dimensionality reduction. None of them reduce the dimensionality of a dataset. Therefore, answers A, B, D are incorrect.

Appendix A ▪ Answers to the Review Questions

12. C. Random Cut Forest is specifically designed for detecting anomalies and rare events in data streams. It creates a forest of trees where each tree is built by randomly selecting and partitioning the data points. LDA is used for topic modeling and is not designed for anomaly detection. IP Insights is used for identifying anomalous behavior in IP address usage but is not a general-purpose anomaly detection algorithm. Factorization Machines are used in supervised learning for recommendation systems and prediction tasks, not for detecting anomalies. Therefore, answers A, B, D are incorrect.

13. B. Latent Dirichlet Allocation (LDA) is specifically designed for topic modeling, allowing you to uncover hidden topics within large collections of text data. The algorithm provides interpretable results by assigning probabilities to words belonging to different topics, making it easier to understand the underlying themes. Moreover, LDA effectively captures the distribution of topics across documents, ensuring accurate identification of the main topics present in the text data. K-Means is used in unsupervised learning to solve clustering problems and is not designed for topic modeling. PCA is a dimensionality reduction algorithm used in unsupervised learning and does not address topic discovery in text data. Random Cut Forest is used in unsupervised learning for anomaly detection and is not relevant for topic modeling. As a result, answers A, C, D are incorrect.

14. C. In unsupervised learning, K-Means is a clustering algorithm that partitions data into K predefined groups based on feature similarity, ensuring that data points within the same cluster are as similar as possible. The results of K-Means clustering are highly interpretable, as each data point is assigned to a specific cluster, and the centroids of clusters provide insight into the characteristics of each group. K-Means is efficient and scalable, making it suitable for large datasets. It can handle high-dimensional data and is computationally efficient. None of the other options are relevant to clustering. Specifically, Random Cut Forest is used for anomaly detection, PCA is used for dimensionality reduction, and NTM (just like LDA) is used for topic modeling. Therefore, answers A, B, D are incorrect.

15. A. BlazingText is designed for text classification and word embedding tasks and is available as an Amazon SageMaker built-in algorithm. BlazingText is highly accurate, efficient, and scalable, making it suitable for large-scale text classification tasks. Sequence-to-Sequence models are generally used for tasks such as machine translation and text generation but may not be as efficient for large-scale text classification. LDA is used for topic modeling and is not designed for text classification tasks. IP Insights is used for identifying anomalous behavior in IP address usage and is not relevant for text classification. Therefore, answers B, C, D are incorrect.

16. B. Sequence-to-Sequence models are specifically designed for tasks like text translation, where input sequences (source text) are mapped to output sequences (target text). These models, often implemented with attention mechanisms and neural networks, provide high accuracy and performance in translation tasks by effectively capturing the relationships between words in different languages. Additionally, this technique helps improve interpretability by highlighting which parts of the input sequence are most relevant to the output sequence. Random Cut Forest is used for anomaly detection and is not designed for text translation. BlazingText is excellent for text classification and word embeddings but not specifically for translation tasks. PCA is a dimensionality reduction technique and does not handle text translation. As a result, answers A, C, D are incorrect.

Chapter 5: Model Training and Evaluation

17. B. In image processing learning, Object Detection algorithms are specifically designed to identify and localize multiple objects within an image, providing bounding boxes around each detected object. Image Classification algorithms are designed to classify an entire image into a single category and do not provide localization of multiple objects. Semantic Segmentation involves classifying each pixel in the image into a specific category, but it is more computationally intensive and less focused on bounding boxes around objects. Factorization Machines are used for recommendation systems and prediction tasks, not for image analysis. Therefore, answers A, C, D are incorrect.

18. B. In image processing learning, Image Classification algorithms are specifically designed to classify images into predefined categories with high accuracy. These models provide clear and interpretable results, assigning each image to a specific category based on learned features. LDA is used for topic modeling in text data and is not applicable to image classification. Object Detection is used for identifying and localizing multiple objects within an image, but it is not focused on classifying entire images into predefined categories. IP Insights is used for identifying anomalous behavior in IP address usage and is not related to image classification. Answers A, C, D are incorrect.

19. C. In image processing learning, Semantic Segmentation algorithms provide detailed pixel-level classification, assigning each pixel in an image to a specific category. This is crucial for tasks that require precise localization and classification of different regions within an image, resulting in high interpretability. Random Cut Forest is used for anomaly detection and is not designed for image analysis. Image Classification algorithms classify entire images into predefined categories and do not provide pixel-level analysis. BlazingText is used for text classification and word embeddings, not for image analysis. As a result, answers A, B, D are incorrect.

20. D. BlazingText leverages word embeddings to represent words as dense vectors in a continuous vector space, capturing semantic relationships between words. BlazingText is optimized for performance, using techniques like hierarchical softmax and negative sampling to speed up training, making it a cost-effective solution. The word embeddings created by BlazingText provide interpretable representations of words, making it easier to understand the relationships between them. Random Cut Forest is used for anomaly detection and does not utilize word embeddings. PCA is a dimensionality reduction technique and is not applicable to NLP tasks involving word embeddings. LDA is used for topic modeling and does not leverage word embeddings for text representation. Answers A, B, C are incorrect.

Chapter 5: Model Training and Evaluation

1. C. Elastic Net regularization is a linear regression technique that combines the penalties of L1 (LASSO) and L2 (Ridge) regularization. This means it incorporates both the absolute value of the coefficients (L1) and the squared value of the coefficients (L2) into the regularization term. LASSO (least absolute shrinkage and selection operator) uses only L1 regularization, which

364   Appendix A ▪ Answers to the Review Questions

can lead to sparse models by shrinking some coefficients to zero. Ridge regularization uses only L2 regularization, which penalizes the squared coefficients but does not perform feature selection. Therefore, answers A, B are incorrect. Answer D is also incorrect because Elastic Net regularization effectively combines the benefits of both L1 and L2 regularization.

2. D. Bayesian optimization uses probabilistic models to predict the performance of different hyperparameters. This allows it to efficiently guide the search process toward the most promising hyperparameter configurations. This optimization technique adapts the search strategy based on previous evaluations, improving the likelihood of finding optimal hyperparameters. This last statement excludes answer B from the list of correct answers. Bayesian optimization typically requires fewer evaluations compared to grid search, making it more efficient. Therefore, answer A is incorrect. Bayesian optimization does not select hyperparameters randomly. Instead, it uses a guided search strategy based on probabilistic models. As a result, answer C is also incorrect.

3. C. The objective function is used to measure how well a model performs with a given set of hyperparameters. Common metrics for evaluation include accuracy, precision, recall, F1 score, and any other performance metric relevant to the task. The goal is not to maximize the number of hyperparameters but to find the optimal set that leads to the best model performance. Although computational cost is a consideration, the primary goal is to optimize model performance. Efficient algorithms like Bayesian optimization help balance computational cost and performance. Hyperparameter tuning focuses on tuning the parameters of an already chosen model architecture rather than determining the architecture itself. Answers A, B, D are incorrect.

4. D. Mean absolute percentage error (MAPE) expresses the error as a percentage of the actual values, making it scale-invariant. This allows you to compare errors across different datasets with varying scales effectively. Mean absolute error (MAE) measures the average magnitude of the errors but does not account for the scale of the data, making it less suitable for comparing datasets with varying scales. Mean squared error (MSE) measures the average squared errors, which can be influenced by the scale of the data, and can also be less interpretable due to squaring the errors. Root mean squared error (RMSE) provides the square root of the average squared errors but still does not address the issue of varying scales across datasets. As a result, answers A, B, C are incorrect.

5. B. Stratified k-fold cross-validation ensures that each fold has a similar distribution of classes as the original dataset. This helps in maintaining the balance of classes in each fold, preventing biases that could arise from uneven class distributions. Stratifying the folds does not increase the complexity of the model. Stratification does not affect the number of folds and does not aim to maximize training time. Therefore, answers A, C, D are incorrect.

6. C. Overfitting occurs when a model is too complex and captures noise or random fluctuations in the training data rather than the actual underlying data distribution. This leads to high performance on the training data but low performance on new, unseen data (represented by test data). This is exactly the scenario in answer C. None of the remaining options indicate overfitting. Therefore, answers A, B, D are incorrect.

7. B. Random search involves randomly selecting hyperparameters from the search space, which can be inefficient, especially in large hyperparameter spaces. It may miss optimal hyperparameter

Chapter 6: Model Deployment and Orchestration   **365**

combinations because it doesn't use any intelligent guidance to explore the hyperparameter space. Random search does not guarantee finding the best hyperparameters as it relies on random selection. Random search does not require prior evaluations. It selects hyperparameters randomly without using past performance data. Random search is inherently nondeterministic due to its reliance on random selection of hyperparameters. Answers A, C, D are incorrect.

8. B. Regularization techniques add a penalty term to the loss function, which discourages the model from fitting too closely to the training data. This penalty term is based on the complexity of the model parameters (weights). By constraining the parameters, regularization prevents the model from learning noise and small fluctuations in the training data, which can lead to overfitting. This helps the model generalize better to unseen data. Increasing complexity would likely exacerbate overfitting rather than mitigate it. Removing training data could reduce the model's ability to learn and generalize properly. Increasing the number of training epochs without regularization can lead to overfitting, as the model may continue to fit the noise in the training data. As a result, answers A, C, D are incorrect.

9. C. Amazon SageMaker Debugger provides tools to monitor and debug training jobs by capturing and analyzing training metrics and model parameters in real time. It offers built-in rules to automatically detect common training issues, such as overfitting, vanishing gradients, and hardware resource utilization problems. Amazon SageMaker Debugger provides visualizations through tools like TensorBoard, making it easier to understand and diagnose issues during training. Jupyter notebooks are not specifically designed for monitoring and debugging distributed training jobs. Spot Instances help reduce costs by using spare AWS capacity, but they do not provide monitoring and debugging capabilities. Disabling Auto Scaling is not related to monitoring or debugging training jobs. It is a configuration setting for managing resource allocation. Answers A, B, D are incorrect.

10. B. The area under the receiver operating characteristic curve (AUC-ROC) is a performance measurement for classification problems. The ROC curve plots the true positive rate (sensitivity) against the false positive rate (1 – specificity) at various threshold settings. A high AUC-ROC score, close to 1, indicates that the model has a strong ability to discriminate between the positive and negative classes. This means the model is effective at distinguishing between the two classes and making accurate predictions. A high number of false positives would typically result in a lower AUC-ROC score, indicating poor model performance. A high AUC-ROC score does not necessarily indicate overfitting. Overfitting can be evaluated by comparing training and validation performance, not just by the AUC-ROC score alone. Similar to false positives, a high number of false negatives would also result in a lower AUC-ROC score, indicating poor model performance. Answers A, C, D are incorrect.

Chapter 6: Model Deployment and Orchestration

1. C. The p3.8xlarge instance type is equipped with powerful GPUs, which are essential for efficiently handling deep learning models and large datasets. By leveraging the computational power of GPUs, the p3.8xlarge instance type can process large-scale models more quickly,

Appendix A ▪ Answers to the Review Questions

reducing the overall cost of training and inference. Additionally, The p3.8xlarge instance type supports multi-model endpoints, allowing you to host multiple models on a single endpoint, which improves resource utilization and cost efficiency. Options A (t2.medium), B (m5. xlarge), D (c5.4xlarge) lack the GPU acceleration required for deep learning models. Answers A, B, D are incorrect.

2. B. Using managed deployment in Amazon SageMaker ensures that you have a scalable, resource-efficient, and low-maintenance solution for hosting your models. Answer A is incorrect because if you require full control over the deployment infrastructure, you might prefer an unmanaged deployment, where you can customize and manage the resources yourself. Answer C is incorrect because managed deployments are specific to Amazon SageMaker and AWS infrastructure, so they are not suitable for deploying models on non-AWS environments. Answer D is also incorrect because if you need to customize the deployment setup extensively, an unmanaged deployment may be more appropriate, as it allows for greater flexibility and control over the configuration.

3. C. Using Canary deployment ensures that you can deploy your critical model update with minimum risk and thorough performance monitoring, allowing for a safe and controlled rollout. Answer A is incorrect because deploying all at once introduces the updated model to 100% of the traffic immediately, which carries a high risk if there are any issues with the new model. Answer B is incorrect because linear deployment gradually shifts traffic in a uniform manner, but it may not provide the same level of fine-grained control and monitoring as Canary deployment. Answer D is also incorrect because partial deployment is less specific than Canary deployment in terms of risk management and monitoring.

4. C. Amazon SageMaker Neo automatically optimizes machine learning models for inference on a wide range of hardware platforms, including edge devices. This ensures that the models run efficiently on various processors and hardware configurations. By optimizing models for edge devices, Amazon SageMaker Neo enables efficient deployment in IoT environments where computational resources may be limited. This reduces the need for manual tuning and ensures high performance without sacrificing accuracy. Amazon SageMaker Neo focuses on optimizing models for inference, not on reducing the cost of training. Although Amazon SageMaker Neo maintains accuracy, its primary advantage is optimizing models for diverse hardware. Amazon SageMaker Neo is designed for model optimization and deployment, not for improving data preprocessing speed. As a result, answers A, B, D are incorrect.

5. A. Using Amazon SageMaker Pipelines ensures that you have an efficient, automated, and integrated solution for managing end-to-end machine learning workflows with minimal manual intervention. Although Amazon Managed Workflows for Apache Airflow (MWAA) is a powerful orchestration service for general workflows, it is not specifically tailored for machine learning workflows and may require more manual configuration. AWS Step Functions is a general-purpose orchestration service for building complex workflows, but it is not specialized for machine learning tasks like Amazon SageMaker Pipelines. Amazon SageMaker Clarify is a tool for detecting bias and explaining ML models, but it is not an orchestration service for automating workflows. Therefore, answers B, C, D are incorrect.

6. D. The inf1.2xlarge instance type is specifically designed for high-performance inference workloads. It provides high throughput and low latency, making it ideal for real-time

applications. Additionally, Inf1 instances are optimized for machine learning inference and are powered by AWS Inferentia chips, which are custom-built for deep learning workloads. This ensures efficient and cost-effective inference. Inf1 instances offer a balance of performance and cost, providing significant cost savings compared to GPU-based instances for inference tasks. Answers A (t3.medium) and B (r5.4xlarge) are incorrect because the former has limited computational power and the latter is memory optimized, making them unsuitable for high-performance inference. Answer C is not the best option because a g4dn.xlarge instance may not be as cost-effective as Inf1 instances for large-scale inference workloads, even though g4dn instances are GPU-based and suitable for training and inference.

7. B. Amazon SageMaker Serverless Inference automatically scales resources based on the volume of incoming requests. This makes it ideal for handling intermittent or unpredictable traffic patterns, ensuring that you only pay for the compute capacity when it's in use. Although Amazon SageMaker Serverless Inference can handle real-time predictions, low-latency requirements might be better served by Amazon SageMaker Real-time Inference endpoints and autoscaling. Amazon SageMaker Serverless Inference is not suited for high-throughput batch processing. For this use case, you should consider using Amazon SageMaker Batch Transform. Large payloads and long processing times may benefit from dedicated instances that can handle the resource-intensive workload more effectively, rather than Amazon SageMaker Serverless Inference. As result, answers A, C, D are incorrect.

8. B. AWS Step Functions is ideal for orchestrating complex workflows that involve conditional logic, error handling, parallel processing, and more. This makes it a robust choice for managing intricate ML workflows with various steps and dependencies. Although AWS Step Functions can automate ETL tasks, it is more powerful and suited for complex workflows. For simple ETL tasks, a service like AWS Glue or Amazon MWAA might be more appropriate. AWS Step Functions does not offer prebuilt templates for ML projects, nor does it perform bias detection and explain model predictions. To leverage prebuilt templates for ML projects, you should use Amazon SageMaker Pipelines. To perform bias detection and explain model predictions, you should use Amazon SageMaker Clarify. As a result, answers A, C, D are incorrect.

9. B. Amazon SageMaker Model Registry provides functionalities such as model versioning, which allows you to keep track of different versions of your models; approval workflows, which enable you to control and manage the transition of models through different stages; and deployment automation, which streamlines the process of deploying models to production environments. These features make it ideal for efficiently managing and deploying models within a CI/CD pipeline. Amazon SageMaker Model Registry does not provide model monitoring and bias detection capabilities. The former is provided by Amazon SageMaker Model Monitor, and the latter is provided by Amazon SageMaker Clarify. It does not simplify data preprocessing and feature engineering. Services like Amazon SageMaker Data Wrangler and Amazon SageMaker Feature Store are suited for these functionalities. Although the Amazon SageMaker Model Registry can be part of a broader workflow that includes AWS Step Functions, its primary functionalities do not involve orchestrating ML workflows. As a result, answers A, C, D are incorrect.

10. B. The Amazon Bedrock Converse API is specifically designed to handle natural language understanding (NLU) and natural language generation (NLG) tasks in real time. This API can process and generate human-like text, making it suitable for applications such as chatbots,

virtual assistants, and other conversational AI systems. Managing and deploying ML models is typically handled by services like Amazon SageMaker Model Registry, Amazon SageMaker Endpoints, and Amazon SageMaker Pipelines. The Amazon Bedrock Converse API is focused on NLU and NLG tasks. Data preprocessing and feature engineering are handled by services like Amazon SageMaker Data Wrangler and Amazon SageMaker Feature Store. Optimizing models for different hardware platforms is typically done using tools like Amazon SageMaker Neo. The Bedrock Converse API does not perform model optimization tasks. Therefore, answers A, C, D are incorrect.

Chapter 7: Model Monitoring and Cost Optimization

1. C. Model drift can cause the model to make inaccurate predictions, which may lead to poor decision-making. Additionally, in regulated industries, failing to maintain model accuracy can result in noncompliance with regulations, potentially leading to legal and financial consequences. Ignoring model drift does not lead to increased computational efficiency. Instead, it can make the model less efficient due to inaccurate predictions. Model drift leads to inaccurate predictions over time because the model's performance degrades as it no longer aligns with the current data distribution. Not addressing model drift does not improve model interpretability. It can actually worsen the model's performance and reliability, making it harder to trust and interpret the results. Therefore, answers A, B, D are incorrect.

2. C. Amazon SageMaker Model Monitor is specifically designed to continuously monitor machine learning models for data quality issues, concept drift, and anomalies. It can automatically detect deviations from expected baselines and send alerts when anomalies are detected. AWS Glue is primarily used for extract, transform, load (ETL) tasks to prepare and transform data for analysis, but it doesn't provide real-time anomaly detection and monitoring capabilities. AWS Step Functions is a workflow service that coordinates multiple AWS services into serverless workflows. Although it can help orchestrate tasks, it doesn't provide continuous monitoring for anomalies in real time data. AWS CodePipeline is a continuous integration/continuous delivery (CI/CD) service for automating the build, test, and deployment of applications. It doesn't provide real-time anomaly detection and monitoring. As a result, answers A, B, D are incorrect.

3. A. Metrics such as mean absolute error (MAE), root mean squared error (RMSE), and receiver operating characteristic (ROC) curve are directly related to evaluating the performance of machine learning models. MAE and RMSE are common metrics for regression tasks, measuring the average error and the square root of the average squared error, respectively. The ROC curve is used for classification tasks, providing a graphical representation of a model's true positive rate versus false positive rate. The metrics specified in options B, C, D are all irrelevant to a model's performance and therefore are incorrect.

Chapter 7: Model Monitoring and Cost Optimization 369

4. C. Poor-quality data can introduce biases and lead to inaccurate model predictions. If the input data is not representative, contains errors, or is biased, the model will learn and propagate these issues, resulting in unreliable predictions and potentially unfair outcomes. Failing to monitor data quality does not enhance model scalability. Monitoring data quality does not directly affect the need for feature engineering. Data quality does not have a direct impact on the speed of model training. As a result, answers A, B, D are incorrect.

5. B. Monitoring network latency ensures efficient data transfer and communication between different components of the ML system. Resource utilization metrics (e.g., CPU, GPU, memory usage) help optimize the performance and scalability of ML models by ensuring that resources are being used efficiently. System anomaly detection helps identify unexpected behaviors or performance issues that could impact the overall health and reliability of the ML deployment. Although important for general application performance and security, aspects such as application load balancing, user authentication processes, and API gateway endpoints do not directly address the specific needs of large-scale ML deployments, such as monitoring real-time data processing and resource optimization. The same applies to interface design consistency, session state management, and cache invalidation. User experience feedback loops, front-end load times, and graphical rendering focus on the end-user experience and front-end performance, which are important but not directly related to the infrastructure monitoring needed for large-scale ML deployments. Therefore, answers A, C, D are incorrect.

6. B. Amazon CloudWatch provides real-time monitoring and observability of your infrastructure. It collects and tracks metrics, logs, and events, allowing you to gain insights into system health, detect anomalies promptly, and track resource usage. This helps maintain the performance and reliability of ML infrastructure by ensuring timely detection and resolution of issues. Automated code deployment pipelines are managed by services like AWS CodePipeline, not Amazon CloudWatch. Amazon CloudWatch focuses on monitoring and observability. Managing serverless function scaling and memory allocation is handled by AWS Lambda, not Amazon CloudWatch. Infrastructure as code (IaC) provisioning and version control are facilitated by services like AWS CloudFormation and AWS CDK (Cloud Development Kit). Amazon CloudWatch is focused on monitoring rather than provisioning infrastructure. Answers A, C, D are incorrect.

7. B. AWS Cost Explorer provides detailed cost analysis, enabling you to track and visualize your AWS spending. By setting up cost and usage dashboards, you can leverage predictive analysis to forecast future spending and set up alerts for unexpected cost spikes, thereby helping you avoid unexpected expenses. Although cross-region replication can enhance data redundancy and availability, it doesn't inherently involve predictive analysis or alert mechanisms to optimize costs. Enhanced monitoring can help improve server performance and optimize resource usage, but it doesn't directly provide predictive analysis or alert mechanisms for cost optimization. Automated backup and recovery solutions ensure data availability and durability but do not involve cost monitoring or predictive analysis to manage expenses. Answers A, C, D are incorrect.

8. C. AWS Savings Plans provide significant cost savings for sustained usage over a specified term (one or three years). These savings are applicable to a variety of AWS services, including

370   Appendix A • Answers to the Review Questions

EC2, Lambda, SageMaker, and Fargate, making them an excellent choice for predictable and sustained ML workloads that require consistent compute resources. AWS Savings Plans do not provide unlimited API call capacity. They offer cost savings for compute usage but do not change the limits or capacity of API calls. Although AWS provides various storage options, AWS Savings Plans focus on cost savings for compute usage, not on flexibility for choosing storage types. AWS Savings Plans do not provide access to dedicated cloud infrastructure. They offer cost savings based on compute usage commitments but do not include dedicated infrastructure. Answers A, B, D are incorrect.

9. A. Real-time monitoring ensures that the model continues to perform accurately even as the data distribution changes over time. It helps detect issues such as model drift, where the model's performance degrades due to changes in the input data. By monitoring in real time, you can quickly identify and address these issues to maintain prediction accuracy. Although minimizing latency is important for user experience, it is not the primary reason for real-time monitoring of model inference. Monitoring focuses on ensuring model accuracy and reliability. Real-time monitoring of model inference is not directly related to automating the generation of training datasets. It is more concerned with the performance and accuracy of the model's predictions. Version control systems are managed separately from real-time monitoring of model inference. Monitoring focuses on the performance of the model in production rather than version control. As a result, answers B, C, D are incorrect.

10. B. AWS Step Functions provides robust workflow automation capabilities, enabling you to coordinate multiple AWS services into serverless workflows. It supports complex workflows with conditional branching, parallel execution, and error handling, making it ideal for orchestrating multistep processes in machine learning pipelines. Amazon GuardDuty is a threat detection service that continuously monitors for malicious activity and unauthorized behavior. It's focused on security rather than orchestrating workflows. Amazon CloudWatch is a monitoring and observability service that collects and tracks metrics, logs, and events. It's crucial for monitoring infrastructure and applications but not for orchestrating complex workflows. Amazon EventBridge is an event bus service that makes it easy to connect different applications using events. Although it can be part of an event-driven architecture, it's not designed to orchestrate complex multistep workflows like AWS Step Functions. Answers A, C, D are incorrect.

Chapter 8: Model Security

1. B. IAM roles are designed to be assumed by any entity that requires them, such as an IAM user, an AWS service, or an application. When an entity assumes a role, it receives temporary security credentials that expire after a certain period. This is useful for scenarios where permissions need to be granted dynamically and temporarily. On the other hand, IAM users are specific individuals or services that require long-term access to your AWS resources. When you create an IAM user, you assign them long-term security credentials (access keys and passwords) that are meant to be used over an extended period. IAM users are typically used for employees or applications that need persistent access to AWS resources. Answers A, C, D are incorrect.

Chapter 8: Model Security   371

2. B. AWS Config continuously monitors and records your AWS resource configurations and allows you to automate the evaluation of recorded configurations against desired configurations. It provides a detailed view of the compliance status of your AWS resources, helping you ensure that they comply with internal policies and regulatory standards. Amazon GuardDuty is a threat detection service that continuously monitors for malicious activity and unauthorized behavior. It is focused on security threats rather than compliance monitoring. AWS CloudTrail records AWS API calls and events for your account, providing visibility into user activity and aiding in security and operational auditing. However, it does not specifically monitor compliance with internal policies and regulatory standards. Amazon Inspector is an automated security assessment service that helps improve the security and compliance of applications deployed on AWS. It focuses on assessing the security of your applications rather than continuous compliance monitoring. Therefore, answers A, C, D are incorrect.

3. C. Security groups are associated with EC2 instances. They control inbound and outbound traffic for the instances they are attached to. Security groups remember the state of the connection. If you allow an inbound connection, the corresponding outbound connection is automatically allowed, and vice versa. On the other hand, NACLs are associated with subnets. They control traffic entering and leaving the subnets. NACLs do not remember the state of the connection. Each rule is evaluated independently for inbound and outbound traffic, meaning that you must explicitly allow both inbound and outbound traffic separately. Answers A, B, D are incorrect.

4. A. The predefined personas using Amazon SageMaker Role Manager are Data Scientist and MLOps. These personas come with suggested permissions tailored to their specific roles and responsibilities within the machine learning workflow. This helps streamline the process of assigning appropriate permissions and ensures that users have the necessary access to perform their tasks efficiently. Answers B, C, D are incorrect.

5. C. AWS PrivateLink allows you to securely access AWS services and VPC endpoint services over the Amazon network without exposing your traffic to the public Internet. This enhances security by keeping the data within the AWS network. AWS PrivateLink does not enable Internet access. Instead, it provides private connectivity. AWS PrivateLink creates private endpoints, not public endpoints. Although managing network traffic within a VPC is important, it is not the primary function of AWS PrivateLink, which focuses on providing private connectivity. Answers A, B, D are incorrect.

6. B. Service Control Policies (SCPs) allow you to define permission guardrails for the accounts in your AWS Organization. They restrict the maximum permissions that any principal in an account can have, ensuring that users and roles cannot perform actions outside of what is explicitly allowed by the policies. This helps prevent accidental or malicious use of AWS resources. Detailed logging of API calls is provided by AWS CloudTrail. SCPs do not handle logging. Encryption of data at rest is managed by services like AWS KMS (Key Management Service) and not SCPs. Monitoring traffic within a VPC is handled by services like VPC Flow Logs and AWS Network Firewall. SCPs do not monitor traffic. Answers A, C, D are incorrect.

7. C. AWS Control Tower automates the setup of a multi-account AWS environment (landing zone) and uses Service Control Policies (SCPs) to enforce compliance with organizational policies, including data residency requirements. SCPs allow you to set permission guardrails

372 Appendix A ▪ Answers to the Review Questions

that apply to all accounts within your AWS Organization, ensuring that data residency policies are adhered to across multiple accounts. AWS CloudTrail provides detailed logs of API calls and user activity, which is useful for auditing and monitoring, but does not enforce compliance for data residency requirements. AWS Config helps monitor and record configurations of your AWS resources and evaluate them against desired configurations, but it does not specifically enforce data residency requirements. Amazon CloudWatch provides monitoring and observability for AWS resources, and Access Control Lists (ACLs) control access to resources, but they do not enforce data residency requirements. Therefore, answers A, B, D are incorrect.

8. C. AWS KMS is a managed service that allows you to create, manage, and control cryptographic keys used to encrypt and decrypt data. In the context of Amazon SageMaker, KMS is used to encrypt data at rest, including training data, model artifacts, and endpoints, ensuring that sensitive information is securely protected. Detailed logging of API calls is provided by AWS CloudTrail, not AWS KMS. CloudTrail helps track user activity and changes to resources. Monitoring the performance of ML models is typically handled by a service like Amazon CloudWatch or Amazon SageMaker Model Monitor. AWS KMS focuses on encryption. Controlling traffic between subnets and instances is managed by security groups and network access control lists (NACLs). AWS KMS does not handle network traffic. Answers A, B, D are incorrect.

9. B. AWS CloudTrail records AWS API calls and activities for your account. It provides a comprehensive log of all actions taken by users, roles, and services in your AWS environment, which is crucial for security monitoring, compliance auditing, and operational troubleshooting. AWS Shield is a managed DDoS protection service designed to safeguard your applications against distributed denial of service (DDoS) attacks. It is not used for logging API calls. AWS CloudFormation is a service for provisioning and managing AWS infrastructure as code. It automates the setup of resources but does not provide logging and tracking of API calls. Amazon CloudWatch provides monitoring and observability for AWS resources. It collects and tracks metrics, logs, and events but does not focus specifically on logging API calls for compliance auditing. Answers A, C, D are incorrect.

10. C. Security by design is an approach where security considerations are integrated into every phase of the software development lifecycle, from initial design to deployment. This proactive strategy ensures that potential security issues are addressed early, reducing vulnerabilities and enhancing overall security. Defense in depth is a layered security approach that uses multiple security measures to protect data and resources. Although important, it does not specifically emphasize incorporating security from the initial design stages. The least privilege principle involves granting users and systems the minimum level of access necessary to perform their tasks. It is a critical security practice but does not encompass the broader concept of integrating security throughout the design and development process. Multifactor authentication (MFA) is a security mechanism that requires users to provide multiple forms of verification to access resources. It enhances security but is not related to the concept of incorporating security from the initial stages of development. Answers A, B, D are incorrect.

Appendix B

Mathematics Essentials

Appendix B • Mathematics Essentials

This appendix provides a self-contained primer on key mathematical concepts essential for understanding machine learning. The topics covered include linear algebra, statistics, probability theory, and calculus. Each section introduces fundamental concepts and contains examples for easy integration into your study materials.

Linear Algebra

Linear algebra is a subject of mathematics focused on linear transformations, which forms the backbone of machine learning. It deals with structures such as scalars, vectors, matrices, and tensors, as well as notions like rank and dimension. A strong foundation in linear algebra is crucial for understanding the underlying principles and rationale behind many machine learning (ML) algorithms.

Linear Equation

In their simplest form, *linear equations* are mathematical expressions of the following form:

$$y = mx + c$$

Here, m is the slope, and c is the y-intercept. Linear equations are essential in ML to model linear relationships between variables.

Figure A.1 illustrates an example of a linear equation.

Scalar

A *scalar* is a single number, typically representing a quantity that has only magnitude but no direction. For example, it can represent temperature or mass:

$$s = 5$$

Vector

A *vector* is a collection of numbers that represent both magnitude and direction. It is usually visualized as an arrow in space:

$$\vec{v} = \begin{bmatrix} 1 \\ 2 \\ 3 \end{bmatrix}$$

The single numbers the vector $\vec{v}$ comprises are denoted by an index, which is used to capture their position. For example, the following

$$v_1 = 1$$

indicates that the first element of the vector $\vec{v}$ has a value 1.

FIGURE A.1 Visualization of a linear equation ($y = 2x + 3$).

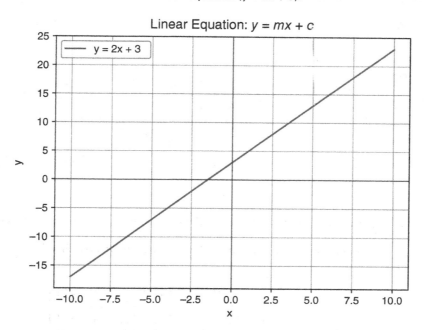

Matrix

A *matrix* is a two-dimensional (2D) array of numbers, which can be used to represent linear transformations or systems of equations:

$$M = \begin{bmatrix} 1 & 2 & 3 \\ 4 & 5 & 6 \\ 7 & 8 & 9 \end{bmatrix}$$

Because a matrix is a 2D array, a given number in the matrix is denoted by two indices: the first to select the row where the number is located and the second to select the column. For example the number 8 in the matrix M is located in the third row and the second column. As a result,

$$m_{32} = 8$$

Tensor

A *tensor* is a generalization of scalars, vectors, and matrices to higher dimensions. Tensors can represent more complex data structures, such as multidimensional datasets in ML or physics.

Appendix B ▪ Mathematics Essentials

FIGURE A.2 Visualization of a 4D tensor.

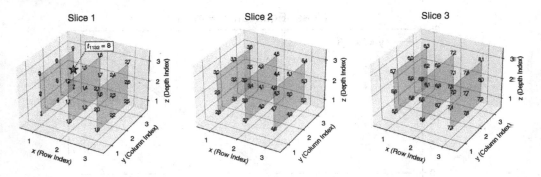

The following tensor T is a four-dimensional (4D) array, and the selection of each element requires four indices.

Notice how rows and columns in a tensor can be vectors of matrices, rather than scalars (single numbers):

$$T = \begin{bmatrix} \begin{bmatrix} \begin{bmatrix} 1 & 2 & 3 \\ 4 & 5 & 6 \\ 7 & 8 & 9 \end{bmatrix} & \begin{bmatrix} 10 & 11 & 12 \\ 13 & 14 & 15 \\ 16 & 17 & 18 \end{bmatrix} & \begin{bmatrix} 19 & 20 & 21 \\ 22 & 23 & 24 \\ 25 & 26 & 27 \end{bmatrix} \end{bmatrix} \\ \begin{bmatrix} \begin{bmatrix} 28 & 29 & 30 \\ 31 & 32 & 33 \\ 34 & 35 & 36 \end{bmatrix} & \begin{bmatrix} 37 & 38 & 39 \\ 40 & 41 & 42 \\ 43 & 44 & 45 \end{bmatrix} & \begin{bmatrix} 46 & 47 & 48 \\ 49 & 50 & 51 \\ 52 & 53 & 54 \end{bmatrix} \end{bmatrix} \\ \begin{bmatrix} \begin{bmatrix} 55 & 56 & 57 \\ 58 & 59 & 60 \\ 61 & 62 & 63 \end{bmatrix} & \begin{bmatrix} 64 & 65 & 66 \\ 67 & 68 & 69 \\ 70 & 71 & 72 \end{bmatrix} & \begin{bmatrix} 73 & 74 & 75 \\ 76 & 77 & 78 \\ 79 & 80 & 81 \end{bmatrix} \end{bmatrix} \end{bmatrix}$$

For example, the number 8 can be denoted as follows:

$$t_{1132} = 8$$

This is because in the tensor T, the element t_{1132} is located in the first row (of matrices), first column (of matrices), third row (of scalars), and second column (of scalars).

Figure A.2 illustrates how to locate the number 8 by "slicing" the tensor:

Rank

The *rank* of a tensor, often called its *order*, is the number of indices or axes required to specify a particular element of the tensor (or the number of dimensions of the tensor as a multidimensional array):

- **Rank 0**: A scalar (a single number) has rank 0.
- **Rank 1**: A vector (a list of numbers) has rank 1.

- **Rank 2:** A matrix (a 2D array of numbers) has rank 2.
- **Higher ranks:** A tensor with rank 3 would require three indices to specify a component (e.g., a 3D array), rank 4 would need four, and so on.

In the previous example, the rank of the tensor T is 4 because you need four indices to locate a particular element.

Statistics

Statistics help summarize and analyze data, providing insights into patterns, variability, and relationships. Fundamental concepts such as mean, median, standard deviation, and correlation are widely used in data preprocessing, evaluation, and feature engineering.

Population and Samples

In statistics, a *population* indicates a complete dataset, whereas a *sample* is a subset of a dataset.

Mean, Median, Mode

The arithmetic *mean* μ is the average value of a dataset, calculated by summing all the values and dividing by the total number of elements. It provides a measure of central tendency but is sensitive to outliers.

The arithmetic mean μ of a population comprised of n data points $x_1, \dots, x_n$ can be calculated with the following formula:

$$\mu = \frac{\sum_{i=1}^{n} x_i}{n}$$

The *median* represents the middle value of a sorted dataset and is more robust to extreme values than the mean. The *mode* is the most frequently occurring value in a dataset and is especially useful for categorical data.

Standard Deviation

Standard deviation σ measures how spread out the data is around the mean. A higher standard deviation indicates greater variability, whereas a lower one signifies that data points are closer to the mean. It is a vital metric in assessing the reliability and consistency of datasets.

The standard deviation σ of a population can be calculated with the following formula:

$$\sigma = \sqrt{\frac{1}{n} \sum_{i=1}^{n} (x_i - \mu)^2}$$

Here, i is a variable that enumerates the data points, x_i denotes a data point, μ is the arithmetic mean of the population, and n is the total number of data points in the population.

Appendix B · Mathematics Essentials

The standard deviation s of a sample can be calculated with the following formula:

$$s = \sqrt{\frac{1}{n-1} \sum_{i=1}^{n} (x_i - \bar{x})^2}$$

Here, i is a variable that enumerates the data points, x_i denotes a data point, $\bar{x}$ is the arithmetic mean of the sample, and n is the total number of data points in the sample.

Covariance

Covariance is a measure of the relationship between two variables, indicating whether they tend to increase or decrease together. A positive covariance means the variables increase together, whereas a negative covariance means one decreases as the other increases. However, covariance does not indicate the strength of the relationship; correlation is used for that.

For a population, covariance is defined as follows:

$$\text{Cov}(X, Y) = \frac{\sum_{i=1}^{n}(X_i - \mu_X)(Y_i - \mu_Y)}{n}$$

For a sample, covariance is defined as follows:

$$\text{Cov}(X, Y) = \frac{\sum_{i=1}^{n}(X_i - \bar{X})(Y_i - \bar{Y})}{n-1}$$

Here, μ_X and μ_Y are the means of variables X and Y for the population, and $\bar{X}$ and $\bar{Y}$ are the sample means.

Correlation

Correlation quantifies the strength and direction of the linear relationship between two variables. The Pearson's correlation coefficient r between two variables X and Y ranges from -1 (perfect negative correlation) to $+1$ (perfect positive correlation), with 0 indicating no correlation. It is widely used in feature selection and understanding dependencies in data.

For a population, the correlation coefficient is defined as follows:

$$r = \frac{\text{Cov}(X, Y)}{\sigma_X \sigma_Y}$$

Here, $\text{Cov}(X, Y)$ is the population covariance, and σ_X and σ_Y are the standard deviations of the variables X and Y, respectively.

For a sample, the correlation coefficient is defined as follows:

$$r = \frac{\text{Cov}(X, Y)}{s_X s_Y}$$

FIGURE A.3 Histogram of normally distributed data.

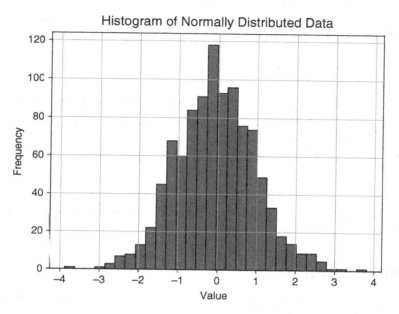

Here, Cov(X, Y) is the sample covariance, and s_X and s_Y are the standard deviations of the variables X and Y, respectively.

Outliers

Outliers are data points that deviate significantly from the rest of the dataset. They can result from variability in the data, errors in data collection, or rare events. Detecting and handling outliers is critical to prevent them from skewing analyses or distorting model performance.

Histograms

Histograms are graphical representations of data distributions. They divide data into intervals (or bins) and show the frequency of values within each bin. Histograms are an intuitive way to visualize the shape of data, detect skewness, and identify potential outliers.

Figure A.3 illustrates a histogram of normally distributed data.

Probability Theory

Probability theory is the branch of mathematics that deals with quantifying the likelihood of events in experiments or random phenomena. It provides a framework to reason about uncertainty in data and models. In ML, probability is crucial for understanding distributions, making predictions, and modeling randomness.

Probability as a Measure Function

Probability can be formally defined as a *measure function* that assigns a value to subsets of a sample space, denoted as S. A probability function satisfies the following axioms (Kolmogorov's axioms):

- **Axiom 1 (non-negativity):** $P(A) \geq 0$ for all events A in the sample space S ($A \subseteq S$ to denote A is a subset of S).

- **Axiom 2 (normalization):** $P(S) = 1$ (the probability of the sample space is 1).

- **Axiom 3 (additivity):** $P(A \cup B) = P(A) + P(B)$ for any mutually exclusive events A and B.

Let S be the sample space, the set of all possible outcomes of an experiment. A **probability function** P maps subsets of S (called *events*) to real numbers, such that

$$P: \mathscr{F} \to [0,1]$$

Here, $\mathscr{F}$ is the set of all events (subsets of S), and $P(A)$ represents the probability of event A, where $A \subseteq S$.

Probability Distribution

A *probability distribution* is a mathematical description of the likelihood of different outcomes in a random experiment. It maps each possible outcome of an experiment to its probability. There are two types of distributions:

Discrete distributions   Probabilities are assigned to distinct, separate outcomes in the discrete sample space by a *probability mass function* (PMF). The PMF assigns a probability to each specific outcome, ensuring that the sum of the probabilities of all possible outcomes equals 1.

For example, the Bernoulli distribution (described shortly) or rolling a die (described in the next section) has a PMF where each outcome (1, 2, 3, 4, 5, 6) is assigned a specific probability.

Continuous distributions   Probabilities are assigned to intervals of outcomes by a *probability density function* (PDF). The PDF describes the likelihood of a random variable falling within a particular range of values rather than assigning probabilities to specific points (because the probability of any single point in a continuous distribution is 0).

For example, the normal distribution (described shortly) uses a PDF to determine the probability over an interval, such as the likelihood that a value lies between a and b.

Example: A Six-faced Die

A good example of a probability distribution is a standard six-faced die. Each face has an equal probability, leading to a discrete uniform distribution:

$$P(A) = \frac{|A|}{|S|}, \ S = \{1, 2, 3, 4, 5, 6\}$$

Here, $|A|$ is the number of favorable outcomes in event A, and $|S|$ is the total number of outcomes in the sample space ($|S| = 6$).

For example, the probability of rolling a 5 (event $A = \{5\}$) is as follows:

$$P(A) = \frac{1}{6}$$

Multiple Outcomes

The probability of rolling an even number (event $B = \{2, 4, 6\}$) is as follows:

$$P(B) = \frac{|B|}{|S|} = \frac{3}{6} = \frac{1}{2}$$

Compound Events

The probability of rolling a number greater than 3 (event $C = \{4, 5, 6\}$) is as follows:

$$P(C) = \frac{|C|}{|S|} = \frac{3}{6} = \frac{1}{2}$$

Complement Rule

The complement of event C (rolling a number ≤ 3) is as follows:

$$P(C^c) = 1 - P(C) = 1 - \frac{1}{2} = \frac{1}{2}$$

Union of Events

The probability of rolling either an even number or a number greater than 3 (event $D = \{2, 4, 5, 6\}$) is as follows:

$$P(D) = P(\{2, 4, 6\}) + P(\{5\}) = \frac{3}{6} + \frac{1}{6} = \frac{4}{6} = \frac{2}{3}$$

Independent Events

If two dice are rolled, the outcome of the first die does not affect the outcome of the second die. For example, the probability of rolling a 6 on the first die and an even number on the second die is the product of the probabilities of each independent event:

$$P(6 \text{ on 1st die and even on 2nd die}) = P(\{6\}) \cdot P(\{2, 4, 6\}) = \frac{1}{6} \cdot \frac{1}{2} = \frac{1}{12}$$

Simulation in Python

The following Python code simulates rolling a six-faced die 10,000 times using random sampling from the possible outcomes [1, 2, 3, 4, 5, 6]. It then calculates the relative frequency of each outcome and plots a bar chart to represent the probability distribution of the die rolls visually. The chart shows how the frequencies approximate a uniform distribution due to the large sample size, demonstrating the concept of probability in action:

```
import numpy as np
import matplotlib.pyplot as plt

# Simulate rolling a 6-faced die 10,000 times
rolls = np.random.choice([1, 2, 3, 4, 5, 6], size=10000)
unique, counts = np.unique(rolls, return_counts=True)

# Plot the relative frequency of each outcome
plt.bar(unique, counts / sum(counts), color='skyblue', edgecolor='k')
plt.title("Probability Distribution of Rolling a 6-Faced Die")
plt.xlabel("Die Face")
plt.ylabel("Relative Frequency")
plt.grid(axis='y')
plt.show()
```

Figure A.4 shows the probability distribution.

FIGURE A.4 Uniform probability distribution.

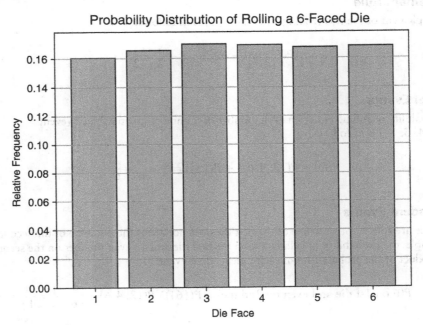

Normal Distribution

The normal distribution is one of the most widely used distributions in ML due to its natural occurrence in many real-world datasets (e.g., height, weight, test scores). It is symmetric, centered around its mean (μ), with a predictable spread determined by its standard deviation (σ).

The central limit theorem reinforces its importance by stating that the mean of a sufficiently large number of independent, identically distributed variables will follow a normal distribution, regardless of the original data distribution.

Many ML algorithms assume data to be normally distributed to simplify computations. The PDF is as follows:

$$f(x) = \frac{1}{\sqrt{2\pi\sigma^2}} e^{-\frac{(x-\mu)^2}{2\sigma^2}}$$

The following Python program generates a plot of the PDF (Figure A.5):

```
import numpy as np
import matplotlib.pyplot as plt
from scipy.stats import norm

# Normal Distribution
x = np.linspace(-5, 5, 1000)
mu, sigma = 0, 1
plt.plot(x, norm.pdf(x, mu, sigma))
```

FIGURE A.5 Normal probability density function ($\mu = 0$, $\sigma = 1$).

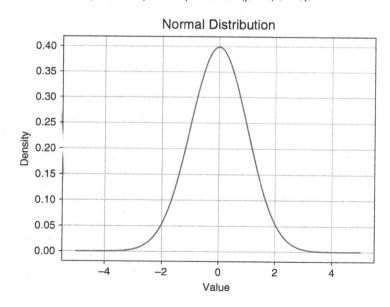

```
plt.title("Normal Distribution")
plt.xlabel("Value")
plt.ylabel("Density")
plt.grid()
plt.show()
```

Bernoulli Distribution

The Bernoulli distribution models binary outcomes (0 or 1) and is commonly used in ML to represent success/failure problems. Examples include determining whether an email is spam or classifying images as cat versus noncat. The key parameter p represents the probability of success (1), whereas $1 - p$ represents the probability of a failure (0). It is widely used in logistic regression and binary classification tasks. The PMF is as follows:

$$P(X = x) = p^x(1 - p)^{1-x}, \qquad x \in \{0, 1\}$$

The following Python program generates a plot of the PMF (Figure A.6):

```
from scipy.stats import bernoulli
import matplotlib.pyplot as plt

# Bernoulli Distribution
p = 0.6
```

FIGURE A.6 Bernoulli probability mass function ($p = 0.6$).

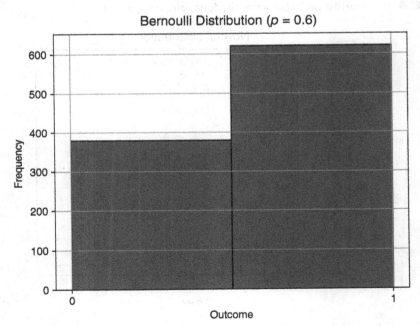

```
data = bernoulli.rvs(p, size=1000)
plt.hist(data, bins=2, edgecolor='k')
plt.title("Bernoulli Distribution (p = 0.6)")
plt.xlabel("Outcome")
plt.ylabel("Frequency")
plt.xticks([0, 1], ['0', '1'])
plt.grid()
plt.show()
```

Calculus

Calculus is fundamental to understanding and implementing ML algorithms. Key aspects like derivatives and gradients are used to optimize models by minimizing errors (i.e., loss functions) or maximizing performance metrics (e.g., accuracy). For example:

- **Derivatives** help measure changes and adjust parameters efficiently.

- **Gradients** form the basis of parameter optimization techniques, such as gradient descent.

- **Maxima and minima** are used to identify optimal solutions in model training.

By leveraging calculus, ML algorithms can adapt and learn from data through iterative optimization processes.

Derivatives and Slope

Derivatives quantify the rate of change of a function with respect to its input, representing the slope of the function's graph at a given point. In ML, this concept is critical for understanding how changes in parameters affect the output.

In its simplest form, the derivative of a single variable function f can be expressed as follows:

$$f'(x) = \lim_{\Delta x \to 0} \frac{f(x + \Delta x) - f(x)}{\Delta x}$$

This formula expresses how a derivative—denoted as $f'(x)$—measures the rate at which a function $f(x)$ changes as its input x changes. The term Δx represents a small change in the input, and the fraction calculates the ratio of the change in the function's output $(f(x + \Delta x) - f(x))$ to the change in input (Δx).

The limit as $\Delta x \to 0$ ensures that the derivative captures the instantaneous rate of change at a specific point on the curve of $f(x)$. In simpler terms, it describes the slope of the tangent line to the function at any given x. This concept is crucial in ML for understanding how a small change in input (features) affects the outcome (prediction).

Figure A.7 visually demonstrates the concept of derivative and slope with a simple function $f(x) = x^2$, showing its derivative $f'(x) = 2x$ at input point $x = 0$.

FIGURE A.7   Derivative and slope ($f(x) = x^2$).

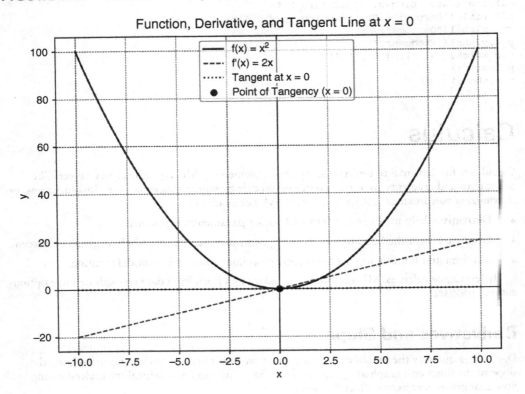

Maxima and Minima

In ML, maxima and minima are essential for optimization, determining where a function (e.g., loss or objective function) is at its peak.

For nonlinear functions, the highest peak or the maximum value refers to the *maxima*, and the lowest peak or the lowest value refers to the *minima*. Put differently, the point x at which the derivative of a function is 0 is defined as the maxima or the minima.

Maxima and minima are the points where the value of the function remains constant: i.e., the change rate is 0.

The concepts of maxima and minima can be global or local, to indicate whether the peak applies to the entire domain of the function (global) or only to a specific neighborhood around a point (local).

More formally, a function $f(x)$ has a local minima at $x = a$ if there exists an interval $(a - h, a + h)$, where $h > 0$, such that $f(a) \leq f(x)$ for all x in that interval.

Figure A.8 visually illustrates these concepts, assuming the function is limited to a domain of positive real numbers ($x > 0$).

FIGURE A.8 Maxima and minima visualizations, for $x > 0$ ($f(x) = e^{(-x)} * \sin(3x)$).

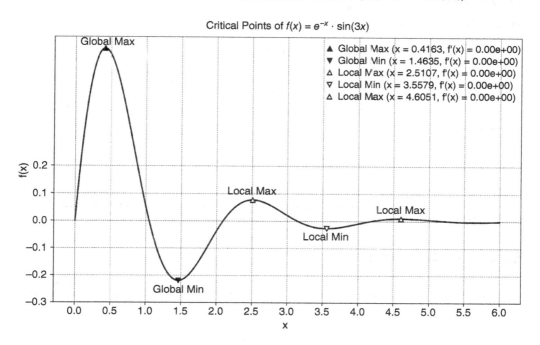

Partial Derivatives

In multivariable calculus, a *partial derivative* measures the rate of change of a function with respect to one variable, while keeping all other variables constant. This is essential in ML for optimizing functions involving multiple parameters, like loss functions.

More formally, for a multivariable function $f(x_1, \ldots, x_n)$,

$$\frac{\partial f}{\partial x_i} = \lim_{\Delta x_i \to 0} \frac{f(x_1, x_2, \ldots, x_i + \Delta x_i, \ldots, x_n) - f(x_1, x_2, \ldots, x_i, \ldots, x_n)}{\Delta x_i}$$

For example, for $f(x_1, x_2) = x_1^2 + x_2^2$,

$$\frac{\partial f}{\partial x_1} = 2x_1, \qquad \frac{\partial f}{\partial x_2} = 2x_2$$

Partial derivatives form the components of the gradient, which is key in optimization.

Gradient

The *gradient* of a function is a vector containing all its partial derivatives. It points in the direction of the steepest ascent of the function.

More formally, for a multivariable function $f(x_1, \ldots, x_n)$,

$$\nabla f(x_1, x_2, \ldots, x_n) = \left[\frac{\partial f}{\partial x_1}, \frac{\partial f}{\partial x_2}, \ldots, \frac{\partial f}{\partial x_n} \right]$$

For example, for $f(x_1, x_2) = x_1^2 + x_2^2$,

$$\nabla f(x_1, x_2) = \left[\frac{\partial f}{\partial x_1}, \frac{\partial f}{\partial x_2} \right] = [2x_1, 2x_2]$$

In ML, the gradient is used to calculate the direction to adjust model parameters during optimization.

Gradient Descent

Gradient descent is an optimization algorithm that iteratively adjusts parameters to minimize a function (e.g., loss function). It uses the gradient to determine the direction and magnitude of parameter updates.

$$x_{new} = x_{old} - \eta \, \nabla f(x_{old})$$

where

- η is the learning rate hyperparameter (step size).
- $\nabla f(x)$ is the gradient of the function.

This process is repeated until convergence: i.e., when updates become negligible or the function reaches its minimum.

Figure A.9 visually illustrates the gradient descent convergence process for the single-variable function $f(x) = x^2$.

In Figure A.9:

- Steps 0, 1, and 2 are explicitly annotated with x_{old} and $f'(x)$.
- All steps beyond 3 are visually marked on the function line but are not annotated to maintain readability.
- Starting from $x = 8$ with $\eta = 0.2$, the algorithm takes 10 iterations to converge, based on the number of steps shown.
- By the 10th step, the changes in x and $f(x)$ are small enough to indicate convergence near the global minimum ($x = 0$).

For your reference, the following Python code shows the plot illustrated in Figure A.9:

FIGURE A.9 Gradient descent convergence process ($f(x) = x^2$).

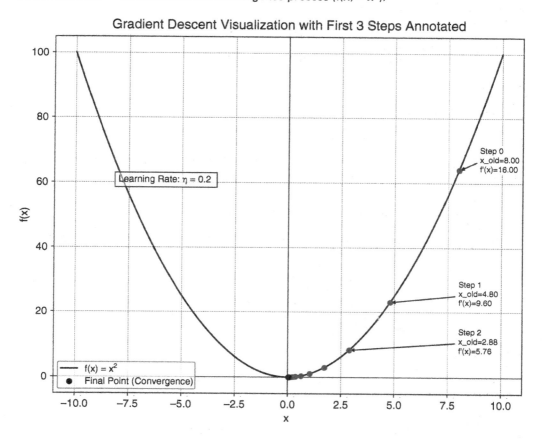

```
import numpy as np
import matplotlib.pyplot as plt

# Define the function and its gradient
def func(x):
    return x**2  # f(x) = x²

def gradient(x):
    return 2 * x  # Gradient: f'(x) = 2x

# Gradient descent parameters
learning_rate = 0.2
x = 8  # Initial point
steps = [x]  # To store the points during the descent
```

```python
# Perform gradient descent
for _ in range(10):
    x_new = x - learning_rate * gradient(x)  # Gradient Descent Update
    steps.append(x_new)  # Track each step
    x = x_new  # Update x for the next iteration

# Generate data for the function
x_vals = np.linspace(-10, 10, 100)
y_vals = func(x_vals)

# Plot the function and gradient descent steps
plt.figure(figsize=(10, 8))
plt.plot(x_vals, y_vals, label='f(x) = x²', color='black', linewidth=1.5)  #
Function plot

# Annotate only the first 3 steps
for i, step in enumerate(steps[:3]):  # Only the first 3 steps
    gradient_at_step = gradient(step)
    plt.scatter(step, func(step), color='grey', zorder=5)  # Plot step points
    plt.annotate(f"Step {i}\n"
                 f"x_old={step:.2f}\n"
                 f"f'(x)={gradient_at_step:.2f}",
                 (step, func(step)),  # Arrow start
                 xytext=(8, func(step)),  # Arrow end (fixed on the right)
                 arrowprops=dict(facecolor='black', arrowstyle="->"),
                 fontsize=8)

# Mark steps > 3 but don't annotate them
for step in steps[3:]:
    plt.scatter(step, func(step), color='grey', zorder=5)  # Mark
remaining steps

# Final point annotation
plt.scatter(steps[-1], func(steps[-1]), color='black', zorder=5, label='Final
Point (Convergence)')

# Add learning rate annotation
plt.text(-8, 60, f"Learning Rate: η = {learning_rate}", fontsize=10,
bbox=dict(facecolor='white', alpha=0.7))

# Axis and labels
plt.axhline(0, color='black', linewidth=0.7)  # Horizontal axis
plt.axvline(0, color='black', linewidth=0.7)  # Vertical axis
plt.legend()
plt.title("Gradient Descent Visualization with First 3 Steps Annotated")
plt.xlabel("x")
plt.ylabel("f(x)")
plt.grid(color='grey', linestyle='--', linewidth=0.5)
plt.show()
```

Index

A

access policies
overview, 343–344
permission boundaries, 345–346
resource-based, 344–345
service control, 346–347
accuracy
classification problems, 199–200
information, 4
ML model selection, 175
model performance
example, 221–230
ACM (AWS Certificate
Manager), 335–336
activation functions, neural network
component, 17
AI (artificial intelligence)
AWS services
chatbots, 113–114
generative AI, 115–124
NLP, 111–113
recommendation, 114–115
visual content analysis, 108–110
compared to ML, 14–16
foundation of, 3
ML, 2
overview, 2–3
services, deploying, 238–245
Services, 15
alarms, model monitoring, 304
ALB (application load balancer), 333
algorithms
Amazon SageMaker,
built-in, 125–126

backpropagation, neural
networks, 18–19
classification, 14
compared to models, 13
data labeling, 94
dimensionality reduction, 157–163
elbow method, clustering
data, 150–153
feature extraction, 67
feature filtering, 68
forecasting, 148–149
image processing, 171–175
image URIs, retrieving, 225
information and, 5
K-means, clustering data, 150–157
k-NN, 136–139
linear regression, 127–129
logistic regression, 130–134
missing values, 70
ML, 5
outlier detection, 74
PCA, 157–163
random forest, 140
regression, 14
reinforcement learning, 14
selection considerations, 106
semantic segmentation, 174–175
supervised learning, 14
support vector machines, 134
textual analysis, 167–171
topic modeling, 163–165
unsupervised learning, 14, 149–167
All At Once traffic shifting, 266–271
Amazon Application Auto
Scaling, 264–265

Amazon Athena, SQL queries, 43
Amazon Bedrock, 16
    foundation model evaluation
        tools, 221
    generative AI applications, 115–124
    marketplace, 116
    pretrained models, 244–245
    tokenization, 93
Amazon CloudFront, 333
Amazon CloudWatch
    ML lifecycle, 11
    model drift, monitoring, 301
    model performance monitoring, 303
    model training metrics, 192
    traceability, 334
Amazon CloudWatch Logs
    Insights, 315–316
Amazon Comprehend
    NLP, 112–113
    pretrained models, 242–243
Amazon Data Firehose, 35
Amazon Detective, 336–337
Amazon DynamoDB, 52–53
Amazon Elastic Block Storage
    (EBS), 51–52
Amazon Elastic Container Service
    (ECS), 258
Amazon Elastic File System (EFS),
    45–47, 118–122
Amazon Elastic Kubernetes Service
    (EKS), 189, 259
Amazon EventBridge, 316–317
    model training, 192
    traceability, 335
Amazon FSx for Lustre, 47–49
Amazon FSx for NetApp
    ONTAP, 49–50
Amazon FSx for OpenZFS, 51

Amazon FSx for Windows File
    Server, 50–51
Amazon GuardDuty, 319–320, 333
    traceability, 334
Amazon Inspector, 320, 333–334
Amazon Kinesis Data Streams, 35–36
Amazon Lex
    conversational interfaces, 113–114
    pretrained models, 243
Amazon Managed Service for
    Apache Flink, 38
Amazon Managed Streaming for Apache
    Kafka (MSK), 36–38
Amazon Managed Workflows for
    Apache Airflow, 275–276
Amazon Personalize
    pretrained models, 244
    recommendation services, 114–115
Amazon Polly, 16
    pretrained models, 241–242
    speech conversion, 110–111
Amazon Rekognition, 16
    image feature extraction, 92
    pretrained models, 240–241
    visual content analysis, 108–109
Amazon Relational Database
    Service (RDS), 52
Amazon S3, 42–46, 63
Amazon SageMaker
    Amazon S3, 43
    built-in algorithms and data formats,
        32–33, 125
    data standardization and refor-
        matting, 78
    hyperparameter space,
        navigating, 196–198
    hyperparameter tuning, 186
    k-NN algorithm, 139

ML lifecycle, 10
ML Services layer, 15
PCA algorithm, 157–163
post-training analysis, 192
remote model training, 189–190
storage services, 42–49
Amazon SageMaker AI Automatic
 Model Tuning (AMT). *See* AMT
 (Amazon SageMaker AI Automatic
 Model Tuning)
Amazon SageMaker AI, 245–255
Amazon SageMaker Batch
 Transform, 10
Amazon SageMaker Clarify
 bias, 96–98
 class imbalance, 96–98
 facet, 97
 model monitoring, 301
Amazon SageMaker Data Wrangler
 dataset splitting, 99–100
 detecting and treating outliers, 73
 image feature extraction, 92
 time-series data, 91
Amazon SageMaker Debugger, 192–193
Amazon SageMaker Factorization
 Machines, 146–147
Amazon SageMaker Feature
 Store, 69, 92
Amazon SageMaker Ground
 Truth, 94–95
Amazon SageMaker JumpStart, 92
Amazon SageMaker Jupyter, 73
Amazon SageMaker Model
 Monitor, 300
 ML lifecycle, 11
 workflow monitoring, 303
Amazon SageMaker Model
 Registry, 273

Amazon SageMaker Neo, 260–261
Amazon SageMaker Pipelines,
 272–273, 277–282
Amazon SageMaker Python SDK
 monitoring model training, 192
 remote model training, 189–190
Amazon SageMaker Real-Time
 Inference, real-time predictions, 10
Amazon SageMaker Savings Plans, 326
Amazon SageMaker Serverless
 Inference, workload traffic
 management, 10–11
Amazon SageMaker Studio, image
 generation, 118–124
Amazon Textract, 16
 pretrained models, 241
 visual content analysis, 108–110
Amazon Transcribe, 16
 automatic speech recognition, 111
 pretrained models, 242
Amazon Translate, 16
 NLP, 111–112
Amazon Virtual Private Cloud (VPC).
 See VPC (Amazon Virtual
 Private Cloud)
AMT (Amazon SageMaker AI
 Automatic Model Tuning)
 hyperparameter tuning, 196–198
 performance example, 221–230
annotating data, 95
ANNs (artificial neural networks), 20
anomaly detection, 149, 165–167
Apache Avro, storing and ingest-
 ing data, 31
Apache ORC, storing and ingest-
 ing data, 31
Apache Parquet, storing and ingest-
 ing data, 31

Index

applicability, knowledge, 5

application load balancer (ALB), 333

artifact repository services, 274

artificial intelligence (AI). *See* AI (artificial intelligence)

artificial neural networks (ANNs), 20

artificial outliers, data points, 71

ASR (automatic speech recognition), 111

asynchronous deployment, managed model deployment, 254

AUC-ROC, classification problems, 202–204

auditing, security, 349

auto-rollbacks, model deployment, 266

automated data labeling, 95

automatic evaluations, foundation models, 221

automatic speech recognition (ASR), 111

autoscaling endpoints
  model deployment, 262–265
  policies, 262–264

availability
  object storage, 43
  storage service selection, 42

AWS
  AI services, overview, 107–108
  compute services, unmanaged model deployment, 255–260
  pretrained models, 238
  pricing models, 324–326
  services
    chatbots, 113–114
    creating data lakes, 63
    generative AI, 115–124
    NLP, 111–113
    recommendation, 114–115

    speech conversion, 110–111
    visual content analysis, 108–110
  services based on data structure, 33–34
  storage layers, 28–30
  storage services, selecting, 41–42

AWS Artifact, Ensuring Compliance, 349

AWS Budgets, 324

AWS Certificate Manager (ACM), 335–336

AWS CloudFormation, 274

AWS CloudTrail, 317–318
  traceability, 334

AWS CodeArtifact, 274

AWS CodeBuild, 274

AWS CodeDeploy, 274

AWS Config, traceability, 334

AWS Control Tower, 346

AWS Cost and Usage Reports (CUR), 323

AWS Cost Explorer, 322–323

AWS DataSync, data transfer, 39–40

AWS Deep Learning AMIs, 15

AWS Glue
  data preparation for ML algorithms, 40–41
  data standardization and reformatting, 78
  jobs, creating, 78

AWS Glue DataBrew
  detecting and treating outliers, 73
  managing missing values in datasets, 71

AWS IAM (Identity and Access Management), 335, 338–343

AWS Key Management Service (KMS), 333, 335

AWS Lake Formation, 63–64
AWS Lambda, 259–260
AWS Management Console, 192
AWS ML stack, 15
AWS Nitro Enclaves, 335
AWS Organizations, 346
AWS Secrets Manager, 335
AWS Security Hub, 321–322
AWS services
    encryption, 335
    NLP, 111–113
    pretrained models, 239–240
    securing, 338–343
AWS Step Functions, 274–275
AWS Trusted Advisor, 323–324
AWS Web Application Firewall
    (WAF), 333
AWS X-Ray, 318–319

B

backpropagation algorithm, neural
    networks, 18–19
baking period, Blue/Green model
    deployment, 266
batch inference
    managed model deployment,
        254–255
    model monitoring, 302
Bayesian optimization,
    hyperparameters, 226
Bayesian search, hyperparameter
    tuning, 209–210
bias
    managing, 210–212
    neural network component, 17
bias drift, monitoring, 300–302

bias metrics, datasets, 96–98
BiasConfig class, 98
binary classification
    AUC-ROC, 202–204
    supervised learning algorithms, 126
binary encoding, 87–89
binning data, 85
BlazingText, 168–170
blue fleet, compute infrastructure, 268
Blue/Green model deployment,
    265–266
bootstrap resampling technique, model
    evaluation, 220
bootstrapping, random forest
    algorithms, 141
Box-Cox transformation, 83
branch nodes, decision tree
    algorithms, 140
bucketing data, 85
build services, 274

C

Canary traffic shifting, 268–270
case studies
    DL applications
        Leidos, 21–22
        Mobileye, 21
    Image Classification
        algorithm, 171–172
    RDS (Amazon Relational Database
        Service), 52
catalogs, data lakes, 62
categorical data, 64
    feature engineering techniques,
        85–90
chatbots, AWS services, 113–114

Index

choose algorithm phase, ML
lifecycle, 8–9
CI/CD pipelines, model deployment, 274
CIA Triad, 335–336
class imbalance
Amazon SageMaker Clarify,
96–98
data labeling, overview, 95–96
mitigation techniques, 96
class weighting, 96
classification algorithms, 14
decision trees, 140
k-NN, 136–139
classification problem metrics, model
performance, 198–202
clustering data
compared to topic modeling, 163
K-means algorithm, 150–157
overview, 149
CNNs (convolutional neural networks)
image processing, 20, 92, 171–174
model selection cost, 176
textual analysis, 170–171
Code Editor, Amazon SageMaker
Studio, 118–122
code repository, Amazon SageMaker
Pipelines, 272–273
coefficient of determination,
207–208
collect data phase
data ingestion and storage,
overview, 28
ML lifecycle, 8
comma-separated values (CSV), 31
completeness, information, 5
compliance, 349–350
AWS services, 34
concentration parameters, 164

configuration, remote model
training jobs, 190
confusion matrix, model
performance, 198–202
containers, dependency
management, 188–189
contextuality, knowledge, 5
continuous data, 64
conversational interfaces, Amazon Lex,
pretrained models, 243
Converse API, 116
convolutional neural networks (CNNs.
See CNNs (convolutional
neural networks)
cost
Amazon Bedrock, 117
Amazon EFS, 45
AWS services, 34
data storage troubleshooting, 54
ML model selection, 176
monitoring, 314–326
object storage, 43
storage service selection, 42
token-based billing, 93
unmanaged model deployment,
255
cost functions, 13
cost optimization monitoring design
pillar, 310–313
cost tracking services, 322–326
CPUs, model deployment
considerations, 256
cross-region inference, foundational
models, 117
cross-validation, overfitting and
underfitting, 217
CSV (comma-separated values), storing
and ingesting data, 31

Index 397

cube-root transformations, 85
CUR (AWS Cost and Usage
Reports), 323

D

data
access patterns, 33
annotating, 95
categorical data, 64
cleaning, 69–79
continuous data, 64
deviation from the mean,
detecting, 71–77
discovery, AWS DataSync, 39–40
discrete data, 64
features, 65
formats
selecting, 32
storage and ingestion, 31–34
image data, 64
imputation, 70
ingestion
overview, 28
services, 34
troubleshooting, 53–54
numerical data, 64
overview, 3
preparation for algorithms, AWS
Glue, 40–41
quality
deduplication, 77–78
monitoring, 300–302
recollecting, missing values, 70
security, 346–349
semi-structured data, 4
skewed data distributions, 75

storage
overview, 28
troubleshooting, 53–54
streaming
Amazon Data Firehose, 35
Amazon Kinesis Data Streams,
35–36
Amazon Managed Service for
Apache Flink, 38
Amazon Managed Streaming
for Apache Kafka (MSK),
36–38
structured data, 3–4
textual data, 64
time-series data, 65
transfer, AWS DataSync, 39–40
unstructured, 4
data augmentation, class imbalance
mitigation, 96
data drift, monitoring, 300–302, 303
data engineering, lifecycle, 28–31
data labeling
automated, 95
class imbalance, overview, 95–96
overview, 94
data lakes, 62
creating, 63
data leakage, 99
data parallel training, 190–191
data protection, 335–336
data splitting
decision tree algorithms, 140
overview, 98–99
data transformation
EDA, 92
ML model training, 65
databases
Amazon DynamoDB, 52–53

Index

databases (*Cont.*)
    data storage troubleshooting, 54
    RDS (Amazon Relational Database Service), 52
datasets
    addressing gaps, 69
    bias metrics, 96–98
    data splitting, 98–100
    date/time features, adding, 91
    deduplication, 77–78
    dimensionality reduction, 157–163
    exporting, 78
    high-dimensional sparse, 146
    linear relationships, 84
    loading, 78
    model training, 66
        compared to model evaluation, 196
    skewness, reducing, 84
date/time features, time-series data, 91
dead-letter queues (DLQs), 192
debugging, model training, 192–193
decision tree algorithms, 140–145
deduplication, dataset streamlining, 69, 77–78
deep learning (DL). *See* DL (deep learning)
deep neural networks (DNNs), 20
DeepAR, forecasting algorithm, 148–149
DeepLabV3, 173
defense-in-depth, 333–334
define problem phase, ML lifecycle, 6–8
deleting outliers, 72
dependency management, local model training, 188–189
dependent variables, 12

deploy model phase, ML lifecycle, 9–11
deployment
    AI services, 238–245
    local model training, 188
derive inference phase, ML lifecycle, 11
design principles, model monitoring, 304–314
deterministic algorithms, compared to probabilistic models, 7–8
Difference in Proportions of Labels (DPL), 97
Digits dataset, XGBoost model optimization example, 221–230
dimensionality reduction algorithms, 157–163
Dirichlet distribution, 163–164
discrete data, 64
distributed file systems, creating, 45
distributed training, 190–191
DL (deep learning), 2–3
    compared to ML, 21
    neural networks, 16
    overview, 16
    semantic segmentation image processing, 174
DLQs (dead-letter queues), 192
DNNs (deep neural networks), 20
Docker, ML algorithm container images, 189
DPL (Difference in Proportions of Labels), 97
durability
    object storage, 43
    storage service selection, 42
dynamism, knowledge, 5

E

EBS (Amazon Elastic Block Storage), 51–52
EC2 (Amazon Elastic Compute Cloud), 256–258
ECS (Amazon Elastic Container Service), 258
EDA (exploratory data analysis), 92
edge devices, optimizing models for, 260–261
EFS (Amazon Elastic File System), 45–47, 118–122
EKS (Amazon Elastic Kubernetes Service), model deployment, 189, 259
Elastic Net, 216
elbow method, clustering data, 150–153
embedding, BlazingText, 168–170
enable traceability security principle, 334–335
encoding data, 85–89
encryption, AWS services, 335
endpoints, 262–265
EOD (equal opportunity difference), 97
epoch, distributed training, 191
equal opportunity difference (EOD), 97
estimators, configuring
  BlazingText algorithm, 169–170
  factorization machines, 146
  k-NN algorithm, 139
  XGBoost algorithm, 145
evaluate model phase
  hyperparameter tuning, 193–195
  ML lifecycle, 9
evaluation metrics, models, 198

events, model monitoring, 303
experience-based knowledge, 5
expert systems, 5
exploratory data analysis (EDA), 92
extreme gradient boosting, 141–145

F

F1 score
  classification problem metrics, 198
  classification problems, 201–202
  model performance, 9, 186, 193
facet, Amazon SageMaker Clarify, 97
Factorization Machines, 146–147
false positive rate (FPR), 201
FCNs (fully convolutional networks), 174
feature attribution drift, monitoring, 300–302
feature engineering
  data types, 64–65
  overfitting mitigation, 217
  overview, 65, 79
  techniques
    structured data, 79–92
    time-series data, 90–92
    unstructured data, 92–94
  underfitting mitigation, 217
feature hashing, 89–90
FeatureHasher class, 89
Featurize datetime transformation, 91
features
  creation and transformation, 68–69
  extracting image features, 92
  extraction, 66–67
  ML models, 11–12
  overview, 65–66

Index

features (*Cont.*)
  selecting
    decision tree algorithms, 140
    model training, 66
  selection, 68
  target variables, 126
file-based storage, Amazon EFS, 45–47
filtering, feature selection, 68
firewalls, network isolation, 347
flexibility, AWS services, 34
FMs (foundation models)
  Amazon Bedrock, 115–124
    pretrained models, 244–245
  evaluation tools, 221
  regional availability, 117
  selecting, 116–117
  support by Converse API, 116
  tokenization, 93
forecasting algorithms, 148–149
formats, data storage and ingestion, 31–34
foundation models (FMs). *See* FMs (foundation models)
FPR (false positive rate), 201
fully convolutional networks (FCNs), 174

G

generative AI, 115–125
GPUs, model deployment considerations, 256
gradient descent, 12
green fleet, compute infrastructure, 268
grid search, hyperparameter tuning, 209

H

hash function, features, 89
hidden layers, neural networks, 18
high-dimensional data, dimensionality reduction, 157–163
high-dimensional sparse datasets, Factorization Machines, 146
holdout set, model evaluation, 220
human evaluations, foundation models, 221
hyperparameter optimization. *See* hyperparameters: tuning
hyperparameters, 186
  Bayesian optimization, 226
  compared to model parameters, 195–196
  DeepAR, 148
  factorization machines, 146
  k-NN algorithm, 136
  neural network training, 19
  Object2Vec, 147
  space, 196–198
  tuning, 12–13, 186, 193–195
    Bayesian search, 209–210
    grid search, 209
    manual search, 208–209
    multi-algorithm optimization, 210
    overview, 208
    performance example, 221–230
    random search, 209
  warm starts, 197
hyperparameters dictionary object, 226
HyperparameterTuner class, 226
hyperplanes, 134

I

IaC (infrastructure as code), 274
IAM (Identity and Access Management),
335, 338–343
identities, 338
image augmentation, class imbalance
mitigation, 96
Image Classification algorithm, 171–172
image data, 64
feature engineering techniques, 92
image generation, Nova
Canvas, 117–124
image processing
algorithms, 171–175
Amazon Rekognition, pretrained
models, 240–241
imputation, outliers, 72
inference processing, 238
inferencing infrastructure, compared to
training infrastructure, 246
information, characteristics, 4–5
infrastructure
monitoring, 314–326
security, 346–349
infrastructure as code (IaC), 274
infrastructure management, 274
infrastructure selection, model
deployment, 246
ingestion
AWS services, selecting, 34
data access patterns, 33
data formats, 31–34
overview, 28
troubleshooting, 53–54
input data channels, defining, 225
input layer, neural networks, 18
inputs, neural network component, 17

intelligence, surveillance, and
reconnaissance (ISR), 173
Intelligent-Tiering storage class, 64
internal nodes, decision tree algorithms, 140
interpretability, ML model selection, 175
InvocationsPerInstance metric, 265
IP Insights, 167
IQR (interquartile range) method,
detecting outliers, 75–77
Iris dataset, 130
dimensionality reduction, 158–160
K-means clustering example, 153–155
k-NN example, 136–139
PCA algorithm, 161–163
XGBoost algorithm, 141–145
ISR (intelligence, surveillance, and
reconnaissance), object
detection, 173

J

job. *See* training job
JSON (JavaScript Object Notation)
semi-structured data, 4
data formats and Ingestion
Techniques, 31–32
Amazon Athena, 43
Jupyter Notebooks, limitations for
model training, 188

K

K-fold cross-validation, 218–220
K-means algorithm, clustering
data, 150–157

k-NN (k-Nearest Neighbors),
    classification and regression
    problems, 136–139
KMS (AWS Key Management
    Service), 333, 335
knowledge, characteristics, 5
knowledge base evaluations, foundation
    models, 221

L

L1 regularization (LASSO), 214–215
L2 regularization (Ridge), 215
label encoding, 85–86
    compared to predictions, 155
labels, 12
Lag features transformation, 91
large datasets, Amazon SageMaker
    Batch Transform, 10
LASSO (L1 regularization), 214–215
latency, ML model selection, 175
lazy loading, Amazon FSx for
    Lustre, 48
LDA (Latent Dirichlet
    Allocation), 163–164
least privilege, 332
Leidos case study, 21–22
lifecycle, data engineering, 28–31
lifecycle (ML)
    AWS tools and services, 15
    collect data phase, 8
    define problem phase, 6–8
    model training, 187–188
    overview, 6–7
Linear Learner algorithm, 127
linear regression algorithm, 127–129
linear traffic shifting, 270–271

LLM-as-a-Judge evaluations, foundation
    models, 221
local training, 188–189
logarithmic transform, 84
    outliers, 72
logging, data storage troubleshooting,
    53–54
logistic function, 130
logistic regression algorithm,
    130–134
logit function, 133
logs, model monitoring, 303
loss functions, 13
    neural networks, 19

M

machine learning (ML). *See* ML
    (machine learning)
Machine Learning Well-Architected
    Lens, 299, 304, 315
MAE (mean absolute error), 206
manual search, hyperparameter
    tuning, 208–209
MAPE (mean absolute percentage
    error), 206–207
MaxAbs scaling, 83
mean absolute error (MAE), 206
mean absolute percentage error
    (MAPE), 206–207
mean squared error (MSE). *See* MSE
    (mean squared error)
mean time between failure (MTBF), 166
migrating data, AWS DataSync, 39–40
mini-batches, distributed model train-
    ing, 190–191
MinMax scaling, 82

Mitchell, Tom, 2

ML (machine learning). *See also*
  algorithms; model training
  AI, 2
  bias, managing, 210–212
  compared to AI, 14–16
  compared to deep learning, 21
  compared to programming, 6
  concepts, features, 11–12
  Infrastructure and Frameworks, 15
  lifecycle, 6–11, 46–47
  model selection criteria, 175–176
  models
    effectiveness, 217–218
    evaluation metrics, 198–204
    generalizability, 217–218
    performance evaluation
      methods, 217–220
    performance optimization, 186
  orchestrating workflows,
    271–282
  overfitting, 135
  overview, 6
  recommendation systems, 6
  Services, 15
  training, data types, 64–65
  unsupervised learning algorithms,
    149–167
  variance, managing, 210–212

MLCOST-27: Monitor Usage and Cost
  by ML Activity, 311

MLCOST-28: Monitor Return on
  Investment for ML Models, 311

MLCOST-29: Monitor Endpoint Usage
  and Right-Size the Instance
  Fleet, 312–313

MLOE-15: Enable Model Observability
  and Tracking, 304–306

MLOE-16: Synchronize Architecture
  and Configuration, and Check for
  Skew Across Environments, 306

MLOps, 274–275
  Security-as-Code, 336

MLPER-13: Evaluate Model
  Explainability, 308–309

MLPER-14: Evaluate Data Drift, 309

MLPER-15: Monitor, Detect, and
  Handle Model Performance
  Degradation, 309

MLPER-16: Establish an Automated
  Re-Training Framework, 310

MLPER-17: Review for Updated Data/
  Features for Retraining, 310

MLPER-18: Include Human-in-the-
  Loop Monitoring, 310

MLREL-12: Allow Automatic
  Scaling of the Model Endpoint,
  307–308

MLREL-13: Ensure a Recoverable
  Endpoint with a Managed Version
  Control Strategy, 308

MLSEC-12: Restrict Access to Intended
  Legitimate Consumers, 307

MLSEC-13: Monitor Human
  Interactions with Data for
  Anomalous Activity, 307

MLSUS-15: Measure Material
  Efficiency, 313

MLSUS-16: Retrain Only When
  Necessary, 314

Mobileye case study, 21

model deployment
  Amazon SageMaker Neo, 260–261
  automating, 277–282
  autoscaling endpoints, 262–265
  dependency management, 188–189

model deployment (*Cont.*)
  example, 282–291
  infrastructure selection, 246
  managed, 247–255
  overview, 238–239, 245–246
  strategies, 265–271
  testing, 265–271
  traffic shifting, 265–271
  unmanaged, 255–260
model drift, 298
  monitoring, 300, 303
model evaluation, compared to model training, 196
model parallel training, 190–191
model parameters, compared to hyperparameters, 195–196
model selection, criteria, 175–176
model training
  compared to model evaluation, 196
  data deduplication, 77–78
  data transformation, 65
  datasets, 66
  debugging training jobs, 192–193
  distributed training, 190–191
  failed, responding to, 192
  features, selecting, 66
  goals, 13
  labeled data, 95
  local training, 188–189
  monitoring training jobs, 191–192
  neural networks, 18–19
  optimizing features, 92
  overfitting, 79
  overview, 186–188
  parallel, 191
  regularization, 214–216
  remote training, 189–190
  setting timeout, 227

steps, 188
  underfitting, 212–213
models
  building, automating, 277–282
  compared to algorithms, 13
  effectiveness, 217–218
  evaluation metrics, 198
  generalizability, 217–218
  monitoring, 298–302
    techniques, 300–302
  performance evaluation methods, 217–220
  tunning example, 221–230
monitor model phase, ML lifecycle, 11
monitoring
  data storage troubleshooting, 53–54
  model drift, 300
  model training, 191–192
  models
    design principles, 304–314
    techniques, 300–302
  security, 349
  Security-as-Code, 336
monitoring architecture, 302
monitoring services, 315–322
MSE (mean squared error), 128
  regression model performance, 205–206
MSK (Amazon Managed Streaming for Apache Kafka), 36–38
MTBF (mean time between failure), 166
multi-algorithm optimization, hyperparameter tuning, 210
multiclass classification, 199
  AUC-ROC, 202–204
  supervised learning algorithms, 126
multicollinearity

Elastic Net regularization, 216
statistical modeling, 135

N

n-grams, textual data, 94
NACLs (network access control lists), 333, 347
natural language processing (NLP). *See* NLP (natural language processing)
natural outliers, data points, 71
network access control lists (NACLs), 333, 347
network isolation, 347–348
neural embedding, Object2Vec, 147
neural networks
    artificial, 20
    convolutional, 20
    deep, 20
    functioning of, 18–19
    overview, 16
    recurrent, 20–21
    structure, 16–18
        neurons, 16–17
    training, 18–19
neural topic model (NTM), 149, 163, 164–165
neurons, neural networks, 16–17
NLP (natural language processing)
    Amazon Comprehend, pretrained models, 242–243
    AWS services, 111–113
nodes, decision tree algorithms, 140
noise in data, compared to outliers, 72
normalization, feature engineering techniques, 80

Nova Canvas, image generation, 117–124
NTM (neural topic model), 149, 163, 164–165
numerical data, 64

O

Object Detection algorithm, 172–174
object storage, Amazon S3, 42–45
Object2Vec, neural embedding, 147
objective functions, 13
observability services, 315–322
OCI (Open Container Initiative), 189
OCR (optical character recognition), 109
OE (operational excellence), 304–306
On-Demand and Batch pricing model, Amazon Bedrock, 117
one-hot encoding, 86–87
one-time loading, Amazon FSx for Lustre, 48
OOB (out-of-bag) data, model evaluation, 220
Open Container Initiative (OCI), 189
operational excellence (OE), 304–306
optical character recognition (OCR), 109
optimization
    algorithms, neural networks, 19
    problems, 12–13
    services, 322–326
    techniques, model training, 195
optimizing algorithms, 12
orchestration tools, selecting, 276
order split, datasets, 99

out-of-bag (OOB) data, model
evaluation, 220
outliers, 69–77, 84
output layer, neural networks, 18
output variables, 12
outputs, neural network component, 17
overfitting, 135
cross-validation, 217
mitigation, 217
model training, 79, 214
oversampling, class imbalance
mitigation, 96

P

parameters, model training, 195
payloads, 238
payment data, compliance
considerations, 349–350
PCA (Principal Component Analysis),
157–163
performance, models,
monitoring, 300–302
performance efficiency monitoring
design pillar, 308–310
performance evaluation methods,
models, 217–220
performance optimization
data deduplication, 77–78
data storage troubleshooting, 54
hyperparameter tuning, 186
Policy-as-Code, security automation, 336
power transformations, 83–84
PPD (predictive parity difference), 97
pre-training bias metrics, 96–98
precision, classification problems, 200

predictions, compared to labels, 155
predictive parity difference (PPD), 97
pretrained models, 240–245
Principal Component Analysis
(PCA), 157–163
probabilistic forecasts, 148–149
probabilistic models, compared to
deterministic algorithms, 7–8
problems, defining in ML lifecycle, 6–8
process data phase
data lakes, 63
ML lifecycle, 8
production variant, Blue/Green
Deployment, 265
profiling, model training, 193
programmatic evaluations, foundation
models, 221
Provisioned Throughput pricing mode,
Amazon Bedrock, 117
pruning, decision tree algorithms, 140
PSP (pyramid scene parsing), 174
purity, decision tree nodes, 140
Python libraries
boto3, creating Amazon Bedrock
clients, 118
pandas, 73
sklearn
FeatureHasher class, 89
LinearRegression, 128
SimpleImputer class, 70–71
StandardScaler, 70–71
Python scripts, model training, 188

Q

quality monitoring, 301
query, Amazon Athena, 43

R

R-CNN (Region-based Convolutional Neural Networks), 173
R-squared metric, regression model performance, 207–208
RAG (retrieval augmented generation), 116
Random Cut Forest (RCF), 166
random forest algorithms, 140, 141
random search, hyperparameter tuning, 209
random split, datasets, 99
random train-test split, model evaluation, 219–220
raw data, 62
RDS (Amazon Relational Database Service), 52
real-time predictions
　managed model deployment, 248–252
　ML lifecycle, 10
recall, classification problems, 200
recommendation
　Amazon Personalize, pretrained models, 243–244
　AWS services, 114–115
recommendation systems, 146–147
ML, 6
RecordIO, storing and ingesting data, 31
recurrent neural networks (RNNs), 20–21, 148–149
reformatting data, 78
Region-based Convolutional Neural Networks (R-CNN), 173
regression algorithms, 14
　decision trees, 140
　k-NN, 136–139

regression problems
　model performance, 204–208
　supervised learning algorithms, 126
regularization
　method comparison, 216
　model training, 214–216
　multicollinearity, 135
regulations, unmanaged model deployment, 255
reinforcement learning algorithms, 14
relational databases, 52
relevance, information, 5
reliability, data deduplication, 77–78
reliability monitoring design pillar, 307–308
ReLU (Rectified Linear Unit), Structure of a Neural Network, 17
remote training, 189–190
resilience
　AWS services, 34
　object storage, 43
resource requirements, ML model selection, 175
ResourceId variable, Autoscaling Endpoints, 265
retrieval augmented generation (RAG), 116
Ridge (L2 regularization), 215
RMSE (root mean squared error), regression model performance, 206
RNNs (recurrent neural networks), 20–21, 148–149
robust scaling, 81–82
Rolling window features transformation, 91
root mean squared error (RMSE), 206
root nodes, decision tree algorithms, 140

S

sagemaker.clarify library, 98
Samuel, Arthur, 2
scalability
  AWS services, 34
  data lakes, 62
  data storage troubleshooting, 54
  distributed model training, 190–191
  ML model selection, 175
  object storage, 43
scaling, feature engineering
    techniques, 81–84
scaling targets, endpoints, 262–264
scheduled scaling, 264
SCPs (Service Control Policies),
    346–347
security
  automation, 336
  AWS services, 34, 338–343
  data, 346–349
  data lakes, 62
  data protection, 335–336
  defense-in-depth, 333–334
  enable traceability, 334–335
  encryption, AWS services, 335
  identity foundation, 332–333
  infrastructure, 346–349
  least privilege, 332
  network isolation, 347–348
  preparation for events, 336–337
  separation of duties, 332
  storage service selection, 42
security by design, 332
Security Group, 333
security identity foundation, 332–333
security monitoring design pil-
    lar, 306–307

semantic segmentation
    algorithms, 174–175
semi-structured data, 4
  AWS services for, 33–34
separation of duties, 332
Seq2Seq (Sequence-to-
    Sequence), 170–171
Sequence-to-Sequence
    (Seq2Seq), 170–171
serverless deployment, managed model
    deployment, 252–254
Service Control Policies (SCPs),
    346–347
SGD (Stochastic Gradient
    Descent), 195
sigmoid function, 130
SimpleImputer class, managing missing
    values in datasets, 70–71
Single Shot MultiBox Detector
    (SSD), 173
single source of truth storage, 63
Site Reliability Engineering (SRE), 315
skewed data distributions, 75
SMB (Windows Server Message
    Block), 50–51
smdebug library, model training, 193
SMOTE (Synthetic Minority
    Over-sampling Technique),
    Class-Imbalance Mitigation
    Techniques, 96
spaces, Amazon SageMaker
    Studio, 118–119
sparse datasets, recommendation
    systems, 146
sparsity, model evaluation, 215
specificity, classification problems, 201
speech conversion, AWS
    services, 110–111

Speech Synthesis Markup Language (SSML), 110
speech to text processing, Amazon Transcribe, pretrained models, 242
speed, ML model selection, 175
split by key, datasets, 100
SQL queries, Amazon Athena, 43
square-root transformations, 85
SRE (Site Reliability Engineering), 315
SSD (Single Shot MultiBox Detector), 173
SSDs, storage, Amazon FSx for Windows File Server, 50–51
SSML (Speech Synthesis Markup Language), 110
   standardization
  data cleaning, 78
  feature engineering techniques, 80–81
StandardScaler class, 70–71
stateful firewalls, 347
stateless firewalls, 347
step scaling, 264
stochastic gradient descent (SGD), 195
stop words, textual data, 93
stopping criteria, decision tree algorithms, 140
storage
  Amazon EFS, 46–49
  Amazon FSx for Lustre, 47–49
  Amazon FSx for NetApp ONTAP, 49–50
  Amazon FSx for OpenZFS, 51
  Amazon FSx for Windows File Server, 50–51
  Amazon S3, 42–45
  Amazon SageMaker Feature Store, 69
  AWS services, selecting, 41–42

data formats, 31–34
data lakes, 62
labeled data, 95
object, 42–45
overview, 28
troubleshooting, 53–54
storage classes, Amazon S3, 44
strategies, model deployment, 265–271
stratified split, datasets, 100
streaming data
  Amazon Data Firehose, 35
  Amazon Kinesis Data Streams, 35–36
  Amazon Managed Service for Apache Flink, 38
  Amazon Managed Streaming for Apache Kafka (MSK), 36–38
structured data, 3–4
  AWS services for, 33–34
  feature engineering techniques, numerical data, 79–85
supervised learning algorithms, 14, 125–126
support vector machines (SVMs), 134
support vector regression (SVR), 134
sustainability monitoring design pillar, 313–314
SVMs (support vector machines), 134
SVR (support vector regression), 134
synthetic data, 96

T

Target Tracking autoscaling, 264
target variables
  features, 126
  ML models, 12

Terraform, 274
test datasets, 98
testing, model deployment, 265–271
text augmentation, class imbalance mitigation, 96
text datasets, topic modeling, 163–164
text processing, Amazon Textract, pretrained models, 241
text-based content, converting into speech, 110
text-to-speech
Amazon Polly, 110, 241–242
textual analysis algorithms, 167–171
textual data, 64
feature engineering techniques, 92–94
time-series data, 65
feature engineering techniques, 90–92
time-series forecasting, supervised learning algorithms, 126
timeliness, information, 5
timeout, setting for training jobs, 227
tokenization, textual data, 93
tools, AWS ML stack, 15
topic modeling algorithms, 163–165
traceability, 334
traffic shifting, model deployment, 265–271
train model phase, ML lifecycle, 9
training datasets, 98
training job, 189
troubleshooting, data ingestion and storage, 53–54

U

underfitting
cross-validation, 217
mitigation, 217
model training, 212–213

undersampling, class imbalance mitigation, 96
Uniform Resource Identifier (URI), 42
unstructured data, 4
AWS services for, 33–34
objects, 42–45
unstructured text datasets, topic modeling, 163–165
unsupervised learning algorithms, 14, 149–167
URI (Uniform Resource Identifier), 42
use cases
Amazon Bedrock, image generation, 124
Amazon CloudWatch Logs Insights, 316
Amazon Comprehend, NLP, 112–113
Amazon DynamoDB, 52–53
Amazon EFS, 46–47
Amazon EventBridge, 317
Amazon FSx for Lustre, 48–49
Amazon FSx for NetApp ONTAP, 50
Amazon FSx for OpenZFS, 51
Amazon FSx for Windows File Server, 50–51
Amazon GuardDuty, 319–320
Amazon Inspector, 320
Amazon Kinesis Data Streams, 36
Amazon Lex, conversational interfaces, 113–114
Amazon Managed Service for Apache Flink, 38
Amazon MSK, 37–38
Amazon Personalize, recommendation services, 114–115

Amazon Polly, speech conversion, 110–111
Amazon Rekognition, visual content analysis, 109
Amazon S3, 44–45
Amazon Textract, visual content analysis, 109–110
Amazon Transcribe, ASR, 111
Amazon Translate, NLP, 111–112
AWS CloudTrail, 318
AWS DataSync, 40
AWS Glue, 41
AWS Security Hub, 321–322
AWS X-Ray, 319
BlazingText, 170
decision trees, 145
DeepAR, 148–149
dimensionality reduction algorithms, 162–163
factorization machines, 147
IP Insights, 167
K-means clustering, 157
k-NN algorithm, 139
LDA, 164
linear regression algorithms, 134–135
logistic regression algorithms, 135
NTM (neural topic model), 165
Object Detection algorithm, 173–174
Object2Vec, 147
Random Cut Forest (RCF), 166
semantic segmentation algorithms, 174–175
streaming data, Amazon Data Firehose, 35
support vector machines, 135–136

V

validation, labeled data, 95
validation datasets, 98
    model training, 196
values, hyperparameter space, 196–198
variance, managing, 210–212
variant. *See* production variant
version control
    Amazon SageMaker Pipelines, 273
    Python scripts, model training, 188
versioning, labeled data, 95
visual content analysis, AWS services, 108
VPC (Amazon Virtual Private Cloud), 337
    network isolation, 347–348

W

WAF (AWS Web Application Firewall), 333
warm starts, hyperparameter tuning, 197
weighted sums, neural network component, 17
weights, neural network component, 17
well-architected ML framework, 9–10
Windows Server Message Block (SMB), 50–51
word embeddings, textual data, 94
Word2Vec model, 170
worklflow, monitoring, 302–304
workloads
    ML and AI capabilities, 15–16
    security identity foundation, 332
    traffic management, 10–11

X

xgb estimator, model performance example, 225
XGBoost algorithm, 141–145
　hyperparameters dictionary object, 226
　model tuning performance example, 221–230

Y

Yeo-Johnson transformation, 83
YOLO (You Only Look Once), 173

Z

Z-score function, 80–81
Z-score outlier detection method, 76–77